The Party Network

The Party Network

The Robust Organization
of Illinois Republicans

Mildred A. Schwartz

THE UNIVERSITY OF WISCONSIN PRESS

The University of Wisconsin Press
114 North Murray Street
Madison, Wisconsin 53715

3 Henrietta Street
London WC2E 8LU, England

Library of Congress Cataloging-in-Publication Data
Schwartz, Mildred A.
  The party network: the robust organization of Illinois
republicans/Mildred A. Schwartz.
336 pp.   cm.
  Includes bibliographical references.
1. Republican Party (Ill.)   I. Title.
JK2358.I3S38   1990
324.2773'04 — dc20   89-40536
ISBN 0-299-12450-9   CIP
ISBN 0-299-12454-1 (pbk.)

Contents

Figures

Maps

Tables

Preface

I came to study the Illinois Republican Party out of a sense of dissatisfaction with the treatment of U.S. parties as defective organizations. Even though my past experience was with political parties in parliamentary systems, where many critics find their models of ideal parties, I felt no urge to disparage the experience of U.S. parties. Because a single party in a single state appeared to be the only way to manage the complexity of party organization in all its manifestations, my selection of a research setting needed to maximize internal variation. Illinois was chosen because it is large, competitive, and internally diverse, and the Republican Party because it is weak in some areas and strong in others. The Republican Party was also a strategic choice because of my longstanding interest in how ideology can test the limits of organization, an interest stimulated by the strains associated with the presidential candidacy of Barry Goldwater, which were likely to be prominent again at the time of this study.

At the time I began my research I was also aware that the Republican Party was developing new organizational forms nationally, making it, more than the Democratic Party, a test case for examining organizational adaptations to change. As a result, today we see

a pronounced new asymmetry between Republicans and Democrats in their arrays of party and associated structures. The last time the party causes differed so decisively in structure was around the middle of this century as a consequence of Roosevelt's joining together machines and unions on the Democratic side, but this time the innovation and advantage are on the Republican side. (Mayhew, 1986, 331–332)

The nature of Republican adaptations, as well as the limits these are likely to encounter, gives my selection the quality of a critical case.

I began to explore some issues of party organization while conducting a departmental graduate practicum on theory and research during the 1978–79 academic year, in which students were introduced to the research process through some umbrella topic. Because students are understandably resentful if they feel they are doing the professor's research, and because they would have to write independent research papers, I refrained from structuring the topic beyond describing it as a study of the Illinois Republican Party. I was so successful in giving them scope for their own interests that there was not a single paper I could use in support of my subsequent research.

Because a practicum should expose students to a variety of research experiences, I was challenged to assemble examples of different kinds of data and to propose collection of others. I was, in the meantime, learning all I could about the Republican Party, and one means was through wide-ranging interviews with party activists. Some agreed to come to class, where they helped demonstrate the interviewing process. The students developed their own interview schedule, and the resulting 21 interviews with ward and township committeemen in Cook County, covering their activities, allocation of time, and assessment of the party, became my compensation for a year devoted to seeing that students completed their requirements.

I was further rewarded by contacts with student Mary Ann Smania and my practicum teaching assistant, Gwendolyn Nyden, both of whom became research assistants of remarkable dedication. Initial research funding came from the Graduate Research Board at the University of Illinois at Chicago. The Institute of Government and Public Affairs helped throughout the course of this study, and I remain indebted to Sam Gove, its former director, for his support and understanding. It was a grant from the National Science Foundation (SES-8013455) from 1981 to 1983 that really made this study possible. Although this support forced me to develop an interview guide so that the three of us, and later Stephanie Rusnak, could collect consistent data, consistency was not bought with structured questions that everyone had to answer but through a range of topics to be chosen from, depending on the type of informant. Informants were allowed to set the pace of the interview and to guide us in the directions where they were best informed. My intention was to obtain richly detailed information about informants' activities, relations with others in the party, and evaluations of those party segments with which they were familiar.

Although initially informants were chosen for their breadth of information through recommendations from friends and colleagues, it soon became possible to make more systematic selections. Formal position, focal points in the party, and attributions of importance by other party activists or by informed observers were my criteria. Later, I added geographic dispersion and even apparent unimportance as ways of ensuring adequate coverage. I drew on all my ties for help in this process, among them my friend Bill Bacon, who first introduced me to financial contributors; my colleague, the late Milt Rakove, who knew the old-timers; my student Gary Andres, who was then interviewing political action committees; but most of all, my colleague James Nowlan, who provided important entree into the party he has long represented and worked for. John Bibby, Cornelius Cotter, and Malcolm Jewel all gave me valuable advice on how to conduct the interviews, and my colleague Barry Rundquist was even willing, on one occasion, to act as an interviewer. In addition, a structured questionnaire was administered by telephone to a sample of precinct committeemen by the Survey Research Laboratory of the University of Illinois in June 1981, and Richard Lipinski helped with its analysis.

Newspapers were a useful source for reports on election issues and participants and, for these, I had the invaluable assistance of a statewide newspaper-clipping archive compiled by the Institute of Government and Public Affairs and additional help from its librarian, Anna Merritt. I also talked to a number of newspapermen about my research, including Basil Talbott of the Chicago *Sun-Times,* Mike Smith and Dan Tucker of the *Chicago Tribune,* Ray Gibson of the *Suburban Trib,* Bill Lambrecht of the *St. Louis Post-Dispatch,* and Franklin Shuftan of Star-Herald Publications. Newspaper people and sociologists have very different concerns and styles, but all those to whom I spoke were invariably helpful.

Electoral data, available either through the Interuniversity Consortium for Political and Social Research or through our own compilations, made with the assistance of Hannele Happala, were supplemented with data on county and party elections through a canvass of county clerks, conducted by the Survey Research Laboratory. Here I was helped by Jack Beggs and my colleague William Bridges.

Information on campaign contributions was supplied by the State Board of Elections with the assistance of its director, Ronald Michelson, and Barbara Mason. The compilation of what turned out to be a most cumbersome but fascinating set of data, to be elaborated in a forthcoming study, was done by Hannele Happala, Richard Lee, Michael Matters, Len Greski, Mary Ann Mowat, and Francine Cannarozzi.

The network perspective as a strategy of analysis owes much to my reading of Laumann and Pappi's (1976) work on community elites, in which they demonstrate the usefulness of thinking about network components as collective as well as individual actors. My strongest inspiration came from my colleague Christopher O. Ross, whose own work on network analysis encouraged me to sit in on his statistics class.

Clearly I incurred innumerable debts in the course of preparing this volume, and some of those to whom I remain indebted have already been mentioned. I especially want to thank those who took time to give me a careful reading of some version of this volume—Christopher Ross, Sam Gove, Fred L. Strodtbeck, Paul Kleppner, Russell Schutt, and Judith Blau. Others deserving of thanks, if only for the encouragement they gave me, include Mary Fennell, my late colleague David Street, R. Stephen Warner, Austin Ranney, Gerald Wright, William Mischler, Leon Epstein, Joseph Schlesinger, David Mayhew, Richard Fenno, James G. March, Howard Aldrich, Duncan McRae, Jr., and Frank Scioli. If I have forgotten anyone, it is not from ingratitude but from the difficulty of keeping track of the large numbers of my colleagues, especially here at the University of Illinois at Chicago, who have been so generous with their help over the years of this study. I thank them all, as I do those Republicans who gave so generously of their time even though they were not sure what I would do with the information they gave me.

The Party Network

1

The Network of Party Relations

What Is a Political Party?

Why does it matter that political parties have been defined in so many ways, ranging from monolithic Communist parties, synonymous with the state, to ephemeral collections of candidates, barely united to contest a single election (Schlesinger, 1965, 764)? It matters because varied definitions make it possible for different observers, even when confined to the United States and writing at the same time, to find signs of organizational decay (ACIR, 1986, 95-162), organizational emergence (ACIR, 1986, 47-94), and stubborn persistence (Epstein, 1986). And all of them may be right, because every definition of a political party implies a theory and every theory shapes what is subsequently observed. I cannot even begin a description of the Illinois Republican Party without an underlying theory for identifying its elements or go on to explain party life without an array of theoretical tools.

The basic premise on which this volume rests is that a political party is an organization. An assertion as commonplace as this may still bring confusion rather than clarity, because organization has multiple meanings, and the perspectives that follow from those meanings may each generate an independent research tradition (e.g., Zucker, 1988; Carrol, 1988). My solution was to search the organizational literature, looking for any vantage points that could be used to explain the character of political parties.

For example, if we follow Scott (1987) and divide contemporary organizational theory into three major approaches, or schools, we can see how each provides a distinct pathway for understanding party life. In the rational systems approach, organizations are defined as structures designed to achieve specific goals in the most efficient way. On the surface, it may be difficult to see any connection between the rational basis of an automated factory or a bureaucracy and that of a political party. Yet a similar principle of rationality can be found in the purposeful character of party organization, aimed at achieving electoral success.

Organizational structure also underlies the natural systems approach, but it is more broadly conceived to take into account organizations' ability to acquire lives of their own, distinct from their founding intentions. In the transition, organizations become institutionalized. Wilson (1973, 13) is led from this approach to consider how voluntary associations, including political parties, are maintained by incentives offered to participants. Like a school or university that may continue to exist regardless of its success in educating students, a political party is also marked by an ability to sustain its organizational autonomy even in the face of electoral defeat.

The third school, the open systems approach, emphasizes process rather than structure and the ability of organizational parts to act independently of each other in relation to changing environmental conditions. Organizations are viewed as "coalitions of shifting interest groups" whose relations are "strongly influenced by environmental factors" (Scott, 1987, 23). This perspective helps in dealing with the existence of shifting coalitions within a party that can be "loosely coupled," that is, they can operate with considerable autonomy without leading to the destruction of the party. The common observation that there is no single hierarchy of authority in a party, almost inconceivable under conditions of a rational organization, becomes feasible in an open system, where hierarchy can refer to the existence of clusters of organizational elements and differences among organizational levels (Scott, 1987, 84). By defining membership in an organization on the basis of activities rather than by formal positions, we can deal with the fact that party boundaries, like those of universities, are typically blurred (Scott, 1987, 82), making it meaningful to think of voters as the essential environment of a party rather than direct participants in its organization.

An eclectic approach to organizational theory sets the stage for reviewing the literature on U.S. political parties and, using the definitions of party found in it, for identifying specific party actors. Once more or less distinct boundaries are established for distinguishing those to be included under the party rubric, a primary description of the Republican Party of Illinois as it was between 1978 and 1981 can follow in chapter 2.

Party Composition

The definition of party which I value as a starting point is one that is broadly inclusive of party actors, regardless of their official status, and emphasizes the primacy of office-seeking as the rationale for party existence. This is provided by Epstein, for whom a party is "any group, however loosely organized, seeking to elect governmental office-holders under a given label. Having a label . . . rather than an organization is the crucial defining element" (Epstein, 1980, 9).

One virtue of this definition is that it encompasses sources of party actors that could be overlooked if only formally specified positions and formally organized groups with a party label were considered. For example, party actors can be found in the guise of interest groups, akin to and even indistinguishable from political parties in their efforts to mobilize supporters, capture government office, and influence legislation. But interest groups have other purposes as well, and only parties "operate solely as political organizations, solely as instruments of political action" (Sorauf and Beck, 1988, 18). While recognizing the unclear distinction between the two, we must still keep them separate (Huckshorn, 1984, 287–290). Only if party and interest group are viewed as independent does it then make sense to look for an interest group that, while retaining its own identity, has permeated the boundaries of a political party. An interest group can be treated as part of a party network when its political actions are directed solely or largely on behalf of a given party. For example, when the National Chamber Alliance for Politics, the political arm of the U.S. Chamber of Commerce, endorsed 100 congressional candidates in 1982, all of whom were Republicans, only the Democrats seemed surprised by the behavior of "an ostensibly nonpartisan group" (Clarity and Weaver, 1984). We can expect a bias toward a single party to be true of many other organized interest groups whose lobbying efforts generally are spent disproportionately with one party.

Spiralling costs of campaigns and candidate reliance on the mass media, especially television, are frequently cited as major sources of party decline (e.g., Crotty, 1984, 75–116). Although they may be, they also provide the context for the emergence of two other kinds of party actor. New methods of campaigning encourage reliance on expert advisors, skilled in the uses of public-opinion polling and the media and adept at political strategy. The presence of technical experts within the party coexists with old skills of door-to-door canvassing and getting out the vote and with traditional functions of candidate recruitment and patronage distribution (Huckshorn, 1976, 97–168). The new activities of experts may be incorporated into existing party positions and groups, but to the extent that they are not, a separate category, that of advisor, is needed for this additional party actor.

New actors are also associated with the vast sums of money involved in campaigns. Since Watergate and subsequent changes in campaign financing laws, there has been a dramatic rise in the formation of political action committees (PACs), often connected with business and industry or with trade associations. The number of PACs and their financial resources are clearly an important change in the political climate, but their presence has not led to the demise of parties, because PACs give their money to party candidates and, moreover, generally favor one party (Sabato, 1984, 88–89). I use the category of financial contributor to subsume both individuals and groups, including PACs, fundraisers, and individuals who make large and regular contributions. Financial contributor, interest group, and advisor are considered to be within a party network when their political activities are carried out solely or largely on behalf of a single party.

Epstein is first useful and then limited in the guidance he offers, because his intention is to provide a minimal definition of party, one that is suitable for comparing parties in Western democracies but covers only those elements that are essential to party existence (Epstein, 1980, 315). Sartori, who begins with a similar definition, criticizes Epstein for leaving us with a definition that has neither explanatory nor predictive capacity (Sartori, 1976, 64). Thus, while Epstein provides a starting point, he offers no criteria for selecting members of a group beyond some unspecified activity on behalf of candidates and no guidelines for mapping relations among members.

Further specification of party composition is available from Sorauf and Beck, who describe U.S. parties as "three-headed political giants – tripartite systems of interactions that embrace all these political individuals. As political structures, they include a party organization, a party in office, and a party in the electorate" (Sorauf and Beck, 1988, 9–10). From these different arenas of operation we discern different functions for actors, allowing us to elaborate the party's governing and programmatic goals, as well as those goals associated with organizational continuity. Sorauf's and Epstein's definitions combined suggest that these functions are incorporated in formal positions and groups, which then become another way of identifying critical actors. In Illinois, positions include the public offices of U.S. senator and congressman, governor, other state constitutional offices, state senator, state representative, and local offices. They also cover party offices: national committeeman, state central committeeman, county chairman, and local committeeman. Groups with leadership or coordinating functions in the legislature – the state Senate and House leadership – or for the apparatus – the Republican National Committee and the State Central Committee – are also identifiable. Since they are separately staffed and assigned a specific range of duties, it is also worth specifying those groups that have solely campaign-related functions: the Republican Senate Campaign Committee, the Republican Congressional Campaign Committee, and as they exist in Illinois, the State Senate Campaign Committee and the State House Campaign Committee. We also need to leave room for auxiliary groups, associated with young people, women, ethnic groups, or special interests, or having specific functions of fundraising. More discretion is obviously needed with these, in the sense that their relative importance is more likely to be affected by the state environment in which they are found.

In chapter 2, the logic of party structure is given concrete shape in the Illinois Republican Party, identified through 23 positions or groups. Each element, or actor, is described briefly and placed in historical context. Justification for choosing these 23 is contrasted with reasons for omitting other positions from the critical analysis. In this scheme, actors are not specific individuals, even when the reference is to unique positions. When speaking of the governor, for example, I include staff along with the role occupant — in the case of this study, for the last three Republican administrations. The same is true with respect to senator, where staff within the state and in Washington, D.C., contributes to defining the position, and here I include past senators and contenders for the office. Some positions typically have many occupants, like county chairman and local committeeman. In such cases, all the occupants are treated collectively for defining behavior associated with the position. A political actor may also be a group, like the State Central Committee, made up of a relatively small number of individuals, or a collection of groups, such as the category of interest group. All these actors are treated in the singular, like an ideal type, in the first part of this volume and elsewhere, whenever I emphasize generic qualities. This is done as a means of penetrating the structure of party organization in a general way, unencumbered, to begin with, by the effects of specific role incumbents or the consequences of district-level variations.

Omitted here is Sorauf's conception of the electoral party as formed by voters. Reasons for exclusion of voters are developed in chapter 2 on grounds now advocated as well by Schlesinger (1985, 1153), who agrees that voters should more properly be treated as part of the party's environment. The arguments of organizational theorists about the importance of environmental contingencies (e.g., Aldrich, 1979) have been demonstrated for parties in a comparative context (Harmel and Janda, 1982) and reinforce the need to consider environmental influences in the study of parties. Voters and their patterns of support are a crucial element of the party's environment, affecting its ability to confront new elections and new events. They are a measure of the party's past behavior with respect to success or failure in winning office as well as a historic link between the electoral sector and other party sectors. Effects of different kinds of environment are presented in chapter 4, which also takes into account relative electoral strength as differential stimuli to the formation and strength of ties among actors. The discovery of such relations also stimulates the systematic decomposition of relevant elements according to local variations in party strength.

The composition of a party generally, and of the Illinois Republicans in particular, covers all levels of the federal structure and both official and unofficial positions. In this approach I am close to Schlesinger's current definition of organization, in which he includes

all of the cooperative, deliberate activities among two or more people aimed at capturing elective office in the name of the party. The organization of party theory therefore rejects the distinction between formal and informal, or prescribed or non-prescribed structures and procedures. (Schlesinger, 1985, 1153)

Because I presume the necessity of giving some scope to the nonelectoral goals of the party, my specific selection of party actors is more attuned to the continuity of party organization than Schlesinger's appears to be when he states, "The basic unit of the political party is the nucleus, which consists of the collective efforts to capture a single office" (Schlesinger, 1985, 1153).

I agree strongly with Schlesinger that party components should be sought in terms of their activities — whether formally prescribed or not — rather than in geopolitical structures per se. But it does not follow then that the only true organizational units are those associated with a candidate seeking office. For example, in referring to the precinct, Schlesinger writes that

the need to record votes or to fill out the formal party structure does not assure party organization in the precinct. For a true nucleus to exist, there must be the expectation that at some time, if not in the immediate future, organizational activity will lead to the capture of the nuclear office. Thus, it is possible for a candidate to run for an office without the development of a true party nucleus if the candidate and his supporters have no expectations that the office can ever be won. (Schlesinger, 1965, 775)

If we were to accept only such nuclei as qualified for inclusion, we would be slighting the significance of party institutionalization. One reason that parties remain important is that they have the state-appointed job of organizing elections. Parties need to create the machinery for nominating candidates to all elected offices, and this task alone, regardless of the chances of winning, can be the basis for the elaboration of an organizational apparatus. The political advancement of ambitious individuals is provided through the avenue of parties. We should remember how the presidential aspirations of people like George Wallace, Eugene McCarthy, and John Anderson foundered after they broke with the constraints of existing parties to mount their own antiparty campaigns. Parties offer virtually the only alternatives to voters, and even where the partisan attachment of individual voters has declined, the limited nature of the choices available to them has not been altered.

The electoral bases of party organization are so pervasive, they can be found in sources other than potentially successful office-seeking. At the same time, there are also party-related activities that do not have such direct ties to elections. For example, representatives in Congress and in state legislatures are elected on party lines and tend act in ways that are discernibly partisan. The president and governors are nominated by parties and act, to some degree at least, as party leaders. Some municipalities are officially run on nonpartisan lines, but that generally does not disguise the partisan affiliation of most officeholders or the partisan relevance of their activities. A case in point is the city of Chicago, notorious for its adherence to party-dominated politics, even though city council elections are based on a nonpartisan ballot. Partly because public officeholders, but also party ones, offer services to their constituents, the continuity of party components has meaning beyond any single election (cf. Sorauf, 1963, 44–45).

Network Construction

Eldersveld has sought to provide a comprehensive definition of a party by combining three prevailing images: "a group seeking power by winning elections," "a group that processes interest-group demands," or "an ideological competitor" (Eldersveld, 1982, 8–11). What is strikingly absent, given Eldersveld's earlier work (1964), is attention to party structure. Structure takes shape through relations among actors—there is no organization without such links. Duverger, associated with the most comprehensive effort at classifying parties along organizational dimensions, downplays by implication the contemporary relevance of Eldersveld's imagery of parties as representatives of class or ideological interests and, further, even their office-seeking goals: ". . . present-day parties are distinguished far less by their programme or the class of their members than by the nature of their organization. A party is a community with a particular structure. Modern parties are characterized primarily by their anatomy" (Duverger, 1963, xv). Sartori (1976, 58) chides Duverger for emphasizing structure through the building of typologies without at the same time producing a compatible definition of party. Perhaps the difficulties of doing both are almost insurmountable; Sartori himself, who promised to deal with organization in a volume separate from his definitional one (1976, 71), has yet to do so. Duverger's formidable work leaves us with a conception that apparently relegates loosely structured U.S. parties to the category of defective organizations.

In support of such a view, it has not been unusual for commentators to look at U.S. parties and conclude that their structure is so decentralized that they can barely function:

Perhaps the best word to describe the structure of each of our two great parties is *feudal,* but it is feudalism with few enforceable pledges of faith, feudalism in which the bonds of mutual support are so loose that it often seems to border on anarchy, feudalism in which one party does not even have a king. (Rossiter, 1960, 13)

But to conclude this is to misunderstand the complexity and consequently anarchic nature of organizational operation in general. The concept of organized anarchy, rather than being an oxymoron, captures what often happens under conditions of uncertainty (March and Olsen, 1976, 24–37; Scott, 1987, 277–282). As Street (1981, 288) has observed:

The existence of an organized anarchy is revealed in all organizations sometimes and in some organizations often on those occasions when decisions must be made despite the ambiguities that exist because preferences are problematic, the appropriate technology unclear, and the roster and involvement of participants in the decisions uncertain.

Following from the organizational literature, which encourages us to abandon tightly integrated organizational structure as the only model of party organization, we can see the opportunities that lie in variation, because "political parties in their internal organizations present all the phenomena and varieties of centralization-decentralization, coordination-uncoordination, of which complex, large-scale systems of human relationships are capable" (Leiserson, 1958, 36). Opportunities are accompanied by tensions, to be sure, but these are found in all organizations. Individual and collective actors face problems and evolve goals that may put them at odds with others in the party in ways similar to those that occur in other social settings:

. . . what is a threat from the system's standpoint is a defensive maneuver from the part's standpoint. Conversely, the system's defenses against these are, in turn, threats to the part's defenses. Consequently, it is to be expected that efforts to reduce the threatening behavior of either the part or the system will be resisted. In short, not only efforts to change the system, but also those directed at maintaining it are likely to entail conflict and resistance. (Gouldner, 1967, 163)

Party actors are only lifeless constructs until they are seen as true actors, engaged in transactions that produce more or less stable links. In the structure I build, I consider party actors and the relations among them as making up a network; a network is both a descriptive conception of the party and an analytical tool for elaborating the consequences of having different participants in positions and groups, differences in the makeup of local districts, and differences in the character of relationships among actors. As Tichy broadly defines it:

The network perspective portrays a society as a system of participants – people, groups, organizations – joining by a variety of relationships. Not all pairs of participants join directly, and some join through multiple relationships. Network analysis examines the structure and patterning of these relationships, and seeks to identify both their causes and consequences. (Tichy, 1981, 225)

Applied to a single organization, the network approach allows it to

be treated as sets of roles linked by multiple networks that transmit information, influence, and affect. Some of these role sets are formal, such as departments and work groups, and others informal, such as coalitions and cliques. (Tichy, 1981, 226)

The network is constructed by the investigator, to be sure, but not in an arbitrary way, because it is defined by specified relationships (Aldrich and Whetten, 1981, 387). In chapter 3, links among actors are first established, based on information about contacts given in self-reports, written records, and observations. That chapter keeps to a general level of analysis in examining the properties of links. Actors are distinguished by their centrality – the number of ways they are connected with others – and their participation in reciprocal relations. Out of the links formed, different patterns of cohesion emerge. Variations in the kinds of linkage produce different consequences for the whole system as well as for its parts (Aldrich and Whetten, 1981, 388). Generalizations that appear in chapter 3, although compared with the literature on network theory, are most closely tied to my specific findings. That is, whatever theory is presented evolves directly from the data.

Conceiving of the Illinois Republican Party as a cast of variably linked party actors also puts us in company with those who see organizations as coalitions of shifting interests (Cyert and March, 1963; Pfeffer and Salancik, 1978). In this perspective, participating individuals and groups come together with different and often competing objectives, and accommodating these different objectives results in an organization that vibrates with change. The possibility of attenuated links and discontinuities among offices and actors is what evokes for us the imagery of "loose coupling" (March and Olsen, 1976).

Relations among Actors

Once I have defined a political party as a network of actors – individual or collective units sharing a party name whose activities have some recognized partisan purpose – we must ask the more critical question: what contribution do actors make to the collective undertaking? To find out how parties work requires examining relations among actors as they go about doing their party jobs.

Factors affecting the existence and nature of ties among elements are either contingent or mediating. Contingent factors stem from the environment in which elements are found, arising either from the political system or from electoral history. Mediating factors, in contrast, are those directly affecting links among elements, based on the resources available to actors.

Among the contingent political factors, the electoral system is especially important in Illinois, because the use of cumulative voting and multi-member districts, in force until the 1982 election, provided unique opportunities for the formation of links. Again and again, we will encounter systemic constraints affecting legislative candidates, differences between candidates for the state House and Senate, and all those actors who have ties with them. It is in this regard that I am most persuaded by Schlesinger's insistence in treating "collective efforts to capture a single office" as the "nucleus" of party existence, and the explanation of "why and where party nuclei will emerge and how they will link up with others" as the "central problem" of party theory (Schlesinger, 1985, 1153).

Tocqueville (1945, 213) was struck by the "feverish excitement" promoted by the frequency of elections in the United States when he visited early in the nineteenth century, and that impression still holds for recent observers. Just as striking is the frequency with which an unusually small number of party labels is used, apparently involving the same parties in elections across levels. Yet federalism, the separation of powers, and the "new politics," by which is meant the emphasis on individual candidates, are generally considered barriers to links across sectors of responsibility, or, in the case of the new politics, even within sectors. I began with no such assumptions, proceeding from the thesis that any formal definition of a relationship, even an exclusionary one, establishes a potential link. For example, different spheres of responsibility separate congressmen from state legislators, and within overlapping geopolitical units, a congressman and state legislator(s) may use the lack of formally specified relations to minimize or preclude contacts. Others, however, will accept a shared constituency as a stimulus to establish bonds. The pervasive effects of the political system environment are dealt with throughout this volume rather than in a single chapter, unlike the treatment of the historical environment in chapter 4.

Although contacts are a simple and straightforward basis for locating links, they are best used for a highly general analysis, and they do not, in themselves, communicate the substance of their decisional origins, the activities they entail, or the relationships they form. For these purposes, we need to specify the media of transaction, found in the special problems faced by political parties, or even in the common problems of all organizations (Tichy, 1981, 231–235). For example, technical problems, requiring that resources be directed to bringing about desired outcomes, are often beset by uncertainty and are met through exchanges of information. Like all organizations, parties face political problems of gaining and retaining control of their resources under changing conditions (Tichy, 1981, 233). If such problems are more central in parties, this may be because parties are a "miniature political system" (Eldersveld, 1964, 1) in which power is the primary medium of interchange. Power is treated in chapter 5 in the sense of decision-making authority. Although this may suggest some hierarchical structure, there is in fact no inherent hierarchy in the party for the division of authority federally or functionally. Power then provides an uncertain link, since it resides not only with those in top positions, but can also be held, and used, by quite minor officials. The literature on organizations is full of examples about how low-level functionaries can control important resources and thereby affect organizational outcomes without either increasing their resources or translating them into higher status.

Because the coercive nature of power can only be applied in limited ways within nonstate organizations, party actors continue to seek other forms of influence. This leads Hennessy, for example, even to dispute the importance of formal gubernatorial powers: "Governors' powers in party organization, I suspect, are more closely associated with (a) patronage, (b) ideology, and (c) presumed voter appeal" (Hennessy, 1968, 32). One general alternative to power is the use of resources to acquire influence by stimulating bonds of personal loyalty. In the party, influence exists in the form of patronage, discussed in chapter 6. Influence through patronage has many manifestations, from low-level government jobs, to honorific appointments, to positions with no formal party affiliation but great party influence.

All organizations have a cultural component through which they strive to meet problems of internal cohesion with common beliefs and congruent values (Tichy, 1981, 234–235). When a party is defined, as Edmund Burke did in 1770, as "a body of men united, for promoting by their joint endeavours the national interest, upon some particular principle in which they are all agreed" (Burke, 1971, 151), U.S. parties appear imperfect. Similarly, Tocqueville described "great parties" as

those which cling to principles rather than to their consequences; to general and not to special cases; to ideas and not to men. These parties are usually distinguished by nobler features, more generous passions, more genuine convictions, and a more bold and open conduct than the others. (Tocqueville, 1945, 182)

He was thus disappointed by their absence in the United States. Others (e.g., Schattschneider, 1942, 35–37) may reject such urgings for ideologi-

cally consistent parties, recognizing that, within any organizational setting, the moral consistency that ideology gives to goals may be bought at
the price of organizational expansion or even continuity. Yet no party exists without some degree of shared beliefs and, for good or ill, there is
no way that a party can avoid the transactional nature of those beliefs.
Ideology, the subject of chapter 7, considers how political beliefs link legislators with each other and with their constituents.

With the exception of salaried officials, the party is not an income-
producing organization for supporting party participants. Yet, as a result
of the costliness of modern forms of campaigning, money is an increasingly important medium of exchange for party actors, as we shall see by
looking at campaign contributions in chapter 8. Contributions provide the
links for legislators with district and corporate interests, with elements of
the party apparatus, across federal areas of responsibility and within the
same sector.

The four media are, at one level, *resources,* either intrinsic to the party,
derived from its surrounding environment, or derived from the larger society. They become agents used by party actors to *communicate* with each
other in choosing among alternatives. Relations in which actors engage
are then defined by the media's *sanctioning* capacity, through which actors
intentionally use power and ideology primarily to punish and patronage
and money to reward.

Each medium is independent, but money, power, and favors may be in-
termingled, since one can be used to acquire the others. They are still separate, however, both logically and empirically. Along with ideology, each
in turn gives a different perspective on how links are forged and relations
elaborated. At the same time, we are able to ask the same questions about
the uses of each medium because of the limited alternatives available to
actors who compete for scarce resources in an uncertain world. Their choices
range between preferences for stability and order or for adaptability and
change. On the side of order, we look for the way resources are used to
maintain existing relations, to limit opportunities for entering new relations, and to cope with dependency by favoring hierarchical modes of relation. On the side of change, we expect resources to be used to challenge
existing relations, to search out new links, and to adapt to uncertainty by
seeking new organizational forms.

The four media of exchange described in chapters 5 through 8 are so
patently parallel to Parsons's four "generalized media of social interchange"—power, influence, value commitments, and money (Parsons, 1967,
297–382)—that one might easily expect parallels in meaning and treatment.
There are many instances when Parsons's conceptions enrich our understanding of party processes. Yet there are also enough differences in interpretation between us to warrant some comment here.

According to Parsons (1967, 274), the media of interchange are symbolic, worthless except for what they acquire from confidence engendered by their use. In my study, media are considered symbolic but also intrinsically valuable, especially power and beliefs. This is because people desire power and they hold to ideological beliefs for their own sake, not only for the reason that power and beliefs can be used to relate to others.

In Parsons's scheme, media circulate as "currency" of exchange, and like any currency, they can be stored or spent (1967, 323). This is not always a meaningful formulation, and Cartwright and Warner (1976, 645–646) criticize Parsons for the inappropriateness of defining power this way. They find his efforts to fit all the media into the same mold to be reflections of "two well-recognized and self-acknowledged aspects of Parsons' cognitive style . . . (1) his evidently deep-seated conviction that convergence is a form of proof and (2) his attraction to, and facility with, analogies" (Cartwright and Warner, 1976, 652). In my view, the usefulness of the four media lies in their separate explanatory power, and any analogies that can be drawn among them are incidental.

Perhaps the greatest source of possible confusion comes from the way we describe our intended use of the media. Parsons wanted to explain some general aspects of the social system, but from the examples he used (e.g., 1967, 337–345), it is not at all clear that he actually needed the media to do so. Cartwright and Warner (1976, 639) argue that the media are not, in fact, explanatory variables. They are better understood as dependent variables which need to be explained themselves. In the context of this volume, it should become clear that, for us, the media in use are very definitely explanatory variables.

Robust Organization

If we, as students of parties, see in organizational theory the path to understanding U.S. political parties, the reverse has not attracted organizational theorists. Schlesinger's observation, made 20 years ago, is still relevant today: "Although political parties provided the basis for the study of organizations for such pioneers as Michels (1944, first published 1915), Ostrogorski (1902), and Weber (1946, first published 1919), parties today stand outside the mainstream of organization theory" (Schlesinger, 1965, 764). Organizational theorists currently pay no attention to parties or, when they do, confine themselves to references to urban machines or to Michels's (1949) analysis of the German Social Democratic Party. Scott, for example, accepts Michels's conclusion that organization means oligarchy. "Most unions, most professional associations and other types of voluntary associations, and *most political parties* [emphasis added] exhibit oligarchical leadership structures" (Scott, 1987, 309). On the contrary, in parties "authority is uncertain and leadership is precarious" (Wilson, 1973, 215), which I too will demonstrate. Some elements of a party may display oligarchical structures, it is true, but even when they do, they do not coalesce into a single hierarchy of authority. So while we may draw on organizational theory to show points of similarity between political parties and organizations as diverse as factories, governmental bureaucracies, department store chains, and universities, ultimately we have to look to parties themselves as the source of theoretical generalization.

U.S. parties may truly be unique organizationally, but if that is so, they need to be viewed nonpejoratively, as Jewell and Olson do when they enumerate four distinctive characteristics. These include the openness of membership criteria, the episodic timing of activities, the constraints imposed by the need for parties to parallel the ecologically based structures of government, and the variability of parties by location (Jewel and Olson, 1988, 48–51). In choosing to study Illinois Republicans I am aware of the possibility that one may speak of "the fifty American party systems" (Sorauf and Beck, 1988, 38–43) without even broaching the variability between the two major parties. The research presented here is a case study with all the limits that method imposes on generalizations. But it is exactly from this kind of method that it will become possible to separate party structure into its general and more variable components.

A party network is not an atomized set of actors. No matter how poorly defined its boundaries, loosely linked its participants, or varied the interpretation of its goals, it remains an organized entity. Moreover, for those defined as party actors, the Republican Party as a source of identification, focus of activity, and wellspring of belief is not in question. The network conception captures what is problematic to them, and hence to us – the kinds of people who best represent the Republican Party, the kinds of activity that best promote the party's interests, and the kinds of ideas that best express Republican ideals. The network of actors opens the problems previously faced when studying parties to the insights of organizational theory, and, at the same time, generates its own party-based theories. The result is intended to put together an appreciation of the unique details of party life among Illinois Republicans with the generic qualities of organizations. In this way I hope to resolve some of the tension between theory and experience earlier identified in studies of decision-making:

Very few reports of organizational decision making strike experienced participants in organizations as unusual. At the same time, many common observations about organizations are pathological from the point of view of theories of organizations. What is mundane to experience frequently becomes unexplained variance in the theories. What is standard in the interpretations of organizations frequently becomes irrelevant to experience. (March and Olsen, 1976, 10)

This volume concludes with the assessment that the Illinois Republican Party represents a robust organization and, in this way, is typical of other U.S. parties. Party organization is robust by being simultaneously complex and protean, elastic and indeterminate. Robustness is the attribute of organization that provides stamina for the day-to-day struggles; it is distinct from the survival benefits that come to an organization from legal guarantees or from greater effectiveness.

Effectiveness itself is assessed by comparing political scientists' judgments about the ideal party system with the results from examination of Illinois Republicans. Both are juxtaposed with organizational theorists' views of what makes for effective organizations. It will come as no surprise that success is evaluated differently, depending on the individuals or groups doing the judging, but in all instances, the criteria used are tied to the party's objectives. The relatively clear and limited goals available to the party form the principal constraints within which party actors operate.

If robustness is separate from the effectiveness of ideal parties, it is also distinct from how changing political realities affect what parties can, rather than should, be. This leads me to ask what makes for adaptive parties, those able to thrive in response to their environments. Now we have to distance ourselves from the Illinois Republican Party, for while it continues to be the basis of my final comments, it was not selected as an exemplar of a highly adaptive party. Its operation in the period studied explains what makes for both greater and lesser adaptability.

A Note on Method

The argument and layout of this volume rest on a diverse body of data. Information on methods is found in the preface, along with my thanks to all those who helped me, and in following chapters, where it appears along with reported data.

The cornerstone of this study is based on 200 informants, interviewed as many as three times and for as long as four hours at a time. I consider these interviews, done with persons whom I call informants in tribute to their knowledge of the Republican Party, the key to understanding how elements hang together and how they work. Many of the interviews were conducted where informants did their party-related work, and along with attendance at campaign rallies, one state convention, and documentation supplied by the state party headquarters of current mailings and minutes of meetings up to 1970, provided opportunities to observe the party in action. Not only did informants tell us what they, as individuals, did or felt about issues or other actors, but we could locate their actions and beliefs according to their placements in the party. They all spoke freely about what they did and what and whom they knew, about their satisfactions, their grievances, and their aspirations.

Anonymity was promised to all informants and respondents, a problem when talking to and about public figures, unlike what is experienced in ordinary surveys, a problem, moreover, in that it is the character of these individuals that gives intrinsic interest to this study. My solution was to use the names of party actors whenever information about them could not be tied to an identifiable source other than a published one. To protect the anonymity of the small number of women informants and elected women officeholders, I used masculine nouns and pronouns throughout to refer to all informants and members of the party network.

By interviewing as many people as we did, observing them in their own settings, and supplementing what we were told with other sources of information, I had checks on reliability. These other sources include a survey of precinct committeemen, designed to give fuller coverage to lower-level party workers and to the diversity of the state, and newspaper reports about local and statewide issues and participants. But best of all, it was the informants who gave the kind of detailed information that an anthropologist might collect for an ethnographic analysis. In consideration of this, I often let informants speak for themselves in unattributed quotations, using their own language to reveal the ways party actors explain their political world.

2

The Illinois Republican Party

The Cast of Party Actors

The Illinois Republican Party network was densely populated during the time frame of the study. Not only were there the expected party officeholders and other activists, but also all public offices had substantial Republican representation from before the 1978 election until after the 1980 election, summarized in Tables 2-1 through 2-3.

Party actors in this chapter are treated as ideal types, in the sense that information about offices and officeholders is of a summary nature, giving only those details about particular individuals necessary for establishing an initial context for network relations and noting sources of information. Later chapters will build on this framework, specifying local and individual variations. To keep track of the 23 actors defined here and the individuals who participate as these actors, readers may consult the appended directory, on pages 287–296.

Senator

From Senator Charles Percy's election in 1966 until Senator Everett Dirksen's death in 1969, the Republicans had the benefit of two senators in Washington. Dirksen, a colorful figure widely known in the state, first achieved congressional office by challenging a group of contenders after entering a primary without official party backing. As senator, he became a central figure in the Republican Party, both nationally and in the state. His concern with state party matters was reflected in the frequent presence of his aide at meetings of the State Central Committee and his own welcomed efforts on behalf of other candidates. Governor Richard Ogilvie appointed Speaker of the House Ralph Smith to fill the vacancy caused by Dirksen's death, but could not prevent a challenge to Smith in the primary election. Although Smith won it with about 80 percent of the vote, the challenge was symptomatic of dissatisfaction within the party, and Smith was later defeated by Democrat Adlai Stevenson III.

Senator Percy's involvement with Republican politics proceeded from a businessman's attraction to Republican positions. His first party office

Table 2-1. Recent Statewide Republican Officeholders

	Tenure
Senator	
Everett C. Dirksen	1950–69
Ralph Smith (appointed)	1969–72
Charles H. Percy	1966–84
Governor	
William G. Stratton	1952–60
Richard B. Ogilvie	1968–72
James R. Thompson	1976–90
Constitutional officer	
Attorney General William J. Scott	1968–80
Comptroller George W. Lindberg	1972–76

Table 2-2. Illinois Republican Congressmen, 1978–1980

Congressman	District	First Elected
Edward J. Derwinski	4	1958
Henry J. Hyde	6	1974
John E. Porter	10	1979
Philip M. Crane	12	1969
Robert McClory	13	1962
John N. Erlenborn	14	1964
Tom Corcoran	15	1976
John B. Anderson	16	1960
Lynn Martin		1980
George O'Brien	17	1972
Robert H. Michel	18	1956
Tom Railsback	19	1966
Paul Findley	20	1960
Edward R. Madigan	21	1972
Daniel J. Crane	22	1978

Total Illinois congressional seats = 24.

Table 2-3. Republicans in the Illinois General Assembly,
1978–1980

	Election Year	
	1978	1980
Senate (Seats = 59)	27	29
House (Seats = 177)	88	91

was as president of the United Republican Fund, a businessmen's group that was, at the time, the sole fundraising agency in the state concerned with supporting the party apparatus. Later he was to run unsuccessfully for the governorship in 1964, first winning a bitter primary race against William J. Scott. Percy had been a major vote-getter in his senatorial races, but this changed in 1978. Deliberately appealing to voters without strong partisan commitments, he alienated those Republicans who wanted him to make the same kinds of appeal they associated with Senator Dirksen. Threats of a challenge in the 1978 primary were strongest from Phyllis Schlafly, well known as a spokesman for conservative causes, who finally did not enter the race. A minor challenge by maverick Lars Daly had little consequence as far as overall results are concerned. More unexpected and therefore more serious was the attack from Democratic candidate Alex Seith, who appeared to eat into the kinds of support that Percy felt he could normally expect. It was a shaken Percy who won, and many Republicans asked if this signalled that he had learned his lesson (Crotty, 1984, 99–105). What they appeared to want was to have him behave like a "true Republican."

A fresh opportunity for the Republicans opened in 1980, when incumbent Senator Stevenson decided against trying for another term. Three candidates competed in the primary: incumbent Lieutenant Governor Dave O'Neal; incumbent Attorney General William J. Scott; and the mayor of Peoria, Richard Carver. Scott, an unusually strong vote-getter, was already under investigation for income tax charges, and his trial was underway during the primary. Even so, he came close to winning the primary race, which was followed by his conviction for tax evasion. The narrowly victorious O'Neal was then unsuccessful against Secretary of State Alan Dixon, the Democrats most popular vote-getter in statewide races.

Most of what is said in this volume about the senator as party actor is necessarily about Senator Percy. Dirksen and Smith are still remembered participants in the office, however, and information about them is used when appropriate, as is information about the three unsuccessful contenders for the senatorial position opened in 1980. Given the prominence of the office, it is possible to draw on public sources. In addition, eight informants directly connected with the office supplied information for this study.

Governor

A party network with an incumbent governor is surely different from one without, a situation ignored in this study. To provide information on the party role of the governor's office, I rely on 18 interviews with individuals holding staff or major departmental responsibilities with one of the three last Republican governors, and some comparisons among the three governors will be possible.

Each of the governors had a different route to office. For William Stratton, it was through varied experience in elected office, including that of state treasurer and U.S. Congress. After two terms as governor, he was defeated in a third try. Richard Ogilvie's sole electoral experience was as Cook County sheriff, from which he built sufficient support to challenge the primary candidacy of John Altorfer, a prominent downstate politician. Coming into office with a well-developed program, Ogilvie introduced the first state income tax, and proceeded to conduct his office with the apparent hope that accomplishments based on new revenue sources would overcome objections to the tax. This was not to be, and Ogilvie served only one term, suffering defeat from an equally short-lived Democratic governor. James Thompson moved to the governorship after his appointment as U.S. attorney, where his most famous case was the prosecution of former Democratic Governor Otto Kerner on bribery charges. Shortly thereafter, Thompson received his party's nomination and went on to win the governor's race for an initial two-year term (Hartley, 1979). When the electoral calendar was changed to hold statewide races in off-presidential years, Thompson achieved even greater electoral support. Popularity with voters could barely withstand the severe test of deteriorating economic conditions, and in the 1982 election, Thompson won by a hairbreadth. While now beyond the frame of this study, Thompson's vulnerability, like Percy's, is an indication of the unstable composition of party positions and, by extension, of the party network.

Since the constitutional change of 1972, the lieutenant governor runs in tandem with the governor, avoiding the earlier situation where the two executive officers could be of different parties. The two still run separately in the primary, and whom the governor wants to be his running mate can be important. Dave O'Neal was the first Republican lieutenant governor under the new system, winning a contested primary in 1976, without evidence that he was Thompson's choice. O'Neal was one of three contenders in the 1980 senatorial primary, and shortly after his defeat in the general election he resigned as lieutenant governor, complaining that it was a "useless" office. Only in 1982 was Governor Thompson's choice a factor in a three-way primary race, when his preference and eventual victor was House Speaker George Ryan. Although not necessarily agreeing with O'Neal's characterization of the office, I will ignore it as a primary actor in the party network, because its occupancy is mainly a means to greater name recognition on the road to another elected office.

Constitutional Officer

Since the constitutional change of 1972, there are now four elected statewide constitutional executive officers in addition to the governor and lieutenant governor: attorney general, secretary of state, comptroller, and treasurer. Each is potentially significant as a focus of independent partisan activity, enhanced, in the case of attorney general and secretary of state, by responsibilities that allow for welcome publicity and offices that have been the sources of considerable patronage. During the time of the study, Republicans were least fortunate in winning election to constitutional offices except for that of attorney general, held by William J. Scott since 1968, from which he built a strong personal following, leading the Republican ticket in 1978. Found guilty of income tax charges, he resigned after the 1980 election.

Only the office of comptroller was held by the Republicans for a single term in the 1970s. The desirable office of secretary of state had last been held by Charles Carpentier from 1950 until his death in 1964. The resignation of Democrat Alan Dixon to run for the U.S. Senate in 1980 opened the way for the appointment of former state representative and gubernatorial staffer James Edgar, who translated that into electoral victory in 1982.

Just as in the case of the governor, one can speculate about the consequences when a party fails to gain constitutional offices. But unlike what we know about the relationship of the governor to the party network based on three administrations, here we are confined to the single office of attorney general, supplemented by some reflections on the Carpentier days. This is the element in the party network with the thinnest base of information. Circumstances surrounding the attorney general's office during the study made it difficult to arrange interviews, so one informant directly connected with the office was our sole source of firsthand information. Fortunately, others who interacted with the office could offer supplementary information.

Congressman

Out of a state delegation of 24 (reduced to 22 in the 1982 redistricting), there were 14 Republican congressmen. Of the three most recent additions, Daniel Crane was a freshman in 1978, winning an open race in what had been a Democratic district. John Porter first won in a special election in 1979, picking up another formerly Democratic seat. In contrast, Lynn Martin continued a Republican tradition, having won the seat vacated by John Anderson when he began his campaign for the presidential nomination. The remainder held well-established positions, two since the Eisenhower presidency. They reflect the political make-up of the state, with none from the city of Chicago; six in the Chicago metropolitan area of suburban Cook County and its collar counties (Congressional Districts 4, 6, 10, 12, 13, and 14); and the remainder from what is usually called downstate.

Experience in the state legislature is the normal pathway to Congress, and nine of the current group have followed that course. Of the rest, John Anderson had previously served as state's attorney, whereas Robert Michel and Tom Corcoran had gained their party experience in the capacity of staff, Michel for the congressman he succeeded and Corcoran for Governor Ogilvie. Only Paul Findley and the two Crane brothers had made their way to Congress without any previous electoral or party experience.

By spending two separate weeks in Washington — one as a three-person team blanketing the offices — and by travelling through the state, we obtained interviews covering all 14 Republican congressional districts. Interviews were with congressmen and their Washington, local, or campaign staff members, either singly or in combination. Use of congressional staff members as sources of information about party matters was often more productive than speaking directly to congressmen. This is analogous to the experience of Richard Thornburg, lobbyist for the National Beer Wholesalers Association: "Too frequently, people in my profession concentrate on the members of Congress. They give them presents at Christmas and everything, and they forget about the staff. But it's the staff — the nuts-and-bolts people — who get everything done" (cited in Keller, 1982).

Within the party network, I see the office of congressman representing a national legislative component, like the U.S. senator, but also a locally rooted one, like members of the General Assembly. The initial discussion treats the congressman in prototypic terms; later the effects of individual variations are considered.

State Senator

The state Senate has 59 members elected for staggered terms. Within a decade, members are divided into three groups with terms of 4-4-2, 2-4-4, and 4-2-4 years. Of the 40 races in the 1978 election, the Republicans won 20. This gave them a total of 27 seats, a minority position. There were 20 races in 1980, so that the Republican victory of 10 seats, including 1 to replace a deceased member, still left them a minority of 29. Republican senatorial seats were located in suburban Cook County, its collar counties, and in the western and central parts of the state. That is, they generally overlapped or were coterminous with Republican congressional seats.

Treated here as a party actor, the state senator is primarily oriented to district concerns, whether they be service to constituents, his own election, or local issues. The composite picture I first draw is based on 16 interviews, some conducted in the home district but most the result of three separate weeks in Springfield, one of which was a three-person team effort.

State Representative

What made the Illinois State representative so interesting was the process by which he was elected. From 1872 up to the election of 1980, every voter had three votes to divide as he or she chose. In the primary election, these votes could be cast for one candidate (i.e., "bulleted"), divided between two candidates, or cast singly for the maximum three candidates, all of one party. In the general election, the choice was generally among four candidates, two per party. If the usual understandings held, every district would elect three representatives, including one from the weaker party, either overtly or with the third ostensibly an independent. The latter situation describes one Democratic district in Chicago during the study period. Normally, however, the stronger party resisted temptations to monopolize candidates (Sawyer and MacRae, 1962).

In 1970, a constitutional amendment prohibited a party from limiting the number of general election candidates to one if more than one had run in the preceding primary. This was intended to discourage "setups," in which voters had no choice beyond the candidates of the dominant party and one of the minority. The voter could distribute his or her three votes by bulleting, dividing them between the two candidates of one party, or giving one each to candidates of one party and the third to the opposite party. From the perspective of the system, the greatest question was whether Republicans elected in Chicago were really adherents of that party or only Democrats in disguise. Although collusion had clearly occurred in the past, particularly in the case of the crime-ridden "West Side bloc" (Nowlan, 1965, 45–46), this was no longer obvious. Questions remained, however, because Chicago Republicans were likely to take positions supportive of their constituents and the needs of the city in ways often more similar to Democratic representatives than to those of suburban Republican ones. The issue then is an ideological one that in no way affects our placement of these minority Republicans in the party network.

The House had 177 seats, now reduced to 118 single-member districts as the result of a referendum passed in 1980, which affected the 1982 election. Representatives were elected from 59 districts coterminous with those for state senator. With the one exception mentioned, every district had at least one Republican representative. During our study, none of the 20 districts in Chicago had elected more than one Republican at one time. The same was true of only 2 out of 10 suburban Cook County districts. After the 1978 election, 7 downstate districts were represented by a lone Republican and after 1980, only 4. In all, 88 Republicans were elected in 1978 and 91 in 1980, the latter number giving them majority status.

In the same way as I have described the position of state senator, my interest in the state representative is tied to his locally rooted party role. Forty representatives were interviewed, initially providing information about the representative as party actor, and later about the diversity of characteristics and activities.

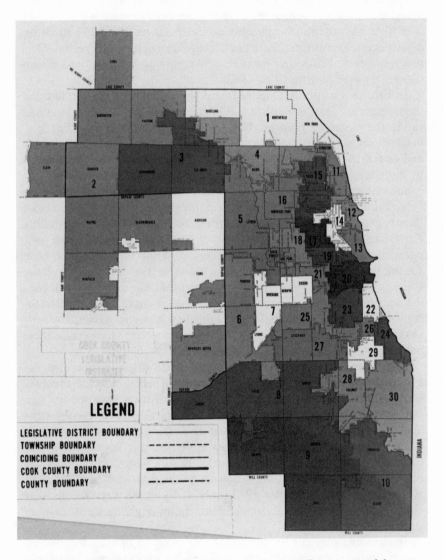

Map 1. Cook County legislative districts; 1971 reapportionment. One senator and three representatives elected from each district. (Source: *Apportionment Maps and Descriptions,* State of Illinois, State Board of Electors.)

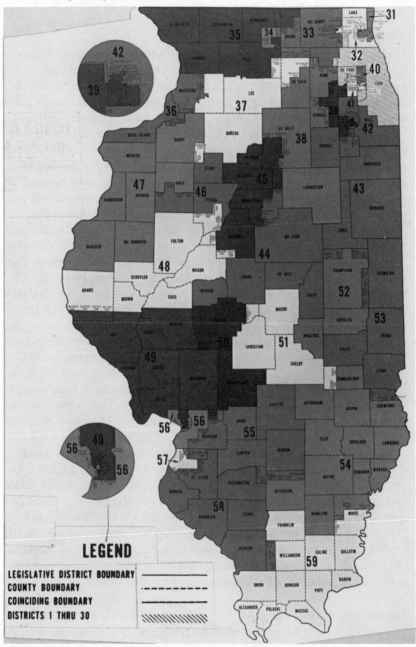

Map 2. Legislative districts other than Cook County; 1971 reapportionment. One senator and three representatives elected from each district. (Source: *Apportionment Maps and Descriptions,* State of Illinois, State Board of Electors.)

State Senate Leadership

It may appear redundant to treat Senate leadership separately from the role of senator, but for the purposes of defining a party network, it deserves this attention. Unlike a senator's primary orientation to his own district, the focus of leadership is on the legislature itself. There its party role emphasizes issues and programs through its own initiative and through that of the governor. To the extent that there is an identifiable Republican program, it takes form in the legislature. When there is a Republican governor, a helpful legislative leadership is essential for the passage of his program. Leadership is also critical to the fortunes of other Republican senators—in committee and commission assignments, support for pet programs, and conferring prestige by introducing administration bills.

The minority position of the Republicans in the Senate during the time of this study precluded their assumption of the Senate presidency. The president, as both presiding officer and majority party leader, has responsibility for setting the Senate agenda (Gove, Carlson, Carlson, 1976, 138–140). With a Republican governor, a minority position can be less of a disability in ensuring the progress of a party program than might otherwise be the case. By the same token, the absence of the presidency, at least during the period studied, placed the leadership in a more subordinate role vis-à-vis the governor and left it without that extra weight of prestige within its own body. Still, given the Senate's smaller size and the greater similarity among senators' constituents, the leadership had an easier time controlling its party members than was true for the House leadership. We may anticipate Republican senators' opposition to their governor; they expressed much less to their leadership.

In a minority situation, the leadership consists of the minority leader, three assistant leaders, and a staff of about 60, of whom only a small number have relevant decision-making responsibility. The Senate minority leader is elected by his peers following each two-year election period, but the frequency of election does not undermine lengthy tenure. Minority Leader David Shapiro held his position following the 1976 election until his death in 1981. He, in turn, appointed assistant leaders, and over the course of the study there was one replacement. Including staff with elected officeholders, five members of the leadership were interviewed.

State House Leadership

The rationale for treating the House leadership as a separate actor is similar to that for the Senate. The two cannot be combined into a single legislative leadership, however, because of the effects of the House's composition. Larger and more diverse in its membership, it presents a less tractable face to its leadership. That leadership then performs its partisan role differently from the Senate leadership. In the study period it was both less supportive of the governor and more heavy-handed in its efforts to control representatives. These characteristics appear to be generally true of the House Republicans (Dunn, 1972; Gove, Carlson, Carlson, 1976, 146–147).

Leadership moved from a minority to a majority situation after the 1980 election, giving the Republicans an opportunity to make George Ryan speaker of the House. Ryan had earlier been minority leader, elected after the 1976 election. As such, his position was more critical than that of his counterpart in the Senate just because it was more difficult. And he often had a more influential role in the House generally, at least until the 1982 election, because the House was more evenly divided between the two parties and the ability to control his own party members was a crucial factor in dealing with the majority party (Gove, Carlson, Carlson, 1976, 142). Control of the speakership means increased formal control over House procedures and, with it, some presumption of impartiality when acting as presiding officer. When that is the case, the majority leader assumes the role of partisan spokesman in the House (Gove, Carlson, Carlson, 1976, 140–141).

In 1978, the minority leader was aided by three assistant leaders, two whips, and a conference chairman. The majority leader in 1980, Arthur Telcser, elected from a Chicago district and soon to be retired under a system of single-member districts, added a fourth assistant leader, also from Chicago. Leadership was supported by a staff of about 80. Altogether seven persons in the House leadership were interviewed.

Local Officeholder

Officeholders elected in municipal and county governments provide another, and often important, level for party activity, where "courthouse politics" still mean a great deal in Illinois political life. Even though some municipal elections are conducted on a nonpartisan basis, with Chicago the most striking example, party affiliations are usually known. Moreover, local offices are often a first stage in a political career. Republican members of the General Assembly with experience in elected municipal, township, or county office made up over 40 percent of the delegation during the study period, and some held local office contemporaneously with their legislative roles. Of the 15 congressmen, 4 had held local office. In order to understand the place of the local officeholder in the party network, I was satisfied to rely on information supplied by 19 who, in addition to other network roles, were current or past local officeholders. This information was supplemented by observations made during a canvass of all county clerks in the state.

If this were a study of the Illinois Democratic Party, I could not excuse my procedure so lightly. The importance of the Democratic organization in Chicago since 1931 (Gosnell, 1937) and its influence on state government under Mayor Richard Daley (Colby and Green, 1979, 15-24) would require much more direct attention than is warranted, for example, by the Republicanism of the local governments of Kankakee, Peoria, or Rockford. My decision still stood even after the 1983 Chicago mayoral election, when former Representative Bernard Epton (District 24), who had entered the Republican primary in what first appeared to be the usual losing situation, found himself competing against the Democratic candidate, Harold Washington.

Anyone familiar with Chicago's history of race relations knew why the odds against Epton suddenly shifted. They knew, too, why the Republican party establishment moved so quickly to bolster his campaign effort. James Fletcher, who had managed Governor Thompson's first campaign, came aboard to direct the general election race, replacing the candidate's daughter, Dale Epton, who had run the primary campaign. Spurred by Fletcher, Republican businessmen opened their checkbooks to finance the campaign. And John Deardourff, of Bailey and Deardourff, the Washington, D.C., political consulting firm that Thompson had used in each of his three races, signed on as Epton's media consultant and chief strategist. (Kleppner, 1985, 200)

But Epton still lost and the effects of his candidacy remain an uncertain legacy for the Republican Party.

National Committeeman

Each state is represented in the national party committee by a national committeeman and committeewoman. They are expected to define state problems, comment on national appointments, act as liaisons with state committees and state officials, and contribute their local knowledge to national campaigns and fund raising efforts. Illinois Republicans select the two committee members at each biennial state convention. Selection of the candidates is made by a special slating committee and ratified by the convention delegates. Since 1976, the national committeeman has been Harold Byron Smith, Jr., and the committeewoman was Crete B. Smith, until her defeat at the 1984 state convention. Despite the division along lines of gender, the position is treated as one here, because all the evidence indicates that the committeewoman's role is regarded as unimportant (Cotter and Hennessy, 1964). My concern is with the committeeman's place in the Illinois party network and not with his relations with other committeemen, who, in any case, "have very little collective identity, little patterned interaction, and only rudimentary common values and goals" (Cotter and Hennessy, 1964, 112).

In general, the national committeeman plays a relatively unimportant role in the party, especially in comparison to the state chairman, who, since 1968, is also a member of the Republican National Committee (Cotter and Hennessy, 1964; Huckshorn, 1976, 204–206). We can anticipate that there will be considerable individual variation, however, just because the limited definition of responsibilities gives scope to those with ambition and ability to enhance the power of their position. This appears to be the case within the Illinois network, where the incumbent committeeman's other positions have contributed to his repute as a power broker. As an elected state central committeeman, Smith played a major role in organizing the financing of the state party apparatus and of legislative elections, gaining, at the same time, recognition as an important party actor in the Washington offices of the Republican National Committee. Meanwhile, his activities generated opposition from a variety of in-state sources, which coalesced into a threatened, but abortive, challenge to his slating as national committeeman at the 1980 state convention.

Republican National Committee

We have separated the national committeeman and committeewoman from the Republican National Committee, because the committee, as a political actor, is more accurately described as an administrative and technical staff, under an appointed chairman, carrying out strategies for party organizational maintenance and electoral success. The role the chairman plays is dependent on the presence or absence of party control over the presidency.

Chairpersons of the party out-of-power have more often been party leaders, in the real sense of the word. The power of the titular party such as former presidential candidates evaporates quickly once they have been defeated. The same is true of former presidents, who are usually willing to assume the role of elder statesman and leave party building to others. Thus the mantle of leadership often falls squarely on the shoulders of the national party chairperson. This situation brings both advantages and disadvantages. Without the presidency, for example, the chairperson has little patronage to dispense and few favors to distribute. But on the other hand, he or she is more likely to be viewed as the real party leader without the added problem of being subservient to the president. He or she is able to concentrate on the daily activities and routines of staff conferences, research, public relations, personnel matters, and establishing diplomatic relations with the congressional leaders. (Huckshorn, 1984, 62–63)

The out-of-power situation prevailed during the study, when the chairman was William Brock. Appointed in 1977 after serving as senator from Tennessee, Brock led the RNC into new and intensified fields of activity, seeking to regain seats in Congress, but also to reach out to special population groups and interests previously beyond the attention of the Republican

Party, and to assist in state and local elections. It is these activities that provide the crucial link between the RNC and Illinois (Bibby, 1979; Cotter and Bibby, 1980). After the 1980 presidential election, Brock was replaced by Richard Richards, who enters the network as well, but less centrally to the analysis.

The Local Elections Committee of the RNC was active in Illinois in a number of state House and Senate elections. Field staff members, typically covering some portion of the Midwest, were involved in advising on all aspects of campaign strategy. They could take the initiative in targeting districts, that is, in deciding which legislative districts warranted special assistance, but they also had to contend with the targeting activities of state-based committees, which did not necessarily coincide with their own judgments.

In general, the RNC also contributed assistance through its research and public relations activities and its skills in campaign training. In these activities, the RNC worked directly with the staff of the State Central Committee. Seven interviews were conducted to cover the offices of national committeeman, Washington-based RNC staff, and local field personnel.

State Central Committeeman

Central committeemen are elected every four years in the party primary in off-presidential years. Their numbers and districts are determined by congressional districting, which has changed the number from 24 at the time of the study to 22 currently. The central committeeman can be viewed in two ways: as making up the State Central Committee and as party spokesman within his congressional district. It is the latter that I emphasize here, because I treat the State Central Committee separately.

In his local capacity, the state central committeeman chairs the district congressional committee, consisting of local committeemen and/or county chairmen, depending on the composition of the district. That is, if the congressional district covers a single county, committee members will be local committeemen; if there are many counties in it, the county chairmen serve; or there could be some combination. While a chairman of the district congressional committee, the central committeeman has no vote, except in the case of ties. One principal statutory duty of the congressional committee is to fill vacancies that occur during the term of a congressman. Beyond that, the central committeeman has considerable scope in defining responsibilities that contribute to furthering party interests.

The ambiguity associated with the central committeeman's role results in considerable competition and conflict. One sign of this was the amount of electoral activity in 1978, when, out of a total of 24 races, only 8 were uncontested. Of the remainder, 3 were open seats and 13 involved challenges to an incumbent committeeman, though none was defeated. Another sign is the recurring efforts to alter the way in which central committeemen are elected, in order to make them more directly responsible to other party spokesmen. For example, in the 1980 state convention, county chairmen unsuccessfully attempted to introduce a resolution changing the method of election by giving themselves the power to serve as electors.

Information about the central committeeman, and also about the State Central Committee, comes from interviews with 14 committeemen. They are not identical in districts with those electing Republican congressmen but are spread more evenly across the state.

State Central Committee

The State Central Committee can also be treated as an independent political actor, made up of elected central committeemen and staff, with the state chairwoman as a nonvoting member. It is in the capacity of administrative unit that the SCC is concerned with party maintenance. Meetings are held regularly to plan election strategy for statewide offices, coordinate with the electoral and policy positions of the legislature, and organize the biennial state convention. In recent years, with an expanded and full-time staff, many of the research, public relations, and campaign training activities associated with the RNC have also been attempted by the SCC with an Illinois locus.

The SCC is headed by a chairman, first elected in a congressional district as a state central committeeman and then elected every four years by his peers. It is an office associated with longevity: Victor Smith was chairman from 1960 to 1973, and Don Adams, its incumbent during this study, from 1973 to 1988. The role of chairman, according to Huckshorn, is one of party leader, constrained by both the presence of an incumbent governor and the possibilities of independence from him. The chairman can then follow one of three possibilities: political agent of the governor, in-party independent from the governor, and out-party independent (Huckshorn, 1984, 78–79). This would suggest that Smith, who held the position without a Republican governor until Richard Ogilvie's election in 1968, had scope for developing into a strong chairman. Although I heard reference to the incumbent chairman as simply "Chairman," without either an introductory article or a personal name, conjuring up the image of a majestic figure, the position is not associated with acknowledged party leadership. This is not necessarily the result of being subservient to the governor, who, as in the case of Governor Thompson, may not show great interest in running the party. Governor Ogilvie was more active in this regard and made efforts to develop a full-time professional staff for the SCC. With his defeat, the SCC retreated from its activities in promoting the "new politics." Their resumption, however, was quite independent of Thompson's election, coming rather from the efforts of some key central committeemen. During the study period, Adams acted as the governor's agent, primarily because he could be a conciliatory spokesman.

Limits on the chairman's authority, and, by extension, on the SCC, have been tied to the method of funding. Up until the mid-1970s the only centralized funding for the Republican Party in Illinois was provided by a single organization, the United Republican Fund. Not only did it exist independently of the SCC, but it also provided all of the committee's operating funds without commitment to a regular budget. In other words, the state chairman was constrained in his planning by the uncertainty of funding. Governor Ogilvie attempted to overcome this problem by gaining control of the United Republican Fund, and when this failed, provided funding to the SCC from his own partisan resources. When these disappeared with Ogilvie's defeat, another attempt was made to subordinate the United Republican Fund to the directives of the SCC, but the renewed effort was also unsuccessful, and a finance committee was set up within the SCC to raise funds for its own operation and its campaign activities. The prime mover in bringing about this change was a state central committeeman, Harold Byron Smith, Jr., whom we have already met in his role as national committeeman.

Information about the SCC comes from interviews with 3 persons directly involved, along with the 14 central committeemen and others who have dealt with the committee. In addition, we had access to informal minutes of SCC meetings from about 1950 to 1970.

County Chairman

Illinois's 102 counties are each represented by a chairman who, after election in the party's primary as a local committeeman, is then elected by his peers for a two-year term. He and his colleagues have responsibility for organizing county-level elections and generally promoting the party's interests, particularly through membership and participation in other district committees of which the county is a part. In practice, a chairman may choose to concentrate his political energies on county elections, especially when Republican prospects are good, because the county still offers an important source of patronage. He has the alternative of active involvement in all political levels. The ambiguous scope of activity limits the ability to generalize the argument that the party's strength and continuity lie in the county organization, because not all chairmen follow expansive policies.

Variation is the key word for describing counties, ranging in size from

Cook, with a population of about 6 million (40 percent of the state), followed by Dupage, with half a million, to Pope, with 4,000, 1 of 16 counties with a population of less than 10,000. They also vary in extent of Republican strength, from the most Republican counties of Ogle, Whiteside, and Dupage, which have an almost firm Republican vote of 75 percent, to Alexander, Union, and Hardin, whose share of the Republican vote is closer to 35 percent. Size affects organization and strength affects participation, both important to the chairman's job. Large counties have central committees with representation that reflects their divisions into cities, towns, and townships. The committees of small counties can directly consist of all elected committeemen. County bylaws may require that all members of the central committee executive be elected committeemen, whereas others may allow chairmen to appoint outsiders. And where the party is strong, filling positions, whether on the executive or in committeemen races, is no problem.

In the course of our interviews with 22 county chairmen, mainly with the best-known and most influential, although not necessarily ones from Republican areas, we encountered individuals who had held their positions for almost a half century. Some turnover certainly occurs, but the norm appears to be stability. Over the period of the study, 76 chairmen in office after the 1978 primary were reelected in 1980.

County chairmen have their own organization, the County Chairmen's Association. Though it has no official status under Illinois election laws, it has in the past been described as one of the pillars of the state party, co-equal to the State Central Committee (Holderman, 1963, 2). We had no evidence that it currently deserves separate attention, however. At best, informants, themselves active in the association, could do no more than promise that it would soon become an important party actor.

Local Committeeman

The concept of local committeeman covers three kinds of positions that vary with geographic locus. In the 101 counties outside of Cook, precincts have the right to elect their own committeeman every two years in the party primary, although in any primary, some positions will have no candidate because the party is too weak to recruit. Cook County elects 50 ward committeemen in the city of Chicago every four years in presidential primaries and 30 township committeemen in the suburbs every four years in off-year primaries. Each ward and township is divided into precincts, headed by appointed precinct captains. Because boundaries are required to be redrawn periodically with population changes, the number of precincts varied slightly even during the course of this study, approximately 6,100 outside of Cook and 5,500 in Cook. The affects of variation in population size and strength of partisanship previously described for counties are similar for these smaller electoral units.

Local committeemen are treated as the embodiment of party fortunes in the primaries, with both the committeemen's and the county chairmen's voting strength in constituent bodies, including the state convention, dependent on the number of party electors they were able to mobilize in the preceding primary. Duties of the committeeman are vaguely defined by statute; their scope is better understood in terms of the organization of the county, personal initiative, and the aggressiveness of the county chairman.

Information about ward and township committeemen comes from interviews with 31 officeholders. Precinct committeemen were found among informants selected for other roles (for example, all the county chairmen), but the major source was a telephone survey with 423 committeemen. The diversity in roles played by committeemen and in the conditions they face does not preclude this initial treatment in prototypic terms. Because the survey was sampled to reflect equal numbers of respondents, divided by size of county and Republican strength, all totals given here and in subsequent chapters are based on weighted averages. The survey revealed that the average precinct committeeman was male, Protestant, of northern European origin, and either a farmer or in a white-collar position. The median age was 55 and the median year of election 1974. Only 19 percent currently held other party offices. In these characteristics, precinct committeemen were both comparable to Althoff and Patterson's (1966) study of a single county and quite similar to the Cook County committeemen. Even more important is the similarity they shared in their contacts with others in the party network.

Republican Senate Campaign Committee

Treatment of the four legislative campaign committees as separate political actors is consistent with Huckshorn's view that at least the two federal ones be considered distinct organizational units (Huckshorn, 1984, 72–74). Located in its own office space in Washington, the Republican Senate Campaign Committee is made up of representative senators and permanent staff engaged in fundraising, campaign organizing, and supportive research. At the time of the study, Illinois had no senatorial representation, and the RSCC appeared to have given little direct assistance to Senator Percy during his 1978 campaign. There was, however, participation along with the Republican National Committee in the 1980 senatorial race. One staff interview is the basis of information, supplemented by interviews with RNC and Republican Congressional Campaign Committee staff members, with whom there is some interchange.

Republican Congressional Campaign Committee

The Republican Congressional Campaign Committee has its origin in the campaign committee of the Union Party (Huckshorn, 1984, 73). In keeping with the larger size of the House and its more frequent elections, the RCCC is a larger, more active, and more influential body than its senatorial counterpart. Each state is represented by one of its House members; during the study period it was Illinois congressman Edward Derwinski (District 4). The staffs of the RNC and the RCCC are housed in the Republican Party's Washington headquarters and, under Brock's chairmanship, were both concerned with increasing Republican congressional representation. The result was some overlap in goals, if not in functions, yet the movement in personnel from one unit to the other did not totally eliminate rivalry.

The RCCC's direct concerns are with fundraising and campaign strategy. If called on for help, the staff will assist incumbent congressmen facing serious challenges in a primary or general election. The committee's special flexibility comes from its field staff, assigned to regions, one of which includes Illinois. The staff has the prerogative of targeting districts that appear likely to swing to the Republican side or to need help in retaining an apparent advantage. Unlike their counterparts in the Local Elections Committee of the RNC, staff members are free to make their own decisions, without consideration of how local party people or the SCC may evaluate their targeting efforts. We were told that staff members in Illinois kept their contacts primarily with the congressional candidates and their campaign managers. Information on these and related activities came from four interviews with staff. In subsequent chapters, to protect the anonymity of informants, I generally refer to the Washington-based committees collectively as the RNC.

State Senate Campaign Committee

Under the aegis of state senate leader Russell Arrington, a special campaign committee was begun in 1966 to aid in the election of state senators. The State Senate Campaign Committee has since played a continuous role in fundraising and campaign assistance to challenged incumbents and, where there is no incumbent, to promising challengers in general elections. This was also clearly an area of overlap with the Local Elections Committee of the RNC.

The staff members of the SSCC are employed by the Senate leadership (which is itself represented on the committee), and, as such, have more limited duties than their national and full-time counterparts in the Republican Senate Campaign Committee. Composition of the SSCC also includes other senators, a representative of the governor, and public members. The numbers of public versus legislative members appear to vary slightly, but the proportion of public members is about half, of whom half in turn hold or have held party office. Public members are prominent businessmen whose place on the committee is often filled by a representative vice president in charge of public affairs or government relations. Information came from interviews with 11 informants.

State House Campaign Committee
The State House Campaign Committee has a history, composition, and mandate similar to that of the State Senate Campaign Committee, except that it has not been as strong or as continuous in its operation. At the time of the study, both legislative committees were active and apparently cooperative, just as they were with the Republican Finance Committee of the SCC. Interviews with 17 informants associated with the SHCC supplied relevant information.

United Republican Fund
Reportedly because of concern over fraudulent appeals for funds, a group of Republican businessmen came together in 1935 to create a fundraising body set apart from political turmoil. It was given its present name of United Republican Fund in 1955. Its sole purpose has been fundraising, deliberately removed from primary election fights or policy issues. Although it has never had statutory recognition, it was for a long time the sole fundraising organ for the party, so that Holderman (1963, 2) considered it one of the three basic units of the party, along with the State Central Committee and the County Chairmen's Association. Monies raised were dispersed to the Republican National Committee, the State Central Committee, and the Cook County Central Committee. An examination of dispersements from 1960 to 1964 indicated that Cook County received most of the funds, followed by the SCC (Nowlan, 1965, 87–114). The favored position of Cook County was the result not only of its greater size but also of the limited fundraising done downstate.

Inroads into the URF's monopoly began in the 1960s with formation of the two legislative campaign committees, and in the 1970s with the Republican Finance Committee tied to the SCC. Today the URF supports the Cook County organization, contributes to some other counties, assists in the campaign expenses of statewide offices, excluding those of governor and U.S. senator, and includes selected legislators. For the period I cover, the various financial committees coexisted in a state of competitive tension. Information came from two direct participants, three opponents, and published reports.

Advisor

Politicians have always relied on trusted personal advisors, separate from the government bureaucracy or the party apparatus, to help them in making plans and decisions that will assist them in their jobs and enhance their careers. What is relatively new is the technical nature of the advice sought in recognition of the greater complexity of government and because of reliance on electronic media for campaigning. The selection of advisors with new technical skills is often based on their past performances — that is, whether the candidates they helped were elected — rather than their personal ties with the candidates. Nevertheless, they are expected to extend their advice primarily, if not solely, to politicians of one party, although Sabato (1981, 24–34) does not fully agree that this is the case. Now, if their loyalty is not ensured by personal ties, it is at least presumed by partisan sympathies. Some differentiation is also made along ideological lines, so that politicians and advisors are matched by their views on issues.

Changes in the style of government and campaigns have in no way eliminated the importance of the older kinds of advisor. But their milieu remains that of selected individual politicians who continue to appreciate the insights of a reliable supporter and the locally based wisdom of a grassroots campaigner. For members of the party apparatus in the State Central Committee and Republican National Committee, and for those political actors involved in leadership roles in campaigning and in the legislature, the old-style advisor is no longer taken seriously.

Advisors have three areas of competence: political issues, media use, and campaigning. Given the emphasis on technical skills, there is often specialization, but some advisors, especially of the traditional sort, will have skills that overlap all three areas. The skills offered are varied, ranging, for example, from organizing public-opinion surveys and interpreting their meaning to organizing individual campaigns. Some advisors have a national reputation, like the firm of Bailey and Deardourff or Market Opinion Research and its then president, Robert Teeter. Others are best known within a local arena, where they regularly serve a small number of clients. But as locals, they are not necessarily deficient in technical skills; they simply operate on a smaller scale.

Those considered advisors here are persons regularly consulted by their clients, but not necessarily paid for their advice, a situation that held for 10 of the 22 advisors interviewed, who were not directly paid by the individuals or groups they helped. Their principal activities and sources of income were separate from their party activities, but they were able to carry out the latter because of the compatibility between the two. What makes this possible is employment in organizations that encourage political involvement (e.g., Republican-oriented law firms), or more often, where the chief executive officer of the organization is strongly committed to the Republican Party or some segment of it, and both he and some of his employees contribute their time to aiding the party. Whether paid or not, the road to becoming an advisor is often prior service in government, where contacts are established and reputations acquired that may then be converted into an advising service.

Although the 22 informants treated as advisors differed in many characteristics, they shared one that makes them amenable to treatment as a single category — their role in providing aid to the party, a role without official status but with wide recognition among elements in the party network. It was through just such recognition that we discovered many of these informants. Both public and party officeholders told us, "You must interview X. Next to the governor, he's the most important Republican in the state," or "Y can really tell you how the party works."

Financial Contributor

Today it is widely believed, and broadly confirmed, that election campaigns run on money (e.g., Alexander, 1980). Although the kind of advice supplied by our category of advisors is sometimes free, when not, it is expensive. Clients have paid from $10,000 to $75,000 to consulting firms, with an additional commission of 15 percent on services ordered through the firm (Sabato, 1982, 43). And whatever the cost of the advice, it requires large expenditures for typical recommendations to be carried out. If television is recommended, and the Chicago voter market is wanted, one could have expected to pay $5,250 for a 30-second commercial during prime time (Crotty, 1984, 97). In contrast, the ABC station in Decatur, serving Decatur, Springfield, and Champaign-Urbana, charged from $150 to $500. For the same length radio message during prime time, charges varied from $312 on WGN-Chicago to $7.50 on WSOY-Decatur and $5.00 on WEIC, serving Charleston and Matoon. A half-page newspaper advertisement cost approximately $13,736 in the *Chicago Tribune,* $814 in the Decatur *Herald-Review,* and $228 in the *Charleston Times Courier.* All prices were in force at the time of the 1980 election and were compiled by McNitt (1982). The costs of running campaigns are not compiled with great accuracy in Illinois, but available information indicates that Governor Thompson spent an estimated $1,936,053 in his 1978 campaign and Lieutenant Governor O'Neal spent $1,270,650 in his losing bid for a Senate seat in 1980. No wonder, then, that regular sources of income are needed for elements of the party apparatus; that candidates drop out of races if they are uncertain about financial support; and that raising money for political purposes has become a full-time job.

One of the major changes in political financing is the vast growth of political action committees connected with corporations, trade associations, and ideological groups (Sabato, 1984). In some instances, these are closely associated with a party, as in the case of a PAC formed to raise (and disperse) money for a candidate seeking the presidential nomination. Other PACs do not have this kind of clearcut association, but they can still be considered at least loosely coupled members of the party network when their contributions are made largely, if not solely, to the candidates of a single party. For example, the Committee for the Survival of a Free Congress, although nominally bipartisan, contributes campaign advice and money almost solely to Republican congressional candidates whom it finds ideologically compatible. Procedures for selecting candidates for support by many PACs associated with businesses include reliance on information supplied by the Republican Party headquarters, especially on which districts will be targeted. Although many business and corporate PACs make at least nominal contributions to local incumbents, regardless of party, the bulk of their money goes to those candidates regarded as most congenial with the company's philosophy of business, and that normally means Republican (e.g., Berry, 1984, 176–178).

Neither the rise of PACs nor federal restrictions on the size of individual contributions have eliminated the importance of individual contributors and fundraisers. Their importance extends beyond the money they actually contribute to the way they serve as leaders of a bandwagon and as highly visible exemplars for encouraging support from other wealthy individuals. In recognition of this, they may be asked to serve as public members of the State Senate and House Campaign committees, and they are, in essence, the United Republican Fund. Such individuals, along with representatives of PACs, made up 19 of our informants.

In this discussion and in chapter 3, the financial contributor as a unit in the party network is defined as one who makes large contributions not limited to a single district and whose primary identification is with the Republican Party or some element of it. In chapter 8, when we look at money as the medium of exchange among network units, we will be able to consider variations among contributors by relying on a detailed analysis of campaign contributions to state legislators based on reports filed with the State Board of Elections.

Interest Group

In the study of U.S. politics, from Arthur Bentley onward, the tradition has been to emphasize the role of interest groups in shaping public policy. This is understandable, given the ways in which interest groups have permeated the boundaries of parties (e.g., Truman, 1971, 270–282). The Republican Party has had a long association with the business community, and this has been important in Illinois for the founding and continued vitality of the United Republican Fund. In addition, we will encounter examples of how business and professional interests have affected party activities, sometimes even in opposition to organized units of the party. One corporate lobbyist, boasting of his influence, recounted how he had been called by Bailey and Deardourff, a firm he considered to exemplify the "atrocities" of current campaign practices:

They are working for Richard Carver, the mayor of Peoria, who wants to try for Adlai Stevenson's Senate seat. Bailey wanted me and others in the business community to dissuade Sam Skinner from running, so that Carver would have a clear field. Skinner [a close associate of Governor Thompson] has also called me. Bailey didn't call Thompson or the State Central Committee. He calls the business community.

Concern over the impact of interest groups became prominent within the Republican Party in the face of the strength of organized ideological, or single-interest, groups. An interest group leader representing the corporate world expressed his assessment:

The troublesome interests are anti-ERA, pro-life, and the Conservative caucus. The Conservatives[1] are supposed to have 25,000 dues-paying members in Illinois. None of these are in the Illinois party but they have the capacity to strongly affect it. Where is this going to leave the economic leaders?

I admitted earlier that the category of interest group as a unit of the party network is the one with which I am least comfortable, because I did not anticipate including interest groups in this study. I did not have any rules for selection, so the 14 interviews with interest group representatives were picked up as part of the search for advisors or financial contributors or for past members of other network units. Eleven were representatives of business, professional, or trade associations, and only three were from the highly influential ideological groups. Lack of representation from the latter is overcome to a degree in chapter 7, where I discuss the components of ideology and their relevance in linking elements in the party network. I rely on interviews with other informants, published reports, and observations of lobbying activities to establish the partisanship of the interest group category and, in chapter 3, its links with other units.

The Pivotal Voter

The tripartite nature of parties, found in government, the electorate, and the organizational apparatus and referred to earlier as the basis for defin-

---

1. It was unclear if he meant the American Conservative Union or the Illinois Conservative Union.

ing the Illinois Republican Party network, might suggest that voters be included in the network. This would follow if voters were to be considered synonymous with the party in the electorate. One could go so far as to say that, because there would be no officeholders elected or apparatus sustained without Republican voters, voters are the party. Such an underlying rationale may be present when political parties are studied through voting behavior. But I agree with Schlesinger (1984) that voters do not belong in the party organization. Exclusion of voters from the party network emphasizes the problem, familiar in organizational analysis, of where to draw boundaries. The solution offered by Pfeffer and Salancik is "that the boundary is where the discretion of the organization to control an activity is less than the discretion of another organization or individual to control that activity" (1978, 32). But this does not help with the special problems of political parties. "Discretion" and "control" are difficult to define where voters, though identified in partisan terms, are still free to give or withhold support, motivated by diverse factors over which parties have little influence. In a sense, Republican voters are analogous to customers of a business in a competitive market (Aldrich, 1979, 225–228).

Voters can be distinguished from members of the party network by the amount of attention they give to their party roles (March and Olsen, 1976, 38–53). Although we can assume variation in political interest, partisan commitment, and willingness to work for the party among both voters and network actors, voters are still distinctive in the infrequency with which they are called upon to display involvement in the party. Voting twice every other year, and perhaps once in one intervening year, is the most they need do to establish their identity as Republican supporters. But even when members of the network participate sporadically as part-time volunteers, they must still allocate more time and effort to some aspect of the party organization than do voters.

One solution to boundary problems is to treat voters as a directly needed resource to be recruited and retained by the party. In this way voters are both a critical aspect of the party's environment and a component of its organization. I take this approach in chapter 4 with respect to variations in voter loyalty to the Republican Party across time, place, and candidacy. We can then ask how the various environments of voter loyalty are related to variations in the coupling of party elements. My general hypothesis is that the two will co-vary; not perfectly, to be sure, but still consistently enough to expect that organizational structures will reflect the environmental conditions they face (Lawrence and Lorsch, 1967).

The ambiguity of party boundaries makes it necessary to recognize that voters are intrinsic to the party while separate (or at least separable) from the party network. It is my hypothesis that, as the electoral center of gravity shifts, so does the structure and performance of the party network.

Offstage Actors

The omission of voters from the party network is justified by their pivotal role as both resource and outcome, affecting and being affected by the network's structure and operation. Omission of other actors was based on different grounds; in the time and place of the study, they played offstage roles, affecting the way network elements are aligned and function without their own participation being at issue.

Among those offstage, only the president displays the characteristics that we would associate with a party actor. The remainder appear to be population categories, like women and young people, but in fact they are representatives of those special interests that all U.S. parties seek to incorporate.

President

The foremost offstage actor is the president. Through the resources at his command, a Republican president can enhance the power of actors who have themselves a more specifically Illinois focus. This happens, for example, when presidential authority is used to quickly validate senatorial suggestions for appointments to federal judicial posts. Interviews and published reports acknowledged that Senator Charles Percy had difficulty with both Presidents Nixon and Reagan, and this, in turn, reflected on his position in the party network. In contrast, Congressman Robert Michel's role as House minority leader was enhanced with the election of a Republican president, and one could anticipate a more powerful role for Michel in the party generally. Even more important are the consequences of direct service to the president, particularly in aiding his election. An example is the reward of ambassadorships to two Illinois fundraisers, John J. Louis and Paul Robinson. Yet such presidential influence, although relevant, still does not make the president a full member of the network.

Taking sides in presidential primaries is a means both for claiming power and for establishing ideological positions. In the 1976 primary, while President Ford won 59 percent of the primary vote and the great majority of committed convention delegates, Governor Reagan's forces established a body of loyal support that provided an important rallying point for continuing opposition within the party network. The crowded 1980 primary ticket had many ties with Illinois, including two favorite sons, Congressmen John Anderson and Philip Crane; Senator Howard Baker, married to the daughter of the late Illinois senator Everett Dirksen; and John Connally, the early favorite of many of the state's leaders. By the time of the primary, however, support for Mr. Reagan had solidified, virtually ensuring his nomination. Still, the timing of support for him remained a litmus test. What these two party elections indicate is the importance of align-ments that presidential candidates generate within Illinois and not so much the activities of the president himself. For example, some of the dispute between the governor and state legislators, between the national commit-teeman and state conventioneers, and between rival county chairmen and state central committeemen was symbolized by their position on Ronald Reagan's candidacy. This is documented in later chapters, especially chap-ters 5 and 7.

Women

Like the president, women in the Illinois Republican Party are also off-stage, but in a different capacity. They are more like stagehands whose work is necessary for the performance of the real actors, but who themselves receive little attention or acknowledgement.

Women hold both public and elected party office, though in small numbers, particularly in party offices (see Table 2-4). Although the national committeewoman, like her male counterpart, is elected by delegates to the state convention, this kind of election is unusual for women in the party, who are normally appointed by elected officeholders. Each central com-mitteeman is empowered to appoint one or more central committeewomen for his district, and the state chairman appoints a state chairwoman. De-pending on the initiative of her sponsor, the committeewoman may assist in fundraising, campaigning, and the maintenance of a Republican pres-ence in the district. The committeewoman may attend meetings of the State Central Committee but cannot vote. The state chairwoman attends regu-larly and takes the minutes.

Party bylaws allow each county chairman to appoint a chairwoman to serve during his term. In the same way, each ward and township commit-

Table 2-4. Republican Women Elected to Office, 1978 and 1980, Compared with Total Republican Representation

	1978		1980	
	Women	Total	Women	Total
Congress	0	13	1	14
State Senate[a]	2	27	1	29
State House	13	88	17	91
State Central Committee	1	24	no race	
County chairman	6	102	5	102
Ward committeeman	2	48	5	50
Township committeeman	2	30	2	30

[a]Because of staggered terms, numbers refer to composition, not to results of that year's election.

teeman in Cook County may appoint one or more committeewomen. Duties and responsibilities of the chairwomen and committeewomen are defined by their sponsors, and in many instances are largely social or even, as one committeewoman described them, "token." The range is considerable, however, as the following report from an unusually active woman indicates:

> My activities include finding election judges.
> I staff the party headquarters and I try to spend a few afternoons a week there. When I'm not there, the answering service refers calls to my home. Questions that people call about concern all kinds of things—I either have to know the answer or know where to refer people.
> I organize and send out yearly mailings to registered Republican for fundraising. I get out the mailing, keep track of money coming in, and send out receipts.
> I attend periodic meetings with others (men and women) in the congressional district—meetings organized to keep track of what is going on locally, to organize districtwide support for candidates.
> I find people to do the official canvass every two years. The purpose is to clean up poll sheets. The canvass is ordered by the county clerk; the canvassers work in teams of two, one from each party.
> I see that the party has precinct captains. . . .
> I organize the endorsement meeting. That's where precinct captains come with delegates, candidates come to speak, and then the delegates vote on whom to support. . . .
> I also organize whatever work has to be done in the township during election campaigns.
> Finally, I organize the annual Lincoln Day dinner—that's the main fundraiser, and we keep it to a $25-a-plate dinner.

The scope of this committeewoman's activities is tied to the complexity of the township in which she works and the deliberate efforts of her committeeman to give her responsibility. We spoke to others who seemed to do nothing more than organize the occasional tea or coffee hour. Which is more typical is hard to say. According to one knowledgeable informant:

> What you do with the position is what you want to do. If you do too little, then you won't continue to have the job of chairman.
> [Can you do too much?]
> Perhaps. It probably doesn't hurt, no matter what you do, as long as you don't want credit.

The crucial distinction is associated with the office, not with gender per se. A woman county chairman is one who occupies a position of relative power, once she has been elected in the party primary and then by the committeemen in her county. A county chairwoman is a woman appointed by her chairman to assume supportive roles. For this reason, and also, as

I stated earlier, to protect the anonymity of the small number of elected women officeholders, masculine nouns and pronouns are used throughout this study to refer to members of the party network.

Party organizations with varying resources and degrees of continuity are present at most local levels, and women participate in them. But typically women also have their own local organizations, some of which are affiliated with the Illinois Federation of Republican Women. Like county chairwomen and state and local committeewomen, they are expected to assist in fundraising, campaigning, and party maintenance, but without the constraints imposed by male sponsors. For a small number of women, these kinds of organized activities have been pathways to elected office. Organized women may be sought out by ambitious politicians, who see them as an important resource in their own efforts to gain office. But no matter how important they are, women and their groups do not have the status enjoyed by elected officeholders or the recognition given to unofficial party actors classified as advisors, financial contributors, or interest groups. We concluded this from the six interviews done with women in segregated positions and from the way in which other informants, both male and female, spoke of women in the party, if they mentioned women at all.

The most prominent Republican woman in Illinois is Phyllis Schlafly, in whom the poise and skills of a former beauty queen and a lawyer are combined to gain her national recognition (Felsenthal, 1981). A former president of the Illinois Federation of Republican Women, her only party office at the time of the study was as precinct committeewoman in Madison County, but through her leadership of the Eagle Forum and her cooperation with the Reverend Jerry Falwell's Moral Majority, she has been able to make her traditional views of women's roles dominant in the Illinois party. During my study, she successfully led the opposition to the Equal Rights Amendment, ensuring its final defeat in the legislature. Republican women lacking sympathy for her position have become either inactive or restrained in their criticism. One informant described her experience: "Recently I had a group of women together and I tried to get them to work for more power in the party, as happens in some other states. But several women sitting in the front row with STOP ERA buttons said that they were happy with things as they are, so I dropped it."

Youth

Young people in Illinois are organized into three groups: Young Republicans, College Republicans, and Teenage Republicans. All these may be characterized as being offstage, because they are explicitly intended as socialization experiences, allowing young people, including those still too young to vote, the opportunity to learn about the Republican Party and the political process before they are expected to assume major party roles. From our interviews, it became clear that membership in these groups is a stepping-stone to later network membership in either the capacity of staff or officeholder, or through acting as an advisor or interest group representative officially outside the party but linked with it. Before becoming part of the network, young people help in various ways, especially in campaigning. Although such help is welcomed and gains later recognition, it does not in itself constitute full-fledged status in the party network.

Ethnic Groups

The United States is an ethnically diverse society; everyone can be identified by ethnic origin, though it does not follow that everyone has a self-conscious ethnic identity, anymore than it follows that every ethnic aggregate is mobilized into a group. For some, ethnicity is not relevant because it has become synonymous with the larger community in the sense that, if we were to continue to use ethnic labels, they would now represent the dominant groups. The mobilization of dominant groups, then, may not be overtly ethnic, but takes place through the actions of surrogate groups — civic organizations, for example — and the policies adopted on their behalf by decision-making authorities (Schwartz, 1981, 23–24). Political parties can be distinguished in analogous ways. With some variation among communities, most self-conscious ethnic groups have been incorporated into the Democratic Party since the New Deal. These include both the newer immigrant groups and racial minorities (e.g., Nie, Verba, Petrocik, 1976, 243–269), though some breaks in these attachments became evident in the 1970s. The remaining groups are the dominant ones and are present in both parties, but proportionately much more important in the Republican Party, both as supporters and as leaders in and out of office.

Awareness of the Democratic Party's advantage with a greater diversity of ethnic groups has prompted Republican activists to speak of the need to broaden their party's social base. This was a message we heard during many of our interviews. It was also part of the strategy of the Republican National Committee, both under Chairman William Brock and his successor Richard Richards. For the RNC, enlisting support from groups not traditionally Republican meant a deliberate outreach program to encourage their support as voters and direct them into office-seeking positions. In the Illinois Republican Party, ethnic fellowship, if not explicitly ethnic interests, is manifested in the following auxiliary organizations: the Nationalities Council, the Black Republican Council, the Hispanic Republican Council, the John Ericson League (the oldest and best organized of all, with members of Scandinavian origin), and the German-American Republican League. In the Midwest, the last two groups can easily be treated as part of the dominant ethnic community.

The existence of such auxiliary groups and efforts to include more ethnic supporters have not appreciably altered the nature of the Republican Party and have not given ethnic groups any more than an offstage role.[2] But even the most sincere intentions on the part of leaders to broaden the party's composition have not overcome perceptions that many ethnic groups are still not welcome. Members of nondominant ethnic groups who were, for other reasons, included in the party network expressed feelings that others like them would have a limited welcome in the party. An informant told of his experiences in this regard.

After Governor Ogilvie's defeat, I was at a party meeting where the X County chairman tried to persuade me to run for office. He said everyone in his county loved me. Then Senator Percy came to the platform and was speaking. The chairman was embarrassing me with his compliments. To quiet him, I said, "Ssh, Percy is talking." "Who's Percy?" I answered, "He's the biggest vote-getter in the state." "Oh that—it's just because he ran against Pucinski [Roman Pucinski was the Democratic candidate for the U.S. Senate and of Polish origin]. No one here would vote for anyone like him." I was really mad. "You bastard," I told him. "You've just finished telling me to run? Who do you think *I* am?"

The Network in Action

The 23 actors introduced in this chapter gained their place in the Illinois Republican Party network in a number of ways. I located them by following advice given in the literature on political parties, especially as I interpreted Sorauf and Beck and Cotter, Bibby, and Huckshorn. I was influenced as well by my open-minded perspective on federalism, in which I was encouraged by my reading in organizational theory. Informants in the study were guides in helping me decide on the relative importance of actors. Throughout the study, including its data-collection stages, continuing analysis went on, weighing accumulating evidence on how a party network should be constituted.

Each actor has been identified as something of a prototype, representing positions rather than persons and collective experiences rather than individual ones. Clearly, these abstractions can be sustained only to a point,

2. At the time of the 1984 national convention, Illinois delegates were still being urged to find a place for more women, blacks, and other minorities. According to Cook County chairman J. Robert Barr, "A better sexual and racial mix in the delegation would show the TV viewing audience that the GOP has a wide political base" (Talbott, 1984b).

and I have tried not to exaggerate common features. References to variations associated with particular individuals, settings, and events are intended to set the stage for the more detailed analyses that will follow. Here what have been brief reports of events and allusions to personal styles or conflicts will contribute, in subsequent chapters, to the substance of how the party appears in action.

3

Properties of Network Links

Contacts

The literature on political parties and organizational theory guided my choice of actors making up the Illinois Republican Party network. There was also a somewhat crude form of empiricism at work, one that provided a cumulative learning experience and helped to change the direction in which some of these choices were made. It operated, as I described in the preceding chapter, to minimize attention to party positions restricted to women, even though my original intention was to describe enough of them to allow detailed comparisons with positions held only by men. Conversely, it functioned to focus more attention on the staffs of party agencies and on Washington-based actors generally, whose centrality was not initially anticipated. The same kind of shift occurred with respect to interest groups, although it did not lead to representing them fully through individual interviews.

A similar kind of empiricism played a role in determining links among network elements. Although earlier research and writing about parties had alerted me to expected links, they did not lead me to rely on formal organizational charts; I looked, instead, for evidence of contacts among party actors. Informants were asked about contacts they had themselves and those they knew of; respondents to the telephone survey were asked about their own contacts. Contacts were also deduced less directly through observations we and others made and through evaluations our informants made about other political actors. A summary measure of the presence of contact was then created based on multiple sources of information about each type of actor. When a majority of these sources reported a contact between one type of actor and another, the contact was assumed to exist, including the cases when the actor category in question involved multiple participants, such as state representative or congressman. In addition, it should be understood that these reports indicate regular contact rather than contact only under highly unusual circumstances.

In the telephone survey local committeemen reported contacts in terms of frequency, whereas informants were more likely to speak of contacts

51

as either occurring or not occurring. In both cases, I anticipated that actors' reports would be affected by such factors as relative status, power,
and social perception, in ways akin to what Blau (1963, 150–152) found
when studying choices made by workers in two government bureaucracies.
For example, actors in lower positions are more likely to report contacts
with those in higher positions than vice versa. Although these kinds of
perceptual biases are considerations in evaluating the reliability of sociometric choices (e.g., Mouton, Blake, Fruchter, 1960a), I begin by assuming
that they pose no problem here. Actors' judgments about contacts, no matter
how idiosyncratic, and even my own interpretations about the existence
of contacts, are treated as given attributes of party processes. To the extent
that perceptions of contacts vary in reliability, they illustrate the pervasiveness of ambiguity and indeterminacy within organizations generally,
occasioned by variations in the positions, beliefs, and competing interests
of individual and collective actors (March and Olsen, 1976).

The major test that should be applied to information on contacts is one
of usefulness: How well do presumed links among actors efficiently describe the party network and account for what is otherwise known about
how the party works? Put this way, the evaluation of contact measures
seems more like a problem of validity (e.g., Mouton, Blake, Fruchter,
1960b), and its test must wait for the conclusion to this chapter. To begin
with, typical contacts among the 23 party actors are used to construct formal properties of the network, from which we can discern centrality, asymmetry of relations, and cohesion among subsets of actors.

All contacts made and received by party actors are shown in Figure 1.
Because we are dealing with collective actors, it is often useful to consider
interaction within elements, for example, among the Illinois congressional
delegation or among financial contributors, but following convention for
the kind of analyses done with such matrices, the diagonal cell entries are
kept at zero. The measures employed should be interpreted more heuristi-
cally than as a serious statistical analysis, since their main purpose is to
give an initial entry point into the world of party actors.

Chapter 2 began by describing the Republican Party network as densely
populated, meaning that Republicans filled most of the positions. The
matrix lends itself to another perspective on density, where it is measured
as the proportion of all theoretically possible contacts (Burt, 1983a, 189).
The density in Figure 1 is 0.47, meaning that almost half the possible contacts among actors were actually made, which further justifies the conclusion that the network was relatively dense.

One reason for contact is to provide services, linking actors through
the services they can contribute either directly to each other or indirectly
to their shared constituents. The latter may be a form of link between a

	senator	congressman	governor	constitutional officer	state Senate leader	state senator	state House leader	state representative	local officeholder	Republican National Committee	national committeeman	State Central Committee	state central committeeman	county chairman	local committeeman	Republican Senate Campaign Committee	Republican Congressional Campaign Committee	State Senate Campaign Committee	State House Campaign Committee	United Republican Fund	interest group	advisor	financial contributor
senator	0	1	1	0	0	1	0	1	1	1	0	1	1	1	0	1	0	0	0	0	1	1	1
congressman	0	0	0	0	0	1	0	1	1	1	0	0	1	1	1	0	1	0	0	0	1	1	1
governor	1	1	0	1	1	1	1	1	1	0	0	1	0	1	0	0	0	1	1	0	1	1	1
constitutional officer	0	0	1	0	0	1	0	1	0	0	0	0	1	0	0	0	0	0	1	1	1	1	1
state Senate leader	0	0	1	1	0	1	1	0	0	0	1	0	0	0	0	0	1	0	0	1	0	0	1
state senator	1	1	1	1	1	0	0	1	1	0	0	0	1	1	0	0	1	0	1	1	1	1	1
state House leader	0	0	1	1	1	0	0	1	0	0	0	1	0	0	0	0	0	0	1	0	1	0	1
state representative	1	1	1	1	0	1	1	0	1	0	0	0	0	1	1	0	0	0	1	1	1	1	1
local officeholder	1	1	1	1	0	1	0	1	0	0	0	0	0	1	0	0	0	0	1	0	0	0	1
Republican National Committee	1	1	0	0	0	1	0	1	0	0	1	1	0	0	0	1	1	1	0	1	0	1	1
national committeeman	0	0	0	0	0	0	0	0	0	1	0	1	1	0	0	1	1	1	1	0	1	1	1
State Central Committee	1	0	0	0	1	0	1	0	0	1	1	0	1	0	0	0	1	1	0	0	1	1	1
state central committeeman	0	1	0	0	0	0	0	0	0	0	1	1	0	1	0	0	0	0	0	0	0	0	1
county chairman	1	1	1	1	0	1	0	1	1	0	0	1	1	0	1	0	0	0	0	1	0	0	1
local committeeman	0	0	0	0	0	1	0	1	1	0	0	0	1	0	0	0	0	0	0	0	0	0	0
Republican Senate Campaign Committee	1	0	0	0	0	0	0	0	0	1	1	0	0	1	0	0	1	0	0	0	1	1	1
Republican Congressional Campaign Committee	0	1	0	0	0	0	0	0	0	1	1	0	1	1	0	1	0	0	0	0	1	1	1
State Senate Campaign Committee	0	0	0	0	1	1	0	0	0	0	1	1	0	1	0	1	0	0	0	0	1	1	1
State House Campaign Committee	0	0	0	0	0	0	1	1	0	0	1	1	0	1	0	0	0	0	0	0	1	1	1
United Republican Fund	0	0	0	1	0	1	0	1	1	0	0	0	1	0	0	0	0	0	0	0	0	0	1
interest group	1	1	1	1	1	1	1	1	0	1	1	0	0	0	0	1	1	1	0	0	1	1	1
advisor	1	1	1	1	0	1	0	1	0	1	0	1	0	0	0	1	1	1	0	1	0	1	1
financial contributor	1	1	1	1	1	1	1	1	0	1	1	1	0	0	0	1	1	1	1	1	1	1	0

Figure 1. Matrix of relations among party actors.

state representative or state senator and a congressman in the same district.

Elections provide a second basis of linkage, giving actors an opportunity to build ties through endorsements, voter contacts, fundraising, or campaign advice. Such linkage can be found in those districts where officeholders campaign together, hold joint fundraisers, or endorse each other. Elections have also justified the importance of advisors because of the technical knowledge they offer for achieving successful outcomes.

A third basis of contact comes from similar positions on issues. Issues can provide the substance for persuasive campaigns by advisors and interest groups, the common ideological underpinnings for state legislators and congressmen, and the justification used by the governor's staff to gather support from legislators.

Centrality

Viewed from the perspective of a particular actor type, the density of network relations is a measure of that actor's centrality, calculated as a proportion of all relations in a network that involves a given actor (Burt, 1980, 92). If the resulting index equals 1, this indicates that the actor is linked with all others in the network; if it is 0, the actor is an isolate, neither making nor receiving contacts — a logically impossible situation for us. Each actor's index of centrality is displayed in Table 3-1, from which we can calculate a centrality mean of 0.47 and a median of 0.43. The five most central actors have contacts with at least 66 percent of the network, and these five will receive first attention.

Unofficial Wing

Since the conviction has spread that elections are difficult and expensive to win, vast opportunities for the assumption of party roles have opened to those otherwise without a legal or formal party position. This seemingly recent phenomenon has had wide publicity resulting from the growth of political action committees, yet recognition of the partisanship of interest groups and their financial counterparts has a long history in U.S. political science, going back at least to the 1908 publication of Arthur Bentley's *The Process of Government.* Financial contributor, interest group, and especially advisor, play different roles and manifest somewhat different degrees of centrality, with financial contributor the most central. They are treated together here because they alone represent what is called the unofficial wing of the party. This wing also has some coherence through overlap in personnel and interests served. For example, directors of corporate PACs frequently serve also as directors of public affairs or government relations, in which roles they direct the activities of lobbyists. When they are also members of the state campaign committees, they can assume advisory roles in evaluating candidates and planning campaign strategy.

Unlike any of the legislative campaign committees, financial contributors, whether corporate or individual, give money to candidates not solely to ensure the election of Republicans, but also as a means for accomplishing their own collective goals. Comparing parties and PACs, one corporate PAC official stated: "PACs and political parties have a lot in common — to get 'their candidate' elected. But the reasons for being part of one of them are different. PACs are financially oriented and have a narrower scope of interests. They also have greater homogeneity in their constituency." In the case of contributors from business or industry, the rationale for giving money is one of self-interest: to support probusiness candidates, especially those running for office in districts with branch plants. Democratic Party

Table 3-1. Centrality of Party Actors

	Index of Centrality
Financial contributor	0.89
Interest group	0.70
Advisor	0.66
State senator	0.66
State representative	0.66
County chairman	0.64
Governor	0.59
Senator	0.55
Congressman	0.52
Republican National Committee	0.52
State Central Committee	0.50
Constitutional officer	0.43
National committeeman	0.43
Local officeholder	0.41
State House Campaign Committee	0.39
State Senate Campaign Committee	0.39
State Senate leadership	0.34
State House leadership	0.34
Republican Congressional Campaign Committee	0.32
Republican Senate Campaign Committee	0.29
United Republican fund	0.27
Central committeeman	0.25
Local committeeman	0.20

candidates may have the same attributes, and consequently some of them also benefit. According to a director of public affairs and member of his company's PAC: "We look for candidates who are for free enterprise, free trade, the advancement of our industries. We support more Republicans than Democrats. Recently, it was 28 to 13."

The choice of candidates to support is often made on the basis of past performance, thus giving an advantage to incumbents. Some members of the unofficial wing do their own targeting, selecting candidates they feel deserve support. A *New York Times* reporter's description of decision-making by the Sun Company PAC before the 1982 election parallels our findings:

Sun's main goal is to help elect pro-business candidates, and in most cases its philosophical choices among pairs of candidates were clear. For example the House Republican leader, Robert H. Michel of Illinois, was predictably preferred over his challenger, G. Douglas Stephens, in the 18th District of Illinois.

The real work of the contributions committee is weighing many factors and then deciding how to allocate its money for the best return. In the case of Mr. Michel, who earlier had received three committee contributions totaling $1,000, it was noted that not only was the Republican leader handicapped by having to spend a lot of time in Washington but also that, because of reapportionment, 45 percent of his district was new. (Hershey, 1982)

Others are satisfied to rely on the directions given by party officials, typically saying, "We follow the lead of the RNC and the state campaign committees. Others solicit us, but we don't follow their advice." Still others may take the initiative in trying to influence the selection of Republican candidates; this was suggested earlier by the 1958 Oregon study which noted the influence of interest groups in recruiting Republican candidates for county office (Seligman, 1961, 79–80). This is an even more likely course for ideological groups committed to single issues or to a generally conservative perspective. An example of the latter is the Committee for the Survival of a Free Congress, founded as a coalition of congressmen, businessmen, and industrialists to oppose what they saw as the liberalism of many congressmen. Possessing a field organization, the committee not only gives money directly to candidates but also enters the district and ensures that there is a campaign organization down to the precinct level. Its choice among Republicans is ideological, and competitive primaries are no deterrent to its participation.

Interest groups, unlike some financial contributors, are always organized entities; some 400 are registered to lobby under Illinois statutes. In advising new directors of state agencies how to deal with lobbyists and interest groups, the executive vice president of the Illinois Realtors Association urges that they "appreciate and capitalize on [the] role of the lobbyist as a two-way communicator between government and interest group" (Cook, 1982, 114). And in describing their activities, he puts them directly in the legislative process:

Sometimes the legislature directs interest groups with fundamentally different positions, such as labor and management, to work together to develop an "agreed bill" outside of the legislative arena. This has been the case . . . over proposed changes in workers' compensation rates. The rationale is that these groups have greater knowledge, larger stakes, and more intense interest in these complex subjects than do legislators. Therefore, it is in their interest to achieve a compromise rather than to leave decisions to an uncertain fate in the legislature. (Cook, 1982, 117)

Cook confirms what had been observed earlier: "Representatives of private groups are physically part of the legislative life" (Gove, Carlson, Carlson, 1976, 122). Reasons for interest groups' centrality include the ability to initiate legislation, identify and create issues, help resolve conflicts between the Illinois House and Senate and among interest groups, and generally provide services to the legislature. In carrying out these activities, interest groups and their representatives become centers of attention for state legislators, creating a sense of obligation extending to attendance at sponsored social events, or even to establishing bonds of friendship. When one legislator was pressed for names of those with whom he had the closest ties, we first reviewed all network members with official status. He made only lukewarm comments about officeholders who had endorsed him, congressmen who mentioned his name when they were at the same meeting, or members of the legislature who helped him or whose voting records were similar to his. None, however, evoked much enthusiasm. Was it possible, we suggested, that he was something of a loner? "No, not really. The person I'm closest to is a lobbyist. We'd kill for each other."

Advisors, when not associated with financial contributors or interest groups, generally supply technical assistance, primarily designed to aid in winning elections. The best known are hired by the State Central Committee, the Republican National Committee, and the campaign committees, as well as by those running for statewide office. Either because advisors have made some initial effort to make their services known or because, once known, they have easy access to party officials, we consider their contacts to be reciprocated.

Lesser-known advisors have a scope of activity in individual races which can become the avenue for recognition in a wider arena. Todd Domke, for example, had worked in county and legislative races for candidates whom he perceived to be conservative. His campaign for Mayor David Nuessen of Quincy as a primary challenger of Congressman Paul Findley in 1980 was partly the result of Domke's dissatisfaction with the congressman and his own involvement in recruiting a suitable challenger. Although Congressman Findley won, Domke moved on to other races, including some outside of Illinois. In Massachusetts, he found Ray Shamie a sound candidate in contrast with the liberalism of Senator Edward Kennedy in 1982. His candidate lost again, but not before Domke impressed some Republicans with his campaign skills. According to Rich Bond, a deputy director of the RNC: "If Kennedy is the Democratic Presidential nominee, Domke's clearly going to be called upon because he knows so much about Kennedy's style and Kennedy's voting record" (Raines, 1982).

Ties between the Republican Party and its unofficial wing extend through most of the network. Links with other network elements occur in the interchange of personnel, compatibility of interests, and expressed desirability of services offered.

State Legislators

State legislators are also highly central but contacts through services, elections, and issues produce a different kind of centrality for them than it does for actors in the unofficial wing. Actors in the unofficial wing provide services intended to be directly convertible into electoral success, and they use their own positions on issues as a test, both before supporting other actors and as a lever of persuasion. Legislative actors, in contrast, are principally concerned with their own elections and have more pragmatic, even short-run, orientations to services and issues, generally confined to district concerns. Unlike members of the unofficial wing, their interactions are often with local-level actors, but are also with those who have central-level roles.

The Illinois legislature now holds yearly sessions, beginning on the second Wednesday in January. The General Assembly customarily recesses on June 30 and returns in the fall for briefer meetings, especially in election years. Committees, however, may meet throughout the year (Gonet and Nowlan, 1982, 73–81). As a consequence, there are a considerable number of full-time legislators. It is difficult to estimate how many, because even those who list another activity as their principal occupation told us that their legislative jobs, done properly, took much of their time. One active legislator, ostensibly in a family-run business, described how biennial elections create conflicts and pressures: "I feel that the best thing would be to have a set term, get a decent salary, and get out. . . . We have three stores . . . but my legislative job is full-time now, and not out of choice." Regardless of how legislative performance is perceived, centrality is undoubtedly tied to the fact that legislative actors are present in the political arena for much of the time.

An election to the General Assembly is held every even-numbered year for members of the House, and three times in a 10-year period for senators, once for a 2-year term and twice for 4-year terms. Legislators, particularly in the House, complain that they are always campaigning, but the result is a high degree of visibility. For senators, visibility is associated with their longer terms. The frequency of elections and the interactions they stimulate with other party actors also contribute to legislators' centrality.

Centrality was also aided, at least until 1982, by the presence of multi-member House districts. In strongly Republican districts, this meant that the party was represented by as many as three legislators. In weak districts, when no other Republican could hope for election, even in county races, one candidate could expect to win a seat in the House. Some people denigrated this kind of minority representation, dismissing it, especially in Chicago, as nothing more than the election of another Democrat in disguise. This was never completely true, however, and some minority Republicans from Chicago could always be found in the party leadership, where they often served as "honest brokers" among party factions and between Republicans and Democrats. An example was Arthur Telcser (District 12), who went from assistant minority leader to majority leader during the period of this study, and then retired after the change to single-member districts. He was appraised by the political editor of the Chicago *Sun-Times* as " a skillful politician. He came out of the weakling Chicago GOP, but made himself one of the most influential Republicans in the House" (Talbott, 1982b).

In understanding the reasons for legislators' centrality, it is more appropriate to consider what the presence of a lone Republican official could mean to party supporters. One such legislator, proud of the personal support he had built, told us: "The county chairman and the central committeeman don't control the party. There is no leadership. The only thing to hold the party together is my position. Local people feel closer to me than to the governor, or any other office." Secure in a safe seat, a legislator could develop an independent base of support that allowed him to act independently of the legislative leadership, the governor, and anyone else he chose to defy outside his district. For example, an incumbent legislator, state Senator Robert Mitchler (District 39), publicly disagreed with Governor Ogilvie, even taking out advertisements to condemn the effects of the governor's income tax policy and becoming, according to a critical informant, "a crusader in the state against the tax." Yet he remained secure in the support he could rely on in the next election. In the words of the same informant, involved in that campaign, "The governor said that we had to defend our position, and that was what I was doing. But we kept our role discreet." Opposing advertisements were placed, without identifying the Governor as sponsor—a procedure possible before legislation on campaign disclosures—and other forms of support were given to the primary challenger. These efforts were to no avail; the incumbent retained his seat.

A similar case occurred under Governor Thompson with a similar outcome. Although the legislator in question, state Senator John Friedland (District 2), had not been totally loyal to the governor's program, he was seen to reflect his constituents' interests and his district legislative committee endorsed him for office:

"A vital issue involved here is the attempt by the executive branch to punish members of the legislature if they do not bow to the wishes of the governor," said Ronald Hamelberg, Barrington Township GOP committeeman, after the Suburban Republican Organization of Cook County voted to "commend" Friedland's voting record. (Egler, 1980a)

The centrality of legislators as party actors does not in any sense mean that they impose unity on the party. They are central as discrete party actors, not as a unified group. For the most part, it is district concerns that define their roles, and these are frequently diverse because of the heterogeneity of the state (Elazar, 1970, 282–316). Looking at roll-call votes for sales tax reduction on food and drugs and on transportation funding, particularly divisive issues in 1979, regional interests were found to dominate over party ones, and this was true for both parties (Everson and Redfield, 1980). Conflicts are frequently found among Chicago, suburban Cook County and its collar counties, and the remaining downstate counties. When columnist Mike Royko epitomized downstate as "Pigkisser County" (Royko, 1981), downstate legislators retaliated with mock war and threatened secession.

Lack of unity contributes to the poor image of legislators generally and probably prevents a full appreciation of their centrality in the party network. They are disparaged as "double-dippers," coming to the public trough twice, when, as elected state officials, they hold other jobs or offer professional services paid for by public funds. In 1979, the Coalition for Political Honesty accused 53 General Assembly members of being double-dippers, implying that they voted "in the interests of the local politicians who gave them their jobs, rather than in the interests of the people who elected them" (Lempinen, 1980).

Also, frustrated by pressures to end a session as scheduled (on June 30), and faced with important legislation at the very end, legislators sometimes engage in clownish behavior. But whatever the justification, that kind of behavior evokes further harsh criticism:

There are legislators who are diligent, knowledgeable, and occasionally effective. It is easier to identify them by comparison rather than total worth, but they are there.

It is more difficult to define those who contribute the *least* to the General Assembly because a vast majority contribute absolutely nothing but the cost of their pay and per diem vouchers. Still, there are some who have managed to thwart, infuriate, and, at the very least, embarrass the legislative process, and those actions have earned them a dubious distinction. (Ciccone, Egler, Locin, 1981, 30)

Some criticism even resorts to appearance as symbolic; a serious, and generally sympathetic, treatment of legislators includes the statement, "In the capitol rotunda, you will see solid kelly green sports jackets and white shoes standing toe-to-toe with black wing tips and sombre pinstripes" (Gonet and Nowlan, 1982, 81). The code word for contempt is often "polyester."[1] Differences in styles of dress are certainly apparent and provide another opportunity to examine legislators' centrality by contrasting four legislators: *A* and *B,* both clad in natural fibers and educated at elite colleges; *X* and *Y,* accustomed to polyester attire and with no more than a high school education.

---

1. Overheard in a popular Springfield restaurant, the day after busloads of polyester-clad constituents had arrived to hold a prayer meeting on the capitol grounds and voice their objections to ERA and abortion: "Yesterday Springfield was the polyester capital of the world. It's a wonder we didn't have a storm after all the static electricity generated."

A described himself as

part of a faction. . . . We're probably better educated than most of the older members of the Senate. Few of them had a college education when we came in. We laughed at their absurdities and they were offended by our attitudes. If we can be described as a group, it is younger, more sophisticated, more talented. It reflects part of the change in style and emphasis in the Republican Party.

None of this self-acknowledged talent, however, was associated with the assumption of leadership roles, even in his faction. *A* handled his district-level responsibilities well, but as one close associate commented, "He does not always play with a full deck," and others who knew him confirmed that he "needed watching."

B was not only more sober in manner but, in a way especially endearing to a professor, also used abstract concepts with ease and even laid out several important hypotheses for this research. His participation in legislative committees was even thinner than *A*'s; he stated that he almost never introduced legislation, and when he did, I found that political commentators tended to disparage it. He was generally content to leave patronage and even campaigning to local officeholders.

In appearance and education, *X* fitted a more negative stereotype, underlined by a tendency to explain events in conspiratorial terms. But his effectiveness as legislator and politician was impressive and included skill in using the whole federal system for the benefit of his constituents. He explained how he went about acquiring favorable recognition in the legislature: "First you have to convince them [other legislators] that you have something that you are interested in. You are an expert on it. Then, when you bring in a bill, they should look to you as a leader."

Our final example, *Y,* was an especially thoughtful man who served as Republican spokesman on several important legislative committees. He presented evidence of effectiveness in dealing with electoral competition and constituent demands. Evidence of his skills from verbatim accounts cannot be reproduced, however, because of both his own modesty and my protection of his identity.

Clearly, clothes do not make an effective legislator, and regardless of style of dress, centrality persists as the result of special attributes and responsibilities. Presence in all districts, frequent elections, emphasis on service, and even parochialism all give legislators a network position that straddles local concerns and central party demands.

Congress

Although the U.S. senator and congressman are not as central as the county chairman or the governor (the latter to be discussed in the following section on asymmetry), the congressional components of the party network deserve attention because of their special claims to centrality. At first sight, their centrality scores, given in Table 3-1, have an intuitive validity, lower than 7 other actors but higher than the remaining 13. But now, having argued in support of state legislators' centrality, I find it easier to ask why Congress does not share this position.

Unlike the state senator and representative, who have the same centrality score, the U.S. senator has a slightly higher score than the congressman. That can be attributed to his statewide arena of operation, which gives him greater visibility and more potential for interchange with other actors over services to constituents. Even though the entire state can be a beneficiary of his services, the likelihood that the provision of services can be converted into party leadership is not great. According to a staff member:

> The senator is in a peculiar position. It is hard for him to keep close ties with his party—he lives in Washington and he is removed from his constituency. This differs from key figures at the state level. For the Democrats, the key posts are local, but for the Republicans, they are state and national. Those are important, even symbolically.
>
> [Isn't there a contradiction—the senator doesn't stay close to the party, but the position is very important to the party?]
>
> Well, let me compare Percy to Dirksen. Dirksen was truly representative of the core of the Republican Party, although he was probably more conservative than the ordinary voter. Percy, however, was a liberal businessman. He's not of the same cloth. He decided—"I'll build my own organization." The Republicans covet the senatorship, but for one of their own.

This informant's explanation of Senator Percy's anomalous role in the party first related it to the general situation of any senator and then tied it to Percy's specific characteristics. The assumption that Percy himself was at fault was often heard in our interviews. A financial contributor, for example, commented: "The senator does nothing for the party. He has a personal following but then does nothing for the party. In part, that's because he has nothing to offer." But we need not accept informants' allegations that Percy was not very important because he lacked resources; otherwise he would not have heard as many complaints about Senator Percy as we did. Nor should we accept complaints as unequivocal evidence that Senator Percy did not involve himself in party affairs. One contrary item, for example, was his contribution to organizing a task force after the 1974 election for party self-study.[2] We can best understand the rela-

---

2. The task force presented a report, "A Party of the People," in March 1975, but its recommendations to broaden the party's base and rationalize its central operations do not appear to have had much impact.

tive centrality of the Senate office by paying most attention to what the first informant said. The accuracy of his judgment is made even more convincing when juxtaposed with comments from an advisor about Senator Dirksen:

In 1950, Dirksen went for the Senate seat. He was a sharp campaigner and he had big-business support, including Standard Oil. Dirksen was a maverick. He didn't go along with the regular organization. He travelled throughout the state, stopping to speak to all the civic clubs. He didn't bother with the politicians.

It seems more accurate to conclude, then, that the centrality of the senator as a type of party actor is conditioned by his limited dependence on party officeholders and local politicians for achieving his own goals. Their resentment is indicative of an imbalance in which they may need him more than he needs them.

The congressman would seem to be even more similar to the state legislators than the senator is; but there is one crucial difference. Instead of being present in all districts, he is confined to those where he enjoys a majority of electoral support. His exclusion from the most populous part of the state — Chicago — can only hurt in assessing his visibility in the network. His broad range of contacts is still largely limited to his local district. This was made evident in the assessment of one congressional aide:

The big surprise of working in the X District is that there are so many people to work with, for example, the aldermen. I'm called by committeemen about appointments, fundraisers, and speaking engagements for the congressman. But then they want something in return. There are two people who have headed the congressman's campaign funding; . . . when they call, they go through me. They feel more comfortable talking to me rather than some more neutral [staff] person. This is also true of Clement Stone and [his associate] Warren Hendrix. When they have some views to express, they talk to me.

We hear from the state legislators. He [the congressman] answers them as he would any constituent.

When asked about Y, who had been a competitor in the primary, the aide replied: "Oh, yes, I should have mentioned him. We try to give him VIP treatment. I always make a point of shaking his hand when he comes to the office."

The breadth of this congressman's contacts are typical, reflecting what he has to offer in services and, to a lesser degree, in election assistance and issue support. There is a tension, however, between the local arena, where he has his electoral support, and his performance in the Washington arena. As with the senator, if he is caught up with duties in Washington, there may be a weakening of links with the home district. One way a congressmen may experience this was described for us by a local party officeholder in terms of a shift from dependence on local-level party organs to dependence on the mass media:

> Candidates fall into two categories — [first] those who are media-oriented. This includes the governor, senator, perhaps some other statewide offices. The party has little impact on them and it can be ignored. Then [second] there are the unknown candidates. This is where the party works — it controls nominations, and now inner factions matter. This county has no exclusive media. . . . Candidates have little chance for just districtwide exposure.
>
> [Does this nonmedia approach apply to congressmen here?]
>
> This is true the first time he runs. He can then be very dependent on the party. But if he runs a mass campaign, if he is colorful, he can run a media campaign. Congressman McClory has been in *Time* magazine; he is minority leader of the House Judiciary Committee — he is important in Washington. . . . Congressman Corcoran doesn't have media attention. But, once he got into office, he had no opposition here; he didn't need the media, and the party became supportive, or at least not troublesome.[3]

The limits on a congressman's centrality are affected by his being restricted to parts of the state where there is a reservoir of Republican strength, unless he can make a personal appeal that overwhelms normal voting patterns. In either case, he can be expected to display a cumulative independence from local sources of party organization. As a party actor, the congressman is a local with a national scope for action. In addition, as we see in Figure 1, contacts with statewide officeholders and the state party apparatus are either absent or unreciprocated. The general effects of this lack of reciprocity bring us to the following section, on asymmetry.

Asymmetry

The flow of contacts between party actors (Figure 1) indicates a high degree of similarity between contacts made and contacts received: 82 percent of all possible contacts were reciprocal. The network, as defined here, captures the generally prevailing mutuality. To the extent that the measure of centrality is an indicator of actors' relative importance, we might expect that the more central actors will receive more contacts that they do not reciprocate, which would conform with research on small groups (Bales et al., 1950; Davis and Leinhardt, 1972). I did my test by looking at asymmetry, measured as the proportion of each actor's paired relations that are not reciprocated, measuring each possible pair only once. That is, for any one actor, lack of reciprocity may be due either to the contacts he made or to those he received (Table 3-2).

---

3. Congressman Corcoran first won the primary in 1976 by defeating four candidates, at least two of whom had local party ties.

Table 3-2. Asymmetry of Relations among Party Actors

	Index of Asymmetry
County chairman	0.27
Governor	0.18
Republican National Committee	0.18
Constitutional officer	0.14
Congressman	0.14
Central committeeman	0.14
State Senate Campaign Committee	0.14
State House Campaign Committee	0.14
Financial contributor	0.14
Senator	0.09
Local officeholder	0.09
State Central Committee	0.09
Republican Congressional Campaign Committee	0.09
State Senate leadership	0.05
State House leadership	0.05
State senator	0.05
State representative	0.05
National committeeman	0.05
Local committeeman	0.05
Republican Senate Campaign Committee	0.05
Advisor	0.05
United Republican Fund	0.00
Interest group	0.00

At first sight, the expected relation holds best for the county chairman, with a centrality index of 0.64 and an asymmetry index of 0.27. The asymmetry index derives from the chairman's receiving contacts from the four campaign committees but not reciprocating, and from his making two unreciprocated contacts, one to the State Central Committee and the other to the financial contributor category. The relatively central governor (centrality = 0.59) provides a second example of the expected relation (asymmetry = 0.18), but the same level of asymmetry is also found in the less central Republican National Committee. The components of asymmetry need elaborating, because they are not all of the same order.

County Chairman

The centrality of the county chairman rests on a clearly defined party constituency, and although he does not always assume leadership, even in his county, he has the potential of being a focal participant. As one county chairman described his duties:

I'm the spokeman here for the Republican Party. I'm responsible for all levels of the party within the state. That means I'm responsible for fundraising, leading the

precinct organizations, and attracting the best possible candidates to run for office.
. . . In my activities with the Northern Illinois Republican Committee [a coalition of county chairmen and ward and township committeemen in Cook and surrounding counties], I do not perceive my role as party leader to interfere with legislation, although this is not a view shared by the other county chairmen. I will interfere if the legislation involves a party matter, like voting, redistricting, or party structure.

As the leader of the core political organization, the county chairman is approached by the campaign committees. There is indirect contact when these committees encourage candidates or their campaign organizations to solicit aid from him. Their own direct contacts are mainly efforts to involve the county chairman in recruiting candidates. One staff member elaborated:

> We meet with chairmen, share information, involve them in the process of recruiting. We try to work with them on recruiting. It's been very unsuccessful. I would advocate bypassing county chairmen. . . . There was one race where we wanted a woman. The chairman went nuts. He wanted his buddy to run.
>
> A county chairman who was a former senator and is now in the House and another who was leader in the House had put together a deal. The campaign committee spent $5,000 for a poll to find what kind of candidate it would take to win, but we were not able to convince them. We lost, exactly as the poll predicted. Then they came and said they were sorry.
>
> Recruitment for the General Assembly is falling flat on its face. My luck with county chairmen is terrible. They're not worried about the party, just about local issues.

This view was echoed by others, including a legislative member of one of the campaign committees:

> We are doing more and more recruiting and we're working with county chairmen, but it is perfunctory. The chairmen are not a good source. But we ask them to have a meeting, and invite everyone who is interested in running. . . . The committee doesn't endorse candidates. But we do pass the word on to the county people about whom we favor.

The contacts received in this fashion are made grudgingly and do not seem to elicit response.

County chairmen need money to sustain a county-level presence, and for this purpose they make contacts with financial contributors. They are, for example, one of the types of actors who regularly approach the United Republican Fund.[4] This study treats the category of county chairman as

4. Nowlan (1965, 91) found that between 1954 and 1964, the United Republican Fund had given 30 percent of its funds to the Cook County organization and 6 percent to downstate counties.

a money-seeker, with little to offer the financial contributor in return, unlike most other actors. In his relations with the financial contributor, he resembles the local officeholder and state central committeeman, but even the local officeholder is more likely to have reciprocal relations when he is in large cities where major businesses and trade associations are located.

I interpret relations between the county chairman and the State Central Committee as going primarily from the county chairman to the SCC because of indications that the former asks for help but does not usually get it. Specific complaints were made about the services that the SCC was expected to provide. Among those we heard, one was: "Several years ago we got a training film. Right now they have nothing for us." Another was: "The SCC is supposed to maintain lists, have mailings available. But when I requested a list, they didn't have it." These complaints are instances of an ongoing rivalry between individual county chairmen and the central committeemen in their districts and between the County Chairmen's Association and the SCC. Both are elaborated later in this chapter as well as elsewhere in the volume, but we will give some content to that rivalry here.

It is not enough to view the SCC negatively or to minimize contact between the SCC and the county chairmen, as one county chairman suggested:

I have little contact with the SCC except at conventions. That is largely because the county organization is politically active, while the state one is [for] service. We are aggressive, they are passive.

A fuller appraisal of the roots of discontent, which supports the direction of contacts I have identified, was given by another county chairman:

The SCC see the county chairmen as a necessary evil. They ignore us when they can. . . . At the 1980 state convention, the county chairmen were ignored on possible nominations for committees. We did not like the heavy-handed way the convention was run. There was a lot of resentment over the blind primary. At our own meeting, we passed a resolution against it. At the convention, efforts to introduce a resolution against the blind primary had been killed in committee. So I got 30 signatures necessary, and introduced a resolution from the floor. There was objection that it would take time. It only took about 40 seconds — it was passed by voice vote.

In trying to account for asymmetry in the party network, we cannot interpret the direction of relations in ways always consistent with small-group research findings. The campaign committees assumed that their initiation of contacts was a sign of their own importance, not the centrality of the county chairmen. Similarly, the county chairmen perceived their one-sided relations with the SCC as symptomatic of that body's weakness. Only the case of making contacts with financial contributors illustrates the anticipated dependency implied by this kind of asymmetry.

Governor

The Governor's asymmetry score is related to four unreciprocated contacts he initiated — with congressman, the State Central Committee, and the two campaign committees associated with the General Assembly.

Describing the governor's relations with the congressman as one-sided does not mean that there is a total absence of contacts arising from individual congressmen. Asymmetry occurs because initiative and necessity lie with the governor. There is some coordination of federally sponsored projects, and congressmen may want help for their constituents. But in most cases, the governor is not the best channel for soliciting help. As one congressional aide noted: "We have contacts with the governor's office, but it makes more sense to hand over issues — for example, a constituent problem that involves the state — to the state representatives." The governor makes most contacts because he wants congressmen to support his programs or those federally initiated ones that affect his state. In other words, he acts as a lobbyist, a role clearly recognized by congressmen and their staffs. In the words of one such informant:

Walker was a great one who wanted legislation his own way. He really pressured for votes. During Kerner's term, the pressure was to lobby for the good of the state. Under him, we were urged to cooperate within Congress for the benefit of Illinois. When Walker became governor, pressure was put on us to vote from a political perspective. Under Thompson, we've returned to voting for the good of the state.

Contacts come from the governor himself, members of his staff, and from the state of Illinois office in Washington, D.C. Personnel in that office keep track of congressional bills affecting Illinois and arrange for testimony before congressional committees. They play a true lobbying role, in company with about half the other states. Although their activities are political, they are not intended to be overtly partisan. There is, in fact, no way of divorcing partisanship from their goals, because they work directly under the governor.[5]

To view relations between the governor and the State Central Committee as asymmetrical is a way of capturing the ambiguity associated with the identity of the party head, the governor's efforts to establish control,

---

5. A brilliant example of state lobbying efforts occurred under Governor Ogilvie, when the state persuaded the Nixon administration to assume federal responsibility for welfare payments (Derthick, 1975, 43–70).

and the SCC's search for independence. The governor makes contacts to signify dominance; the SCC refrains from doing so to maintain some autonomy. We see this in the retrospective assessment of an informant who has actively participated as a staff member for both the SCC and the governor.

When the governor is a Republican, he is the titular head of the party. This can lead to fights with the SCC when the chairman is strong. This was most acute when Stratton was governor. When Ogilvie took over, the SCC was not strong. Stratton controlled the SCC. This led to the chairman, Stanley Guyer, a very sharp lawyer, resigning. He was replaced by Vic Smith, who was innocuous. Later, Guyer was sorry he resigned — he had been opposed to Stratton running for a third term. Guyer felt that, then, without a Republican governor, the chairman had an opportunity to rebuild the party. Smith never did this — he was ineffective.

Governor Stratton's dominance is confirmed by Nowlan's (1965, 22) earlier study of the Illinois Republican Party.

Governor Ogilvie as well tried to put his stamp on the SCC by taking steps that might otherwise have been taken by different centers in the party, or possibly by the SCC itself. As one staff member put it, "Ogilvie ran the party." When asked what that meant, he said:

In his case, when he became governor, it meant that the party, which had had one or two people in Springfield — Ogilvie brought in pros. He hired five or six people and gave them a budget. He got rid of those who objected. He felt that, since he was governor, the ultimate decisions were his. For example, when it came to fill Dirksen's position, he asked around, but then he was the one who decided to appoint Ralph Smith to the Senate.

The SCC's ability to hire its own autonomous staff and elect a chairman, who is, symbolically at least, the state party leader, is a structural impediment to the governor, making even his relative success neither conclusive nor enduring. This is illustrated by another example from the Ogilvie administration, given by an RNC informant:

The Illinois Party [i.e., the SCC] struggled very hard to become a professional organization. I'm told they have raised their standards recently. The party went through a reorganization attempt in 1969–70 that was a great success. Then the party backed away. The program for professionalization was dropped, and only two or three were left at headquarters.

Asked why the party backed away, he replied:

I'll answer with an example. In 1972 there was a vacancy for a University of Illinois trustee. The SCC met to select from two candidates. One was a banker from the Chicago area, a loyal Republican, and very able. The other was from southern Illinois. The first one was asked what he had done for the party — how many precincts he had walked. He was supported by Ogilvie, though not formally endorsed. The second one had been a county chairman, etc. He promised the committeemen football tickets. He was the one who was nominated. I felt the SCC was very shortsighted. The SCC has not been able to get out of the nineteenth century. It demonstrates all the negative aspects of patronage, although I believe in patronage. The SCC believes that you need to break people's arms to get them to participate. Ogilvie understood the party, and he fought it. Thompson understands it, but he can't control it too well.

These examples give the rationale for gubernatorial contact with the SCC. Even so, governors may vary in the ways in which they behave toward the SCC. As the last informant later went on to say:

For Thompson, the situation is different. Thompson's way of doing things is to dabble in the party. Party is more of a burden to him. He wants to have prominent roles. . . . Thompson doesn't want to control the party. He wants to keep it at bay, quiet. He wants to keep it not worth a shit, so long as it doesn't give him trouble.

If this means that Governor Thompson takes much less initiative in making contacts with the SCC, it still does not increase the likelihood that the SCC will contact him.

The unreciprocated contacts with the State Senate and House Campaign committees arise from the presence of "observers" on the committees who are the governor's personal representatives. They keep him informed of campaign strategies and serve to indicate his willingness to assist legislators seeking reelection. There is no particular need for the committees to reciprocate. Moreover, their own commitment to incumbents would place them in overt conflict with the governor should he choose to make an opposing primary endorsement.

Lack of reciprocity appears to be associated with the governor's efforts to strengthen his own position through control over other party actors. His success in this increases the likelihood that they will support or carry out his programs.

Republican National Committee
The Republican National Committee plays a less central role than any of the preceding actors, but, like the governor, it initiates four unreciprocated contacts. Two of these are with the state senator and state representative, stimulated by the committee's efforts to increase Republican representation, regardless of local conditions or judgments. One staff member described typical activities:

The Local Elections Committee went about its job systematically. We sent people around to find out about the legislature and to target likely districts. Then we prepared profiles on target areas. We used these to help in recruiting candidates. . . . Candidate recruitment is still the weakest link. People get "hacked" if the RNC anoints someone. We go to the county chairmen with the results of our analyses — we use these to try to sell the chairmen on types of people needed. But if someone wants to run, and feels it's his due, there isn't anything we can do about it.

Some of the national staff's activities were so unobtrusive, they were barely noticed by candidates. Even candidates and campaign managers who had benefitted from the staff's work did not find it important enough to mention. At best, candidates and managers spoke of their pleasure that so much money had been raised in their districts — money that was directly, though not solely, the result of national targeting. One beneficiary, when told that we had interviewed national staff, volunteered, "It's my feeling that the field staff is useless. They come in for a day and leave. They seem more willing to help if they know and like you." But then he admitted, "A young man from the RNC was quite helpful." It is for such reasons that I consider the RNC's legislative candidate contacts unreciprocated.

The other unreciprocated relations, with the two state campaign committees, were tied to the RNC's resources of money and services, offered with strings attached. The campaign committees were not passive, however; they, in fact, decided on districts to be targeted and expenditures to be made. RNC field staff was then told the committee's decisions. One member of the field staff told us: "The Illinois people were not enthused about my going into districts, or talking to candidates." Relations in Illinois were, in general, quite different from what had been intended by a policy of actively affecting state races through offering resources but holding the purse strings. The Illinois campaign committees were successful in evading restraints, using the RNC but making no efforts to involve it in their deliberations.

Constitutional Officer

The matrix of contacts gave the constitutional officer a below-average centrality score. This ranking was probably due to the special circumstances of the study period, when Attorney General William Scott was not only the single Republican constitutional officeholder but was also in legal jeopardy. The legal problems, in particular, enhanced the likelihood that existing contacts would be ignored or denied, as the following comment by a county chairman implies: "Scott has no friends. Everyone is standing back, letting the bullets hit him. He was never around when he was needed. . . . He was arrogant, surrounded by a little clique. He didn't give local groups a piece of action." It was time to belittle Scott with comments about his being "a loner," "never a party man," or "never a leader," but the informant who said the following missed the tenacity of Scott's support: "Scott was never much of a campaigner. You never saw him around at political events. I could never understand how he was able to get so much support." Even while the newspapers were publicizing Scott's personal and financial problems during his trial, he still was second in the three-man primary race for U.S. Senate in 1980, with 34 percent of the vote compared with the winner's 42 percent. He retained the loyalty of many county chairmen in that race and enough financial support to prompt a disgruntled evaluation by someone close to Mayor Richard Carver of Peoria, the third-ranking candidate: "Scott kept Carver from winning. He preempted all the fundraising sources outside of Peoria. . . . none of the big names in Chicago would go for Carver, people like Beré, Malot, Swearingen, Abboud" (industrialists and bankers). W. Clement Stone held a fundraiser for Scott to help defray his legal costs and gave him a job when he was released from prison (Simon, 1981).

Because there was both strong criticism of him and great personal loyalty to him, it was difficult to define Scott's contacts. These difficulties were compounded by the residue of relations originating at the time when Scott, as treasurer, was the sole Republican statewide officeholder. We know that such occasions are opportunities for leadership and also for rivalry, as observed by a longtime county chairman: "When Carpentier was secretary of state, he was the only Republican who was visible in state government. The *Tribune* called him 'Mr. Republican.' . . . Carpentier was a real irritant to the county chairmen. He literally dictated party policy without consulting the rest of us."

One aspect of leadership potential is control over patronage. Scott was said to have, at times, provided jobs for about half the central committeemen and county chairmen, allegedly using his resources in a more partisan fashion than did Carpentier. Yet the minutes of State Central Committee meetings at the time record dissatisfaction with Scott for not sharing information about jobs or soliciting applicants from among party actors. The importance of allowing for indirect patrons, in the sense of allotting jobs to party actors who can then dispense them independently of the original patron, is elaborated in chapter 6.

I used the SCC's complaint as my basis for designating an absence of contact between the constitutional officer and the SCC and central committeeman. Yet the place of the constitutional officer in the party network is too interesting to be slighted here by uncertainty about his centrality, and the same is true, I believe, with respect to asymmetry. Although the constitutional officer's asymmetry score is identical with those of five other actors, all the unreciprocated contacts were received by him, a characteristic shared only with the highly central financial contributor. But the ratio of unreciprocated to reciprocated contacts for the financial contributor is 0.08, whereas it is twice that (0.19) for the constitutional officer, suggesting a greater significance for the latter. I explain the contacts initiated by the county chairman, local officeholder, and central committeeman to the financial contributor as efforts to gain stable and reliable sources of funds from those who make large contributions in more than one district, in order to build their own centers of power. Such a straightforward explanation is not as readily available for unreciprocated contacts initiated by the state Senate and House leadership and by local officeholders to the constitutional officer.

It is quite usual for all statewide officeholders to have their own legislative agenda (Gove, Carlson, Carlson, 1976, 148). When constitutional officers and governors are of the same party, it is still possible that their agendas will not be totally compatible; Scott, for example, was opposed to Governor Ogilvie on social welfare policies, and Ogilvie retaliated by trying to persuade the Constitutional Convention of the value of an appointed attorney general. In the face of such rivalry, the constitutional officer is likely to bypass the General Assembly leadership in its designated role as legislative voice for the governor. Scott, we were told, used his "own people in the legislature." This raised the need for the leadership to consult him in order to plan the legislative agenda and possibly to minimize conflict with the governor.

Contacts from local officeholders are stimulated by needs for services to individual constituents or their communities and by desires to share in the vote-getting abilities of the constitutional officer. I could not determine exactly how these contacts were treated, but I based my judgment of nonreciprocity on statements that denigrated Scott for his unwillingness to help others in the party and the fact that there was no contrary evidence of the kind I had, for example, from county chairmen.

Direction of Contacts

In most past research, direction has been the main criterion in the interpretation of asymmetrical relations. The general finding was that lower-ranking participants made more contacts to higher-ranking ones than vice versa. In our network, however, when the number of actor-initiated asymmetrical relations is subdivided into the greater or lesser centrality of the actors, the results are equal—12 unreciprocated contacts made by the more central actors, and the same number by the less central. The only notable similarity to previous studies is the total absence of such relations for six of the more central actors compared with three of the less central. Perhaps these findings are affected by a poor fit between what is meant by "rank" and "centrality" in the party network. My own judgment is that the meaning of "asymmetry" is dependent on both the direction and the substance of contacts.

Substantively, almost all pairs of asymmetrical contacts can be classified as either requests for help or efforts to give direction and dominate. The former includes all requests for assistance, support, or added resources; the latter includes unsolicited advice, attempts to affect decisions, and offers of reward for forthcoming behavior. Requests for help account for nine dyads: county chairman and financial contributor, county chairman and State Central Committee, central committeeman and financial contributor, senator and central committeeman, local officer and financial contributor, local officer and constitutional officer, state House leader and constitutional officer, state Senate leader and constitutional officer, national committeeman and advisor. Efforts to dominate effect 13 dyads: governor and congressman, governor and SCC, governor and State Senate Campaign Committee (SSCC), governor and State House Campaign Committee (SHCC), Republican National Committee and state senator, RNC and state representative, RNC and SSCC, RNC and SHCC, SSCC and county chairman, SHCC and county chairman, Republican Congressional Campaign Committee (RCCC) and county chairman, Republican Senate Campaign Committee (RSCC) and county chairman, RCCC and central committeeman. More-central party actors (governor, RNC) initiate contacts with others in order to dominate; less-central actors (national committeeman, local officer, state House leader, state Senate leader, central committeeman) initiate contacts primarily to request help—all in conformity with my expectations about the relation between centrality and the rationale for contacts. But because efforts to dominate are more prevalent, we find that even less-central actors (SHCC, SSCC, RSCC, RCCC) try to dominate.

It was not possible to classify the contact made by the congressman to the local committeeman, because it appeared to subsume both requests for electoral assistance and encouragement of a sense of dependency. Ambiguity was also present in the unreciprocated contacts from the senator to the congressman, contacts much more likely to be reported by the senator's office than vice versa. One congressional informant dismissed existing contacts with contempt made obvious by the tone of his voice: "They say that when Dirksen was alive, he used to have meetings with congressmen. Some have this complaint with Percy [that he doesn't meet with them]. But he comes over when we ask him." Although I suspect that the lack of acknowledgement of reciprocity by congressmen is a sign of their independence, and therefore also one of the senator's efforts at dominance, I decided against any classification.

Asymmetrical relations were infrequent but clearly important. They were complex in meaning, appearing not only as expected requests for help but also as attempts to influence other actors. When contacts made are not reciprocated, they can, at times, be interpreted as efforts to protect autonomy. They are, in a sense, rejections of the efforts made by others to dominate. Because they can have such different meanings, it seems advisable to set aside asymmetrical contacts now.

Cohesion

Subsets

The original matrix was treated like a sociogram; that is, it was squared and cubed (Luce and Perry, 1949; Luce, 1950) and permutated to produce the symmetrical matrix in Figure 2. That matrix, which contains only reciprocated contacts, emphasizes the existence of one large subset and a chain of five smaller ones. A subset is made up of at least three actors, all of whom have reciprocated contacts. Each subset is as large as possible, given the property of reciprocation (Kemeny, Snell, Thompson, 1966, 403). Subsets defined this way are usually called cliques (e.g., Moore, 1979), but I avoided using this term because of the connotation that cliques are real groups. These subsets, in contrast, are forms of relationships among classes of actors. In addition, cliques usually imply close relations, but the relations among members of party subsets need not be.[6] All I have required is that they have more or less regular contacts. As examples have shown, some of these contacts can be displays of conflict, some can be quite impersonal exchanges of information, and others may be accidents of legal requirements or geographic proximity. Subsets, then, are neither work groups nor friendship cliques; rather they are congeries of actors whose party roles bring them into contact with each other.

The largest subset, located in the middle of the matrix, consists of seven actors: state senator, state representative, senator, governor, advisor, interest group, and financial contributor. This is the party core—the actors whose identities and activities define the Republican Party. It is a curious group, made up, on the one hand, of a state and national legislative component and a state executive component and, on the other hand, of an unofficial and extralegal component. Of all the members of the subset, only the governor is widely recognized as a party leader. Yet public leadership is probably not a crucial issue in establishing the focal nature of this subset. What is at stake is the ability of these actors to *be* the Republican Party, to personify its goals, and to lead it in directions that they favor, whether or not this is congenial to other party actors or to the public at large.

Arraying the actors in the core subset from left to right captures a crucial dimension of the matrix, contrasting localness, prominent in the left

---

6. Laumann and Marsden (1979, 714) present similar justifications for avoiding the concept of clique.

Column key (1–23): 1 state central committeeman, 2 local committeeman, 3 local officeholder, 4 United Republican Fund, 5 county chairman, 6 constitutional officer, 7 congressman, 8 state senator, 9 state representative, 10 senator, 11 governor, 12 advisor, 13 interest group, 14 financial contributor, 15 Republican National Committee, 16 State Central Committee, 17 national committeeman, 18 State House Campaign Committee, 19 State Senate Campaign Committee, 20 state House leader, 21 state Senate leader, 22 Republican Congressional Campaign Committee, 23 Republican Senate Campaign Committee.

Row	1	2	3	4	5	6	7	8	9	10	11	12	13	14	15	16	17	18	19	20	21	22	23
state central committeeman		0	0	1	0	1	0	0	0	0	0	0	0	0	1	1	0	0	0	0	0	0	0
local committeeman	0		0	1	0	0	1	1	0	0	0	0	0	0	0	0	0	0	0	0	0	0	0
local officeholder	0	1		1	1	0	1	1	1	1	0	0	0	0	0	0	0	0	0	0	0	0	0
United Republican Fund	0	0	1		1	1	0	1	1	0	0	0	0	1	0	0	0	0	0	0	0	0	0
county chairman	1	1	1	1		1	1	1	1	1	0	0	0	0	0	0	0	0	0	0	0	0	0
constitutional officer	0	0	0	1	1		0	1	1	1	0	1	1	1	0	0	0	0	0	0	0	0	0
congressman	1	0	1	0	1	0		1	1	0	0	1	1	1	1	0	1	0	0	0	0	1	0
state senator	0	1	1	1	1	1	1		1	1	1	1	1	0	0	0	0	1	0	1	0	0	0
state representative	0	1	1	1	1	1	1	1		1	1	1	1	0	0	0	1	0	1	0	0	0	0
senator	0	0	1	0	1	0	0	1	1		1	1	1	0	0	0	0	0	0	0	0	0	1
governor	0	0	1	0	1	1	0	1	1	1		1	1	1	0	0	0	0	0	0	0	0	0
advisor	0	0	0	0	0	1	1	1	1	1	1		1	0	1	0	1	1	0	0	1	1	1
interest group	0	0	0	0	0	1	1	1	1	1	1	1		1	0	1	1	1	1	1	1	1	1
financial contributor	0	0	0	1	0	1	1	1	1	1	1	1	1		1	1	1	1	1	1	1	1	1
Republican National Committee	0	0	0	0	0	0	1	0	0	1	0	1	1	1		1	1	0	0	0	0	1	1
State Central Committee	1	0	0	0	0	0	0	0	0	0	0	1	0	1	1		1	1	1	1	0	0	0
national committeeman	1	0	0	0	0	0	0	0	0	0	0	0	1	1	1	1		1	1	0	0	1	1
State House Campaign Committee	0	0	0	0	0	0	0	0	1	0	0	1	1	0	1	1	1		1	1	0	0	0
State Senate Campaign Committee	0	0	0	0	0	0	1	0	0	1	1	1	0	1	1	1	1		0	1	0	0	0
state House leader	0	0	0	0	0	0	0	1	0	0	0	1	1	0	1	0	1	0		1	0	0	0
state Senate leader	0	0	0	0	0	0	1	0	0	0	0	1	1	0	1	0	0	1	1		0	0	0
Republican Congressional Campaign Committee	0	0	0	0	0	1	0	0	0	0	1	1	1	1	0	1	0	0	0	0		0	0
Republican Senate Campaign Committee	0	0	0	0	0	0	0	0	0	1	0	1	1	1	1	0	1	0	0	0	0	0	

Figure 2. Matrix of reciprocated relations.

part of the matrix, with centralness, prominent in the right part. This dimension captures not only the location of actors or the arena in which they are most active but also an aspect of function. That is, it is tied to functions that are independent and autonomous, prominent in the upper half of the matrix, versus those that are centralizing, prominent in the lower half. The character of these functions can be traced both for actors in the core subset and for those in the smaller, linked subsets.

At the lower, centralizing end of the diagonal there are two linked subsets, tying together financial contributor from the core with the RNC, SCC, and national committeeman, and tying the last two named with the State House and Senate Campaign committees. A central arena and centralizing functions go together.

At the upper left side of the matrix are three smaller linked subsets, tying the state senator and representative with the congressman; the constitutional officer, county chairman, and United Republican Fund; and the county chairman, United Republican Fund, and local officeholder. The local arena dominates, even for the statewide constitutional officer, reflecting his limited role in the party network, at least at the time of this study. In a different way, the congressman is also a local figure, despite his Washington venue, as was anticipated by his lack of reciprocation with the senator. All these actors have in common a drive to keep their positions independent and protected from the dominance of other party actors.

In both the upper third and lower third of the matrix we find actors whose vectors extend through to the border of the matrix. At one end, the central and centralizing roles of the financial contributor and interest group are interwoven with virtually all other actors with similar party interests. At the other, the two state legislators are linked with almost all local and autonomy-seeking actors. In addition, the county chairman has a similar vector, confirming that he has his own power net.

These subsets summarize the properties of network relations, separating local from central actors, and those attempting to integrate party activities from those defending their own spheres. They also identify the party core along with important, but less focal, subsets.

Relational Models

Each party actor is tied to the network through contacts with a limited number of others. These selected contacts make up structures of relations when viewed from the perspective of particular actors, in the sense of giving shape or form to the network. An examination of only those contacts that are symmetrical indicates that even the same number of contacts can produce different structures. It is these structures that are each actor's relevant party world.

The two actors with fewest contacts are the state central committeeman and the local committeeman, each of whom regularly interacts with four others. Figure 3 shows how their worlds differ. Chapter 2 anticipated the finding that the central committeeman participates in two separate worlds. As a model of relations, I call this an articulated set, because the central committeeman is an articulation point whose removal would make for an unconnected graph (Flament, 1963, 39). The local committeeman, in contrast, is part of a single, interrelated structure, termed a closed set (Emerson, 1972, 82).

In theory, the structure of the central committeeman's world places him in the position of broker, able to mediate between the two subgroups he connects (Burt, 1980, 91; Granovetter, 1973; Boissevain, 1974, 147–161).

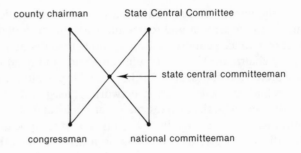

Articulated Set

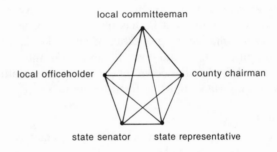

Closed Set

Figure 3. Relational models.

In fact, however, he is often dismissed as "powerless," "useless," and "irrelevant." Although the local committeeman may also be characterized as useless, he does not normally receive the same amount of criticism as the central committeeman, nor is it voiced with the same indignation. Focusing on the structures of which they are a part, we can look for reasons explaining contrasts.

Both central and local committeemen are elected directly in the party primary, precinct committeemen every two years, ward and township committeemen every four years, and central committeemen every four years. This election schedule is a source of dissent and conflict for central committeemen, but not for local ones. In 1978, as was noted in chapter 2, of a total of 24 races for central committeemen, only 8 were uncontested. Of the remainder, 3 were open races and 13 represented challenges to the incumbent. In our survey of precinct committeemen, we asked simply if anyone had ever run against them, so we do not have the same framework of a single year. Nonetheless, it is clear that precinct committeemen races are less competitive, because only a quarter of the sample answered that they had ever been in a competitive race. Moreover, election of central committeemen through the primary process is viewed by many county chairmen as somehow detached from party control, as one chairman's statement illustrates: "I feel it ought to be a party obligation to say who is a state central committeeman. Now the committeemen don't have an obligation to the party."

Over the years there have been a number of proposals to change the way in which central committeemen are selected. During the 1980 state convention, county chairmen attempted to introduce a resolution giving themselves the power to serve as electors. When this failed on a voice vote over objections to the chairman's ruling, the County Chairmen's Association moved to the legislature. According to a spokesman:

We decided to start it in the House, because the Senate chairman of the Elections Committee was not expected to be helpful. Bob Winchester [a legislator close to the county chairmen] is chairman of the House Election Committee. George Ryan [the House speaker] said he was 100 percent behind it. Then things changed. Celeste Stiehl became a member of the committee and her husband is a state central committeeman. . . . We needed nine votes on the committee and there were nine Republicans. But Susan Catania [Chicago] is one, and she's unpredictable. Phil Bianco [Chicago] is one—he's a state central committeeman—and he's there because the Democrats want him. The Northern Illinois Republican Council backed us. . . .

None of the apparent support was sufficient, however, even to get the bill through the committee. Subsequent efforts to change election methods finally succeeded, to take effect in 1990. But in explaining the contrasting worlds of central and local committeemen, their similar modes of election are not at issue except in the way they are a major point of complaint in regard to central committeemen.

A better explanation can be found by examining functions and their consequences. Local committeemen serve as foot soldiers in recurring campaigns. Although there are some differences in their reports of what they do, depending on the size and Republican strength of their counties and presumably on the organizational styles of their county chairmen, there is also considerable uniformity. Using weighted averages, over 90 percent of the precinct committeemen surveyed reported that, during the most recent election, they had distributed campaign literature, and over 75 percent had distributed posters and conducted voter-registration drives. Asked about what they believe to be their most important activity as committeemen, more than half said it was getting out the vote, and under a third emphasized voter registration. In other words, election-related activities are their major functions. If they perform these activities well, the committeemen are a great asset to their party and its candidates. If they do not, they are merely superfluous. The same, however, cannot be said of the central committeemen.

The central committeeman's job is defined in quite specific terms with respect to responsibilities. But when these responsibilities are translated into support for the Republican Party and the election of candidates, the leeway allowed makes for an ambiguous definition of activities that opens the way for conflict. As one aggressive central committeeman put it:

While the county chairman is the elected head, I'm the symbolic second-in-command. Often there are strong differences between us. This could be over legislation — for example, on the so-called blind primary [for 1980 national convention delegates]. The county chairman was for it, but I was opposed. I took my case to the county executive here and won. . . .

I'm trying to make this job important. I make decisions by consulting with the rank and file, what I call party loyals. This is a point of difference with my predecessor state central committeeman. I believe this consultation gives more power to the job, because I'm speaking for more than just myself. I have popular support. . . . I'm an activist. I see my role as one where others see me as being active. I bulled my way into position, and I've made the job more influential.

Such activities may or may not be helpful; they are never neutral.

Another illuminating example is from the perspective of a congressman close to his district:

The central committeeman's job is supposed to be one of overseeing the counties in the district, being the liaison with the county chairmen. He should try to make most events in the district and encourage registration. But [Committeeman] X is the focal point of frustration and anger. . . . It's a sore point with this office. The central committeeman is supposed to be a healer and a leader. Instead he is a divisive factor. . . . The central committeeman job is being wasted.

When the central committeeman is inactive, that too evokes criticism and resentment.

The divided world of the central committeeman is one that cannot easily be bridged, largely because of the constraints in carrying out his job that arise from overlap with other actors. Furthermore, those with whom he interacts may not want to use him as a mediator because, as in the case of the county chairman and the State Central Committee, they are competitors; and in the case of the congressman and the national committeeman, they are perceived as irrelevant to each other. The local committeeman, in contrast, operates in a more consistent world of mutually dependent actors, joined by their local interests.

Only one other instance of an articulated set occurs, as part of the State Central Committee's contact structure. Its nine contacts are also divided among two five-member and two four-member closed sets. But it is the articulated set that draws attention to the manifold difficulties of the SCC.

The SCC, as it articulates between the national committeeman and the central committeeman on the one hand and the state Senate and House leadership on the other, symbolizes the division between the party's administrative and its legislative or programmatic roles. The three actors who make up the curiously isolated party world personify the reasons why, "when there's reference to the party, it's as a little building in Springfield," as one involved informant complained. Among the causes for this isolation are the anomalies associated with the SCC's constituency and its responsibilities. The problems of constituent relations have already been suggested in discussing the individual state central committemen and the criticisms aroused by their election in party primaries. The outcome of the battle over election procedures was also indicative of the SCC's limits in its relations with the legislative leadership.

Within the state party's nexus, the national committeeman derived special importance, because in the time of this study, it was Harold Byron Smith, Jr., who was also a central committeeman and the moving force in setting up the SCC's Finance Committee. It was widely recognized, according to one informant, that "Smith represents a lot of influence centered in one person. He plays multiple [party] roles and he is in touch with the business community." His unusual visibility also made him vulnerable to attack, whether the underlying issues were the activities of the SCC itself, his support for John Connally in 1980, or even the governor's role as party leader. The effect, however, was to put the SCC on the defensive. At the 1980 state convention, Representative Donald Totten (District 3), also a township committeeman and leader of the Reagan forces in 1976 as well as 1980, attempted to unseat Smith as national committeeman. A participating central committeeman informed us:

I supported Harold. He is the best thing we have going for us. He's got lots of clout at several levels. It would be a tragedy to lose him. I made no secret that I was pro-Smith; we had our ducks lined up.

When asked why there was opposition, he continued:

Basically, it was from Totten, who is a Reagan champion. Harold headed up the Connally campaign. Totten felt he had acquired power in the state because of Reagan's success in the primary. But he didn't have it. He wanted to rub the governor's nose. . . . I don't deny Reagan's strength, but I didn't think that was all that mattered. Totten did. He deluded himself that he was more powerful than the governor.

The Totten forces agreed with this assessment of why they challenged Smith but then withdrew Totten's nomination for national committeeman before it was presented to the convention:

There were a number of things in contention at the convention [in addition to the national committeeman]: Who is going to be chairman of the delegation? Who is going to head the delegation if the chairman is not there? Who will be among the at-large delegates? You don't throw up only one ball on which to negotiate. So we threw up four balls.

Tension between the two worlds of the SCC has been anticipated in the previous discussion of its unreciprocated relations with the governor, particularly when these implied the possibility of a strong state chairman emerging in competition with the governor. The SCC remains constrained by the way its functions have evolved. As one key state central committeeman assessed them:

The SCC is a deliberative body. It doesn't have any authority. It doesn't have any hierarchical relation to anything else in the party. . . . What the SCC is trying to do is important in the campaign sense. The SCC is the official party body. This is a resource. The SCC could take postures as the leading Republican voice in the state. As a resource, it could be used for pulling together other resources. . . . The problem of the SCC is that its work is only known by those with whom it's intimately involved. It's not seen by the average county chairman or legislator, not unless we do something they don't like. The SCC doesn't get brownie points.

One issue on which the SCC tried to exert influence was the composition of the delegation to the 1980 Republican National Convention. Although a number of the major party figures in the state, particularly some of the business leaders, initially favored John Connally for the presidency, Ronald Reagan's candidacy had a strong and early lead because of the organizational support that had been generated, tied to his 1976 bid. The governor was careful not to make an endorsement, but it was known that many of those close to him were Connally supporters, and this presumably had a bearing on his own preference for an uncommitted slate of convention delegates, which he would head. The legislature passed a bill—later to be made irrelevant by the primary outcome—permitting the Republicans to use a "blind primary" in which national convention delegates were not identified on the ballot with the name of the presidential candidate to whom they were pledged (Kieckhefer, 1979). The SCC also passed a motion in the bill's favor. This issue then became tied to some of the negative feelings about the SCC, even within that body. As one member saw it:

We [the SCC] don't do much. We should be plotting, making decisions. The SCC was more important in the past. County chairmen used to take their lead from the SCC—now the county chairmen are stronger. We do a certain amount of fund-raising, and organize the Republican nuts-and-bolts work. There is some policy-making, but our most recent venture, on the blind primary, was a big "boo-boo." I voted against it.

In the SCC an executive committee makes decisions. It includes Harold Byron Smith, Dave Brown, Dave Martenson, Tom Anderson—there may be some others. Then they announce what we are going to do.

When asked whether this was a formal executive, he replied: "No, it just happens. Now we seem to be marking time. No one says we ought to be doing anything, so I'm not."

Opportunities for the emergence of a strong SCC chairman are limited, stemming from the constraints of the SCC's constituent base and the need for playing a mediating role. These were well summed up by two observers, both of whom contrasted the current chairman, Don Adams, with Harold Byron Smith. The first was a member of the unofficial wing of the party:

Don Adams isn't going to lead this party into anything the least bit different. He's a compromiser, he won't offend anyone. H. B. Smith has great ability, but he has to walk around carrying eggs in both hands. He has to be careful to avoid having his legs cut off.

The second was an active county chairman whose earlier comments had been highly critical of both the SCC and his own central committeeman, particularly the latter. He ended on a more moderate note that gave greater credence to his remarks:

If it weren't for Harold [Byron Smith], there would be no SCC. He raised a lot of money, but he doesn't pay any attention to the way money is spent. He doesn't want to be state chairman, and there is no one else to take that position.

I know a lot about the SCC . . . but then [during Governor Ogilvie's tenure] it was 400 percent better than now. Now, they [the staff] are really arrogant and insulting. They're condescending, especially the executive director. Don Adams— he's fine because he doesn't make any waves; he doesn't offend anyone. It's a thank-less job, in a way. He doesn't direct the staff—the executive director runs things.

Leadership, whether from the state chairman or the SCC itself, is also constrained when directed to the legislature. Legitimately, it comes into play only over matters seen to affect the party organization, for example, on the blind primary. Otherwise, SCC members are treated as intruders by the legislative leadership. According to a legislative spokesman:

The SCC wants to be directly involved in campaign races, but we don't [want them]. . . . They are not capable of doing legislative research on someone's record.

. . . I told the director to stay the hell out of here. I'll give you an example. They want to know what are the ramifications of a piece of legislation. They come over, spend two hours blundering around. They should call me, I could get them the information in 15 minutes.

By introducing the notion of relational models as a property of network cohesion, we can encompass the fact that each party actor has his own network of relations, with its own roots and its own implications. Each relational subset assumes its meaning through its constraining qualities; that is, the actors in each subset take part in a more or less discrete set of relations, and it is the structure of this set that points up the limits on their actions and the restraints on their assumption of responsibilities.

Network Exploration

At the outset, I argued that the accuracy of judgments about links between party actors is not a major issue because they are bound to vary, depending on the perspective of who is judging. That makes the resulting description of links conditional, it is true, but in ways that are logically coherent. If we accept usefulness as the primary criterion, then my inductive exploration, based on tools of network analysis, did result in a number of concise ways of characterizing the party network.

Because I have examined a single party, it is hardly surprising that I found relations among actors to be dense. Yet individual actor types make a differential contribution to that density and, on the basis of contacts, the unofficial wing, state legislators, county chairman, governor, senator, congressman, and the Republican National Committee are seen as most central. When the matrix of relations is treated like a sociogram, the party core is narrowed to seven actors, locating county chairman, congressman, and RNC in connected sets.

The statistical summary of centrality and cohesiveness is enhanced by the explanations offered by informants, who also helped me discern major themes in the life of the Republican Party. Two distinct dimensions stand out with respect to how activities are organized — central arenas of action in contrast to local ones, and efforts at centralization in contrast to those aimed at retaining autonomy.

Burt (1983b) argues that instead of using sociometric analysis for uncovering cliquelike subsets, as I did, it is preferable to concentrate on network positions to produce structurally equivalent clusters of actors, in which each element in a cluster is linked to others in the party network (but not necessarily to each other) in similar ways. That is, clusters are made up of actors with shared contact patterns. In fact, I did a cluster analysis based directly on data in Figure 1 and also on a derived social distance matrix (Burt, 1976). Neither result, however, is as useful as what can be learned from Figure 2. The first cluster analysis produced a single large cluster of structurally equivalent actors that is too undifferentiating. In addition, several of the residual elements are too important, by measures of centrality and cohesive subsets, to be set aside. The second analysis had more intrinsic meaning but without the same relation to core actors that the sociometric analysis revealed. Moreover, structural equivalence did not allow the discernment of the two dimensions that were otherwise so helpful in organizing activities and positions.

Burt suggests that cliques (our subsets) be treated "as a special type of jointly occupied position" (1983, 263). That is, a clique can itself be a single element in a cluster of structurally equivalent elements, but this is not useful here because we are dealing with collective actors who have already been assigned the same position. I have, in fact, presumed a kind of structural equivalence by conceiving of the Republican Party as a network; theoretical and substantive concerns therefore focus on relations among the actors themselves.

Although contacts were assumed to rest on requirements for service, associations through elections, and common perspectives on issues, an examination of unreciprocated contacts uncovered another feature of such relations. Informants revealed that requests for help, rather than being more prominent, were outnumbered by attempts to give direction to other actors, interpreted as efforts at domination. The importance of power relations was also implied in the discussion of cohesion, particularly in contrasting aims of centralization with local autonomy. We can anticipate that power will be a recurring theme in the Republican network.

Though this chapter has moved beyond the straightforward depiction found in Chapter 2, it is also largely descriptive. I have provided a good deal of explanation for each pattern of network links, but always in an ad hoc fashion, without calling on any underlying theory. The chapters that follow are quite different. They build on these descriptions to deal with the issue of why particular forms of relationship occur.

4

Environments of Party Actors

Constituency Environments

Party actors conduct their political lives in environments that supply them with necessary resources while shaping and constraining their activities. In their most elemental form, environments are created by actors' constituents, who provide the bases that enable actors to attain their positions and the resources that legitimate them. Constituents are therefore a constant concern; continuing efforts are required to maintain them as dependable resources. And precisely because they are so valuable, constituents are objects of competition among actors.

The variety and changing nature of environments are approached here through four questions: Who makes up various actors' constituencies? How distinct are constituencies in having separate geopolitical identities? How much commitment as Republicans do constituents demonstrate? How large are these constituencies? Answers to these questions enable us to consider the consequences of environments for party actors.

Each type of constituency raises its own problems and demands, and responses to them contribute to setting categories of actors apart from each other. Because constituency types are internally differentiated, especially geographically, actors both within and among collective categories will face either separate constituencies or ones they share with others. And this situation in turn stimulates conflict or cooperation. Constituents' commitment to the Republican Party defines what actors can rely on as dependable support, affecting the decisions they make on how available resources should be used and on their ability to control factions. Finally, the size of constituencies has direct implications for the power of actors, as it does for the likelihood that actors will deal with a homogeneous social base of support.

Types of Constituents

In chapter 2, where the actors making up the party network were defined, voters were relegated to the party environment, the argument being that, no matter how important voters are, they are not at the core of the party because they can only react to decisions made by others. At the same time, it is voters who are the single most important feature of the party environment, determining the fate of the party as it seeks to carry out its governing and programmatic goals. There is a crucial distinction between those actors who have direct links and those who have indirect links to voters; only elected officeholders have direct links. The electorate itself may be divided into primary or general election voters. Local committeemen (and indirectly the county chairmen) and central committeemen are tied to the primary electorate; the environments of all other officeholders are defined by the general electorate. The remaining actors have their first-order ties with other kinds of constituents. For the state Senate and House leadership, the constituents are legislators.

The election of county chairmen by local committeemen ties the former to the organizational apparatus at the county level. Yet because the county chairman too has an electoral constituency, I generally find it more meaningful (as will be seen later in Table 4-2) to treat the county chairman as dependent on the electorate. The State Central Committee, the Republican National Committee, the national committeeman, and the advisor have state-level constituencies in the party apparatus.

Because of the peculiar role played by the United Republican Fund, I see its environment as primarily one of special interests, that is, the business community; and because of its self-defined sphere of activities, I place it at the county level. Interest groups and financial contributors may also operate at this level, but my own concern has been with those who have broader constituencies. Because the campaign committees at both state and national levels are dependent on financial contributors, this study categorizes their primary constituents as special interests. They are assigned to the most inclusive geographic sphere, because constituents are diversely, if not evenly, distributed.

The most obvious thing to say about these relationships is that party actors have different kinds of constituencies, with 9 directly linked to the electorate and 14 to other interests. Those with direct ties to the electorate give precedence to their constituents, in the sense that they are primarily concerned with their own elections and reelections. This is hardly surprising, nor should it be cause for complaint, because winning elections is the mainstay of the Republican Party. Yet absorption in seeking election is a frequent cause of complaint when it is experienced as neglect of other kinds of party concerns. These can include failure to help other candidates, lack of willingness to support programs extending beyond one's own district boundaries, compromises in ideology, unavailability to county chairmen or other officials, or just a general disinterest in party traditions. Dependence on the electoral connection leads then to the division of actors according to their goals.

The electorate itself is not of whole cloth. As Snowiss (1966, 628) has observed, dependence on the primary electorate means dealing with an even narrower than normal slice of the Republican voting public. Local and central committeemen then have a direct relation with voters who may be helpful as party workers without reflecting the kinds of support other officeholders need to achieve their elections. The general electorate itself manifests parallel differences, in that voters at a local or district level are often more homogeneous than those found in a broader arena and are more likely to display parochial kinds of orientation. These distinctions were expressed by one observer of Senator Percy's relations with others in his party: "Senator Percy has a very broad base of support, from labor, all ethnic groups except Irish Catholics. . . . Percy is sort of an outsider. He is not one of the boys. But if he were he wouldn't be able to win reelection. He needs his broad base." The understanding of this informant was that the Republican Party also needed Percy's broad base if it wanted to hold the senator's seat.

Dependence on the electorate means that actors are tied to an uncertain and volatile source of support, one that may remain committed to the Republican Party but still turn against particular incumbents whenever it feels neglected or abused. Common responses to why incumbent officeholders faced real or threatened primary challenges were: "They didn't feel he came around enough," or "He didn't pay enough attention to his constituents." This is not to say that this was the principal reason for a primary challenge or for success in displacing an incumbent, but it indicates the widespread belief that the electorate is fickle and readily provoked to threaten officeholders. This belief inspires challengers to enter races and constrains incumbents to spend their resources in paying attention to constituents.

Those whose principal ties are with other interests operate in other worlds, no matter how well they understand that what they do has an electoral impact. This was captured in the comment of a dedicated financial contributor and party activist with no formal party office:

I have no interest in electoral politics. While it is true that I am involved in the Connally campaign, my real model is George Shultz. It is appropriate to try to excel in some field, like business or academia, and then be asked to take on a public service job. After that, you should return to your own field.

This form of political ambition can be expressed only by those utterly removed from electoral politics. It is a perspective associated with self-images of greater selflessness, dedication to Republican principles, and with even greater integrity than found among politicians. As such, it implicitly denigrates those engaged in political callings that require them to deal directly with the electorate.

More frequently, the nonelectoral environment is associated with making the conduct of politics a rational set of activities. Whether in fundraising, recruiting candidates, planning campaigns, or guiding legislative programs, the emphasis is on strategic planning, both immediate and long range. But to plan does not necessarily produce success or even greater rationality. What planning does provide is a common perspective for all actors dependent on constituencies distinct from the electorate. Activities associated with planning are also centralizing, as I indicated in chapter 3, when considering the nature of contacts among actors.

Generally, actors in this nonelectoral arena would deny any centralizing goals, but at least one informant, associated with the local elections committee of the Republican National Committee, was more candid:

We try to use our expertise to help local people become better candidates, and we give them money. In some states we hire the candidates' field force, in cases where they want to have local help. Some states wanted our money directly, but we didn't make our contributions that way. We felt that would be contrary to what our constituency [those who contribute money for the RNC's work on local elections] wants. They want to take control over elections, at least to a degree, out of the hands of the state apparatus.

Rationalizing the party through reliance on such activities as coordinated fundraising and polling of voters, centralized decision-making in the targeting of districts and the selection of candidates with proven vote-getting ability, and a general orientation to the long-range goals of the party can be the predominant objectives of those with constituencies separate from the electorate. These activities, however, do not necessarily lead to success.

From the perspective of those who deal directly with the electorate, especially with that segment which votes in general elections, other party actors may be too concerned with protecting their own positions or the status quo. Their goals, in short, have to do with maintaining their own component of the organization. In the words of one observer:

The Republican party means a country club group, some conservative ideologues, some people who feel drawn by community service, and some attracted to patronage. The problem is, they're not hungry. Politics shouldn't be for patronage, or a hobby. You want a hunger to win elections.

People like the state chairman would rather be in control of the party, even if it's small, than be in the majority. Therefore, to them, winning is not crucial.

The importance of elections themselves, and the overriding importance of winning, gives these events a special urgency in the lives of those whose fortunes are directly dependent on them. The electoral constituency consequently has a greater claim to legitimacy than do the others. Party actors were open to criticism, at least in part, because they lacked this constituency. For example, county chairmen, whose constituencies were ambiguous, were disparaged because they could not help the governor by delivering votes for the General Assembly, or were bypassed by congressional candidates because they lacked vote-getting ability. Technical advisors, whether part of the official or unofficial wing, were criticized as outsiders, unaware of local voter concerns. As one long-time participant put it: "There just can't be too much time spent with voters. All these young guys don't realize this. People now don't appreciate this." The "young guys," in turn, looked down on the state and local party apparatus as unwilling to adjust to a new political era. A staff person, experienced in both Washington and Illinois, echoed the complaint about a lack of hunger to win:

The problem with the Illinois party is that they still are filled with old hacks. They are scared of new, creative people. They feel threatened and they should be. . . . *X, Y,* and *Z* [well-established county chairmen] will fight change very hard, and they have. But the party organization will have to change, and then there will be a bloodbath. That will happen when the time comes and there is a new, bright state chairman who knows that you hire someone to write a newsletter because he does the job well, not because his mother is county chairman.

From these and similar comments, we can conclude that lack of direct ties with the electoral constituency encourages mutual distrust.

Separation versus Overlap

Table 4-1 lists all the actors in the Republican network according to both their predominant constituencies and their spheres of activity. The latter category leads to consideration of relations among actors within the same sphere as well as actors whose ties with constituents put them in different geopolitical arenas. For these comparisons, I begin with Schlesinger's language:

(a) Some constituencies are *congruent,* that is, both sets of voters are the same: e.g., all the elective officers of a county face the same electorate, and governors and United States senators both face the state electors at large. (b) Other constituencies have an *enclaved* relation, that is, one constituency is a subset of the other, as with the presidency and senators, or senators and congressmen of the same state (except for congressmen elected at large). (c) Finally there are *disjoint* constituencies, that is, there are no overlapping voters. (Schlesinger, 1965, 787)

Schlesinger confines himself to constituencies made up of voters; it is my intention to include in Table 4-1 party actors whose principal environment is of a nonelectoral character. This will raise a number of problems, but

Table 4-1. Relation between Constituency and Geopolitical Sphere

Sphere	Constituency				
	Primary Electorate	General Electorate	Legislature	Apparatus	Special Interest
Precinct	local committeeman				
County	county chairman[a]	local officeholder		county chairman[a]	United Republican Fund
Legislative district		state representative state senator			
Congressional district	state central committeeman	congressman			
Statewide		senator constitutional officer governor	state Senate leader state House leader	State Central Committee Republican National Committee national committeeman advisor	State Senate Campaign Committee State House Campaign Committee Republican Senate Campaign Committee Republican Congressional Campaign Committee interest group financial contributor

[a]There is some ambiguity about where to locate the county chairman, because he has two kinds of constitutents.

Table 4-2. Distribution of Party Actors by Separation or Overlap of Constituency

Constituency Type	Degree of Separation or Overlap		
	Disjoint	Congruent	Enclaved
E	local committeeman	local officeholder	state central committeeman–local committeeman–county chairman
L		local committeeman	
E	state central committeeman	county chairman	
C		state representative	governor–congressman–state senator and/or state representative–local officeholder–county chairman
T	local officeholder	state senator	
O		state representative	
R	congressman	senator	senator–congressman–state senator and/or state representative–local officeholder–county chairman
A	state senator	constitutional officer	
T		governor	
E	county chairman	state central committeeman	constitutional officer–congressman–state senator and/or state representative–local officeholder–county chairman
		congressman	
O	national committeeman	financial contributor	Republican National Committee–State Central Committee–county chairman–advisor
T		interest group	
H			financial contributor–United Republican Fund–State Central Committee–Republican National Committee–State Senate Campaign Committee–State House Campaign Committee–Republican Senate Campaign Committee–Republican Congressional Campaign Committee
E			
R			

92

it will also enrich our understanding of how different kinds of constituencies affect relations among actors. Although I follow Schlesinger's lead in distinguishing between congruent and enclaved constituencies, I also use the more inclusive concept of "overlap" to consider any situation where actors encounter overlapping constituent environments.

Disjoint Constituencies

Schlesinger uses "disjoint" to refer to separate electorates linked to the same category of political actor. Table 4-1 allows us, if we wish, to speak of disjoint constituencies when these are separated by type; I do not do so because I dealt with the effects of separate types of constituencies in the preceding section. In this section, when I refer to separation or overlap of constituencies, it is always with respect to a single type of constituent, whether made up of voters or other kinds of interests.

Schlesinger's concern is whether voters respond similarly despite geographic separation — for example, in terms of national or regional trends (Schlesinger, 1965, 793). My concern, in contrast, is with party actors, and how they are affected by the disjuncture in their constituencies. It is easiest to begin with those actors who have electoral constituencies, of which I identify six with geographically separate constituents in Table 4-2. Of these, I have little to say about the local officeholder, because data collection was only incidentally aimed at its members.

Each local committeeman is elected by primary voters, separated into precincts, wards, or townships. State central committeemen and congressmen face voters divided by congressional districts, although the former do so only in primary elections. State senatorial candidates have constituents divided into 59 districts. Although county chairmen are classified in Table 4-1 as principally linked to a nonelectoral environment by virtue of election by local committeemen, in this situation they can be considered more like other officeholders, with their electorates divided into separate units.

Within each of the six categories of actors, we might assume that disjunctures in constituent environments will lead to party actors' indifference to each other's concerns. Why should an Adams County chairman care about a chairman in Woodside? One obvious reason is that they, like the other five categories of actors, have an arena for joint activities in which there is institutional pressure for cooperation. For local committeemen, it is the county organization; for county chairmen, the County Chairmen's Association; municipal or county government for local officeholders; Congress for congressmen; the state Senate for state senators; and the SCC for state central committeemen. The existence of an organizational unit like Congress is sufficient in itself for predicting that there will be some sense of collegiality among a category of party actors. Additional factors are the similarity in constituents' demands and the common experiences of gaining office through elections. It is not that the contents of the demands are the same or that pathways to election are identical; rather, it is that everyone in the same category is constrained by similar environmental pressures.

In the case of state senators and congressmen, collegiality is enhanced by the campaign committees, committed to the support of incumbents regardless of ideology, closeness to others in the legislature or Congress, or even competence. Support is intended for incumbents facing a challenge or otherwise occupying shaky seats. For example, when Congressman Findley faced his Democratic challenger in 1978, after surviving a serious primary battle, he called on and received help from the Republican Congressional Campaign Committee, even though he was not considered a well-integrated member of the state delegation. There are also suggestions that the urge to extend assistance may go beyond clear need. One informant, privy to some of the deliberations of the state campaign committees, reported how personal bonds of friendship could be a consideration: "Senator X is a member of the State Senate Campaign Committee, but he is not part of the leadership. He advocated that money from the SSCC be given to his buddy Senator Y. That's ridiculous. But he probably got it. They wouldn't tell me how the money was distributed."

Aside from those dependent on electoral constituencies, only the national committeeman has disjoint relations, established in comparison with other national committeemen. In Illinois, however, it makes no sense to speak of his constituents in terms of either separation or overlap.

Congruent Constituencies

Congruent environments (as well as enclaved ones, discussed below) are more varied in character and consequences than disjoint constituencies. Multimember districts created congruent constituencies for Republican state representatives in 30 districts out of a possible 59 after the 1978 election and 33 after that of 1980. Republican state senators shared constituents with one or two Republican state representatives in 29 districts over the same period. In off-year elections, state central committeemen and congressmen have district-level congruence in primary elections. Local officeholders, local committeemen, and the county chairman draw support from coterminous primary electorates at the county or lower level. The whole state provides the congruent constituencies of the governor, U.S. senator, and constitutional officers. Removed from similar electoral dependency, financial contributors and interest groups may still be dependent on other kinds of congruent constituencies.

For Schlesinger, the significance of congruent electoral constituencies lies in their impetus for the creation and strengthening of formal organizational entities linking interdependent offices. That is, constituency congruence leads to interdependence among officeholders. He proposes

that the strength of the particular formal organizational unit (strength equals level of activity and direct involvement of the organization in three phases, nomination, campaigning, and government; unit equals the associational leaders, as, for example, county chairmen or state central committee, conventions, and so on) is positively related to the electoral interdependence of the offices chosen by the organization's constituency. (Schlesinger, 1965, 788)

Information gathered during this study gives clearest evidence of Schlesinger's proposition with respect to local-level offices. But even in this instance, I am prepared to say only that congruence is associated with formal party organization at the county level. I cannot, however, make any assumptions on this basis alone about the relative strength of organization. For all other electorally dependent offices, we more often find an unwillingness to acknowledge interdependence or to institute regular forms of cooperation. In exploring reasons for this, I examine each set of actors with congruent constituencies in turn.

Multimember legislative districts with cumulative voting had provided Illinois electors with the opportunity to have virtually guaranteed representation from the weaker party. For candidates of the stronger party, when voters were expected to return two representatives, there was, at best, a guarded sense of community of interest. Typically, each attempted to carve out his own base of support from the same partisan pool. This was done most overtly when supporters were asked to "bullet" vote, that is, to cast all three votes for one candidate. Information from our interviews for 29 of the districts in which there were two Republican representatives shows that the norm was for independence in campaigning, fundraising, and contact with constituents. Representatives told us that, at the most, they worked together on district bills, or that they were even considering some joint activities, because, as one said, "I feel closer to this young man [the new second representative] than I have to any other representative."

More often representatives seemed surprised at the suggestion that cooperative activities leading to shared organization would be reasonable. "We're not all the same," they said, or "Other counties in the district have their own man." Some went so far as to describe their running mates as "enemies." A freshman representative told us ruefully, "I thought we were running together. Later I found we weren't." Listening to a group of legislators who were discussing common problems, we heard strong agreement with the view that "the biggest problem in multimember districts is competition from your seatmate in the same party. There is great rivalry and egocentrism." Whatever two representatives in a single district gave to overall party strength was offset by the loss of individual importance, perceived when there is only one. In a candid expression of regret by a representative who had gained a partner, we heard: "I have good relations with the governor. . . . But now the governor has to deal with both of us. It will take away from some of my credit in getting things done." These assessments of intraparty competition are generally not present in single-member districts; they more closely resemble the situation in Italy under a system of proportional representation:

Once nominated, the office seeker's principal electoral enemies are not candidates of other parties, but other candidates of his own party, with whom he must compete for the preference votes that determine which candidates will be elected. This means that each candidate must attempt to develop an independent campaign organization and access to resources beyond those provided by the party to all the candidates. (Katz, 1980, 108–109)

The State Senate Campaign Committee was a factor in promoting collegiality in the state Senate, where there are disjoint constituencies, but the State House Campaign Committee seemed to reinforce divisions. A staff member, familiar with the two campaign committees, contrasted them:

The SSCC is the stronger. That's partly because of its history—it was founded earlier, it had the support of Senator Arrington—but it's also tied to the structure of the House, with its multiple members. That makes for jealousy in House races, where everyone wants to be number one. For example, the incumbent representative in a targeted district had to be persuaded not to hog all the votes.

Cooperation between rivals could be achieved, but at the cost of providing funds or other resources to the incumbent, even if they were not needed. This was confirmed for us quite unselfconsciously by one representative in a safe seat:

I got money from the SHCC in 1976. I was on the committee then, but that's not how I got it. Before 1974, when I was the only representative who made it, the SHCC decided we should try to get the other seat back. The committee was going to give the candidate $3,500. I said I had to get the same, so I got it.

In four instances where representatives had congruent constituencies, there was clear evidence of shared organization. In three cases, initiative for cooperation came from the county level and, in the fourth, from a township organization, supporting Schlesinger's analysis of how formal organization grows at this level. It is also relevant that county and legislative districts were largely coterminous, so that congruence of constituency was not just a feature of the representatives' experience.

The situation of the state senator and state representative is somewhat different, because they are not such direct rivals. Even so, the general tendency discerned through our interviews was for their organizations to be independent. Some of the pressure for independence presumably occurs through the habits set by representatives, and also through the likelihood that one of those representatives will eventually aspire to the Senate seat. Rivalry was augmented by the prospective reapportionment into a smaller, single-member House. Representatives waiting, patiently or not, to take over from their senators apparently do not experience conditions in which shared organizations can flourish.

Although I assumed constituencies are congruent for the U.S. senator, governor, and constitutional officers, congruency is likely to be more potential than real. Each candidate who faces the statewide electorate may attract quite different constituents, as is evident from numbers alone in Table 4-3. In 1978, Attorney General William Scott was able to win the largest share of the two-party vote. In contrast, Susan Sharp, running for secretary of state against the best vote-getter on the Democratic ticket, Alan Dixon, received only 26 percent of the vote. Even if we disregard the three unsuccessful candidates for constitutional office, we are still dealing with three very different campaigns. Although those running for the offices of governor, U.S. senator, and attorney general may not overtly express the kind of rivalry that underlies the campaigns of state representatives, it does not take much imagination to infer that differential vote-getting ability is still a sore point. The ability of constitutional officers to gain widespread voter recognition and support, regardless of what they may actually achieve in their offices, is important, because it can be used as a stepping stone to more visible office. In 1980, Republican William Scott and Democrat Alan Dixon both entered their parties' primaries, each convinced that he could win election to the U.S. Senate. Dixon won the Democratic nomination and the Senate seat, and Scott might have won on the Republican ballot had he not been in trouble with the IRS. Governor James Thomp-

Table 4-3. Republican Vote for Statewide Offices, 1978

	Percentage of Two-Party Vote
Attorney general	65
Governor	60
U.S. senator	54
Treasurer	47
Comptroller	47
Secretary of state	26

Source: State Board of Elections, *State of Illinois Official Vote* (Springfield: State Board of Elections, 1978).

son, though less popular than Scott, used his vote-getting ability to convince some supporters that he would be a serious contender for the presidency. In contrast, Senator Charles Percy found himself with a much thinner margin of victory, and a body of rivals in both his own and the Democratic Party who felt that he could be picked off.

Statewide office-seekers who perceive that they are drawing on different constituencies have little inclination to assist each other. In the 1972 election, Governor Richard Ogilvie's campaign staff recognized that he was in trouble and tried to benefit their candidate by linking him with President Nixon. They were successful to the extent that there was reliance on staff personnel with simultaneous attachments to both Ogilvie and Nixon. An advisor recalled that only staff members' threats of resignation overcame objections from "the Washington people [who] were very unhappy if more emphasis was not put on Nixon." The 1978 primary race for comptroller might at first appear to provide a better example of interdependence, but it was illusory. John Castle, running against former House speaker W. Robert Blair, was said to have been "handpicked" by Governor Thompson (Peoria *Journal Star,* 1978a) and promised financial support by the Thompson campaign organization (Griffin, 1978). The governor's endorsement became a major campaign issue (e.g., St. Louis *Globe-Democrat,* 1978), and Castle was forced to affirm his independence. Election results do not indicate that fully congruent constituencies were successfully created. Castle won the primary with a mere 51.9 percent of the vote and was soundly defeated by his Democratic opponent in the general election.

Congruence at the primary level is assumed for the state central committeeman and congressman, because they run in the same congressional district. We can examine the extent of this congruence by looking at the vote won by central committeemen as a proportion of the total vote for congressmen. In 9 of 24 districts, candidates for central committeeman received more votes than did the congressional candidates. These were all districts in which Republicans had little chance of winning the congressional seats. Otherwise, central committeemen had smaller electoral constituencies, though often close to the congressmen's when the latter were unchallenged. Where there was no incumbent and a strong contest for Congress — in the 10th and 22nd districts — or a challenge to the incumbent — in the 13th and 16th — then participation in the congressional election was notably higher.

Contests for the state committeeman's office did not have much impact on the overall turnout. In all instances that I know of, central committeemen and congressional races were quite independent. One might assume that in those districts where there is a congressional contest, especially where an incumbent is challenged, as happened to Congressman John Anderson in the 16th District and Congressman Robert McClory in the 13th, there will be some association with the race for central committeeman. In fact, however, although there were contests for the central committeeman post in those districts, we have no information that one race was directly related to the other through joint campaigns or even endorsements. Instead, containment of several counties in one congressional district may have been more of an issue (a phenomenon discussed below under "Enclaved Constituencies"). Robert L. Hess, candidate for state central committeeman in the 13th Congressional District, pointed out during his campaign that Lake County was the home base of both Congressman McClory and state Supreme Court Justice Moran: "Party unity and strength in a large area must depend on equal representation by all of the three counties. . . . The state central committeeman should come from either Kane or McHenry counties" (Campaign Briefs, 1978). Dr. Hess did not mention that the home base of his own opponent, Margaret Hart, was also in Lake County.

Table 4-2 suggests that congruent constituencies representing special interests might link the financial contributor and interest group categories. Where this linkage occurs we can expect to find organizational evidence of interdependence, as in the formation of trade associations or other similar umbrella groups with associated PACs. A nonelectoral context, then, can also be the basis for supporting Schlesinger's thesis about stimuli to organization.

Enclaved Constituencies

Dependence on overlapping constituencies is characteristic of the local committeeman, county chairman, and state central committeeman, simply because congressional districts are normally larger than counties; the exception is Cook County, where congressional districts find themselves enclaved. In a couple other instances, congressional districts and counties are about the same size. Other overlapping chains of electoral constituencies join the congressman, state senator, state representative, local officeholder, and county chairman, and because their constituents are also part of a statewide electorate, connect them separately with the governor, U.S. senator, or constitutional officers. Enclaved constituencies are also characteristic of party actors dependent on nonelectoral constituencies. The county chairman, State Central Committee, Republican National Committee, and advisor are linked together through their use or provision of technical services. Dependence on those providing financial support produces the longest chain of enclaved actors—the State Central Committee, the Republican National Committee, the four campaign committees, the United Republican Fund, and the financial contributors themselves. Financial contributors are included to the extent that they, too, can be considered to have constituents—others who are financial contributors like themselves; this is easiest to envision with respect to PACs or other corporate contributors.

A high degree of conflict is found in enclaved constituencies apparently because different interests within the most inclusive unit have less-inclusive territorial bases from which to build alternative or rival organizational forms. Enclaves themselves do not cause conflict, but they do allow incipient conflicts to be expressed in terms of grievances that unite a geographically bounded constituency.

In the discussion of how sets of party actors develop through contacts, we were not concerned about whether contacts were friendly or not, but only about their existence; nor were we concerned with internal variations among classes of actors. Even so, we were able to ascertain that one dimension which enables us to distinguish among actors represents a pull between centralization and local autonomy. By considering how relations among actors are affected by the nature of their constituencies, we now come to see how the centralization-autonomy dichotomy may be tied to enclaved constituencies.

Informants at all levels of the party network were very much alert to the consequences of enclaved constituencies. At times they saw these as creating opportunities, which is exemplified in the comment of one county chairman: "There is a problem keeping voters apprised of what is going on. But there is a benefit for me. I have four representatives and two state senators. That means I have more people to talk to and to ask for help."

The boundaries associated with enclaved constituencies can provide opportunities for action that could not otherwise be carried out without stimulating a great deal of internal conflict. For example, we were told of a situation where party activists were unhappy with the incumbent county chairman. He had been in office for a long time and had acquired considerable support, despite his lackluster performance. To challenge him directly during the county convention, when local committeemen vote for a chairman, might have been successful, but it would have led to a great deal of ill feeling. Instead, opponents entered a challenger in the primary election to run against the county chairman in his own precinct. At that level he proved vulnerable, and his primary defeat led to his loss of eligibility for the chairmanship.

The earlier discussion of conflict associated with the congruent constituencies of state representatives also alluded to the importance of territorial bases of support. Similarly, this issue occurred in the case of challengers in congressional districts. Where challengers arise, their entering primary elections may be justified as giving representation to particular regions within the district that have otherwise felt excluded from the attention of representatives currently in office.

The overlap in constituents among state central committeeman, county chairman, and local committeeman underlies one of the most frequently expressed areas of conflict in the party network. The central committeeman's role arouses an unusual level of competition. In the 1978 primary, county chairmen ran against incumbents in two districts, and in a third, a county chairman was a challenger in an open race. All three were unsuccessful, but in two Cook County districts, incumbents were successfully challenged by ward committeemen. There are no simple explanations for these results, but in the seven districts where comparisons were possible, six of the losing candidates, including two county chairmen, came from counties that made up a relatively small part of the overall district.

In the most complex story of challenge in the central and local committeemen nexus, the challenge did not lead to the incumbent's defeat; but it did reveal, in unusually clear form, the importance of using a geopolitical base for mounting an attack. One of the main actors was Harold Byron Smith, Jr., who was not only the incumbent central committeeman in the 12th Congressional District but also the major organizer of the State Central Committee's Finance Committee and the national committeeman. In other words, he represented in one person several party roles, as well as being a strong liaison with Governor Thompson. His principal opponent was Donald Totten, committeeman for Schaumberg Township, but also state representative for the 3rd Legislative District, Illinois chairman of the 1976 Reagan for President Campaign, and general opponent of Governor Thompson. The 12th Congressional District included 11 separate jurisdictions, and after redistricting in 1972, there was no resident central committeeman. To ensure resident representation, township representatives formed a separate corporation with its own president; but in the 1974 primary, when Smith, a resident of the district, was elected central committeeman, there was a reversion to the older form of organization, even though the corporation was kept alive as a legal entity.

At a meeting in July 1978, Totten proposed that, because Smith was so busy, there should be a corporation president separate from the central committeeman. The vote was postponed, and when called, all voting members abstained except for four committeemen. These committeemen, representing the townships of Schaumberg, Elk Grove, Palatine, and Wheeling, succeeded in reviving the corporation as a parallel, if not rival, organization to the 12th Congressional District organization. Why these four? The most common response focussed on Donald Totten and his quarrels with Governor Thompson, particularly on how these related to their ideological differences.[1] For the remainder, it was suggested that the Elk Grove committeeman, who became corporation president, joined the revolt be-

---

1. No one suggested that Totten's aborted challenge to Smith as national committeeman had anything to do with this earlier conflict.

cause "he doesn't like things unless he is the leader," and the others were united through their conservatism. Altogether, it was said, "they formed a marriage of convenience." What was left unsaid was that all four committeemen had a common bond through the disjoint constituencies they had in the 3rd Legislative District. On whatever other grounds they may have been united, the geopolitical base of their enclaved constituency gave them an arena from which to act in concert.

Three further chains of actors with enclaved constituencies demonstrate links between the state and the local districts leading through the offices of governor, constitutional officer, or U.S. senator. Regardless of which statewide office is involved, there are congenial relations throughout the chain, with statewide candidates or officeholders providing help in campaigning and offering other services. If there are complaints, they come from those in the district who feel that statewide candidates do not do enough for them.

Other tensions found among actors in these three overlapping chains are generally minor, but where they exist, they are most often associated with the congressman. One influential party actor argued that congressmen are "not used effectively as a center of the political force in this state." Congressmen, in turn, can be expected to want to play a more central role. From his study of congressmen and their district parties, Olson notes that

even with an independent electoral base, most congressmen want to cooperate with the district party and are willing, to a point, to share their personal resources with the district party in a cooperative campaign. The electoral relationship established in the initial campaign tends to extend to successive elections as well. (Olson, 1978, 261)

Yet those county chairmen who commented on relations with their congressmen were inclined to see them as peripheral to their jobs, especially in contrast with state representatives. As one county chairman put it:

The congressman does little for you as county chairman. He doesn't get down to the grass roots. He doesn't deliver what the state representatives do. And the state representatives come around.

State legislators often have ties with their congressmen if for no other reason than the provision of services to constituents. Yet overlap in the constituents on whom they depend also generates some competition. Because the General Assembly is a customary route to Congress, both sets of actors in the relationship are mindful that ambition may produce rivalry. One congressman who expected to recruit candidates for the state House and Senate told us: "The district doesn't like this. I have to be concerned about recruiting because I don't want a future opponent campaigning against me at home. It's really self-serving [for me] to have good candidates in the General Assembly." A state senator, accounting for cool relations with his congressman, said, "My congressman is always worried I'll run against him." Even where such ambition is not present, there are other grounds for rivalry. One state representative, linked with three congressmen, noted, "They are my competitors, in a sense. We're after the same sources of money."

Congressmen also have a link with local officeholders, who may too be a source of challenge. In the course of this study, Congressman Robert McClory was challenged by Dr. Richard L. Verbic, the mayor of Elgin, and Congressman Paul Findley by David Neussen, the mayor of Quincy. In each instance, the challenger represented an urban center and county separate from the incumbent's major bases of support, and although both challengers lost, they managed to garner some 40 percent of the primary vote.

Congressmen are criticized by other political actors with whom they are linked through overlapping constituencies if they do not take a strong interest in local affairs, but closeness to the district makes them vulnerable to the aftermath of factional fights. Congressman Philip Crane was remarkably skillful in staying clear of the dissension associated with the governance of the 12th District party organization and the role of the central committeeman; Congressman Robert Michel had to mend fences after supporting an incumbent legislator in one enclaved legislative district who then suffered a primary defeat. In another district, we were told of the need to keep some distance from local party actors engaged in a "tong war," and in yet another, a candidate complained that, when the townships in a large county in his district kept up continuous internal warfare, any position he took labelled him a maverick.

The fifth chain of actors—the Republican National Committee, State Central Committee, county chairman, and advisor—is tied to enclaves made up of the party apparatus. Specifically, where there is conflict, it is associated with dependence on constituents who are candidates for public office, and the center of tension is the RNC. Although relations between the SCC and the typical county chairman frequently undergo strain, the issues that divide them are not related to this form of constituency dependence. The main source of contention between the RNC staff and other actors is over contact with candidates. One former staff member recounted his experiences, saying they were part of "deliberate moves to keep me from participating. For example, I wanted to meet with candidates along with state staff, but they wouldn't set up meetings for me. Or when I heard about meetings with candidates, and I tried to go along, then they were cancelled."

Informants attributed efforts to exclude RNC staff from direct contact with candidates to resentment for the presentation of new ideas by out-siders. Local party actors, whether operating statewide or in particular districts, often found themselves confronting young, even boyish-looking men, identified as representing Washington. As one RNC staffer described it:

We walk a tight rope. We're in a bind when we go into a district. We tend to get respect because we're from Washington, but we're also outsiders. The flack we get is not usually from the candidate or his campaign manager, but from others. . . .

We are on their territory. That always raises the possibility of [our] developing a closeness with the candidate. People in the district want to develop this close-ness. It can be cultivated [by us] in either of two ways. There are positive ways — for example, by giving money to the candidate — you give something valuable. Sometimes there are negative ways — we have something negative to contribute, like rumor — you ingratiate yourself by showing you're in the know.

The procedure of the field representative is to demonstrate that he is not trying to get close to the candidate. Then, if you have some ideas you want to communi-cate, how you do it varies with whom you are dealing. If you are dealing with the campaign manager, you can be up front. But if it is a local committee, then you may need to do this indirectly.

The final set of actors with overlapping constituencies consists of finan-cial contributors, the four campaign committees, the United Republican Fund, the State Central Committee, and the Republican National Com-mittee. They are all dependent on constituencies made up of financial con-tributors (treating contributors here as part of the environment and not as direct party actors), and the major issue they face is control over the use of financial resources. As far as we could ascertain, the RNC and the Republican Senate and Congressional Campaign committees are autono-mous units that compete for funds; but they are also clearly cooperative, sharing lists of contributors and transferring dispersement authority when required. We were given similar information for the SCC and the two state legislative campaign committees by an informed participant: "The House and Senate Campaign committees and the SCC Finance Committee are all elements of the same package. The legislative committees should be subcommittees of the SCC, but they are not, although they operate almost as though they were." For the remaining relationships, there are three points of stress in the financially dominated chain of actors — between the SCC and the URF; between the RNC on one side and the SCC and State Senate and House Campaign committees on the other; and between the financial contributor as party actor and all others in the subset.

The SCC Finance Committee was originated to ensure the certainty of financial resources for the operation of the SCC, along with clear party control, whereas the rationale for establishing the URF was to ensure existence of a fundraising body separate from political turmoil. The URF's long history does not obscure the basically anomalous nature of its operation: when it was the principal fundraiser, those who performed the party's business, whether in the apparatus or the government, had no control over how money was raised or dispersed. Governor Ogilvie was prominent among those who tried to change these arrangements. One former URF chairman described his dismay at a meeting he attended in the governor's mansion:

. . . the reason for the meeting, I soon discovered, was to bring the party's financing more directly under the Governor's control and to this I objected stubbornly. The Fund, I argued, had to be independent if it were to function effectively. The Fund, I stated, lived on forever, while governors, senators, and state legislators came and went. People gave to the Fund because it served all the Party, not an individual or a clique. Nobody in the Fund sought anything; no one had personal ambitions. The Fund was audited and was . . . clean as a whistle. How many political organizations can say that? (Fetridge, 1976, 78–79)

Members of the URF continued to protest their detachment from the wheeling and dealing of politics, but the resentment of politicians also led to the feeling that their past neutrality had been a mistake:

We never tried to get back anything in return for our support. We couldn't get people we supported to help us. For example, I wanted to get someone's son a congressional internship, but Senator Percy [a former URF president] didn't even answer my call. Now we may endorse in the primaries. Now we put some strings on our money. That was our mistake—we were too gentlemanly.

The response of the SCC in setting up its own finance committee, and the expanded and more rationalized activities of the two state legislative campaign committees, effectively removed the URF from participation in support of the SCC and of any centralized actions on behalf of legislative races. However, the URF continues to support individual state senators and representatives on the basis of whatever judgments it makes of their need or worthiness. Changing roles, however, have not eliminated tension between the URF and the SCC.

Strain between the RNC and the congressional campaign units and the SCC and the state campaign committees is perceived to arise from the efforts of Washington-based groups to control the conduct of campaigns in Illinois. It was readily recognized that Washington staff members would not come into a state as passive observers who made no demands. Local opposition was seen as a natural response to the local elections committee of the RNC, and strategies devised to counter it were described by a participant:

In forming the new program, [RNC Chairman] Bill Brock decided that offers of expertise and people would be more successful if we could put our money where our mouth was . . . in a lot of places, we bought our way in in the first year. We could be the single largest contributor to a campaign. People then had to pay attention to us. Illinois was the exception.

[Was this because money was not needed?]

No, they did need the money, but they wouldn't admit it. . . . In order to allow us to participate in the program in Illinois, we gave away our right to dictate what was done with the money. There were no strings attached in Illinois.

Problems were more acute for national staff working in state races, but were not confined to such campaigns. The practice was to "give money, advice, and services directly to the candidates. We can also give to the state party, but we did not do so in Illinois." In all instances, the policy was to "tie strings" to the dispersement of funds. In Illinois, these efforts at control were largely repulsed in state elections, and were successful only in national elections where the field staff could make direct contact with the candidates.

Presumed effectiveness in working for the election of Republican candidates should enhance a unit's ability to acquire and sustain support from contributors. Actors whose environmental dependence rests on financial contributors are vulnerable because of their continuing need to mount the kinds of campaigns now considered adequate — using professional polling organizations and advertising campaigns and saturating the media. Actors lacking the financial resources cannot compete in this demanding world.

Financial contributors are not only elements in the party environment. They are also treated as full members of the party network when they are responsible for large and multiple contributions and identify with the Republican Party. Like other actors in the set with whom they have constituents in common, their importance lies in their ability both to acquire resources and to direct their use. In other words, financial contributors have the capacity to make their own decisions about how the money they raise or contribute should be spent. In the case of PACs, contributions can be made following the lead of the party, for example, by funding those candidates in districts the party has targeted. Financial contributors also told us that they have their own agendas for making contributions, targeting districts where they have plants, where there are concentrations of members of a trade or professional association in which they are involved, or where they select candidates on the basis of issues or ideological dispositions.

Participation by independent financial contributors is an asset to the party when they give help in targeted races or, in primaries, when campaign committees are reluctant to enter but where there is a clear party favorite. Participation may appear less valuable to the party where it just adds to the coffers of incumbents yet, as we were told by a financial contributor, "we make contributions to incumbents even when it's a safe seat. We do this to build relations."

Selectivity based on issues or ideology primarily serves the interests of contributors and their affiliated groups (chapters 7 and 8). For example, the Committee for the Survival of a Free Congress, with its own field staff, has the capacity, according to an informed observer, "unlike the Republican National Committee or the Republican Congressional Campaign Committee, to stick its neck out in a primary in support of one candidate," regardless of local sensibilities. Efforts of single-issue groups to try to control or redirect the party into unduly narrow directions understandably aroused the concern of many party staffers and politicians.

Independent contributors with a bias toward incumbents do not confine themselves to Republican candidates. In congressional races between 1976 and 1978, corporate PACs gave more money to Democrats than to Republicans. Like Illinois financial contributors, on the national scene, "the prevailing attitude is that PAC money should be used to facilitate access to incumbents" (Hucker, 1978b). Since the Democratic Party has come to dominate Chicago politics, the Republican Party traditionally has had to contend with the waywardness of its natural constituency. The role of financial contributors produced especially harsh comment by state Representative Bernard E. Epton, shortly before he retired from the restructured legislature in 1982.

Republican businessmen are a joke. They are subservient to the Democratic order. . . . [Cook County Republican Chairman J. Robert] Barr has tried again and again to get them off their fannies. . . . If Stalin were here and doing well, they would give him money. They are a bunch of paper tigers. (Sweet, 1982)

A different example of the independence of some financial contributors was manifested in the early days of the 1980 presidential campaign, when there was great enthusiasm in the financial community for John Connally. An informant in this group spoke of the "fairly nifty group supporting Connally in Illinois. Businessmen have come out [for him] early, and made a refreshing commitment. I believe there is a lot of untapped excitement around." Another told us that many large contributors across the country were persuaded that Connally was the right man for them: "There was tremendous peer pressure from the business community. Connally can mesmerize the corporate leaders." This kind of support for Connally led supporters of Ronald Reagan to worry that the 1980 race would be a replay of 1976, in which their candidate would be upstaged by the party qua financial establishment.

Still another way in which financial contributors can emerge as independent actors is to assume the role of political entrepreneur. This normally happens within the confines of a single district, although there it is not necessarily confined to any one level of government. While he could give no instances of ever having supported a Democrat, one such entrepreneurial financial contributor described himself as selective in his support: "I'm more oriented to the candidate than to the party." I tried to determine how he made choices about whom to support: he soon made it clear: "There has to be personal contact for me to help." One way this occurs is through a connection with a district in which the informant lives. Historically, such entrepreneurs have had a disruptive influence on Republican Party politics. Reviewing their activities for two decades up to the mid-1960s, Snowiss found:

The party simply does not know when a prosperous businessman will decide to embark upon a political career or support a non-organization Republican for some office. . . . Public spirited businessmen have upset regular Republican organization expectations on all levels of government in Illinois — from the ward or township to the governorship. (Snowiss, 1966, 632)

The most famous Illinois-based entrepreneur, and also one who has channelled some of his contributions through the United Republican Fund, is W. Clement Stone. The premise on which his contributions are made is a commitment: "a magnificent obsession, that I would try to change the world and make it a better world for future generations." He attempts to achieve this goal by the contribution of funds to politicians of his choice, including the $5.5 million that helped elect Richard M. Nixon to the presidency (Martin, 1980). During the time of this study, Stone contributed $25,700 to 30 state legislative candidates, giving the largest amounts to incumbents but also contributing $500 each to 10 first-time candidates. His largest contribution to an individual totalled $6,000 to Donald Totten. This is curious, because Totten was not challenged during this period or otherwise in obvious need, and Stone gave at least $4,000 of this money during the time that Totten headed Ronald Reagan's Illinois presidential campaign, although Stone was then pledged to John Connally. Another noteworthy contribution was $1,000 to John Friedland during the 1980 primary period, when Friedland was running to retain his state Senate seat, to which he had been appointed, against a challenger supported by Governor Thompson. Were these contributions signs that Stone was attempting to shape the direction of the Illinois party? At the least, such contributions present a different avenue for action, one that is distinct from the organizational efforts of the party apparatus and its associated campaign committees.

Where members of the same category of party actors are dependent on disjoint constituencies, the ecology of constituencies has the effect of making them likely to have collegial relations with each other. Where constituencies are congruent, interdependence is fostered among actors found either at the county level or in constituencies that are not solely of an electoral nature. Otherwise, congruence is associated with independence, manifested by actors having separate campaign and service organizations. Enclaved constituencies, perhaps because they can lead to disputes over territorial rights, engender rancorous relations among political actors. Such relations emerge and continue where participating actors find resources in their own enclaves.

Commitment

The ability to count on loyal constituents, concentrated in relevant geo-political units, assures party actors of resources comparable to money in the bank. We may consider such situations as ones where actors face environments of certainty.

Ironically, there is also certainty produced by the lack of committed constituents. Republican ward committeemen in many Chicago wards knew they had a hopeless task in general elections. Sometimes this was the case only in local elections, but in some wards lack of support for the Republican Party extended to all offices. Such statements as "This is a Democratic ward" or "We get a larger vote tally for state offices than for local ones, but still the Democrats win the ward" summarize these situations.

In my study I anticipated that the greatest uncertainty with respect to the outcome of appeals for support—whether electoral, financial, or in terms of authority—would occur where constituents favored Republican candidates, causes, or factions about half the time. I also expected uncertainty to be great where the social base of support was variable or heterogeneous (Scott, 1987, 128).

Some of the differences discussed earlier, related to the consequences of having different types of constituents, can now be explained by the differential commitment or loyalty of those constituents. Earlier, the differences between the state Senate and state House leadership were attributed to differences in the character of the two chambers (chapter 2); these differences can now be placed in the context of commitment with the additional observation that senators are more loyal to the party as a statewide entity, as well as to their leadership, than is true of their House counterparts. As a result, Senate leaders can rely on a more certain constituent environment, whereas House leadership emerges from an ability to take advantage of factionalism, as a House spokesman affirmed:

You have to consider the House make-up. The Republicans are downstate, conservative, opposed to leadership from the Chicago area. There is an opposition from suburban Cook County. They had several candidates for leadership. . . . the Cook County people don't always stick together. So downstate could put it together. . . . I would say suburban Cook County is a faction. For example, they are by themselves in opposition to the RTA [Regional Transportation Authority]. They are left by themselves on many legislative issues. As a result they challenge the leadership.

Similarly, differences inherent in having primary compared with general electoral constituents, discussed above, now appear to be due partly to differences in commitment. That is, the local committeeman, county chairman, and state central committeeman typically have more committed constituents from among primary-election voters than do other elected officeholders.

Financial contributors as constituents also differ with respect to commitment. Comments made earlier in this chapter about fundraising were echoed by other informants who complained that the party suffered from the weaker commitment of the business community — the party's natural constituency — compared with the greater consistency in support from trade unions for the Democratic Party. This complaint has been substantiated by other observers (Hucker, 1978b).

Schlesinger's hypotheses about the effects of commitment are couched in terms of competitiveness in electoral results and tied to his discussion of enclaved constituencies. Translating these terms into the concepts used here, we can interpret him to predict that conditions of certainty in winning will lead to independence among actors in overlapping geopolitical settings, with independence manifested as factionalism: "This conclusion is supported by Key's (1949) study of southern one-party states which found the Democratic organizations there weak and fractionated despite and presumably because of their unfailing support by the electorate" (Schlesinger, 1965, 789). Where, instead, there is uncertainty because of closely contested races in enclaved situations involving one large and one smaller unit, "one expects the highest level of cooperation, since both face similar needs. Between such organizations there will probably be the greatest interchange of personnel and also the greatest agreement on policy stands" (Schlesinger, 1965, 789). Although my earlier discussion on the effects of separate versus overlapping constituencies indicated that ecological interdependence frequently leads to organizational independence or competitiveness, we cannot be certain that this will also be the case when constituents' commitment is taken into account.

The first need was to establish some systematic way of measuring constituent commitment. Systemization confines us to the electorate, and thus to effects on elected officeholders, although commitment and factions are relevant for other actors, as I indicated in earlier examples. The procedure followed, adapted from McCarthy and Tukey (1978), was used by Jack Beggs and myself (1984) to trace trends in partisan electoral loyalty to president, governor, U.S. senator, and congressman. The method uses medians to measure long-term state (or office), year, and county effects, gaining the advantage of minimizing the consequences of extreme but unusual voting results. For the present analysis, data from 1948 to 1976 general elections were used to establish the historical context of party commitment in each county. Results can be interpreted as the customary Republican vote in each county, expressed as a percentage, for the office in question.

Because my interest was in the certainty of commitment, I presumed confidence in an election outcome if the Republican vote for the four offices had traditionally been 55 percent or above. In a parallel fashion, certainty of losing was assumed where the customary Republican vote had been 45 percent or below. Within this 45–55 percent margin, I postulated that party actors felt there was a chance of winning or losing, and I defined this as a realm of uncertainty. Of course, party actors may have felt quite confident despite past experience, or they may have worried even when history had been kind, but this need not concern us here. Using the procedures outlined, I found 41 counties that were historically certain winners for the Republicans, including 4 of the 5 collar counties around Cook County — Dupage, McHenry, Kane, and Lake — and the remainder in the northern and central portions of the state. Only four — Johnson, Washington, Edwards, and Pope — were in the southern half of the state. An additional seven counties conformed to my standard of certainty for three offices, of which four were in the south and deviated from the Republican norm only in congressional elections. These 48 counties are counted together as certain winners for Republican candidates. The two certain Democratic counties were St. Clair and Madison, part of the greater St. Louis area. Another five were strongly Democratic except on the presidential vote; four of these were southern counties and the other was Cook. This gave Republicans seven counties that they could treat as certain losers. The remaining 47 were centers of maximum uncertainty.

Key defined faction as

any combination, clique, or grouping of voters and political leaders who unite at a particular time in support of a candidate. Thus, a political race with eight candidates will involve eight factions of varying size. Some factions have impressive continuity while others come into existence for only one campaign and then dissolve. (Key, 1949, 16)

Intuitively, we might prefer a definition that puts more emphasis on those factions with long-run effects, as Benedict (1985, 365–366) points out in his review of factionalism in nineteenth-century U.S. politics; but Key still provides an empirically useful starting point.

My count of factions, following Key's guidance, covered the 1978 and 1980 primary elections and gave each county an index of factionalism computed by summing the number of candidates in each race and dividing by the total number of races. A county that was part of a single legislative and a single congressional district would have 12 races in this period — 2 congressional, 1 state central committeeman, 4 state representative, 1 state senatorial, and 4 county races, the last based on information obtained from a canvass of county clerks.[2] Where a county was part of more than one legislative or congressional district, the number of relevant races increased accordingly. The index ranges from 1.00 — signifying no factions — to 2.80, with a mean of 1.82, a median of 1.80, and a standard deviation of 0.367. If we use the standard deviation to determine cutting points, then only Bureau County, in the northwestern quadrant of the state (factionalism index = 1.00, indicating that, on the average, it had no factions), is less than 2 standard deviations from the mean on the side with few factions. On the extremely factionalized side, using the obverse criterion, there are four counties: McHenry in the north and McLean, Piatt, and Menard in the geographic center.

Looked at individually, counties have unique properties. For example Cook, classified as a certain loser, has a factionalism index of 2.02, whereas Bureau, a certain winner, has no factions. Still, dividing counties into three categories, depending on the chances of Republican victory, leads to increasing factional scores in the expected direction. The seven counties classified as certain losers have a score of 1.58; the 46 uncertain counties score 1.71; and the 48 certain winners have the most factions, scoring 1.95. These are significant differences (F (2,98) = 7.70, p < .001), where the statistical significance emerges from the contrast between certain winnters and all others. Further support for the Key hypothesis comes if Cook County is subdivided into Republican and Democratic areas. Based only on votes in the 1978 and 1980 congressional and legislative elections, Republican areas had a factionalism score of 2.40 and Democratic areas, a score of 1.77.

When the commitment of loyal supporters gives party actors a sense of certainty that they can win, this can lead to factionalism because the value of the outcome is clearly high. Someone in the party is going to win public office, so the stakes involved in running are worthwhile. Even the rancor aroused by competitive primaries can be tolerated in committed districts, because it will have little impact on general elections, an observation that has been found to hold generally (Pierson and Smith, 1975, 561–

2. The canvass was conducted by mail, and one county clerk refused to supply information, forcing us to drop one "uncertain" county.

562; Jewell and Olson, 1988, 130). Party office in such supportive constituencies also becomes increasingly worthwhile because of the enhanced likelihood of rewards of patronage and prestige. All this promotes a sense of confidence among network participants, leading some actors to feel that, because they are successful, they must also be right and others in the party network, even though they face different competitive situations, must be wrong. This argument is used to explain the factionalism associated with disputes between local candidates and statewide officeholders, as one informant described:

Suburban [Chicago area] Republicans don't like Thompson, as they didn't like Ogilvie or Percy. This is not realistic. Suburban officeholders don't face competition, and this keeps them unrealistic. Other Republican officeholders, even when conservative, are more pragmatic.

Within a district, certainty of winning may be associated with a kind of parochial independence. That is, winners assume their own conception of Republicanism, which then goads others to mount a challenge. The following description by a participant indicates how this takes shape at the municipal level:

The village council had been elected as Republicans, but then they abandoned the party. They had raised taxes, and there were a lot of issues about which people were unhappy. So the local Republican Party endorsed a slate for the coming village election. Even though the incumbents were Republicans, once elected they had nothing more to do with the party organization.

The self-confidence that goes along with certainty of winning makes actors unwilling to accept new ideas or ways of doing things. New candidates wanting acceptance in the existing organization frequently have a difficult time. Those already entrenched feel they have the resources to resist any challenge. Security associated with a stable base of support also leads to conviction that the old ways are the best. Discussing his experiences in trying to give advice in a strongly Republican district, one member of the Washington-based party field staff described how certainty of winning affected willingness to change: "The X Congressional District is a Republican one, with a strong organization, and some sophistication. That makes it more confrontational. They had a new candidate but they wanted him to run like the previous one, just using new techniques."

Size

In the development of political parties, the size of constituencies has been a major factor contributing to their modern form. In Britain, for example, political parties began to have their contemporary organization after the

Reform Bill of 1867, when an increase in the size of the electorate led what were essentially parliamentary factions to transform themselves into bodies that could mobilize a mass electorate and compete in vote-getting (Epstein, 1980; Sartori, 1976).

Size is a measure of power generally, nowhere more explicitly than in the life of Illinois political parties. The number of primary election ballots distributed to voters is directly translatable into the voting power of party officeholders. Article 7-8 of the State of Illinois Election Laws, in force in 1978, makes this direct connection between ballots and power for state central committeemen and for local committeemen. The same rule is invoked in all central and district committees, so that representative officeholders have weighted votes, depending on the number of ballots distributed within their immediate jurisdiction. Article 7-9 specifies that the preceding primary election vote be the basis for allocating the numbers of delegates eligible to vote at state conventions. The blatancy of equating power with size of constituency led one informant to disparage the County Chairmen's Association as "ridiculous. Each county chairman has only one vote. This means that chairmen from sparsely populated counties have the same power as those from densely populated ones."

Equally relevant is the fact that constituency size has consequences for control. Smaller counties are perceived to be easier to control, requiring fewer resources to stay in touch with constituents. They are also, in a related fashion, easier to ignore. This is exemplified by the experiences of one legislator, who saw the major base of his support as coming from a large, industrialized county that would, almost alone, assure his election. In his case, however, the temptation to ignore the small-county voters was overcome by the relative ease with which he could stay in touch with these constituents: "I have an office there and I go there every week if I can. I stop at the drug store, the bank, the barber shops. I keep the office open one day per week and the farmers come in and look around."

With increased size, there is a greater likelihood of diversity among constituents, representing a multiplicity of interests. This has been well recognized for the state as a whole, whose 102 counties vary not only internally but also sectionally (Elazar, 1970, 282–316; Monroe, 1980). The difficulties associated with these variations were particularly evident to those party actors in positions where they could make comparative assessments. Accounting for his judgment that the party apparatus was structurally weak, a party actor attributed it to the fact that "the state is so large and diverse. You don't have the homogeneity of, say, Iowa." Another observed:

One of the greatest challenges in Illinois is that downstate you're in the South, and then even there, there may be four kinds of South. This is a more heterogeneous, and hence difficult, state than most. This has produced a vacuum at the top of the party historically. The longer the vacuum exists, the harder it is to deal with. We get some county chairmen who assume inordinately large roles. By and large county chairmen tend to be compromise people. As a result, the state chairman is going to be someone who won't offend anyone. He will not be someone like Ray Bliss in Ohio.

To the extent that it goes along with diversity, size makes for difficulty in organizing and campaigning. This is true for the state as a whole, as well as for constituent parts. One means of ensuring greater uniformity in campaign efforts is through endorsements whose function is to make clear that there are party choices deserving of time, effort, and votes. From the perspective of party actors in either the formal organizational structure or the unofficial wing, endorsements may take the form of targeting, in which particular candidates are designated as the objects of special concern. Targeting is generally not public information, but it is part of the information given to PACs and other financial contributors. For the voting public, and for those party actors most directly concerned with them, endorsements are made public in order to ensure maximum support.

In general elections, endorsements are guidelines for ensuring voters' partisan consistency; in primary elections, endorsements are affirmations of organizational control over candidate recruitment. In the latter case, endorsements may follow as a matter of course when no alternative candidates are able to appear on the ballot. Endorsements in competitive primaries are more difficult to predict at the same time that they are more important for the competitors. In either instance, we would expect that primary endorsements would be more frequent in larger districts, more likely to be heterogeneous in population, and hence more prone to divergent interests that require guidance. This suggests the greater difficulty of organizing campaigns in larger counties, and the consequent need for the cues given by endorsements. Larger size is associated, as well, with the greater likelihood of an ongoing organizational apparatus, which in turn is more likely to have the means to control the recruitment process.

My expectations were confirmed when we asked precinct committeemen outside of Cook County, "Do you give support or approval to candidates in the primaries so as to persuade others to vote for them? That is, do you ever personally endorse candidates in the primaries?" Seventy percent of the committeemen in the largest counties agreed that they made endorsements, compared with 59 percent in midsized counties and 49 percent in small ones. Focussing only on 1980, the scope for endorsements altered, given both new opportunities and new sources of conflict. For example, because of the "blind primary," in which convention delegates were not identified by the presidential candidates to whom they were pledged, it would appear that larger districts again had greater need for direction.

Yet committeemen who endorsed in that year's primary were more likely to endorse if they were in small counties — by 61 percent — than if they were in medium-sized or large counties — 54 and 50 percent, respectively. Here the power of the larger counties was reflected in the alignment among their county chairmen, the State Central Committee, and the state legislative leadership, making endorsements by local committeemen redundant. Instead, it was in the less powerful small counties that committemen had more opportunity to indicate their displeasure with the blind primary and the choices it entailed (an example was given in chapter 3).

The comments of party actors and the evidence from the committeemen surveyed can be interpreted as part of the ambivalence associated with size of constituency. On the one hand, a large constituency provides strength for actors, both directly and as a measure of their prestige in the party network. On the other hand, a large constituency is harder to control and requires the expenditure of scarce resources on keeping a presumably diverse body of supporters reasonably satisfied. A number of actors, almost all in the central arena of operations, talked seriously about the need for the Republican Party to broaden its social base; to pursue voters who normally vote Democratic but who might have the potential for becoming aligned with the Republicans. Included were groups such as blue-collar workers, blacks, and Jews. We even heard the argument that failure to go after such groups would be a serious handicap for the future of the Republican Party. Blame for not previously attracting such support might be laid to the parochialism of local party officials, but a more basic issue is at heart. It is the understandable reluctance to change what is known, comfortable, and secure for what is unknown and uncertain.

Diverse Environments

Environmental differences have consequences for the legitimacy of party actors, with electoral constituencies enhancing that legitimacy. In a society that values popular participation and frequent elections for choosing leaders and policies, it follows that those party actors who share in such valued activities will always have a superior claim to legitimacy. Yet finding that actors who have nonelectoral constituencies are involved in efforts to rationalize party activities suggests an alternate pathway to legitimacy, arising from a rational-legal basis of authority. If, as Max Weber alleged, rationality is the pervading force in Western society, movements to rationalize, especially through the adoption of bureaucratic forms, should have strong appeal on grounds of their own legitimacy. No doubt they do, but the full rationalization of the Republican Party will always be blocked by the greater strength of traditional bases of authority. In short, I consider attachment to elections in itself a manifestation of devotion to U.S. political traditions, just as I do, in different ways, the attachment of voters to political parties.

If tradition is not sufficient to sustain legitimacy, we can expect movements toward rationalization to be further stymied by the charismatic characteristics of elections, where the personal appeals of highly persuasive politicians sweep aside arguments for rational organization.

> Since all emotional mass appeals have certain charismatic features, the bureaucratization of the parties and of electioneering may at its very height suddenly be forced into the service of charismatic hero worship. In this case a conflict arises between the charismatic hero principle and the mundane power of the party organization, as [Theodore] Roosevelt's [1912] campaign demonstrated. (Weber, 1978, 1130)

Tradition and charisma remain powerful forces. Compared with them, rationality as the basis for party organization is a weak competitor.

The extent to which constituents are geographically separated fosters modes of response by party actors that are evocative of organizational strategies used in other settings for managing task environments, that is, those relevant to the goals that must be fulfilled (Dill, 1958, 410). We found that actors confronting an environment made up of similar, but geographically separate, constituents were inclined to respond to each other in helpful, collegial ways. These responses grow out of the recognition of common problems and common fates, manifestations of a form of interdependence. What this means is that "interdependence exists whenever one actor does not entirely control all the conditions necessary for the achievement of an action or for obtaining the outcome desired from the action" (Pfeffer and Salancik, 1978, 40). By proferring assistance to each other, party actors interact in a kind of "contracting" behavior, analogous to the interaction among organizations, where contracting is "the negotiation of an agreement for the exchange of performances in the future" (Thompson, 1967, 35).

Those party actors with identical constituents tended to protect themselves by adopting strategies that emphasize their independence. These are like the uses of bargaining by other organizations. "They are competitive as opposed to cooperative techniques (see Thompson, 1967: 32–37), aimed at assisting the organization to retain its independence" (Scott, 1981, 194).

Overlapping constituents were frequently associated with rivalry among linked actors. Such actors can be compared to large, complex organizations that adopt "buffering strategies . . . to help seal off or cushion the technical core from disturbances in the environment" (Scott, 1987, 185).

The principal analogue to a technical core in the party is the provision of electoral candidates, and even those actors not directly dependent on an electoral constituency have a stake in that goal. Examples of buffering strategies are attempts to stockpile resources of support or to level fluctuations in the resources received (Scott, 1987, 184).

As stated earlier, settings in which there is certainty of support from constituents tend to create competitive relations among relevant actors, which can be manifested in factions. In the economic world, this is similar to the way bountiful markets attract spinoffs from the original participating businesses as well as from competitors (Aldrich, 1979, 163). From the perspective of the market, potential rewards are high; from the perspective of competing businesses, only some will survive. Yet if we treat the Republican Party as a single, large organization, then the emergence of factions is counterintuitive. Pfeffer and Salancik (1978, 68) hypothesize that environments characterized by concentrated power and authority and by scarcity of resources will foster conflict among social actors. In contrast, dispersion and munificence should lead to low levels of conflict. My findings, however, are exactly the opposite. The unique nature of stable electoral resources and the opportunities for intraparty dissension make the environmental conditions for the emergence of factions within a party almost incommensurate with the experiences of other organizations.

Large constituencies provide greater power to actors who enjoy them, just as "it seems reasonable that those who contribute most to maintaining organizational resources would develop power in the organization" (Pfeffer and Salancik, 1978, 232). For example, a study of the University of Illinois–Urbana found that greater departmental power was associated with greater access to outside grants and contracts. Those external resources also enhanced departments' prestige, and the power thus gained was deployed to acquire a greater share of the university's budget (Pfeffer and Salancik, 1974). In parallel ways, we can expect that representatives of larger constituencies will have power to draw on a larger share of the party's resources.

Power is not just a matter of control over resources, as we shall see in chapter 5. It requires the ability to cope with contingencies by using resources wisely (Hickson et al., 1971). Most directly, a large support constituency must be translated into an assured source of votes, when and where they count. But it is also likely that the more supporters there are, the more diverse their demands. We can understand this as the environmental counterpart of conditions making for intraparty factions. Size of constituency then raises problems of control.

Constituent environments are important generally because of the ways in which they provide resources for party actors. Resources are also intrinsic to the party system itself or they may be part of the more immediate environment of the political system. But regardless of how they are generated, the ways resources are used provide additional explanations of relations within the party network. These matters are dealt with in the following four chapters.

5

The Uses of Power

Media of Interchange

Political parties in Illinois find their legal justification in the fact that they provide avenues of orderly choice for public office; the law does not favor any party. Within each party, however, desirable outcomes are distinctly partisan. A party wants to field candidates compatible with its aims and have them elected, to shape government policy in its mold, and to elect party officeholders to sustain its organization. To these ends, party actors need to be linked into a functioning network. With no set answers to the best form of relations among party actors for contributing to collectively desired outcomes, we anticipate that the extent of mutually beneficial exchanges will vary, given the diversity of actors operating in competitive and uncertain environments.

Within the framework created by party goals, actors make recurring and limited choices that affect the stability and adaptability of network relations. We can observe these choices as answers to three questions: Are existing relations maintained or challenged? Is access to new relations emphasized, or are limits to relations enforced? Will dependence, resulting from environmental uncertainty, lead to choices of orderly relations through hierarchy or of new forms of organization?

Choices made with regard to the maintenance of existing relations, access to new ones, or dependence on others, and reasons for them, provide the organizing themes for this and the following three chapters. It takes that much coverage to find answers to our three questions, because transactions among actors involve four different media of exchange: power, patronage, ideology, and campaign contributions.

The particular media involved in exchanges, whether among individuals or collectivities, are determined by their social context. For example, Tichy (1981, 229) lists the media making up the "transactional context" of organizations as expressions of affect, influence, information, and goods and services. For this study, literature and observations on parties led to isolating power, patronage, ideology, and money as media of interchange.

Beginning with the medium of power, the consequences of its use are examined for problems of dependency, access, and maintenance.

Sources of Power

Power is defined here as the ability to make binding decisions on behalf of a political party or some component of it. In parties, the sources of power and the ability to exercise it are highly ambiguous. As Schlesinger has noted, ". . . in parties more than in any other type of formal organization, the official lines of authority are suspect, and there is always implicit the question, Who is the 'real' leader" (Schlesinger, 1965, 777). Sorauf documents how these ambiguities range from local to national levels of party organization (Sorauf and Beck, 1988, 77–98, 147–152).

It is hardly surprising, then, that in Illinois, as elsewhere, party actors have differing perceptions of the locus of authority. Most commonly, it was the governor who was selected as the principal power-holder, because he "creates the party." But, as described in chapter 3, when the party does not elect the governor, and many times even when it does, the state central chairman is recognized as the titular head of the party. For the most part, however, this office has not been a powerful one in Illinois, whether or not its occupant competes with the governor, although some actors continue to recognize its potential. The U.S. senator was also acknowledged to be a powerful figure in the party network, mainly because of activities associated with the late Senator Everett C. Dirksen. But even those who disparaged Senator Percy had to admit that he communicated an image of power by virtue of his vote-getting ability and his national stature.

Other informants emphasized that "real power lies in the hands of county offices." The ability of legislators to get things done and the capacity of the legislature to be, as one participant described it, "a forum for change" were also associated with power. Those described as advisors and financial contributors were also presented as playing crucial roles. For example, at the conclusion of one interview, I was admonished to be sure to speak to an individual with no formal position tied to the party, because "next to the governor, he is the most important man in the state." We had indeed interviewed him and judged him to be highly influential, evidence of the ambiguous and multiple sources of power for Illinois Republicans.

Power derives from the formal structure of authority, in which the right to give orders and make binding decisions is attached to specified positions or offices through custom and rules. But power can also be exerted without recognized rights, in which case it lacks legitimacy, though not potency. The fact that power spills over from any formally designated authority has led to the more general thesis that power is not a fixed capacity. It lies with individuals and units that have control over valued resources. Information is one such resource, giving power to those who have access to it or who can control its channels. In other words, power derives from the ability to cope with organizational uncertainties (Pfeffer, 1981, 238–241).

The power advantage that rests with those who have control over "critical uncertainties" (Aldrich, 1979, 94) occurs when they engage in activities and decisions that prevent what would otherwise be serious problems for the organization. The standard example comes from Crozier (1964), who observed the unexpected power of maintenance engineers in a highly routinized tobacco factory, where virtually the only remaining uncertainty was associated with the breakdown of machinery which they alone knew how to repair. From this and similar examples, Pfeffer offers advice on how to increase or retain power:

This may be done by destroying sources of information relevant to how the job is done (e.g. the destruction of maintenance manuals as described by Crozier), developing specialized language and terminology which inhibits the understanding of the job by outsiders, and by restricting the distribution of knowledge concerning how the task is accomplished. (Pfeffer, 1977, 257)

I was careful in chapter 3 not to speak of either centrality or cohesion as direct measures of power. Caution was also dictated by the way in which conditions affected the relation between asymmetry and power. All that is now justified theoretically by the concept of critical uncertainties, which allow power to those without either formal authority or visible centrality. At the same time, illustrative material gave clear evidence that there is often correlation between contacts and power. Informants revealed, through their equation of visibility with power, a similarly imperfect form of correlation with centrality. Those mentioned most often as powerful were also in the top half of the centrality scale, but in more or less reverse order, and to the neglect of both the Republican National Committee and congressman. My search for cohesion produced a core subject of seven actors, almost all of whom were recognized as powerful by informants, yet the interest group category was overlooked by them. We can conclude, then, that visibility, centrality, and cohesion are three related, but still different, means of designating powerful actors. In this chapter I consider formal structure and control over uncertainty to be the most inclusive ways of locating power in the party. Cases of power use described in previous chapters are reexamined along with new information.

In speaking of powerful individuals, we normally refer to the structural determinants of their power. That is most obvious in the case of formal authority, but it is equally true of any capacity to deal with uncertainties.

Yet how is it possible to speak of politicians without leaving room for individual ambition? Granted that virtually all politicians are ambitious, that in itself is not a source of power. Power arises from the opportunities and constraints found in party structures and their environments; these are the crucibles from which individual ambition flames out (Schlesinger, 1966, 3). Ambition is relevant to the use of power where individuals take advantage of the opportunities presented. This entails the ability to manipulate rules (Mechanic, 1962) and engage in activities for which there is no ready substitute (Hickson et al., 1971, 218). Ambition is most easily expressed by those not otherwise constrained by collective norms or loyalties.

Open-ended interviews are the principal and most appropriate means for examining the uses of power. Because we did not have to ask directly about power in the course of questioning informants about their own activities and relations with others in the party, the candor of responses developed from the interview situation itself. We normally interviewed more than one informant in many networks of relations, so we did not have to depend on information from a single perspective. In this sense, we were able to follow the admonition that "power is best exercised unobtrusively, and must consequently, be diagnosed in a similar fashion" (Pfeffer, 1981, 243).

Formal Structure

With the sole exception of the unofficial wing of the party, the authority of office is associated with all types of party actors. But because of its origins and stated purposes, the United Republican Fund's authority is questionable and should probably be excluded. By extension, Table 4-1 suggests that all those with special-interest constituencies, including the campaign committees, are not appropriately treated in the formal authority structure. Also, the local committeeman, local officeholder, and national committeeman can easily be set aside because, even though they have authority, they can exercise it only in a very narrow sphere. This leaves 12 categories of actors—governor, state Senate leader, state House leader, constitutional officer, senator, congressman, state senator, state representative, county chairman, state central committeeman, the State Central Committee, and the Republican National Committee—with electoral, legislative, and managerial constituencies generally recognized as conferring significant legitimate authority.

Dependency

The division of U.S. political parties into sectors based on ecological and federal distinctions, and into positions based on a functional division of labor, creates many loci of power. To the extent that units within the party are able to establish a domain, defining what they do, where they do it, and whom they serve (Thompson, 1967, 26), the exercise of power stays within formally prescribed limits, but only to the extent that actors carry out their roles with some degree of insulation. As organizational theory points out, however:

> The domain claimed by an organization and recognized by its environment determines the point in which the organization is dependent, facing both constraints and contingencies. To attain any significant measure of self-control, the organization must manage its dependency. (Thompson, 1967, 37–38)

Translated into our frame of reference, this suggests that actors with recognized dependency on others in the party network will try to use their power resources to manage those dependency conditions. One illustration is provided by the relations between the governor and his legislative leaders.

A governor is dependent on his party's legislative leaders to move his bills through the legislative process and enact the programs on which he bases his reputation as an effective leader. On their part, legislative leaders whose party holds the governorship rely on that office for enhancing their positions through visibility gained in the legislature and with the public, and through increased bargaining power from the extra resources provided by their connection with the governor. Clearly these are conditions that encourage cooperation. But mutual dependence also creates uneasy tension among partners, in which each tries to assert his own authority and delimit the power of the other. So Senate Minority Leader James "Pate" Philip responded to a possible extension of the state income tax by informing the governor in the fall of 1983 that he would receive no support.

> I've told the governor . . . if you think you're going to get us in that position, you're wrong. There won't be one Republican to vote to extend that tax. Now we're all running for reelection. We all said it was temporary—and it better be. . . . You couldn't get a vote out of my 26 members if your life depended on it. (Ross, 1984, 30)

The governor and legislative leaders are not only separated by constitutional powers, but they also have their own bases of support. Once elected to the state Senate or House, members jockey for position until some are able to acquire authority from the support they gain from their fellow members. In each chamber, and for each party, the principal legislative leader is elected by his caucus, and he then goes on to appoint assistant leaders. Both election and appointment are independent of the governor's approval. One informant, describing the process from his initial selection to this eventual incorporation into the leadership, said:

> You give your support to the person who is running for minority leader or House speaker, and then you are given patronage in return.

In my — th term in the House, I didn't support the guy who won as leader. Later, I was asked to be the ranking Republican on the ——— Committee, even though I didn't support the leader. It was because I was the only acceptable person. . . .

[How did you get into the leadership?]

I have clout.

[What is clout?]

George Ryan picked me and others . . . so we wouldn't run against him for House leader. That's true of all the others in the House leadership. We are now in the fold, and we bring our people in. Clout is people who trust me. I don't lie; I work hard — so there are 10 or 11 people who stick with me. . . . Some people look to me as a leader because of my stand on issues. They may not be in a position to vote their conscience [the way I am]. So I was picked by George Ryan, even though he disagrees with me, because I have a following.

The current leadership role of Senator Philip, in a style described as "blunt, often abrasive, but never ambiguous," is seen as a reflection of the "size, scope and strength of his political base of support" (Ross, 1984, 30).

Once in a leadership position, service to the governor can be of such dedication, especially on key bills, that the governor, in turn, acquires a "political debt." This was purportedly the basis on which Governor Ogilvie appointed Speaker of the House Ralph Smith to fill a vacancy for the U.S. Senate and later pushed for his election to that post. A contested primary, although resulting in an overwhelming victory, "used up lots of the governor's capital." Many people considered the Senate candidate a liability and were apparently vindicated in their evaluation when he lost to the Democratic candidate. According to one participant, "The night before the election, those of us in the campaign tried to figure out how the campaign could win and the candidate lose." In this instance, the governor's containment of competition for an office over which he had initial control probably contributed to his own loss of power.

It is also the case that effective legislative leaders exert control over the governor. Members of Governor Ogilvie's administration describe how they "worked hard on creating a Republican legislative program." In this they were in harmony with the Senate leader Russell Arrington. An informant close to the process told us how:

Senator Arrington used his personal clout to get a cohesive Republican program. He didn't like the idea of a binding caucus. He preferred having a program and then scaring people to keep them in line.

But in the end, the mutual dependence that this created became the focus of animosity from rival power-seekers. Our informant continued:

Governor Ogilvie had been close to Senator Bill Harris. But Bill was chafing under Arrington's leadership. Bill felt it was time for a change. And he wanted to be Senate leader. I tried to tell Bill that, while his complaints about Arrington were valid, the governor would support Arrington. Bill thought he still had the votes, and ran for the leadership in a bitter contest. Then, two weeks after the leadership election, Arrington had a stroke. Bill became Senate leader two years later, but he could never bring the caucus together. Some of the Arrington people were bitter, even with me. They suspected that the governor could have gotten Harris out of the race, but in fact he couldn't.

The governor exerts his authority over the legislature by his ability to confer tangible favors and more symbolic rewards through association with the prestige of his office. In this he is not restricted to dealing with legislative leaders or even with his own party. He is aided by the expectations of many legislators, who, as one informant put it, "don't really care about issues. They are more concerned with who gets appointed or whether they're informed about jobs in their district." But dependency remains and becomes a source of competition whenever divisive issues arise. Two prominent ones in recent years have been concerned with regional problems focussed on Chicago and its suburbs and collar counties, and with the Equal Rights Amendment.

To deal with regional problems, the Northern Illinois Republican Committee was founded to tie suburban and collar legislators to their county organizations. At times, it has met regularly to discuss pending bills of interest and to decide on voting strategy. According to one participant: "The proof of our success was that we were able to tie up some of Governor Thompson's legislation. Thompson didn't like this and decided to put up a challenger to the . . . county chairman." Regional transportation issues remain a thorn in the side of suburban Republicans, and they feel they lose in their struggle with the governor whenever a transportation bill is passed that signifies a deal has been made between Chicago Democrats and downstate Republicans.

The Equal Rights Amendment battle, on the other hand, worked to the advantage of those opposed to the governor, including the then speaker of the House and the former lieutenant governor, who kept the amendment from passing despite the governor's endorsement (Felsenthal, 1982, 141).

How actively leaders take the initiative in opposing the governor is related to how they see their roles. Some leaders believe that they must stick with the governor no matter what:

There are a lot of Republicans, especially in the Senate, who don't subscribe to the kind of party loyalty that means support for the governor's bills. I feel strongly about it, even if I think that the legislation offered is bad. The governor is the head of the party in the state. When there is opposition to him, I very seldom allow any of the leaders in the Senate or the caucus to change my mind, even if it means that I have to go it alone.

Other leaders take a more independent position:

I have an obligation to promote the governor's programs, to be his floor man. But it depends on the issues. Take ERA. I don't vote for it — it's opposed in my district — though the governor leans on me. . . .
[What happens when you disagree with the governor?]
There are two ways to handle this. I can be for it, or FOR it. I don't go out to defeat him in the first instance, but I don't press people to vote for his bill.

Because a governor and his party's legislative leaders have different arenas of action and depend on different constituencies, they may develop opposing interests even while conditions make them interdependent. These circumstances make power the medium of interchange for coping with dependency. From these illustrations and materials discussed in earlier chapters, we can find at least 27 instances of power used to deal with dependency between dyads with formal authority. The governor was the heaviest power user, relating to 7 out of 11 possible actors through power. State legislators, county chairmen, and congressmen each had from five to six power links. The senator was notable in having only one link.

Access

Like many organizations described by Benson (1977), political parties are rife with contradictions over the distribution of responsibilities and rewards, even though their formal structure would appear to preclude this. In the case of Illinois Republicans, these situations are most notable with respect to relations between county chairmen and state central committeemen. Contradictions in roles and responsibilities arise because of actors' modes of election and vague statutory definitions. During the 1980 state convention, for example, I observed how county chairmen, as official convention delegates, attempted to present a motion changing the way in which central committeemen are elected. The central committeemen, who have responsibility for convening and running state conventions, were then able to declare a voice vote as insufficient to carry the motion. Power is associated with both offices, but neither was strong enough to overwhelm the other.

Relations between county chairmen and state central committeemen represent instances where formal authority is used to limit or restrict the scope of other actors. Limiting actions in this case functioned to sustain the status quo. Not only were the county chairmen blocked by the authority of the central committeemen during the convention, but they were later unable to enlist enough support in the legislature to ensure passage of a bill to change the mode of election. I suspect that this was due less to the countervailing power of the central committeemen than to the preference of a variety of actors, in and out of the legislature, for retention of existing arrangements. If I am correct, these party actors help restrict the power of both county chairmen and central committeemen, leaving greater flexibility to those actors who rely on a general electoral constituency.

A search of all our data found five dyads where problems of access were associated with power use. Except for the possibility of conflict between the governor and constitutional officer over access to sources of support, access was primarily of concern to actors in the party apparatus.

Challenge

Organizationally defined responsibilities associated with particular positions and accepted as legitimate authority are the mainspring of power for establishing dominance. Paradoxically, they may also be the milieu out of which challenges to authority occur. Legitimacy is a transactional process, linking leaders and followers, and specifying what is appropriate for both:

Legitimacy norms specify the orders to which subordinates are expected to comply — and hence support the exercise of power — but also identify demands that the power wielder cannot appropriately make of subordinates — and hence limit the exercise of power. In sum, legitimacy norms cut both ways: they permit greater and more reliable control of subordinates within certain limits, defined as appropriate areas of control . . . and they restrict the exercise of power to these areas. (Scott, 1987, 287)

The absence of a clearcut hierarchy of authority in U.S. political parties produces situations in which the legitimacy of actions can be challenged in two diametrically opposite ways. In one, roles are expanded to assume responsibilities that make authority more consistent from one perspective, but illegitimate from another. The presence in parties of multiple centers of authority, a condition shared with many other organizations, creates ambiguity about who is in charge, and encourages challenges from those who believe prerogatives have been overstepped.

In the opposite way, legitimacy is challenged when authority is perceived as used in too restricted a fashion. This is, on the surface, a question of the effectiveness of authority, in terms of how well a job is being done. But it is also a question of legitimacy, in the sense that authority is not being used appropriately. The preceding condition of multiple centers of authority still does not quell concern that the party is not getting the leadership it needs.

Those who exercise authority may see a need to enlarge their powers in order to carry out general organizational goals. This happens, for example, when a party has captured the highest office in its sector and the incumbent tries to improve the party's governing capacity by defining who should be party candidates. At some time, every top officeholder makes a bid to consolidate power by demonstrating that he "runs the show." Existing authority will be challenged, however, by competitors when they find it stretched beyond its legitimate boundaries. Ranney gives two instances of competition associated with presumptions of excessive authority by Governor William Stratton:

> Before the 1958 primary . . . the party's slate-makers, under Stratton's direction, passed over ultraconservative incumbent Warren E. Wright for renomination for state treasurer and instead slated Louis E. Beckman. Wright, however, refused to be dumped, entered the primary on his own, and campaigned vigorously against Stratton's "bossism." He managed to secure a good deal of *sub rosa* organization support downstate, and in the primary defeated Beckman handily by 373,876 to 286,893. . . .
>
> Late in 1959, Stratton announced that for the Republican nomination for U.S. senator in the 1960 primary, he would support progressive Chicago attorney Samuel E. Witwer, the man who had done most of the organizing of Stratton's campaign for legislative reapportionment. This was too much for many party regulars. Not only did Witwer seem far too radical to be a worthy spokesman for true Republicanism, but they also resented what they regarded as Stratton's dictatorial effort to impose his candidate on the party. Consequently, Witwer was challenged in the primary by two strong opponents, both supported by groups of regulars from the party's right wing, and several weaker ones. (Ranney, 1960, 32)

Reactions to such gubernatorial slate-making are often critical. If a governor endorses candidates in a primary, he runs the risk of arousing a challenge from those who feel he is interfering in local party matters. For statewide offices, an endorsement may be interpreted as evidence that the candidate is merely the governor's representative. I gave the example in chapter 4 of the efforts by John Castle, candidate for comptroller, to define his independence after receiving the governor's endorsement. One informant told us how he hesitated to ask for endorsement for a statewide office, because the governor had already made several, to some objection from other party leaders. He felt it best to wait—"I don't want his embrace now"—and, as a consequence, lost the opportunity to run. Too-active campaigning on behalf of legislative challengers may lead to accusations that the governor is overstepping the authority of the executive by interfering in legislative races.

I have related examples of the governor endorsing challengers to incumbents, one in Governor Ogilvie's tenure and the other in Governor Thompson's. The latter example can be elaborated in the present context on the uses of power in challenging situations. According to an informant, Governor Thompson told him that "it was suggested that he was losing the pulse beat of the suburbs, and that he should be more involved politically. This seemed to be a test case. I said to him, 'Campaign against Democrats, not Republicans.'" Publicly as well, the governor spoke of the need to exercise authority in order to demonstrate his power against challengers. "Munching on an alfalfa sprout salad after a gym workout last week, Thompson talked about why he got into a race that pits him against local party officials: 'For years I've been hearing Republicans say I've got to be more political. This is the race'" (Talbott, 1980).

My own reconstruction suggests that support for the primary challenging candidate was an opportunity for the governor to take on what was mistakenly seen as an easy target and, in that way, give notice to more formidable opponents that the governor was in command. It was probably also in anticipation (again mistaken) of how legislative reapportionment would later divide Chicago suburbs and collar counties. Safe in another part of the state, one politician pronounced the judgment of those who felt that they better understood party politics: "The governor made a mistake getting active in the primary. And then his choice lost. It hurt him."

Yet by taking this action, the governor appeared to have made one point. His rival, Donald Totten, was also hoping to move to the state Senate in his district (3), but feared the governor's counterattack. The form this would take was already clear from efforts to persuade incumbent state Senator David Regner to step aside in the 1980 primary and allow Susan Sharp, the unsuccessful candidate for secretary of state in 1978, a clear field. Regner was known to be interested in retiring. "As the Dec. 21 deadline for withdrawal neared, Thompson's strategy became more clear. Bob Kjellander, his patronage chief and top political advisor, met with Regner. A top job in the Department of Law Enforcement was discussed—and rejected" (Manning, 1979). Sharp quickly withdrew, recognizing that she had no chance against Regner. But more to the point was evidence that Regner was truly interested in retiring and held on to his seat in the primary only to protect it for Totten, who ran and won in the 1980 general election.

Such examples indicate that the nature of party networks and the responsibilities that go with them make ambiguous the precise definition of legitimate authority. From the perspective of challengers, excessive authority turns out to be inadequate authority when a leader fails in his objectives. We are made conscious of this paradox in reviewing a particularly astute political advisor's assessment of Governor Thompson's performance prior to the 1980 primary:

If you're governor, you must run the government. You don't have cabinet government, where people set policies for different departments. Thompson doesn't want to run the government. He does nothing, he's a spectator. He'll do what he likes and [not do] what he doesn't like, for example, to deal with the budget.

When challenges to formal authority arise, they are not the result of dependency, as I elaborated earlier in the relations between the governor and legislative leaders, but stem more straightforwardly from conflicts over control. In the examples used, gubernatorial efforts to punish rank-and-file legislators who did not treat the governor's program as a party program were clearcut policies of control; they aroused objection because they were so openly exercises in power.

Similarly, when a major officeholder attempts to demonstrate his control over the administrative arm of the party, alternative sources of power may be invoked by those who expect to enjoy longer terms of office (Schlesinger, 1965, 778–780). To some degree, because the past always looks rosier than the present, the three living Republican governors were often rated as party leaders in reverse order to the recency of their tenure. One of the sharpest critics drew his comparisons between Governors Ogilvie and Thompson:

Thompson wants to have prominent roles, like chairman of the Illinois delegation, but that's it. He took no position on the U.S. Senate candidates [in the 1980 primary]. For Ogilvie, it was straightforward: punish your enemies and reward your friends. For Thompson to go against [state Senate incumbent] Friedland was inconsistent.

Yet whatever the accuracy of this assessment of Thompson, it does not give the total picture for Ogilvie. Although he tried to control the party apparatus and to strengthen the central committee with a professional staff, his accomplishments were fleeting and did not survive his term of office. As a Washington staffer observed, "Ogilvie in 1968 tried to build a power base for himself through the state party, but he didn't succeed." To the extent that authority was at stake, those who questioned its legitimacy were, in the end, more successful. They illustrate yet another way in which the authority structure both fosters its own avenues for the uses of power and its own challenges.

Data reviewed here and in preceding chapters have revealed 12 cases where power linked pairs of actors under challenging conditions. Half of these involved the governor, whose role in the party bears striking resemblance to formal authority in another loosely coupled organization, the American university.

The American college president . . . is resented because he is more powerful than he should be. He is scorned and frustrated because he is weaker than he is believed capable of being. If he acts as a "strong" president, he exposes his weaknesses. If he acts as a "democratic" president, people consider him timid. (Cohen and March, 1976, 197)

It should be safe to generalize, then, that when criticisms were directed against Ogilvie and Thompson, we were, at the same time, hearing about how formal authority in the party structures its own sources of dissatisfaction.

Uncertainty

Dependency

Power resources emerge out of the uncertainties and contingencies associated with the environment in which the party network operates and the environments created by interaction among party actors as representatives of sectors and positions (Lawrence and Lorsch, 1967; Aldrich, 1979, 57). It is here that the medium of power, used for coping with dependency, intersects with the medium of money. Money, in large amounts and steady flows, is the route to decreasing the normal uncertainties of candidate appeal and performance, organizational continuity, and electoral fortunes. Among Illinois Republicans, the search for stable sources of money has been complicated by a long monopoly over fundraising and dispersement by a group, the United Republican Fund, determined to be apolitically Republican.

My earlier accounts of the origins of the URF and of its relations with other party actors recorded that inroads into the URF's monopoly were introduced in the 1960s by means of two state legislative campaign committees. Because both committees were concerned with legislative races, they left the URF the bulk of its self-appointed responsibilities. But complaints remained about "secretive old men," and arguments grew for more stable sources of funding, needed to establish a comprehensive machinery of the party's central office and to respond to demands for technical assistance in campaigning. These arguments and demands were met in the 1970s with the establishment of the Republican Finance Committee, based on the central committeemen and tied to the State Central Committee, but still without the demise of the URF.

The URF continues to support the Cook County organization, contributes to some other county organizations, and assists in the campaign expenses of state offices other than governor or U.S. senator. There is evidence (presented in chapter 8) that the URF also gives directly to legislative candidates. However, the URF no longer contributes to the SCC, defining itself as "a bone in the throat of the SCC." Leaders of the URF see their continued locus in the business community as a virtue, attributing the increased competition in fundraising to the personal ambitions of specific individuals. Their connections with the business establishment in Chicago led to a sympathetic editorial in the *Chicago Tribune,* which criticized those Republicans who contribute mainly to "stars" running for major offices:

The only help for many of these forlorn candidates has come from the United Republican Fund, an independent fund-raising organization dedicated to supporting Republican candidates on the basis of merit and need, regardless of prominence.

As sometimes occurs when big Republican stars are ascendant, the U.R.F. is now under attack. The stars are unhappy with the way it is allocating the funds, which is another way of saying that they don't like its independence. . . .

As long as the U.R.F. is working to support candidates at all levels, to put the party's and the public's interests before those of a few ambitious individuals, and to remain independent of party factions, it is helping to maintain a healthy two-party system. And it is doing its job. (*Chicago Tribune,* 1978)

URF leaders agreed that "there were accusations against the URF, that we were arrogant and independent," but they admitted no wrongdoing. Instead, they attributed criticism to their special position: "We are still resented because of our independence from the political leaders." But critics had a less benign view, as a financial contributor associated with the campaign committees told us:

Take the case of fundraising and the URF. Where did it get its charter? The fund is more conservative than the party in this area [Cook County]. The kind of administrative costs they have are unconscionable. It's a group that acts like it is run by old men and their fathers. We can't justify that kind of organization. It engages in dead-in-the-water actions.

Support for Ronald Reagan in 1980 from prominent URF members and appointment for two of the fund's former officers, Daniel Terra and Paul Robinson, to ambassadorships seem to have given the URF a brief rise in influence. Its members responded to criticisms with their own hints about the SCC Finance Committee, saying that it is "not clear what they are doing with the money they raise." Nor do they yet appear willing to give up control over resources. After data collection for this study ended, new information emerged before the 1982 primary that dependency on an uncertain electoral environment was helping the URF retain power by its ability to threaten both the Cook County party organization and county candidates:

First, the URF has threatened to yank all aid from the Cook County Republican Central Committee if chairman Bob Barr tries to raise any substantial money on his own. Second, with only three weeks to go until the county election, the URF hasn't yet given help to any county candidates. (Talbott, 1982c)

By the next month, a truce had been called, and announcements were prepared heralding the merger of the URF and the Republican Finance Committee with respect to fundraising in Cook County (Talbott, 1982d). However, less than a year later, reports appeared that the merger had never worked, and the Cook County party began its own fundraising committee (Talbott, 1983b). Subsequently, the split seemed to deepen, when the URF took an even more overtly conservative stance, symbolized by the appointment of executive director Mike Adelizzi, formerly linked to Governor Thompson's rival, Donald Totten. "'If a group is viewed as conservative, it can raise more money,' Adelizzi said. 'Conservatives will give to conservatives. What conservative would contribute to Gov. Thompson?'" (Talbott, 1984a).

The power of the URF lies in its ability to raise funds in the business community, and this is a power it does not choose to give up. As long as the electoral and organizational functions of the party are heavily dependent on money, URF contributions to candidates and county organizations will be welcomed; URF money is as good as money from any other party source.

Access

Winning an election is an individual goal that also serves an organizational purpose. Yet we would be hard pressed to find a politician who considers his own election secondary to the victory of a party ticket, and electoral strategies are built on such particularistic outcomes. There would need to be a special kind of collective commitment to bring about the adoption of a different position — one like that found in the Republican National Committee under William Brock or, at times, in the State Central Committee. Candidates are free to cultivate their own support even when doing so appears to preclude support for others. Power is sought to reduce the uncertainty of individual election outcomes through monopolizing or otherwise gaining access to party workers and by attracting recognition for services.

Chapter 4 considered the consequences of overlapping constituencies, and here we can examine this situation from the perspective of control over resources. Overlap among levels and districts lends merit to the efforts of an existing apparatus to supply workers and otherwise look after all party candidates. In one large county that includes a number of electoral districts we were told by the county chairman: "No volunteer organizations are needed here. The congressman could go on vacation from now to the election. He would have nothing to worry about." This conforms to Olson's findings (1978, 246) about the activities of tightly organized district parties. Integrated campaigns are also possible and present even in more loosely structured overlapping districts. But offers to share by those who have already cultivated their own support will likely be late in the campaign.

Evidence from our interviews led me to conclude that competition over available workers is quite common, because there is always an advantage to having help from those who are clearly committed. As one candidate put it:

You have to have both volunteers *and* the county organization. The candidate needs to project an image that's separate from the party. People don't vote along party lines so much. That means the committeemen can only do so much [for you].

In another district with strong county organizations, both legislators and the congressman had built their own loyal work force, and according to a legislator:

There is some animosity against my organization, as there is against the congressman's. But I have to have my own organization. Those committeemen who work [for me] do it out of love. They can't be motivated by patronage any more. You have to have your own people — those who are your personal representatives. They are not necessarily in the party — maybe half are in the party organization.

Emphasis on the importance of volunteer workers, motivated by special issues or ties to candidates, is sometimes interpreted to signal the decline of political parties. This idea was expressed, probably in a self-serving way, by an advisor: "Parties can't elect anyone anymore. Campaigns are built on candidates. Now we have citizens' committees, not a Republican Party. Governor Thompson personifies these developments. The media force this. Now a candidate builds a personal organization." This is not, however, the impression I am left with, because efforts to limit contacts among party workers were around long before the intrusion of the mass media into campaigning. In a diverse state like Illinois, different kinds of candidates are successful with different constituencies, and the party is never able to fully control such differentiated relations. In addition, once officeholders become entrenched, normally the only way they can be removed is to go outside the existing structures. If candidates then compete over the support of workers, they are responding to political realities.

In one strongly Republican area, where the party apparatus works for a ticket, Senator Percy was not popular. We were told by a party officeholder: "Our people were up tight with him on the last election. I had to write a letter to my precinct captains to deliver the vote. I argued he was better than Seith [the Democratic candidate]. Sometimes you have to choose a lesser evil." For Senator Percy to have relied solely on such workers would have been foolhardy. Although Governor Ogilvie's efforts to placate county chairmen included consultation on picking local campaign chairmen, there was still a recognition of the limits on help received: "We would ask them, 'Who is the strongest Ogilvie backer here?' There were some risks to this. One county chairman gave us his brother-in-law, which was a guarantee that nothing would happen; another gave us the town hooker." Using power to obtain access to workers while limiting the access of other candidates may seem unduly power-oriented. But if refraining from using power appears more conciliatory, it still does not evoke loyalty from those tied to existing organizational units.

The campaign of Dave O'Neal, the incumbent lieutenant governor and then candidate for U.S. senator in 1980, demonstrates the importance of establishing access to committed workers. Without a strong cadre of workers tied to him, his campaign strategy was to make use of existing organizations at the local level. According to an advisor:

When Dave O'Neal ran for the lieutenant governor in 1976, in the primary against Joan Anderson, he visited all the county chairmen. He is a strong organization-political person. As lieutenant governor, he has spent the last four years reinforcing party ties. Thompson is not very party-oriented. Dave has gone to all the party functions, both on his own and as a surrogate for the governor. He has made an enormous number of friends. . . . people approached me with lots of offers of help. There were people offering repayments for Dave's help in their campaign.

To see how well this strategy worked, I rechecked the survey of precinct committeemen, where they were asked about the kind of campaigns that received most of their effort; committeemen ranked the O'Neal race a low fifth out of six possible campaigns. Although O'Neal won the primary with a narrow margin, he was decisively beaten in the general election.

Obviously, not all campaign strategies that rely on party officeholders and the workers they recruit will fail, but there is that risk when the candidate enters, as O'Neal did, after a divisive primary, plagued by accusations of improper campaign behavior and of running a lackluster campaign. The resources of workers, unaffected by ties of personal loyalty, will be expended where they will do the most good for those workers, if not for the party.

In the exchange between officeholders and the electorate, officeholders attempt to increase the stability of their support through the services they provide. Because of the separation of roles and responsibilities, voters do not always recognize who should be given credit for benefits received. That degree of insulation allows some slack in how officeholders behave, translatable into limitation on how credit is distributed. For example, an individual with a problem concerning social security payments could approach the local committeeman, who might either direct the constituent to the appropriate office or act as the constituent's intermediary. If he does the latter, he may also choose among contacts at the federal level. Although these kinds of contingent relationships may not be important to everyone, to some they are a conscious mechanism in the competition for support. One state legislator spoke of relations with his congressman as deliberately distant, even though the two were of the same party: "Philosophically, we're not of the same mold. . . . I don't respect the congressman. When constituents have problems, I send them to Senator Percy. I know they will be helped and dealt with competently. I don't want the congressman to get credit."

At the organizational level, choices must also be made. In one well-organized congressional office, in a district where the congressman is known to rely on the local apparatus for campaigning and to work closely with state legislators, a staff member told us that there is still some selection: "We probably work most closely with *B*. He runs a good office. We also work with *S*, who runs a good office too. The others don't, so there is no one to contact, no organization for getting things done." Related interviews made clear that those legislators chosen for contact because they had the appropriate infrastructure (although there were also personal ties) were the ones who received credit for the successful completion of a district project that required federal and state cooperation.

Choices of this sort are a manifestation of power, both by those who make the choices and by those who benefit from them. They maintain and strengthen existing ties among party actors and, where they are used to give credit for a job well done, enhance the power of recipients. Conversely, if choices serve to limit credit, they also limit the ability of the deprived actors to demonstrate their own power.

Challenge

Strategies for increasing organizational effectiveness through imposing greater rationality in operations often take the form of increased centralization and control (Scott, 1987, 37–40). Organizational units may attempt to resist such efforts, and this is especially likely in loosely coupled systems, where units are able to act autonomously. The existence of different goals and styles of politics, producing a contrast between what Huckshorn (1976, 97–168) calls the old and new politics, is associated with the uncertainties of electoral fortunes and public tastes. If the new ways are intended to reduce that uncertainty, they also engender conflicts with an older generation of politicians who still believe their ways are best.

We saw earlier that national party staff agreed that Illinois was an unusually difficult state in which to work, and some went so far as to express their hatred for those with whom they had been in contact. In contrast, there was not even a single spontaneous comment about national staff from any of the party actors with whom they dealt. Complaints by national staff were not against candidates but against virtually everyone else in the party apparatus. To understand why these complaints occurred and why the state apparatus could ignore the national staff, we shall consider the process by which national staff attempted to promote centralized control.

Echoing the language of the population ecology model of organizations

(Aldrich, 1979, 28), one informant described the national task as "finding a niche with existing structures and interests."

We would normally look to the SCC as the next level for dealing with, but that doesn't happen in Illinois. Don Adams is a great guy, but you can't define him as a power-broker. But there is a strong County Chairman's Association and it always gets a nod or curtsey from candidates. There are also strong elected officials.

National staff members have much to offer in money, services, and advice, plus a certain amount of maneuverability. They can decide on how these contributions will be made because they have the capacity to target districts, a capacity premised on the understanding that they have congressional and even state legislative races to themselves. According to a national staffer: "No one cares about state legislative races. State central committees care about the governor — he's the source of patronage. County chairmen care about county races, where they have the patronage." Available benefits are distributed with restrictions attached, our informant continued: "We don't just send money. We support expenditures for mail, media, and survey research. But we also control how the money is used. For example, we want to know who does the service and what they do."

In practice, however, things work differently. In Illinois, at least, the existing legislative campaign committees care very much about legislative races. Decisions about expenditures and which districts to target are first made in the state and then presented to field staff. All this causes most acute problems for national staff working in state races, but problems over control of resources are by no means confined to those races. In searching the comments of informants for explanations of problems that were not simply attributable to personality difficulties, I found allegations that most stemmed from the treatment of Washington-based personnel as outsiders. Organizational explanations were also suggested: existing ways of doing things had been satisfactory, and therefore any willingness to adapt to new circumstances was minimal. I have already referred to the successful Republican district that felt strong enough to be "confrontational" with national staffers and their new ideas.

This perspective was also said to apply to the state generally. In the words of an informant who had worked at both the state and national levels:

The Illinois party people haven't been hungry enough to change. They have had a moderate level of success. There have been some attempts to move forward a little — by party-building, registering new voters, targeting, media programs, survey research — but then they don't take the next step.

If national party actors see reluctance to take advice as resistance to needed change by those at the state and district levels, "jealous of power and wanting to maintain it even if it means losing," those at the state and district levels see it as protecting both their current positions and the prerogatives of existing sectors.

In the course of their encounters, national staff members have learned guidelines for survival. One rule is to make as few contacts as possible with the state party apparatus. This is easiest in cases that involve congressional campaigns or where there is little existing organization. A second rule is not to get close to the candidate. This is easiest where there is a strong campaign manager who will accept suggestions directly, but more difficult where a campaign is run by the local party apparatus. One national staffer said:

We don't play political games. We don't try to get attention in the areas where we work. My boss needs to know that I'm doing a good job, but no one else does. If the candidate wins, then I get my back patted here [in Washington]. I'm not a politician, and I don't care for local exposure.

This may be a primer for avoiding conflict, but it does nothing to stop challenges to existing relations. These go on because of the continuing push toward a greater rationalization of party campaign activities, making them more interchangeable and giving scope to the same group of opinion pollers, media advisors, and producers of campaign literature and advertisements. To the extent that the carriers of this rationalizing message from Washington can be resisted, it is largely by those party units — the legislative campaign committees — that are themselves committed to a similar goal of rationalization and have enough of an infrastructure to pursue it. In other words, there are at least two sets of challengers to the status quo, each with a capacity to cope with electoral uncertainties.

Ambition

Dependency

Ambition, in my view, is not in itself a source of power, but rather the personal trigger that affects the uses of power. This position still acknowledges that all politicians, virtually by definition, are ambitious, yet recognizes that they vary in the extent to which their personal qualities and abilities are utilized in finding and drawing on power resources. Ambitious actors have resources of support that are not contingent on those of their opponents. These may derive from their participation in civic activities or local government, their involvement with other organizations, or their ties with party actors in other sectors. Such sources of support are especially important for those actors attempting to enter new arenas.

One well-known example is Everett Dirksen's election to Congress after defeating incumbent William E. Hull in the 1932 primary. "If Hull had great wealth, control of the local party, and the favor of the newspaper publishers and editors, Dirksen had the American Legion, a growing political force in Illinois and the nation" (MacNeil, 1970, 42). The American Legion district, of which Dirksen had become commander, was, fortunately for him, identical in its boundaries with the 16th Congressional District; its division into 36 posts provided an organizational base for mobilizing support. In our interviews, whenever we encountered officeholders who had gained their positions by either first challenging incumbents in the party primary or, in open races, overcoming the lack of endorsement by local organizations, we were given evidence of the importance of ambition coupled with alternative sources of support.

Ambitious power-seekers are also quick to appreciate the usefulness of new sources of support. This was exemplified by one primary challenger whose essential conservatism on social issues went along with a pragmatism about his competitor's enemies: "The incumbent was anti-ERA. I didn't really care about ERA, but I decided it was O.K. as an issue. I could then take advantage of the pro-ERA forces in my district." Such party actors are prepared to go on the offensive, looking for the particular weaknesses of their opponents and using the strengths they have acquired from their own ties with constituents. When they fail, it is often attributed to their brashness and insensitivity. When they succeed, the initiative fuelled by their ambition is evidence that they were correct to act, and whatever shortcomings that were previously held against them are generally forgiven by the victorious party.

When ambition is separate from winning office or changing position, individuals can establish a sphere of influence built on their apparent concern for the collective good of the party. This happens at times to county chairmen with static ambitions. Entrenched in their own sector of county responsibilities, they are insulated from pressures faced by party actors with broader ambitions. They are then freer to use the power associated with their ability to deliver votes and to speak from experience than they might be if they wanted those resources to increase the likelihood of enhancing their own future in the party. The kind of power they have was described in terms of personal affiliations ("close friends to whose political careers I devoted time") or influence ("I got Charles Percy to run against Charlie Carpentier in the gubernatorial primary").

Disinterest in office ambition for oneself gives a certain credibility to efforts to influence others, and may produce, as we found with long-time county chairmen, regular pilgrimages from presidents, governors, and contenders for these offices, seeking advice and support. Comparably, wealthy businessmen, who establish their party credentials through contributions and advice, can satisfy their political ambitions by affecting recruitment of candidates, organization of fundraising, and decisions about how resources should be distributed.

Access

Campaign strategies can be approached with more certainty where information about constituents is incorporated, including information about past behavior. Data on primary and general elections, available in publications of the State Board of Elections, are one such source. Details of county elections, particularly outside of Cook County, including those dealing with party offices, are not published but kept instead by county clerks, themselves elected in partisan elections. Although others in the counties may keep tallies of votes, these are not official until attested by the county clerks, who then report results to the State Board of Elections. In order to obtain these data for use in this volume, we canvassed all county clerks, asking for results of the 1978 and 1980 primary and general county elections, including elections for local committeemen. In two instances, the county clerks could not be persuaded to supply what is public, though not published, information. Because both clerks were Republicans, we next approached the district congressional offices where we were already known. With some embarrassment, aides admitted that their offices had no influence on the clerks, and that they too had been refused information. One told us that his congressman had had to obtain a court order to dislodge election information. That county remains a blank for us, whereas we were successful in the second only by imposing on the good will of another influential Republican.

When using a mailed questionnaire, a refusal rate of 1 or 2 out of 102 would generally be considered extraordinarily good. For us, however, it remains a failure to complete a data set. Yet, more important, it reveals a way in which individuals normally not thought to hold positions of power in the party organization can use their authority to thwart access to valuable information. I consider this among the limiting ways in which power can be used when it is driven by ambition, because there is really no other explanation. Supplying the data was no easier for any of the other clerks, many of whom recorded results by handwriting them on ledger sheets. Evidence that they objected not only to professors searching for free data but also to influential members of their own party suggests that the small world in which they operated had an importance to them out of proportion to their actual role, and they used one of the few ways at their disposal to demonstrate their power. No reward would follow this demonstration that they were gatekeepers of desirable information; it was apparently sufficient that they could thumb their noses.

Challenge

Ambition is found among all politicians, but in some it resides to a greater degree than in others. Moreover, it is probably significant to the political system that there is such differential ambition, motivating newcomers to believe that they are able to take on demanding roles in the political arena. We expect, then, that ambition is more likely to be strong among outsiders — those not tightly integrated into the party machinery or the party sector in which they want to mount a challenge. One prototype of such an ambitious outsider is Congressman Philip Crane, who emerged as a presidential hopeful in 1980 from his leadership of the American Conservative Union. Although enjoying a safe congressional seat, he is recognized as "not a candidate of the mainstream," and being a Republican is, for him, an identity secondary to his conservatism (Robinson, 1978). Even in a rather consistently conservative congressional delegation this is unusual, as it is among other Republican Party actors in the state who identify themselves as conservative. Congressman Crane, his brother Daniel, and Paul Findley were unique in the 14-member Republican delegation in their lack of prior party connections through state or county office or partisan employment. The consequence of this kind of initial independence is a continuing independence within the party network.

Like Philip Crane, the ambitious challenger is likely to be one who has his own resources, some degree of sectoral insulation protecting him from dependence on his opponents, and at least some status as an outsider. As one successful challenger said, "If the party were strong in my district, you wouldn't be talking to me." In a sense, I have given a general description of every successful politician who has not simply moved through the ranks.

How Power Is Used

Power can be seen as the most important of the four media of interchange, even though each is analytically and empirically independent. Characteristics of both independence and greater importance pose no problem if one thinks of all resources converting into power (Scott, 1987, 283). An even more fundamental reason for attributing primacy to power is inherent in parties themselves. Regardless of the diversity of goals distinguishing one party from another, or distinguishing one set of actors from another within each party, every genuine political party exists to obtain office (Epstein, 1980, 9). Thus, by definition, a party is an organized entity for seeking power. Power is the motor force of parties and the common coin of relations among party actors. At the same time, if it is so important, why did so many instances of its use lead to equivocal outcomes? To answer, we need to reconsider how different actors are affected by different sources of power.

Among the 12 actors designated as making up the formal authority structure, problems of dependency were more frequent than were those of maintenance-challenge or access-limit. Even the unobtrusive ways we gathered information on power (presumably missing some data) still left dependency as the most prominent issue.[1] This suggests its almost generic quality, because, by definition, "power resides implicitly in the other's dependency" (Emerson, 1962, 32).

The governor had relations with the largest number of actors and was also the one most often involved in challenging relations. The county chairman was engaged in a power grid with eight others, in which issues of access and challenge, as well as dependency, were characteristic of his links. The state senator, state representative, and State Central Committee had power relations with six others, and the congressman with five. In contrast, the senator had power relations with just two others. To interpret these findings, we must confront the meaning of data presence or absence. Does the absence of information about a pair of actors mean that they were not linked by power or that the link was simply not observed? Conversely, does the presence of data mean that the example presented is typical of power use or only a randomly selected instance? My answer is fundamental to the weight I assign to these forms of data as valid evidence — the absence of data probably means the absence of power relations, whereas their presence probably means typical kinds of relations, though without regard to frequency. In other words, the governor typically relates to others in the authority structure by using power. He does not always use it effectively in the sense of achieving his ends, but his efforts at domination appear to require a continuing show of muscle. The senator, on the other hand, despite accounts of how powerful this office is, seemed to have little opportunity or inclination to use power, at least while the office was held by Charles Percy.

Authority is the favored concept when one wishes to convey the sense that power is exercised under constraining norms of legitimacy. The presumption is that a structure will emerge where

a set of dyadic power relations between the superior and each subordinate is transformed by the emergence of legitimacy norms into a multiperson control structure with each subordinate now participating in the control of each of his or her colleagues. Peer group controls are harnessed in the support of the power structure. (Scott, 1987, 286)

1. Of 66 dyads, a conservative estimate omits 6 as logically irrelevant. This leaves dependency the stimulus to power use in nearly half the pairs.

A power structure, in this sense, implies a hierarchy of authority. In the party network, however, there is legitimate authority without hierarchy. The absence of a clear hierarchy, and the concomitant diffusion or decentralization of power, has at least two roots — the origins of power in uncertainty and the limited sanctions available to authoritative actors.

The ability to cope with uncertainty transcends formal office and provides a fuller capacity for using power. By taking into account situations described in previous chapters along with those described here, we find that virtually all actors have been users of power stemming from uncertainty. Information was lacking only for the national committeeman and the House and Senate leadership. Because of the greater fluidity of situations involving uncertainty, I am much less sure that I have captured all typical instances, and the absence of information about these three actors adds to my uneasiness. Even so, it is clear that the uncertainties of electoral and legislative fortunes, and the difficulties they create in sustaining an organizational presence, help to create a large number of bases for the exercise of power. This makes the Illinois Republican Party like other complicated organizations, which are expected to

exhibit more organizational politics than the less complicated ones, for complexity means more or deeper interdependencies and therefore more points of contingency. Similarly, we would expect the organization which is open to the environment at only a few points to contain fewer political positions than the organization facing a heterogeneous environment on a variety of fronts. Thus, in proportion to the total membership of the organization, we would expect the hospital or university to have a wider political base than the army division or the manufacturing division of an industrial firm. (Thompson, 1967, 129)

Because of these multiple power sources, party actors holding positions of authority cannot establish the kind of hegemony that permits a hierarchy to emerge. In some sense, the experience of the Illinois Republican Party may be an exaggerated form of what happens in other party systems. For example, a 1974 study of influences on legislators' voting decisions found that state legislators assigned greatest importance to cues from personal friends and specialists within the legislature, followed by those from interest groups. Legislative party leaders ranked 6th out of 11 possible influences and governors ranked 10th (Uslaner and Weber, 1977, 429–431). Even in Britain there is often internal conflict, because "the two chief claimants to ultimate authority in enunciating party policy are the party in Parliament, and the Annual Conference of a party" (Rose, 1974, 264).

In the final analysis, power rests on the ability to impose fearsome sanctions. Party actors, however, have only relatively mild sanctions at their command, and even the severest of these are not the monopoly of authoritative actors. Under conditions of strict party government, deviants can be threatened with expulsion from the party caucus, a threat generally regarded as serious enough to keep most parliamentarians in line but unavailable in most U.S. situations. In Illinois, the governor can use his power positively, by publicly showing support for other actors. But when he attempts to use sanctions, such as campaigning against legislators, he is likely to fail. He appears to be most effective in using negative sanctions when they are applied in his own sphere of activity, that is, against other statewide candidates or officeholders.

Legislative leaders have similar problems in devising ways of dealing with deviants. As a member of the leadership put it:

Pressure [on rank-and-file legislators] is positive when we assign sponsors for appropriation bills—this looks good. Problem types are pulled off bill sponsorship. The best way to exert pressure is to change someone's office, or get them off a committee. That ticks them off.

But "ticking someone off" is not very likely to bring him into line. And it was made clear to us that harsher alternatives, such as threats of electoral punishment, are inappropriate.

It did not appear that other actors, in an official capacity, could impose any sanctions severer than the withholding of support. This is no trivial threat, but, in fact, a county chairman who says that he will not support a candidate often cannot prevent him from finding other sources of support. Sanctions are always limited where there are alternative resources available. Thus the blocking of information, even by those whose power stems solely from control over uncertainty, is often more potent than the sanctions of those who have only authority behind them.

In all the instances examined, power was essentially a medium of control, limiting links among party actors, exploiting dependency, and either challenging those enjoying stable positions or parrying such challenges. These controlling or restrictive uses of power arise regardless of whether power stems from the formal authority structure or from abilities to deal with uncertainty. In only one case was power used in ways that revealed positive instead of negative possibilities. This occurred when links among actors were enhanced by giving credit to others in the party network for services performed. In general, we can expect the negative side to predominate, so that power is more customarily used to restrict the sharing of credit.

To find ways in which relations among party actors are given positive reinforcement we must look to a different medium of interchange. We find this in chapter 6, where we examine how patronage is used to establish and reward loyalty.

6

Patrons and Patronage

The Nature of Patronage

Patronage serves as a medium of interchange among party actors in fundamentally positive ways, put to use by patrons as an incentive and as a reward. In this respect, it is parallel to Parsons's concept of influence (1967, 363) when it is used to "appeal to a subjective sense of obligation" (1967, 364). And in describing political machines, the historical home of patronage in urban America, Merton emphasizes that "politics is transformed into personal ties. . . . The precinct captain is forever a friend in need" (Merton, 1957, 74). Yet we must be alert to the possibility that, in creating bonds of loyalty, patronage may also become a source of tension whenever the loyalty it evokes is restricted to a patron who does not project it into the larger network.

The positive character of patronage is separate from any negative evaluations made about the effects of patronage on the political system. These include the association, made almost by definition, among patronage, urban political machines, and corruption (Eldersveld, 1982, 149), or the argument that patronage is an inefficient way to recruit workers and provide services, bringing only meager benefits to the party that uses it (Sorauf, 1959, 125). Patronage is frequently recognized as having negative consequences even by party actors most involved with it. As one such informant told us, "a patronage job is one that makes 10 people unhappy and creates one ingrate." Donald Udstuen, the patronage chief under Governor Ogilvie, still complains:

Since leaving government after Ogilvie's defeat in 1972, I can assure you that I can count on one hand the number of people who have come up to me to thank me for what I or Governor Ogilvie might have done on their behalf. This is out of somewhere between twelve and fifteen thousand people who were placed on the payroll during Ogilvie's administration. Yet still to this day, it's rare that I don't go to a political event that someone doesn't come up to me and introduce themselves to remind me about some job they should have gotten, but didn't. (Nowlan, 1982, 57)

146

Without denying the significance of such consequences, we also recognize that the reason patronage persists as a medium of interchange is to promote loyalty.

To the extent that patronage is basically a positive medium, in contrast with power, we would expect it to be used in ways that emphasize the positive side of the three forms of interchange. That is, it should function to establish links among party actors, not to limit them. Similarly, it is anticipated that patronage will help to maintain relations, not to challenge them. In coping with dependency, patronage is expected to create bonds of dominance and subordination.

Why is dominance considered a positive form of link? To begin with, theory and research both attribute centrality to the dominance of the patron. For example, Lemieux's effort at conceptual clarification, made in connection with a comparative analysis of patronage, affirms that the superordinate position of the patron relative to his clients is a key element in defining any patronage system (Lemieux, 1977, 22–27). From the perspective of an empirical examination of how patronage was used to distribute jobs in New Haven, Johnston concludes, "Bosses remain bosses by maintaining an imbalance of obligations in their favor" (Johnston, 1979, 395). If such points still do not establish why dominance should be interpreted positively, it is because we may not have recognized that its opposite is not equality, but something closer to anarchy. This became evident in chapter 5 when considering how power, generated either from the formal authority structure or from organizational uncertainty, was typically associated with conflict when used to cope with dependency because of the lack of clearly established authority or dominance. Dominance, then, is expected to be a positive outcome of the uses of patronage, because it gives order to relations among actors and makes clear their mutual obligations.

In this chapter, I define patrons as any individuals or organizations, within or outside of government, who provide jobs to persons who qualify, at a minimum, because of their partisan affiliation. Patronage, then, includes appointments to public service jobs, boards, agencies, commissions, or the like, whether paid or unpaid, as well as to private-sector jobs. In short, regardless of other qualifications necessary for appointment, attachment to a political party is an irreducible requirement.

My focus is solely on jobs and not on other kinds of favors that might also be regarded as patronage. In arriving at this definition, I have been guided by standard dictionary definitions. For example, *Webster's New World Dictionary* defines patron as "a person, usually a wealthy and influential one, who sponsors and supports some person, activity, etc." Patronage is "the power to appoint to office or grant other favors, especially political ones," or "offices or other favors distributed through this power." I am also in company with Epstein (1980, 104), who agrees that it would be too simple to think of patronage jobs as confined to government, though he may not have exactly the same understanding of private-sector patronage when he includes contracts for business and preferential treatment in licensing. The special favors covered by the concept of "preferment" (Sorauf, 1984, 92–93) also suggest the ambiguous boundaries between a political party and the private sector, but they are not really part of what I mean by patronage, because they generally refer to forms of preferment only marginally like jobs. Probably most important, in ways that I will go on to demonstrate, is the fact that my definition makes manifest those meanings of patrons and patronage that are part of the experience, though not necessarily the vocabulary, of political actors.

The single outstanding characteristic of patronage today is its ambiguity. It might be assumed that, in this study, ambiguity originated in the variety of definitions presented, with my own simply different from those used by political practitioners, as they are from those of some other students of patronage. But although it is true that there are differences in usage, these are not in themselves sources of ambiguity. Rather, these differences are evidence of its presence. This is demonstrated by Wilson in connection with attitudes toward patronage:

The amateur politician's attitude toward patronage is ambiguous — not so much because he openly rejects while secretly coveting the chief reward of the professional, but because the very meaning of patronage is itself ambiguous. Every amateur politician — by definition — rejects outright low-paid governmental jobs which require that little or no time be spent on the ostensible duties of the office but much time on partisan work. These jobs — the "no-show" jobs — are what all the New York reformers would like to see abolished and what the California liberals are happy to find largely absent in their state. On the other hand, almost any amateur would be flattered to be offered the post of Ambassador to France, Secretary of State, or Director of the Budget. In between the low-paying, no-show job with the Department of Public Works and a prestigious cabinet office, there are a larger number of posts which are hard to define as being either "patronage" or "nonpatronage." (Wilson, 1966, 200)

Thus the sources of ambiguity lie in the content of patronage itself: "To the amateur, patronage generally is bad — but which jobs are 'patronage' in the bad sense of the word?" (Wilson, 1966, 201).

I commented on organizational ambiguity in chapter 5 with respect to power-holding and its uses; we will find beliefs and values clouded in ambiguity in chapter 7, and ambiguities associated with campaign contributions in chapter 8. So why construct this chapter around the ambiguities of patronage? It is because patronage confronts those who study it and those who use it with ambiguity of a qualitatively different sort, rooted in conflicting interpretations of its value and even its existence.

Is patronage good or bad? Fish (1904, 156) saw in the spoils system — the instrument for using patronage — a reflection of the "triumph of democracy," while Key (1964, 369) considered patronage necessary for the support of U.S. political parties, and some nostalgia remains for the accomplishments of the political machine and its reliance on patronage (e.g., Lowi, 1968). Opposition to patronage continues as a hallmark of political reform, though Sorauf (1959, 115) wondered whether political scientists had abandoned their moralistic opposition. Yet, not long after publishing this uneasiness, he went on to express another concern, relating the criticism of patronage to the devaluation of politics generally:

An increasingly middle-class American political culture, by looking with disfavor on the rewards of patronage and preference, has accelerated those reform movements which preach their elimination. So also has it demeaned the prestige and status of the patronage job. Similarly, the American political culture discounts the prestige of many elective positions. (Sorauf, 1964, 93)

Whether good or bad, there is general agreement that the amount of government patronage in the United States has fallen sharply (e.g., Sorauf and Beck, 1988, 103–105). Illinois went along with this shift by imposing a state civil service system in 1905. But what was initially covered by that legislation had little impact on the growth of bureaucracy or on the patronage that went with it. The first real step in dealing with the changed character of state government came with the introduction of a new personnel code under Governor Stratton and the establishment of a Department of Personnel in 1957. That change produced a good deal of grumbling from party officeholders, but patronage was probably not seriously diminished:

In many states patronage is still an important source of the governor's influence on party; the received wisdom of the political science profession is that patronage, overall, is a declining factor in American politics, but, like most of the received wisdom, this supposed fact has not been demonstrated. It may be that given the expanded number of state and local employees, and the increasing politicization of the health and welfare sectors of our economy, the trend is toward more rather than fewer patronage jobs. (Hennessy, 1968, 32)

At least until the Thompson administration, Illinois retained the image "as a leading patronage state, with up to 15,000 jobs (about 20 per cent) potentially available" (Crane, 1980, 82). The more recent work of Nowlan, both a political scientist and an insider, suggests that some element of patronage remains widespread: "Patronage considerations affect almost every vacancy that arises among the corps of 70,000 employees who work for the governor" (Nowlan, 1982, 55).

Patronage also exists at the county and municipal levels of administration, and except for the Chicago machine, there is not much known about its operation. For Chicago we have Gosnell's (1937) landmark study, ably supplemented by Rakove (1975). But even now, after important court challenges to the uses of patronage (Elrod v. Burns, 1976; Shakman et al., 1979), there is still uncertainty about how much patronage the Cook County Democratic organization can distribute. According to Richard Simpson, both a colleague and a former alderman, estimates of 20,545 jobs, presented to the court in the depositions supporting Shakman, are probably low. The Shakman decision has not eliminated patronage, but it has introduced new elements of uncertainty with regard to constraints over hiring and firing.

It would have been useful to estimate levels of patronage among our informants and respondents in order to establish a firmer basis for generalizations. The difficulties encountered in trying to do this are probably indicative of why overall patronage figures are so elusive. About a quarter of our informants were found to have held government patronage jobs, either in the past or currently, and perhaps another 10 percent were in private-sector patronage. But even our lengthy interviews were incomplete with respect to job histories and political experience, and we could surmise private-sector patronage only after our analysis had begun, since the possibility that such patronage exists goes virtually unrecognized by party activists. When we discovered that some beneficiaries of paid government patronage also held second, and even third, jobs in the private sector, we became particularly wary of generalizing, since it was only our own persistence that led us to instances of multiple job-holding. For precinct committeemen, we could find no way to uncover patronage-holders within the constraints of a relatively brief telephone interview.

Considerations of this kind, and the premise that patronage is not of great importance to Republicans today, led to data-gathering that gave no direct attention to it. Informants, however, had different concerns and soon communicated them. Among the problems they cited was the advantage that accrued to Chicago Democrats because of their ready access to government patronage, and the inadequacy of the Republican governor's response to the need for dispensing patronage. There were also complaints about the role of trade unions in performing roles as extragovernmental patrons for the Democrats, an advantage unavailable to Republicans. Yet the kinds of jobs some of our informants held, and the frequency with which particular organizations provided employment for party activists, began to suggest that the Republicans had at least analogous patrons. Even while some people told us that party functioning was crippled by the decline in patronage, others said that they had more patronage jobs to offer than they could fill. Patronage was described as a highly desirable resource, one that can never be excessive, but there were also skeptical views expressed, emphasizing the deleterious effects of patronage. My conclusion is that, although patronage is evidently an important issue, party actors operate with competing definitions and explanations.

Of all the media, patronage is the most opaque, and I anticipate that this will result in greater potential for usage by party actors. Information supplied by informants led us to ask: Who are patrons and what constitutes patronage? Ambiguous answers were then related to how patronage is used to establish new network links, maintain existing relations, and create dominance. The findings reported will qualify any expectation of a totally positive usage of patronage, because the loyalty created is differentially applied to network members.

Identifying Patrons

Virtually all actors in the party network can be patrons, either directly, through their control of vacant jobs, or indirectly, through their ability to effect the dispersement of jobs given to them by other patrons. Furthermore, patron roles may go unrecognized. Patrons, then, can be one of four types, depending on the directness with which they control jobs and whether or not they are acknowledged as patrons.

Establishing Links

The primary source of patronage in Illinois, according to our informants, is the governor. As the major patron, he is also the major focus of complaint. Informants perceived Governor Thompson as one who "doesn't believe in patronage." The more charitably inclined described him as coming to appreciate the importance of patronage, but felt that he had gone about its sponsorship and organization slowly and ineffectively. As one committeeman summed it up:

Thompson has tried to develop a patronage organization — I was going to say, very clumsily, but that's too judgmental. The governor went through five personnel directors within the first three years of his office and until the sixth, more effective, appointment. So he's developed an organization for patronage, but he has done it poorly.

As a patron, the governor plays a linking role, reaching out to party actors and tying them to him. For example, before the 1980 state convention, Bob Kjellander, Thompson's "sixth" patronage chief, referred to above, used his vacation to travel through the state and visit about 90 county chairmen. Kjellander's "tour of duty," presumably with the governor's blessing, was interpreted as a gesture signalling a more sympathetic attitude and the promise of additional patronage. More directly, it was also interpreted as a means for ensuring that the county chairmen, in their roles as convention delegates, would remain loyal to the governor in any dispute that arose over the election of national convention delegates, the national committeeman, and changes in bylaws.

The governor's links with county chairmen also involve an acknowledgement that they play indirect patron roles within their own counties. That is, they use the jobs allotted them to ensure a working organization that will, in turn, prove beneficial in electoral campaigns.

Indirect patrons may also be legislators, and they too are important to the governor as he establishes network links. Because legislators may dispense patronage indirectly, that is, by passing it on to their county chairmen, they may continue to be unrecognized as patrons. This was evident on the few occasions when informants mentioned state senators and representatives in connection with patronage and dismissed them as of no consequence. But they remain important. According to one knowledgeable informant, otherwise skeptical about the value of patronage:

Patronage is more valuable for the governor in building legislative support than in building electoral coalitions. [Patronage chief] Bob Kjellander would argue that it's also of value in the electoral game. . . . It is more important to help [legislators like] Bob Winchester or Sam Vinson with jobs, because they will reciprocate. County chairmen can't help unless they get good turnout in primaries; then they are important.

Linking functions can be performed by other party actors, and these in fact fall to constitutional officers when there is no Republican governor. When Secretary of State Alan Dixon, a Democrat, resigned to run for the U.S. Senate in 1980, there was real ambivalence in his own party, and for good reason: with a Republican governor holding the authority to fill the office before a general election, the Democrats stood to lose their most crucial source of statewide jobs. From 1964 to 1968, when William Scott was the highest ranking statewide Republican officeholder, he employed about half of the state central committeemen and an undetermined number of county chairmen on the state payroll. This was interpreted as an effort "to keep the party alive." But a review of the SCC minutes at this time indicates that the state central committeemen saw this more as a way for Scott to build his own following; members complained that he did not inform them of job openings in ways that would allow them to serve as indirect patrons. By playing such roles, they would have had a more overt channel for maintaining relations within the party network. Instead, Scott's virtual monopoly over patronage helped him develop ties that seemed suspiciously like a personal following.

The uses of patronage to establish links operates primarily in aid of the patron. Any unit of the party that benefits does so, in effect, after the patron has obtained what he wants, whether it be support for reelection, legislative approval, or access to information. This pattern is suggested as well in the example of Senator Dirksen:

> The battling over appointments was routine for Dirksen. He had been hustling for patronage appointments for all of his years in Congress, and he had met with more than his share of success. He had even persuaded President Johnson to appoint one of the senior partners of his law firm in Peoria, Robert K. Morgan, to the federal bench. He had placed, or had helped place, friends and allies in many federal agencies, and the persons so located became, in a way, part of the senator's personal network throughout the federal establishment. They were persons on whom he could call, and they provided him with a private apparatus of information and help.
>
> "Golly," he said at one point, "if I didn't know people all over the government, I'd have wasted a third of a century in this city." (MacNeil, 1970, 352)

Patrons use patronage to develop ties with party actors, who then assume the role of clients. This kind of relation is implied when the governor or constitutional officer dispenses patronage to county chairmen, who are then obligated to help him win reelection. But there is also a sense in which links are established among patrons themselves, emphasizing reciprocity among near-equals rather than the obligations of dependents.[1] When county chairmen and state legislators are given access to jobs for patronage purposes, they become indirect patrons, but the indirect aspects of their control over jobs is only analytically interesting. To their clients, it is irrelevant how the patrons acquired their status. For direct patrons, their original clients — now transformed into patrons — are valued because they have mobilized a new chain of clients, obligated to some component of the party network, and presumably available to them as well.

One way in which interchange among patrons takes place is through information and recommendations about jobholders. Employees of private-sector patrons, for example, come to their positions through recommendations by congressmen, legislators, or governors, generally after some service to them. The job history of one prominent private-sector patronage holder indicates his avenue of mobility and the responsibilities he faced. In both respects, his experiences were quite typical.

---

1. This discussion has benefitted from an unpublished manuscript by John Padgett, in which he elaborates the relations between oligarchy and clientage in the Roman Republic.

After the Republican defeat (and the loss of position on Governor Ogilvie's staff), I went to work for the *X* Company. My assignment was like *Y*'s [the current holder of this position]. I handled government relations and public affairs and part of my job was to get involved in the state Senate campaign.

Links among patrons may be established across types of party actors, as I have already described, and also within types. This occurs, for instance, among private-sector patrons, eager to develop ties with others like themselves in order to enhance their access to the party network. One manifestation was observed by a Republican National Committee staff member, perturbed by what he felt to be excessively close ties between business and politics in Illinois.

The corporate world of Chicago is closely nested with the political world. This is true more so than in other states, in terms of the nesting of the political party structure. The Chicago-area Public Affairs Association is mostly concerned with politics. [When I would attend] it was like a meeting of precinct people. For example, *X* and *Y* [two prominent private-sector jobholders who serve as surrogates for their patrons] were right in the heart of the party organization.

Maintaining Relations

Patrons who provide private-sector jobs belong to the party network in their capacity as advisors, financial contributors, and interest groups. When they make patronage appointments, they give employment in corporate departments of government and public affairs, in PACs, and in trade and professional associations. Those appointed — while paid by trade and professional associations, businesses and corporations, and major law firms — actively take part in political campaigns, engage in fundraising, advise on campaign strategy or policy, and recommend the distribution of PAC funds. They may participate either in tandem or as surrogates for their chief executive on the Illinois State House and Senate Campaign committees, along with public and party officeholders; or they may, in effect, perform as unofficially designated party staff. It is for these reasons that I consider private-sector patrons, though they may be unrecognized by other party actors, as serving to maintain relations in the party network, even to the extent of helping sustain the party apparatus.

Indirect patrons need jobs to maintain the local party apparatus and keep a strong base of support. Speaking of an earlier period of Republican politics in Chicago, one committeeman recalled:

When we had precinct captains, it was important to fill election judges' jobs and to do door-to-door selling of the virtues of the party. If the party was not acceptable to the person, then the captain would sell the candidate. Now, however, because our officials are not patronage-oriented, it is much more difficult to get workers. I must use, instead, letters for campaigning rather than canvassing.

A recurring theme in our interviews is the necessity of establishing close and continuous ties in Springfield. Because the center of patronage is in the state capital, those who regularly spend time there have an advantage in learning of patronage opportunities. There are obvious advantages, then, to county chairmen who have jobs in Springfield or to legislators who want to have jobs at their disposal. Next best is to have someone from the local party organization who can travel to Springfield regularly or who at least has easy telephone access to the governor's office or to departments. In all cases, regularity of contact was deemed essential. For those seeking patronage, the ability to offer electoral support and dedicated party workers where it appears to matter and — perhaps most important — to provide legislative or organizational support is what counts. An active role in such bodies as the County Chairmen's Association or evidence of some following in the legislature is apt to increase the possibility of achieving positive results from a patronage search concentrated on the governor's office. Some indirect patrons so actively pursue jobs that they deserve to be called patronage masters.

Legislators who are also county chairmen are more likely to assume the role of patron. The most common sequence is for participation in the county organization to stimulate an individual's concern for patronage, and when he then becomes a new legislator, he arrives in Springfield with an existing set of priorities. But I also found instances where a legislator, already conscious of his patron role, then sought to consolidate his ability to dispense patronage by running for the county chairman's office. Because several counties make up a single legislative district in the less densely populated parts of the state, a representative who is also a county chairman becomes at least first among equals in his relations with other county chairmen in his district.

Among those held up as patronage masters were legislators who had an agenda for their districts that included the establishment of state facilities and the improvement or creation of state-supported public goods. These become resources for providing regular employment to workers who reciprocate with their campaign efforts. Such resources also provide opportunities for local merchants and businessmen, whose campaign contributions are money and prestige. Adoption of such patronage-master roles involves conscious stratagems, openly expressed by one legislator as: "I am a patronage legislator." He meant by this that he kept close ties with the governor's office and with departments to ensure that his information about job opportunities was always sound, and he also lobbied for permanent facilities or other projects that would provide a continuing source of jobs in his own district.

Successful efforts by masters mean building the equivalent of fiefdoms, whose maintenance requires sustained attention. Nowlan, a former member of the state House, remembers the behavior of C. L. McCormick, "an almost legendary 'patronage haw,' a politico who can whiff the scent of a patronage job in his territory the second it becomes vacant" (1982, 55). McCormick represented a downstate district whose economy was closely tied to the availability of state jobs:

I noticed that at least once each week C. L. would excuse himself during a lull in our afternoon legislative session to go down to the governor's office. Following each trip, he would return with a smile and note the newest patronage plum he had garnered: it might be a "weights and measures" inspector with Agriculture or a beauty shop investigator with Registration and Education. (Nowlan, 1982, 55)

Such an aggressive approach to the addition of state jobs can extend to state facilities, and those who have mastered the process have been undeterred by the encroachment of the Shakman ruling limiting patronage appointments. Other legislative responsibilities are often subsumed or made secondary to ensuring success in maintaining a fiefdom. During the last legislative session covered by this study, one legislative patron described how he was putting all his energy on acquiring a new state facility, even calling on his congressman for help in finding data with which to contest decisions made by the state bureaucracy. Ultimately, he said, "I am helped by my position in Springfield and my seniority."

The congressman and the U.S. senator constitute another category of unrecognized patron. Earlier I noted some inclination on the part of our informants to dismiss congressmen as not central to state party organization just because they had no patronage available. In addition, complaints about lack of senatorial patronage could have been related to life under the Carter presidency, when most of our interviews were done. Yet both congressmen and their counterparts in the state legislature described locally based projects that required federal action and consequently placed congressmen in the position of patron. But if acquiring contracts to build or repair dams and bridges, establish an Amtrak stop, or otherwise aid local businessmen is the substance from which patronage flows, these activities may more often be interpreted as services to the community, and may not, in fact, represent a large number of jobs. It is true that, compared with congressmen in other states, the ability of Illinoisans to locate large-scale federal installations in their districts has been modest. But I suspect that the more likely reason for the lack of identification of congressmen as patrons is the result of prevailing role definitions that emphasize the provision of services rather than the creation of employment opportunities, though the two may overlap. To the extent that patronage exists, even when unrecognized, it has a maintaining role. If it were used to establish independent links, then I would have expected to hear complaints like those in Olson's 1965–66 study, in which patronage was a frequently contentious issue between congressmen and their district party leaders (Olson, 1978, 252).

Dominance

For a patron to be dominant, he must be certain that he can rely on his clients for help; he wants and expects their personal loyalty. This puts a governor in a peculiarly difficult situation: he controls the bulk of patronage in the state, yet he cannot use it without arousing antagonism from other patrons, especially indirect ones dependent on his largesse for their own patronage resources. The result, as one informant put it, is that "Republican governors have always been accused of using patronage to their own benefit rather than to build the party."

Benign interpretations of frequently heard complaints about Governor Thompson recognized that times have changed and resources have become more limited while demands have remained insatiable. One such interpretation was:

There are a lot of complaints about Thompson for not paying enough attention to the party, for not helping with the organization. This may mean that he doesn't give complainers enough jobs. I don't know how unique he is in that regard. Ones who have been around in the Stratton administration speak of him as the model. But in Ogilvie's time, people complained about his "whizz kids," those around him who weren't party old-timers.

Less benign interpretations accused the governor and Attorney General Scott of shortsighted neglect of party interests:

Let's contrast Lou Kasper [Chicago ward committeeman and city chairman of the Cook County Central Committee] and Governor Thompson. Kasper is an old-timer, a part of the patronage system. Thompson is for himself only. This contrast personifies the party today. One represents too much party; the other, too much self-interest. I would also include Bill Scott with the governor [as self-interested].

Such critical informants do not accept arguments about changing times and continue to see meaningful contrasts among the last three Republican governors. In the words of one local committeeman:

Stratton favored the party in his appointments, Ogilvie was second, and Thompson is third. Thompson is not as strong a party person. The party has suffered as a result. He is not building up the party. . . . he brings in people from out of state, instead of hiring in Illinois. Half the department directors are Democrats. The county chairmen resent that.

Yet making county chairmen angry is exactly what a governor has to do, at least some of the time, if he wants to demonstrate his dominance. This is because dominance is not just a matter of relations with subordinate clients but also with rival patrons (Lemieux, 1976, 22). County chairmen cannot be ignored in this regard simply because they are not patrons on their own. For one thing, they can get some patronage from other sources. But more important, once chairmen acquire resources, they can use them almost at will, and this may entail building their own machines. It is then that county chairmen, or similar indirect patrons, become serious rivals to the governor. The dilemmas in control that are then created are well captured by Sorauf:

. . . only one organ of the party is apt to gain from any one specific political appointment. And it is a matter of vital concern in understanding the effects of patronage to know just which party organ or leader, on what level of the party structure, reaps the reward. Patronage, therefore, by bolstering local centers of power and entrenching the political lords in their local fiefs, by preventing unity on candidates and policy, may be used as a weapon in intra-party squabbles just as easily as it may be used to create intra-party cohesion or vitality. (Sorauf, 1959, 123)

The governor's rivals can include constitutional officers, especially when they, as in the case of Attorney General Scott, have their own legislative agenda and their own patronage-oriented clients. Within the legislature, rivals are also the legislative leaders of his party. Relations between the governor and legislative leaders were discussed in chapter 5 as instances of dependency associated with the structure of authority, but these relations are also part of patronage interchanges, in which the legislative leaders, as patrons, control a number of critically placed jobs.

Dominance of the governor is extended through the activities of an effective patronage chief, who maintains constant liaison with the departments that are the source of jobs, both for budgetary control and to ensure that the governor's programs are carried out. These two goals can be accomplished by having, within major departments and separate from their directors, a "key man" with final say over personnel decisions:

The key man is usually an administrative assistant to the director and is not assigned to the agency personnel office. He or she serves as liaison to the patronage director, monitors personnel actions, relays vacancy information, and represents patronage interests within the agency. The patronage director maintains lists of prospects, their sponsorship, backgrounds, and the geographic areas in which they are willing to work. The key men provide weekly updates on anticipated vacancies and new job classifications. (Nowlan, 1982, 57)

Surprisingly, this kind of arrangement is not always recognized as tied to the patronage system. For example, its operation under Governor Ogilvie was described to us by a member of that administration as separate from the mechanisms for putting the governor's appointees into civil service positions:

Patronage was a minor part of our political job. Our patronage officer was very effective. There was minimum interference from patronage considerations in the operation of the agencies. [We] brought a lot of good people into government. It was then our idea, after work in the Bureau of the Budget, to feed them into various agencies. We then created new positions for them, in which they served as management people. Their first loyalty was to the Ogilvie administration.

That jobs for those whose "first loyalty was to the Ogilvie administration" were not considered patronage is still another indication of the ambiguity to which I have referred. Without the strong traditions of a neutral civil service, epitomized by Max Weber's prototype of the Prussian bureaucracy, dominance is more likely where all jobholders are assumed to have a partisan taint, and are treated accordingly. So Governor Ogilvie's patronage chief could say:

People often ask if it bothered me that I was involved in firing some twelve-to-fifteen thousand people from their jobs. I can honestly say it never did, for two reasons. First of all, virtually all the people I had a hand in firing, whether they were in exempt jobs or in the Personnel Code, were people who got their jobs through politics in the first place. Now, over the years they may have tried to "professionalize" themselves by getting under the code; but in effect they were political people, and we were replacing them with political people. I think the old adage that "if you live by the sword you die by the sword" fits in very well here. (Nowlan, 1982, 57)

The dominance of private-sector patrons would seem to be unimpeded by considerations of accountability that affect public officeholders. By hiring people with previous connections to government, private patrons may hope to gain financial advantage. "Leading political figures can make money by taking advantage of business opportunities through inside information, or from business given to them by government favoritism or a desire on the part of customers to be well rewarded by the party organization" (Wolfinger, 1974, 95). But this is probably not the most significant factor in the creation of private-sector patrons. The desire to express a particular philosophy of government, to make the Republican Party more "business-like," to encourage particular candidates, and to influence specific policies were, in our experience, more prominent. Private-sector patrons who hire those active in election campaigns, College Young Republicans, or ideological groups like Young Americans for Freedom or the Committee to Elect a Free Congress, do so to reflect their own ideological predispositions more than because they expect any immediate advantage from these partisan connections.

Private-sector patrons have the advantage, then, of hiring whom they wish without regard to the interests of indirect patrons or other clients. So Clement Stone could appoint Dwight Chapin, convicted for offences associated with the Watergate breakin, as editor of his in-house journal; or he could appoint William Scott after the former attorney general had served his jail sentence but before he could practice law again (Simon, 1982). But one general constraint that inhibits private-sector patrons is the small number of positions they can offer as their equivalent of patronage. Even the most avidly Republican chief executives or senior partners will not be likely to hire only Republicans. For example, when former vice president Walter Mondale was looking for a law firm to join, the firm of Winston and Strawn, well-known for its Republican leanings, hired him for its Washington office. Because business exists for profit, no firm is likely to have more than a few people, at any one time, working on campaigns instead of attending to the enterprise.

Forms of Patronage

Patronage ranges from low-paid and unskilled government jobs; through appointments to high-status positions, whether paid or unpaid; to jobs in the private sector. And as is the case with patrons, some of these jobs go unrecognized as forms of patronage. As I go on to demonstrate, there is some tendency for particular kinds of patronage to be associated with specific uses in the interchange among actors.

Establishing Links

Using patronage to establish links means reaching out to attract new support or to intensify otherwise lukewarm support. Most of the patronage used in this way, as far as we could determine, is provided through government jobs and hence is also in the category of recognized resources. Workers so employed function to ensure the electoral victory of the party, a view supported by an informant active in all election levels, and not only in Cook County:

The absence of patronage hurts the Republican Party. If you accept that the Democratic Party controls approximately 45,000 patronage jobs, and that each patronage job is worth approximately 10 votes, the Democratic Party has about 45 percent of the vote in the bag, assuming it takes a million votes to win in Cook County. The Republican Party starts out with only about 30 percent of the vote guaranteed through patronage; it's hard to compete against those odds. If the patronage was equal, or if there was no Democratic patronage, then things would be different. As it is, Cook County has become a one-party county in the last 10 years. The Republican Party is made weaker in the county because of its lack of public offices [as sources of patronage].

A downstate legislator, complaining about the governor's hiring policies, felt that patronage is essential for motivating workers at the local level: "We need to get people to work for us down in the precincts. We need to reward people with jobs, even summer jobs." In Cook County, the complaint was, "I cannot get workers without some patronage jobs to help them want to work for the party."

Some lower-level party officeholders, however, felt that the absence of patronage is salutory, even if not totally desirable. They felt it creates a distinctive environment for party action, with more emphasis on candidates, ideology, and a greater commitment to participation. Under this system, work is done for the party with greater enthusiasm. According to a local committeeman:

The party is generally loosely composed of volunteers. Its strength is built on individual loyalty. The Republican Party has patronage jobs, but jobholders are not required to get the vote out to retain their jobs. The Republican Party is then better able to come up with new ideas. It isn't trapped by old ideas because there is no worry about losing a [support] base if jobs are eliminated.

Such officeholders were spared the apparent indignities experienced by a former county chairman:

The [patronage] jobs that are available are those that are not filled within the state organization. That means they are generally at the entry level, or they are jobs without any succession — they're dead end. But a lot of people think there are jobs available. So I was besieged by job seekers. They would get insulted and irate if I told them there was nothing. They would call constantly, night and day, even three in the morning. Then when occasionally the governor's office called with a good job, you could give it to only one person. The whole thing is thoroughly unpleasant and counterproductive.

Another manifestation of how patronage is used to establish links is exemplified in the activities of patronage master C. L. McCormick:

When the Vienna Correctional Center opened in 1969, there was a patronage payroll spot for a chaplain at $1,000 a month. Since the center was in Johnson County where C. L. was county chairman as well as local legislator, I called him to see who he would recommend for the position.

C. L.'s first comments were that he already knew it was vacant and that we had to deal with this situation carefully. If he picked *one* of his preachers and gave him a $1,000-a-month job, that would make all the other preachers mad and probably create problems for the preacher with his own flock.

Therefore, C. L. came up with a unique solution that solved everyone's problem. Instead of having one chaplain, we ended up with four. The salary was split four ways. That way we could appoint Baptist, Methodist, and Lutheran ministers, and a Catholic priest. Each complemented his meager salary at his home church, four denominations could be represented instead of one, and old C. L. made four preachers and their parishioners happy. (Nowlan, 1982, 55)

One form of unrecognized patronage is the result of changes in party emphasis from direct contact with voters to contact through the electronic media, relying on experts in campaign management, fundraising, and public-opinion polling. Some of these technical experts have been incorporated into the party apparatus as full-time employees. But because most of them are needed only some of the time, tied to the periodicity of elections, it is common for parties and individual candidates to hire specialists when they are needed. When party or public officeholders, or employees of the Republican Party at the state or national level, told us whom they hired, or when we asked extraparty experts for whom they worked, it became clear that services were available on a partisan basis. It is certainly possible for professional fundraisers, advisors, or pollsters to work for candidates of both parties, but it is more usual for them to emphasize their partisan connection. Purchase of needed services is a new form of patronage, guaranteed by the partisan dependability of the specialists. Yet because this exists as unrecognized patronage, to whom is loyalty owed? That is, does a designated polling organization or media placement agency form bonds with particular party functionaries — its counterpart within the party apparatus — or with the candidates it was hired to help?

A governor needs a nucleus of people to help him develop his program, take over departments, communicate with legislators and other interest groups, and ensure his reelection. To these ends, patronage, in all its forms, is an important linking mechanism. In contrasting Governors Stratton and Thompson as party representatives carrying out such activities, Governor Thompson is perceived to be weaker. Typical of this view are the words of one legislative informant:

Some people feel there should be a flow of patronage, yet I don't think this is true now. A lot of people don't even want the jobs if they are available. At the higher levels, they don't pay enough. A lot don't want to be in the public eye. But there are other kinds of complaints. Some people feel they should have jobs for which they're not qualified. Governor Thompson came in from scratch. He had not built up a core of good people that he could draw on, that are loyal, that he can have confidence in. Governor Stratton wasn't like that — he had people, he was ready to go.

Governor Ogilvie was frequently held up as a model of the efficient creator of a dedicated staff. Yet his ability to establish links with a staff did not prevent his being a one-term governor. According to a former staff member and current advisor:

In Sangamon County [the seat of the state capital], no Governor seeking reelection has carried it since 1944. But Ogilvie carried Sangamon in 1972. We had the patronage, the apparatus with us, and a strong citizens group. . . . The defeat of an incumbent governor says something about patronage, but I don't really know what.

Maintaining Relations

It would appear preferable that, as an economic stimulus, "patronage . . . be used as an *incentive* to extract more work, rather than as a *reward* to compensate for past attainments" (Wilson, 1961, 376–377). Our informants differentiated between the two uses of patronage and recognized the value of patronage as an incentive for establishing links. But for purposes of maintaining relations, patronage was seen by them as more effective when used as a reward. According to another of our patronage masters, positively gleeful about the number of jobs he could dispense, "Patronage is what makes the party strong." To a Cook County legislator, asked about weaknesses in the party, it was all in "the way the party operates: They do not take care of the people who elect them. They do not care about their workers — their precinct captains. Elected party officials give jobs to the families of their large contributors, not to their party workers." This complaint speaks to a dilemma generally faced by a party when considering how to regulate and control those on whom it depends to carry out its goals: Who should be rewarded, workers or contributors (Sorauf, 1964, 89)? If it were to be the former, the Republican Party would have a "built-in army of workers, like the unions" in relation to the Democratic Party.

Patronage jobs in government — and they can be low-level ones — are important for maintaining relations among the rank and file of party activists. The relative frequency with which they are used in this way is problematic, however, because of both the decline in the numbers of such jobs and the questionable value attributed to patronage-selected party workers who, under the constraints of the Shakman et al. (1979) decision, need not fear loss of their jobs if they do not help the party. A county chairman with a strong organization expressed the ambivalence patronage arouses:

How much patronage is there? Very little. We are offered a lot of patronage jobs from the state, such as state highway worker, and also at the township level. We don't have people to fill them. I can't ask a professional to go shovel snow. We do have a lot of housewives who work over at the county complex. One woman worked for X for 10 years and then refused to hand out campaign literature at the railroad station with me.

Boss Plunkitt epitomized the view that patronage is essential to reward activities on behalf of the party: "You can't keep an organization together without patronage. . . . Men ain't in politics for nothin'. They want to get somethin' out of it" (Riordan, 1948, 51). This idea is still widely shared in Illinois, especially among those who have the task of recruiting and motivating party workers, as one old hand commented:

Now the committeeman is a sort of eunuch. He has no clout and no patronage to dispense. So why should anyone want to be a committeeman? . . . The old system was good. I don't like freezing people into jobs. The old system worked better by turning people out with the government. Now we have a situation where incumbents are entrenched.

These proponents of patronage see it as a more equitable system, rewarding those who support the victorious party and ensuring the removal of uncooperative opponents. Instead of a merit civil service providing a skilled and efficient work force, they believe that jobs are really better done under patronage. The government gets "good value" with patronage, because it is both economical and efficient. An influential committeeman gave the following analysis:

The destruction of patronage has had definite fiscal impact. This is because a new governor or president can't fire people, so he needs to layer in another group of people. This increases the inefficiency and cost of government. I feel that, with public scrutiny, we could go back to patronage. Now productivity is low because people have job security. This costs money.

Another important maintaining function of patronage can be support of potential candidates for public office, giving them a protected position where they wait for the most auspicious time to run. Relatively high-level, well-paid government jobs are appropriate for this purpose. Yet the sense of our informants was that Republicans did not do enough to foster the candidacy of good people. According to one critical committeeman:

Republicans don't help young men with political aspirations the way Democrats do. If an ambitious young Democrat loses, the party can look after him with a patronage job, and keep him politically active. When the same thing happens to us, Republicans say, "Isn't it too bad that *X* was defeated?" – but then he's on his own.

We were told that some of this kind of placement, described as warehousing, does occur: "Bill Scott was known to warehouse Republicans – those who are getting ready to run or who have been defeated. He makes a place for them." The most famous candidate helped in this way was Governor Thompson, originally hired by Attorney General Scott in 1969 as chief of the Department of Law Enforcement and Public Protection.

Private-sector patronage, closed to the scrutiny of jealous party actors or censorious reformers, might appear to be ideal for maintaining relations with potential candidates, but it is not clear from our information that it helped more than a few officeholders. According to a jobholder in an organization that we identified as a patron, and who participated in a number of time-consuming party offices and activities, the fault lies in the insensitivity of Republican businessmen:

People who support Republican Party principles don't understand the need to work at politics. . . . If an employee desires to run for public office, he should not be penalized; there should be no loss of seniority or other benefits within the corporation. This need is especially true [for those wanting to run] for state offices. This arrangement would be analogous to our having "labor statesmen."

Dominance

Patronage acts to develop dominance when it is used to create an orderly environment in which mutual obligations between patrons and clients are clearly defined. This happens most readily when there are large numbers of public-sector jobs under partisan control, as was recognized by those party actors who argued that patronage makes for a more responsive public service. It is hardly a surprising view for former patronage chief Don Udstuen:

You need to change people throughout any agency on a regular basis in order to have it be responsive. How often have we heard the old saying in politics "it doesn't matter who you elect, everything stays the same." That's because it's very difficult under the code to change the day-to-day managers. There's nothing wrong with shaking up the bureaucracy every four or eight years, whenever a new governor comes in, and turning over some new faces. It's healthy for the people and the taxpayers. (Nowlan, 1982, 57)

Such responsiveness was seen by an advisor who had been in the Ogilvie administration as an aid in developing more cohesive political parties, linking party platforms and governmental programs:

[Now] I'm pessimistic about the possibilities of change in our system toward one of stronger parties. I see flexibility, and flexibility may not mean patronage. Lots of people don't want the guff of patronage, but patronage is an important means for ensuring responsiveness for carrying out the policies of a new government. You have to be able to fire the old crew and hire your own people. . . . In this state government, it's partly a problem that Thompson has abdicated and partly the result of the Shakman decision. Thompson woke up to the need to take control two years after coming to Springfield, but it's probably too late. Ogilvie went into state government with a team of 75–80 — they had been with us in Cook County. . . . Our institution of the Bureau of the Budget helped too. We then had two

ways of ensuring that policies were carried out – through having our people in charge
and around, and through budget supervision.

An active local party officeholder implied that patronage-inspired responsiveness would lead, as well, to philosophical coherence:

I personally would prefer that there be more jobs. When the term "patronage" is
employed, it's an emotional term. The purpose of the movements heretofore had
been to eliminate patronage, but they were intended to eliminate patronage from
the other group. Until the Republicans and Democrats get together, not in the sense
of political platforms, but in the structure of government, the country will continue to head down a shadowy road. I would strongly encourage our republican
system to use more of the patronage system. I don't think that the patronage system is sufficiently implemented. The courts and judges don't answer to anybody
now. Whoever owns the judges intellectually, runs the country.

The dominance created by patronage is also well understood by those
who avoid involvement with it, as an influential county chairman demonstrated: "I've never been on the state payroll, and I refuse to take a patronage job. I'm retired now but I've made my money through my work in
building up my business. I've never taken money from the government . . .
never in my political career have I used my position to get a payroll job."
When he went on to say how much he would have liked to run for public
office, but could never afford to because it would have meant being away
from his business, we asked, "And yet you've refused patronage?" He replied: "Honestly, I would have loved getting the money, but then I would
have been beholden to my benefactor. That's not for me. I'm no rebel or
revolutionary; I just couldn't stand being beholden to someone else. Patronage will do that."

The potential for widespread patronage no longer exists, its decline accelerated by an increasingly well-educated population and a technically ad-
vanced economy. The lack of job skills required in the typically low-level
government patronage job and the often poor opportunities for advancement make such jobs "unsatisfying for the more educated party members,"
and for others, an insufficient inducement to contribute to party activities.
Patronage jobs in the private sector have their own contraints. Rakove told
us that, in 1938, when he wanted to apply for a job with Sears, he was
refused an application form until he produced a letter from his alderman;
he came to suspect that the need for political endorsements across a whole
range of jobs may have been prevalent at least until the 1970s (Rakove,
1975, 112–113). Today, however, patronage job opportunities in the private
sector are quite limited, again because of the increased demand for technical qualifications. Opportunities for dominance through patronage are then
more likely to occur when they exist as a kind of "organizational slack" –

unused resources that can be drawn on to increase efficiency and competitive advantage (March and Simon, 1958, 126).

Although slack, in the form of patronage, may not be great, it is especially important when associated with high-status appointments, including unsalaried ones. For example, at the federal level, as patronage jobs have decreased, there has been an increase in "political non-jobs," honorary appointments high in prestige (Sorauf and Beck, 1988, 105–106). Within the state, there are about 2,000 possible appointments to boards and commissions which, properly distributed, can influence the community from which appointees come, and thus help in raising funds for the party. It is in this context that the governor as patron has principal, if not sole, authority. But here, as well, Governor Thompson is perceived not to have made the best use of his patronage capabilities. One patronage-holder in the private sector, closely tied to party operations, observed: "The governor is slow in doing some things. He seems reluctant to fill a lot of positions. There are about 200 commission and agency positions to be filled." A committeeman attributed this slowness to

the lack of recognition of the importance of the patronage system, for example, that there are a lot of appointments to boards. These are given to Democrats. This doesn't give recognition to capable people in the Republican Party. Newspapers are at fault—they imply that because a person is a Republican, and he is appointed by a Republican, he's not capable, that his job is given as a pay-off.

Although this committeeman interpreted the lack of recognition in several quite different ways, his complaint is relevant to us in confirming the incomplete recognition of the patronage potential in high-level appointments, honorific or not.

When high-level appointments are used as patronage, they foster dominance for the patron who dispenses them and for the segment of the party network involved. The meaning of patronage as a medium of interchange derives from creation of mutual loyalties and obligations which extend beyond a single patron and his client. As we implied when discussing indirect patrons, patronage is used effectively when its beneficiaries are able to extend the chains of relations in the party network. For low-level jobs, this may translate into a designated number of votes in a precinct, gained through the obligation of the jobholder to help in election campaigns. For high-level appointees, like Wilson's amateur politician pleased to be named ambassador, the chains are expected to draw in large contributors or organized interests to whom the party wants to appeal. Yet there is no obvious quid pro quo. The recipient of symbolic patronage does not appear to be a client with clear obligations, but someone whose loyalty is freely given, according to the perceptions of an appreciative county chairman:

Whom do I admire in the party? Harold Byron Smith, the national committeeman and ITW [Illinois Tool Works] chairman. Also several of his counterparts. They are people who have little to benefit them from party work, but they are working hard for free enterprise. They give their time and money—they are the voluntary structure out there. Clem Stone is one of those. He doesn't have to do it. There are thousands of Clem Stones all over the state. The people who give the most ask the least.

Although neither Smith nor Stone necessarily held symbolic patronage positions during the time of this study, the views expressed about them exemplify how such people are perceived. Unlike a lowly precinct worker, their motives are not impugned, nor, by extension, are their patrons criticized for attempting to build a personal following. Instead, both they and the patrons who reward them are enveloped in an aura of selfless loyalty to the party. In this respect, the suspicions voiced by a state convention delegate seemed atypical, even to him: "I objected to the choice of Clement Stone as an at-large national convention delegate. One person shouldn't have that much influence. Most of the committee disagreed. People felt that he had helped them, had provided opportunities, and had helped the party."

The Ambiguity of Patronage

The wide range of Republican patrons and patronage, the imprecise ways they are identified, and the competing evaluations they evoke all justify treatment of patronage in terms of ambiguity. Because ambiguity over goals, understanding, history, and membership is present in other kinds of organizations (March and Olsen, 1976, 12), we have some guidance in interpreting the manifold ways in which patronage is used as a medium of interchange.

The persuasive qualities of patronage can be used to enhance the controlling impact of power, so that party goals can be more easily defined by those in leadership positions. But though party actors agreed that patronage *can* be used in this way, there was considerable disagreement over whether it should be so used and, if it is, for the maintenance of which leaders. For example, some legislators insulate themselves from patronage demands by defining their goals to be initiation and furtherance of legislation, whether in the interests of the state, particular groups, or their own districts. Their leadership is maintained through the rejection of patronage, where others in the district, generally county chairmen, take on patron roles and look after legislators by attempting to translate patronage into votes.

Statewide officeholders who choose to follow the model of legislators who abjure patronage soon find themselves in trouble. Not only must they accept the need for patronage, but they must also establish criteria for relating to others in ways that give precedence to their own goals: protecting their leadership, bargaining with others to support their programmatic objectives, and encouraging electoral support.

For local-level party leaders, the rationale for demanding patronage is to attract workers for the party who then are instrumental in getting out the vote. Electoral goals are emphasized as more important (and respectable) than building up an organizational apparatus. For patrons with government jobs to dispense, allocation should be in ways that maximize support from voters (Wilson, 1961, 373–374). Patronage is most useful when it goes to marginal, or swing, districts, where it can serve as an incentive to both workers and voters. However, the bargaining power of party leaders in such districts may be weaker than that found in traditionally Republican areas. Patronage then is offered as a continuing reward for past performance.

Demands can be strong and effective even in weakly Republican areas, because local leaders have established some independent power in the state party organization or the legislature. Patronage in such cases is used to sustain the local organization and enhance the status of the local leadership. Competing goals then make for flexibility in distributing patronage but leave unresolved the incompatibility among contending leaders, some of whom inevitably feel that their treatment has been unfair and whose loyalty is thereby diminished.

Private-sector patrons have special advantages because they need not account for how they use patronage. They can, in effect, use it solely to enhance their own claims to party leadership. But for the very reason that the patronage they offer is outside of party control, they are still dependent on some access to both the party apparatus and the party in government. Their efforts to link patronage with personal ambition or ideological goals may flounder just at this point, where competitors more solidly within the structure emphasize the need to sustain the party through working for existing goals.

As March and Olsen point out, "It is hard to see the connections between organizational actions and their consequences" (1976, 12). Ambiguity then arises over understanding events and explaining causal relations. I was struck, for example, by the understanding, expressed by a ward committeeman, of the differential advantage enjoyed by the Democratic Party in Chicago: "The Republican Party has a hard uphill fight in Chicago. We are facing a patronage army of 100,000. That includes policemen, firemen, teachers, and all city workers. It's fighting an army with a small band of volunteers." Whenever Democratic victories are attributed, as this committeeman did, to Democrats' access to almost unlimited patronage, affected Republican leaders are going to make great demands for patronage themselves, remain largely unsatisfied, and attribute their own lack of success in attracting workers or voters to forces beyond them (Rakove, 1975, 163–190). This creates a form of inflexibility, in which party actors protect their meager resources and discourage any change. Key described an analogous situation in the South, where Republicans deliberately kept their organization weak and support from voters limited in order to protect their own claim to whatever limited patronage was available (Key, 1949, 292–294).

Ambiguity also emerged in explanations of how Democrats foster political ambitions among likely candidates compared with what is done by Republicans. The conception that potential Democratic candidates may be nurtured in patronage appointments, and that trade unions, by serving as patrons, provide another niche for them, goes along with the view that Republicans have virtually no such havens. The lack of recognition given to private-sector patrons and the patronage they offer suggests that party leaders are not consciously using these sources for fostering candidate recruitment. There was even some suggestion in our interviews that, if candidates were to come out of such private-sector positions, they would be faced with prejudice for not having done their apprenticeship directly in party roles.

Ambiguity about an organization's history occurs because past experiences and events are treated selectively in determining what is relevant to contemporary experience. History is a way of conceptualizing how organizations learn from experience (March and Olsen, 1976, 54), but it is also a source of myths and illusions (March and Olsen, 1976, 59). Nowhere is the ambiguity more prominent than in regard to assessments of the last three Republican governors. Interpretations of history suggest that William Stratton was the governor most responsive to the need for patronage and James Thompson the least. Whether or not these are valid interpretations, they constitute a shared myth that the past was better than the present. Myths that reinvent history can do this in ways that encourage group solidarity and lead to the emergence of a shared ideology. My examples, however, suggest that those who place their emphasis solely on the advantages of the past help create an environment that devalues innovation and the contributions of new participants.

Why should the past seem so desirable in retrospect? One answer is tied, no doubt, to the real decline in patronage. But other reasons, probably more germane, have little to do with patronage itself and more with the route to the governorship; the extent to which that route has been embedded in the party network's core, including a reliance on the party apparatus;

and subsequent relations with all segments of the party. Of the three governors, Stratton's career was most closely tied to the party (Ranney, 1960, 30–32) and Thompson's least. Accounts of the history of patronage, then, symbolize the consequences of different career lines and the intraparty relations these engender. Governor Thompson's personal history in the party has created disadvantages for him that have then encouraged beliefs about his comparative inadequacies as a patron.

Ambiguity associated with what March and Olsen term organization, meaning organizational participants and patterns of participation (March and Olsen, 1976, 94), surrounds the identity of patrons. We have seen how ambiguity operates to focus attention, and in some instances hostility, on the governor and away from other patrons, including legislators, congressmen, and even county officeholders. With less attention, these other patrons can play a low-key role with respect to patronage and offer it to a less critical clientele. In general, lack of recognition of who patrons are means that some of those with their own patronage resources, whether in government or the private sector, have a period of freedom to consolidate their power and emerge as claimants to a major leadership role. Such ambiguity can be especially beneficial to private-sector patrons who build up a reputation for political astuteness and a following without the constraints felt by those who seek elected office.

Membership ambiguity also enters when questions are raised about who is most deserving of inclusion in the party network and, consequently, who should be rewarded with patronage (Sorauf, 1964, 89). This is part of a pervasive tension between pragmatism and principle, and its articulation is often tied to position in the party network. For example, among self-reported motives for participation by activists in Wayne County, Michigan, "volunteerism" was most frequent at the upper levels of the party apparatus, whereas "self interest" predominated among the lower levels (Eldersveld, 1964, 273–276). This contrast was evident in the tone of a congressional aide who deplored the ineffectiveness of the county organizations within his district:

I blame it on the patronage system. Party officials don't represent anything other than job seekers. For example, in one of our counties, over half of the committeemen are public jobholders. I thought we were getting to the point where party people were more issue-oriented, but it just isn't so.

Patronage, then, not only is the means for linking actors and maintaining relations but also, like power, has the potential to limit and challenge membership in the party network.

The crowning ambiguity lies in the imperfect recognition given to patronage as a means of creating mutually reinforcing obligations. The nega-

tive implications of the patron-client interchange were captured by Samuel
Johnson, nursing his own grievances, in his definition of a patron as "commonly a wretch who supports with insolence, and is paid with flattery"
(McAdam and Milne, 1963, 285). It is this resentment aroused by patrons
and patronage that paradoxically also helps explain some of the tenacity
of patronage and its capacity to take on new manifestations as honorary
appointments and private-sector jobs when older forms of patronage dis-
appear. It is because of the personal obligations inherent in patronage relationships that patron surrogates and their trusted lieutenants are able to
emerge. Mutual dependence and trust are possible across all kinds of positions, from unskilled workers tied to those who they are convinced are the
only source of jobs, to highly skilled workers eager to be close to the center of power. These may sound like quasi-feudal relationships, but such
feudal elements have not totally disappeared in modern societies generally
any more than they have in political parties. The need for personal loyalty
and loyalty to principle never disappears, and parties continue to need them
as much as ever. Patronage remains a means for creating bonds to build
up the personal and organizational capital that is one of the ingredients
for sustaining a party network.

7

Republican Ideology

Conservatism Rampant

Values are conceptions of the desirable (Kluckhohn, 1951) used in organizations as criteria for selecting goals (Scott, 1987, 15). The value-laden character of goals symbolically defines the organization and provides a focus for the identification of its participants (Clark and Wilson, 1961). In a political party, relevant values make up an ideology, that is, a set of beliefs about the nature of individuals and society, distinguishing the desirable by providing an explanation of events and a blueprint for action. This conception of ideology is familiar to students of politics (for example, Wasburn, 1982, 235), though not necessarily to those students of organizations who consider ideology solely in its explanatory capacity and not in its evaluative one (Beyer, 1981).

In the planning and execution of this study, ideology was the mirror of patronage. Where I initially saw declining patronage as relatively unimportant to Republicans, I gave a preeminent place to ideology because of my interpretation of the polarizing effects of the Goldwater presidential candidacy in 1964 and its continuing legacy in Ronald Reagan's effort to unseat President Ford in 1976. Ideology and the internal conflicts it appeared to generate then became central to my earliest theoretical premises about how the Illinois Republicans should be studied, leaving virtually no place for patronage. Chapter 6 tells how my shift in perspective occurred, with the result that I came to treat ideology as one medium of interchange, more or less on a par with the others.

The first indications of the continuing importance of patronage came from party actors themselves, and subsequent analysis revealed how the diversity of patrons and patronage is associated with a high degree of ambiguity about the place of patronage in the party network. Ideology, in contrast, is more monolithic, in the sense that conservatism dominates the Republican Party.

One sign of this dominance is evident from the ratings given by explicitly ideological groups like Americans for Democratic Action on the liberal side, or Americans for Constitutional Action on the conservative, using the voting records of congressmen. Although the correlation between party affiliation and ideological position is not perfect, it is sufficiently strong to separate the majority of each party into two distinct ideological camps (Huckshorn, 1984, 274–278). Poole (1981) used ratings of U.S. senators made by 32 groups over a 10-year period to obtain a single ideological dimension, accounting for 80 percent of the variance. His subsequent analyses confirm, for Congress as a whole, general disappearance of moderate central positions, making conservatism the Republican norm (Poole and Rosenthal, 1984). My own analysis of Congress in 1979 and 1980 used only four groups — Americans for Democratic Action, Americans for Constitutional Action, AFL–CIO, and Chambers of Commerce of the United States (Tarrant, 1980, 1118; Keller, 1981, 516). Consistency in rankings was especially high in 1979, accounting for 95 percent of the variance in a single dimension. The same dimension accounted for 76 percent of the variance in 1980 and, in both years, clearly divided the Illinois parties on ideological grounds.

Members of the state legislature have been ranked with comparable results. Combining ratings, based on roll-call votes in the 81st General Assembly (mainly in 1979) by seven groups — Illinois Environmental Council, Illinois Manufacturers' Association, Illinois Public Employees Council, Independent Voters of Illinois–Independent Precinct Organization (the Illinois affiliate of the Americans for Democratic Action), Illinois Political Action Committee (the Illinois Chamber of Commerce), Illinois AFL–CIO, and Illinois Conservative Union — each using from 10 to 20 roll calls, produces a single dimension of liberalism-conservatism, accounting for 79 percent of the total variance. Our state rankings divided Republican from Democratic state senators without any overlap. In other words, the seven ideological groups basically agree that Illinois Republican state senators were all conservatives. I would not have expected the multimember Illinois House to divide so cleanly, yet a similar analysis of their ratings produced only 4 inconsistent Republican representatives, who ranked with Democrats rather than with the remaining 84 Republicans.

Thoughtful commentators on U.S. values note that these are full of inconsistencies, including the conservative ones espoused by the Republican Party. Conservative columnist George Will, after the 1980 Republican convention, saw these encapsulated as "a dilemma of conservatives":

The difficulties with the Republican position . . . derive from the fact that foreign policy depends on domestic factors, on values, discipline, confidence, morale — in short, national character. The Republican platform stresses two themes that are not as harmonious as Republicans suppose.

One is cultural conservatism. The other is capitalist dynamism. The latter dissolves the former.

Republicans see no connection between the cultural phenomena they deplore and the capitalist culture they promise to intensify; no connection between the multiplying evidence of self-indulgence and national decadence (such as pornography, promiscuity, abortion, divorce and other forms of indiscipline) and the unsleeping pursuit of ever more immediate, intense and grand material gratifications. (Will, 1982, 36–37)

Yet even those who concern themselves with moral issues, more often found in the "New Right," find ways to join with the "Old Right" in nurturing the conservative roots of the Republic Party. As James C. Roberts, executive director of the American Conservative Union, has attested:

. . . on matters of principle and policy there is no *major* difference between these groups and individuals. Except for columnist Kevin Phillips (who argues that conservatives should embrace big government as a means of rewarding conservatives and punishing liberals), I know of no conservative leader who does not champion limited government and individual liberty. Similarly, both Old Rightists and New Rightists favor a reliance on the market economy and both subscribe to traditional morality.

On any given issue of national importance Old Rightists and New Rightists will be found to be on the same side. (Roberts, 1980, 7–8)

The essential unity of American conservatism is also confirmed in social science analyses (Himmelstein, 1983, 21).

Even though not all Republicans are conservatives or agree on the meaning of conservatism, some form of conservatism is the party's overarching system of beliefs and values, symbolized by the frequency with which party actors use it for identification. For example, three-quarters of the weighted sample of precinct committeemen interviewed by telephone answered that most voters in their precincts would prefer conservative candidates, just slightly greater than their own preference.[1] An analysis of delegate preferences for presidential candidates from 1940 to 1968 puts Illinois among the most conservative states, although it apparently departed from this pattern in 1976, when 40 percent of the primary vote for Reagan translated into only 11 percent of the delegates (Munger and Hoffman, 1980). The absence of stronger support for the clearly conservative Reagan is not so much a denial of Illinois's essential conservatism (President Ford himself was not part of the progressive wing of the party) as it is an indication of the range of internal issues that divided the party.[2]

1. I tried, through several pretests of the questionnaire, to find a better way of differentiating ideological preferences, but without success.
2. If survey results from rank-and-file Republican supporters are any indication, they suggest that preference for either Reagan or Ford was virtually independent of ideology (Munger and Hoffman, 1980, 12).

By defining ideology as a system of values, we begin with a recognition of how it embodies the rationale for an organization's existence, inspiring the confidence and loyalty of adherents and attracting converts to its cause. But when put to use, especially in the form of sanctions, ideology has quite a different aura. Like power, ideology uses negative sanctions to activate commitments; however, the coercive sanctions associated with power are manifested by the withholding of resources, whereas those associated with ideology involve moral judgments. In other words, power is used to prevent or achieve dominance, in its ultimate form, by exclusion of opponents from the Republican Party — a sanction normally left to voters rather than to the authority structure. Ideology also holds out the threat of exclusion from some segment of the party network, but in the form of ordering the moral worth of members. Senator Percy, for example, was denigrated as not really a Republican, who would help the party only if he left it.

Ideology is linked with power through the capacity to define legitimacy, but the two are not always compatible, like what Max Weber saw as strains arising between moral leaders and political power (Parsons, 1969, 452). Chapter 5 provided illustrations of ideology justifying challenges to authority because leaders' lukewarm conservatism led to judgments that they were unworthy. Ideology gives primacy to the party, not as a vehicle for winning votes or gaining office, but as a moral community.

At a general level, value commitments operate to maintain the integrity of a social system's basic design (Parsons, 1969, 446). In a parallel way, ideology is a medium for promoting the value integrity of the Republican Party, currently manifested as some form of conservatism. Although the general integrity of a conservative value system was not in question during this study, party actors varied in their beliefs about the best ways to maintain conservatism.

Conflict over how conservatism should be expressed is the channel for using ideology as a medium of interchange, manifested in two ways, analogous to Parson's distinction between intensity of commitment and value-generalization or scope (Parsons, 1969, 445). Among party actors, assumptions about commitment are the means for differentiating purists from pragmatists. The scope of ideological standards is reflected in the issues and leaders that symbolize their application. As we examine these two dimensions in this chapter — purists versus pragmatists, and issues and leaders — we follow in the path of power as a negative medium. That is, we expect ideology to be used to limit ties among party actors and to challenge existing relations. In addition, we anticipate that dependency will be exploited as an arena for choice based on principle, not expediency. If actions taken result in conflict, and not in the establishment of order, participants can be expected to consider this a reasonable price for preserving the integrity of conservative values.

Purists and Pragmatists

At the end of an unusually bitter national convention, Senator Barry Goldwater, the 1964 Republican presidential candidate, threw back on his opponents their criticism of his extremism: "I would remind you that extremism in the defense of liberty is no vice. And let me remind you also that moderation in the pursuit of justice is not virtue." The results, of course, were not those he wished to achieve (Mayer, 1967, 538–546). They came to epitomize a crucial distinction in the Republican Party, one between purists and pragmatists. From interviews with delegates to that convention, Wildavsky arrived at two ideal types. Purists are distinguished by

their emphasis on internal criteria for decision, on what they believe "deep down inside"; their rejection of compromise; their lack of orientation toward winning; their stress on the style and purity of decision — integrity, consistency, adherence to internal norms. (Wildavsky, 1965, 395)

Professional politicians, whom we call pragmatists, do not differ from purists in the content of their conservatism but in the fervor with which it is expressed:

The belief in compromise and bargaining; the sense that public policy is made in small steps rather than big leaps; the concern with conciliating the opposition and broadening public appeal; and the willingness to bend a little to capture public support are all characteristics of the traditional politician in the United States. (Wildavsky, 1965, 396)

When only seven informants in our study described themselves as moderate or middle of the road, but avowedly conservative party actors could still complain about "ultraconservatives," it became clear that the major issue was differences in commitment similar to what Wildavsky found.

Limiting Ties

The demand for ideological purity leads, on the one hand, to the creation of cohesive groups acting as dedicated carriers of beliefs and, where appropriate, as proselytizers; and, on the other, to the fostering of factionalism over the question of who is the true believer. In the experience of one wary member of a governor's staff, the backbiting prevalent in the party could be attributed to the fact that "ideology makes haters. These people have a burning knowledge that only they are right. This is as true of liberal Democrats as conservative Republicans. This is clear, because when one of these extreme groups captures the national party, they always lose."

Stated in less exaggerated form, the tension between purists and pragmatists revolves around the willingness to compromise. An informant directly involved described the major problem in the General Assembly as
lying in

divisions between the very conservative in the suburbs [of Cook County]. They
are very critical of the governor, for example, on the transportation [the Regional
Transportation Authority] issue. They also blame the leaders — George Ryan in the
House and Dave Shapiro in the Senate. Ryan, as House minority leader, first ran
against Bill Walsh, a suburban candidate from the 6th District. The divisions over
issues often bind together downstate legislators against the suburbs. The Senate
situation is similar to the House with regard to the ideological division. Subur-
banites are on the outside. They're archconservative.

After he described conservatism in terms of opposition to such social issues
as the Equal Rights Amendment and gun control, it became apparent that
this informant saw no major substantive differences in the conservatism
among Republican legislators, and he confirmed the conservatism of George
Ryan, particularly compared with Governor Thompson. Important differences, instead, are ones of commitment. He concluded: "Downstate Republicans are pragmatic. Archconservatives, however, won't compromise.
They are so philosophical."

My combined analysis of the rankings provided by the seven interest
groups indicates that divisions are more complex than our informant described and occur mainly within regions. For state senators, comparisons
are laid out in Table 7-1, in which Districts 33 and 38 are classified as downstate, although they are also partly adjacent to Cook County — by the location of McHenry County in 33 and Kane in 38.[3] As statistics in the table
show, a one-way analysis of variance is not significant, and that is also
the case with comparisons between pairs of groups. In other words, as a
group, neither suburban Cook County nor collar-county legislators are
any more conservative than those downstate.

Shifting to the Illinois House, Chicago can be added to the comparisons in Table 7-2, because the multimember House always had minority
party representation. Results are statistically significant, entirely because
of the presence of Chicago legislators, whose mean conservatism score of
27 is sharply at variance with that of Republicans in other parts of the
state. Yet notice that Chicago includes not only Republican Susan Catania,
ranking 166th down the conservatism index along with the most liberal

---

3. This classification is similar to the one used by Van Der Slik and Brown (1980, 118).
I also did a second analysis, grouping Districts 33 and 38 with the collar counties, but this
made little difference.

Table 7-1. Ideological Rankings of State Senators, by Region, 1979

	District	Score		District	Score
Suburban Cook County			Downstate		
Nimrod	4	160	McMillan	47	169
Regner	5	153	Maitland	44	158
Walsh	6	151	Weaver	52	138
Graham	2	126	Shapiro	37	128
Ozinga	8	113	Sommer	45	117
Becker	7	106	Grotberg	38	116
Keats	1	102	Bloom	46	104
DeAngelis	10	97	Coffey	53	86
Moore	9	89	Schaffer	33	69
Rhoads	6	69	Martin	34	68
Collar counties of Cook			Davidson	50	53
Philip	40	154	Rupp	51	17
Bowers	41	129			
Mitchler	39	123			
Berning	32	120			
Geo-Karis	31	30			

$F(2,26) = 0.366$, n.s.

A factor analysis for the entire Illinois Senate was done, based on ratings by seven interest groups, and factor scores were multiplied by 100. All Republicans scored higher than any of the Democrats.

Democrats, and Charles E. Gaines, ranking 138th, but also Elmer Conti, John McAuliffe, and Philip W. Collins, ranking 18th, 25th, and 26th, respectively.

To the extent that our informant's description was correct, it was because he could find examples of vocal ideological purists in suburban Cook County and the collar counties — John J. Nimrod, David J. Regner, Richard A. Walsh, and James "Pate" Philip in the Senate; and Penny Pullen, Donald Totten, William D. Walsh, and George Hudson in the House. These are among the same names given to us earlier by a leader in the Illinois Conservative Union: "Daniels, Keats, Hudson, Pullen, Totten, and Collins define the conservative roll calls as far as the ICU [Illinois Conservative Union] is concerned. Totten in particular is the leader." At the same time, purists represent districts in other parts of the state, and even the consistency of purists can vary with issues. Although, clearly, ideologically based factionalism contributed to divisions in the General Assembly, they were not always associated with regions.[4]

4. An analysis of roll-call votes in the 80th General Assembly, covering 1977 and 1978, and based on a sample of all regular legislation that reached final passage for which no more

Table 7-2. Ideological Rankings of State Representatives, by Region, 1979

	District	Score		District	Score
Suburban Cook County			Downstate *(cont.)*		
Pullen	4	173	McMaster	47	133
Totten	3	150	Neff	47	133
Walsh	6	143	Ackerman	45	129
Boucek	6	139	Woodyard	53	128
Birkinbine	1	138	Friedrich	55	126
Matula	7	126	Schuneman	37	124
Huskey	8	120	Swanstrom	35	121
Klosak	7	116	Bower	54	117
Bluthardt	5	115	Waddell	33	110
Friedland	2	112	Borchers	51	109
Piel	10	107	Campbell	53	109
Hallstrom	1	105	Wikoff	52	108
Grossi	10	90	Ebbesen	37	108
Macdonald	3	70	Ropp	44	101
Stanley	2	66	Watson	55	101
Mahar	9	53	Anderson	45	96
Barnes	8	47	Winchester	59	95
Schlickman	4	32	Hallock	34	95
Chicago			Vinson	44	92
Conti	18	127	Ryan	43	91
McAuliffe	16	118	Stiehl	57	89
Collins	30	117	Rigney	35	88
Peters	15	88	Steele	56	81
Abramson	14	83	McBroom	43	74
Wolf	17	70	Bell	36	64
Capuzi	19	65	Dunn	58	63
Bianco	25	64	Reilly	49	55
Margalus	23	39	Skinner	33	49
Stearney	20	38	Jones	50	44
Meyer	28	36	Oblinger	50	38
McCourt	11	8	Johnson	52	34
Epton	24	3	Polk	36	9
Kucharski	27	0	Collar counties		
Molloy	21	0	of Cook		
Telcser	12	−49	Hudson	41	161
Sandquist	13	−51	Reed	32	137
Gaines	29	−92	Davis	42	118
Catania	22	−144	Hoffman	40	115
Downstate			Deuster	32	113
Hoxsey	38	161	Kempiners	39	103
Sumner	46	155	Schoeberlein	39	89
Ewing	38	155	Griesheimer	31	80
Kent	48	142	Frederick	31	77
Simms	34	142	Leinenweber	42	76
Robbins	54	139	Daniels	40	67
Tuerk	46	133	Dyer	41	−10

$F(3,87) = 12.028$; $p < .001$

A factor analysis of the entire House was done, based on ratings by seven interest groups, and factor scores were multiplied by 100. One Republican was at the bottom of the Republican distribution, and four others were grouped with Democrats.

It is more difficult to describe the ways in which ideological purity limits ties among congressmen because of the need for interaction in a state delegation. At least publicly, there were comments about ideological opposites as friends, despite my own — probably misguided — expressions of disbelief. Erickson (1982, 168), citing experimental evidence on how the creation and maintenance of a similar attitude structure are tied to the attractiveness of interaction among those who disagree, suggests an explanation — that the commonalities presumed by those interacting account for the greater enjoyment of discussion among political opponents. In quite opposite ways, it is also difficult to deal with purity because of the potential divisiveness of single issues (elaborated in the section "Issues and Leaders," below). One example, told us by a congressional aide, relates to Minority House Whip Robert Michel, generally considered staunchly conservative: ". . . when the Hyde amendment [opposing federal funding for abortion] was first offered, and Michel was against it, he was picketed by pro-lifers. Now he supports Hyde, but he is still not for a pro-life constitutional amendment."

A congressman who had told us that he saw the Illinois delegation as cohesive without being in total agreement on issues, and who had described himself as conservative on economic but not on social issues, was then reluctant to identify with the stances of others: "Why should I have to use John Anderson or Philip Crane [presumed opposites] as my standard? I'm my own man." Another well-placed informant, comparable to the one previously quoted on divisions in the state legislature, gave at least a partial ordering of congressmen. First he said, "There are few philosophical differences. . . . Senator Percy is the one who is most out of line, he and Congressman Railsback." Then he went on to say that John Anderson was "the odd man out." Pressed, he reconsidered: "In ordering people according to their integration into the delegation, it is Percy, Anderson, and then Railsback. Then I would put McClory, followed by Findley" (the order is from the least to the most integrated).

Discussion with these informants made clear that ideology is at least one underlying premise in the assessment of congressmen, but it is not the only one. We can compare the preceding ranking with one produced from rankings based on factor scores derived from the ratings of four interest groups for 1979, shown in Table 7-3.[5] Congressman McClory may

---

than 80 percent voted on the winning side (Van Der Slik and Brown, 1980, 109), found that Republicans display less party loyalty than do Democrats, and also more internal factionalism (Van Der Slik and Brown, 1980, 117). These findings are not directly comparable to those for our study, because our ratings are based on a much more selective number of bills that interest groups had already judged to have an ideological content.

5. I used the 1979 ratings because they match best with our informant's time perspective, in which he felt it was too soon to rank newly elected John Porter. The factor analysis

Table 7-3. Ideological Rankings of Congressmen, 1979

	District	Score
D. Crane	22	142
P. Crane	12	141
R. Michel	18	129
T. Corcoran	15	116
H. Hyde	6	106
R. McClory	13	99
G. O'Brien	17	97
J. Erlenborn	14	90
E. Derwinski	4	78
J. Anderson	16	61
E. Madigan	21	54
T. Railsback	19	36
P. Findley	20	27
(Senator C. Percy		− 10)

A factor analysis for the entire Illinois delegation was made, based on ratings by four interest groups, and factor scores were multiplied by 100. All Republicans scored higher than any of the Democrats.

have stood out to our informant because of more personal habits of interaction rather than any deviation from conservative orthodoxy. McClory has been characterized as "independent and unpredictable" (Ehrenhalt, 1982, 354). Involved in the Judiciary Committee's impeachment proceedings against President Nixon, he was highly selective in taking positions on the charges, in ways that appeared to epitomize his career: "It was a nationally televised example of McClory's career-long march to his own drummer, one that can look heroic at times and merely willful at others" (Ehrenhalt, 1982, 355). Similarly, Congressman Madigan may have escaped notice as less of a purist because of a generally low profile. He may also have been helped by a reputation of being among the "best backroom operators" in Congress, according to a poll taken by columnist Jack Anderson (MacKay, 1981).

But Table 7-3 still confirms the limiting qualities of ideology in Congress. Senator Percy is set sharply apart from the rest of the delegation, as others had long complained. Although my own ratings are based on a single session, and need not be stable over time, they are indicative of enduring ideological divisions, supported by Poole's 10-year analysis of 48

---

for 1980 appears less consistent with other sources, because it lowered scores for the Cranes, especially compared with John Erlenborn. The inconsistency of the 1980 ratings was entirely due to the procedure followed by the U.S. Chamber of Commerce for that year (Keller, 1981, 512).

senators, where Senator Percy ranked a low 14th out of 20 Republicans on a conservatism scale (Poole, 1981). In the House, Findley and Railsback stand apart, as do, to a degree, Madigan and Anderson, by being much less conservative than the delegation norm. At the other extreme, the Crane brothers are also distinctive, although they were never mentioned as non-conforming. Yet we picked up some suggestions of discomfort with their positions by other conservative congressmen. One spoke of his unhappiness with those conservatives who, by their disparagements, act to demean Congress. The example he gave was Daniel Crane, who had a bumper sticker reading, "It's after ten. Do you know where your Congressman is?" Now that we know where Congressman Crane was—in bed with a 17-year-old congressional page (Warren, 1983)—our informant may have been conveying even more of a message than we realized at the time of the interview.

The requirements for purity limit contacts by interest groups, financial contributors, and advisors with candidates for elected office. These kinds of political actors offer their resources to candidates selectively, as I noted in chapters 3 and 6, where I alluded to the relevance of ideology with respect to the activities of private-sector patrons. In interviews with advisors or with those who use their services, each mentioned that at least some element of ideological disposition was present in the process of choosing with whom to work. A Republican National Committee staff member was quite explicit:

I prefer working with Market Opinion Research because they give you information and work with the full range of ideologues in the Republican Party. They don't try to dictate strategy the way [Arthur J.] Finkelstein [and Associates] and a couple of others do, who only serve conservative candidates.

Advisors with a national clientele are readily identified by their commitment to the conservative cause (Roberts, 1980, 303–317), and so are those who work within the confines of the state. Ideological compatibility between advisors and candidates is a mutual concern, perhaps even greater on the part of the advisors, concerned that their technical skills be used only for objectives with which they are in philosophical harmony.

The many conservative organizations that act as pressure groups in the political system must be distinguished from the Republican Party (Roberts, 1980, 39–56; Himmelstein, 1983), even though their primary channel of influence is through the party. Organizational separation is a concomitant of the restricting role they play within the party, by the precedence they give to beliefs over the continuity of the party itself. Roberts speaks with favor of those who work within Congress—the House Republican Study Committee and the Senate Steering Committee—because of the way they emphasize ideology:

The existence of these organizations has proved of inestimable benefit to conservatives in both houses who were often out of synch with the elected leadership. In addition, the committees have been valuable sources of information for conservative organizations, apprising them of the likely timing of the introduction of important legislation and giving them advice on how to lobby particular members most effectively. (Roberts, 1980, 54)

A similar distribution of loyalties was suggested in the General Assembly by a member also active in the Illinois Conservative Union:

The relationship between the ICU and the Republican Party is zero. . . . I identify myself first as conservative and then as a Republican. The Republican Party is a pain in the ass. It's a means to an end toward more limited government. Parties are an anachronism.

His words indicate that conservative organizations put their agendas above concerns with party unity or compromise. When the staff member with the Committee for the Survival of a Free Congress spoke of the committee's ability to support candidates in primary elections, an activity normally eschewed by formal party units except in the case of incumbents, he was concerned with the ideological benefits, not the consequences for party cohesion.

Further limits are imposed by financial contributors, especially those I labelled earlier as entrepreneurs, when they use ideological guidelines in deciding on the distribution of funds. As with advisors and interest groups, ideology is an important basis for dividing financial contributors (Roberts, 1980, 67–82). This extends to those who specialize in fundraising, where conservative themes have become most prominent with such direct-mail specialists as Richard Viguerie (1981). Professional fundraiser Bruce Eberle, also a board member of Young Americans for Freedom,

concedes that the Republican fund appeals are almost always based on conservative issues. A moderate-to-liberal pitch tends to do very poorly, he admits — a fact that dictates conservative-oriented letters for the GOP committees, even when the chairman of the committee is an unabashed liberal, as is the case with Republican Senatorial Campaign Committee Chairman John Heinz. (Roberts, 1980, 63)

Although clearly a self-serving assessment, it is relevant in revealing the way in which pressure for purity affects the raising and distribution of money. In the narrower context of Illinois Republicans, a similar trend is at work. Corporate contributors tend to support not only incumbents and safe seats but also those with a philosophy generally supportive of business or free enterprise. Ideological interest groups, even more explicitly, attempt to distribute their resources to candidates who emphasize either a conservative orientation or sympathy toward particular causes. Money itself is used as a medium of interchange in positive ways, but ideology limits its availability.

Challenging Relations

Senator Percy's vulnerability to challenge from purists was not serious until 1984, when Congressman Tom Corcoran faced him in the primary (Talbott, 1983a). Percy was able to deflect that challenge and won with 62 percent of the vote. In 1978, however, there had been considerable nervousness in the Percy camp when Phyllis Schlafly threatened to enter the primary. A prominent member of Percy's campaign staff agreed that

Percy was most vulnerable in the primary, where conservatives are most likely to vote. Conservatives were opposed to his vote on the Panama Canal, ERA, etc. My first job was to preclude having Phyllis Schlafly enter the primary. We did this by persuading 44 or 45 county chairmen attending the annual meeting that they should endorse Percy before the primary. I feel the county chairmen did not want a disruptive primary. That endorsement was unprecedented. There were also phone calls from Illinois Republicans that tried to persuade her to withdraw.

Schlafly's participation as a leading figure in the conservative movement would have represented the first time Senator Percy had to defend his ideological pragmatism within the party's own electoral forum (Howard, 1978, 9; Boczkiewicz, 1977). Asked about this possibility at a press conference announcing his own presidential candidacy, Congressman Philip Crane described Senator Percy as "out of touch with the party's mainstream," and assumed "Percy could have been defeated in his bid for renomination if he had been challenged by conservative Phyllis Schlafly of Alton" (Watson, 1978).

During the time of this study there were five congressional races in which incumbents were challenged, and in all of them, ideological issues were at stake. In the 1980 challenges involving Congressman Edward Derwinski in the 4th District and Congressman John Erlenborn in the 14th, both incumbents easily beat their challengers, with 83 and 81 percent of the vote, respectively. Two of the other races were more serious, and the fifth was somewhat ambiguous.

The ambiguous case involved Congressman Robert McClory in the 13th District, challenged both in 1978 and 1980. As we have already noted, although his votes in Congress may not have been so far from the conservative ideal, his behavior generally set him apart from other conservatives. His 1978 challenger, Elgin mayor Richard Verbic, was a self-described fiscal conservative (Stevenson, 1978), but in fact had stronger claims to identity as a purist and was assisted in his campaign by conservative fundraiser Richard Viguerie. Verbic's ability to win 41 percent of the primary vote was almost matched by McClory's 1980 challenger, state Representative Calvin Skinner. While in the state House, Skinner also built a reputation as a maverick, but his score of 49 gives him a ranking of 70th on the ideological scale, toward the bottom of the Republican half of the scale. Yet during the congressional campaign he was described as "a loud conservative who relishes taking on the government as an underdog" (Schilling, 1980). His principal theme was opposition to the Regional Transportation Authority, an important concern to local conservatives, which he attempted to convert into a national issue (Schilling, 1980). In addition, and unlike McClory's congressional vote, he campaigned in opposition to gun control, gaining funds from the Gun Owners of America PAC. Altogether, evidence may not be as unequivocal as we would like, but we can still be fairly confident that ideology was a strong component in the challenges mounted in the 13th District.

Joseph P. Savard, who challenged Edward Derwinski in the 4th District, pitched his campaign to what he said was the bogus character of Derwinski's conservatism. Savard focussed on Derwinski's congressional voting record, particularly his support for spending bills and for the revised Panama Canal treaty (*Star* Publications, 1980). For other observers, it also appeared that Derwinski's claim to conservative purity had been weakened by the Panama Canal vote (Ehrenhalt, 1982, 331). But as already noted, Savard was not able to shake the vast majority of Derwinski's supporters. The same strength was shown by John Erlenborn in the face of a challenge from William Grossklass, who was dissatisfied with Erlenborn's voting record and attacked him for departing from conservative principles.

The most notable challenge from an ideological purist in 1978 came in the 16th District, where former evangelical preacher Don Lyon attempted to unseat Congressman John Anderson. Anderson, who had himself begun his congressional career as a strong and moralistic conservative, even proposing a constitutional amendment to declare the United States a Christian country, had by then become less of a purist, especially on social issues. Lyon could thus attack him for supporting the Panama Canal treaty, gun control, federal abortion funding, and homosexual rights, all issues that serve as litmus tests for conservatives. Although Anderson overcame the challenge, it was a bitter primary fight that left him with 58 percent of the vote (Peoria *Journal Star,* 1978b; Hucker, 1978a).

Purity played an important role as well in 1980, when Quincy mayor David Nuessen challenged Congressman Paul Findley in the 20th District. Findley, like Anderson, had once been an unimpeachable conservative. "Over 20 years in the House, Findley had moved out of his initial Farm Belt conservatism into an unpredictable pattern that leaves him consorting with Palestinian rebels one day and preaching free enterprise economics the next" (Ehrenhalt, 1982, 371). In a campaign that covered Findley's apparent distance from his constituents and from other party actors, and his inexplicable fascination with the Middle East, Nuessen always emphasized his own conservatism, including his support of Ronald Reagan and Philip Crane (Manning, 1980). Findley won, but with only 56 percent.

Past the time frame I allotted for this study, two other instances of congressional challenge appeared, pitting purists against pragmatists. In 1982, after the old 19th District had been redrawn into the 17th, the most conservative member of the state Senate, Kenneth McMillan, challenged incumbent congressman Tom Railsback. In an area with unusually high unemployment in the farm implement industry, Railsback could no longer count on his normal support from the United Auto Workers. Although Railsback had maintained a strong district office and generally tried to play a broker role between different wings of the party, as he had done in the House between Democrats and his own party's conservative wing (Ehrenhalt, 1982, 368), support was weak. Compared with McMillan, he was not a conservative. His loss, with 49 percent of the vote, was probably aided by allegations of impropriety in sharing a weekend house with lobbyist and *Playboy* model Paula Parkinson (Ehrenhalt, 1982, 369; Chicago *Sun-Times,* 1981b). Moral issues were prominent again in 1984, but this time Congressman Daniel Crane may have been protected by his ideological, if not his moral, purity. Crane was able to turn back the primary challenge mounted by state Senator Max Coffey, retaining his seat with 66 percent of the vote (Locin, 1984). He lost, however, to his Democratic opponent.

I did not find similar evidence of ideological challenges in state and local offices, although they may have occurred. More obvious were challenges to incumbent legislators which involved specific issues (treated in the section "Issues and Leaders," below) rather than general purity.

Dependency

In the conservative value system, dependency on other party actors and the electoral environment is met with principled choices, exemplified by the 1964 Goldwater slogan, "A choice, not an echo,"[6] intended to convey the distinctiveness of a program that would not stoop to promise what might be pragmatically popular. Put this way, there is an implied expectation of dominance resulting from these choices, and although that outcome may follow, it is secondary to the importance of being right. Purists recognize and are prepared for the consequences of their position. In the words of a public officeholder:

6. This was the title of Phyllis Schlafly's (1964) self-published campaign pamphlet, credited with helping Barry Goldwater win the presidential nomination, although he has never given her credit for her help (Felsenthal, 1981, 178).

A party that's basically conservative has a more difficult time dealing with differences in opinion. It is by nature more oriented to what you believe. The Democrats are more compromising and inclusive, almost by definition. I would rather be a minority party, and stand for principles, than have power.

In general, the demand for ideological purity discourages interaction among party actors and encourages a sense of exclusiveness on the part of those who feel they best represent the party ethos. Extrapolating from Blau's (1977, 138–139) analysis, Beyer (1981, 173) feels "organizations must make a strategic choice between growing and adopting generally accepted ideologies, or staying small and developing a distinctive ideology." This choice poses a serious dilemma to any organization, but for a political party that wants to stay competitive, and particularly to win office, the advantage would appear to lie with pragmatism. That advantage is offset, however, by two contrary tendencies: the demonstrable success of purists in district offices and the persistence of ideologues as party activists.

It is not difficult to find congressmen, state legislators, and local officeholders with strong claims to ideological purity who are able to win and retain office without difficulty. They have found a niche where their particular beliefs and values are congruent with those of other party actors and supporters with whom they are linked. Problems arise, however, when purists try to generalize beyond their niche and argue that their form of ideology has widespread utility as a means of interchange.

Ideologues, once they become involved in an organization or movement, are characteristically highly committed and work with a level of energy virtually unaffected by setbacks, which they, in any case, define as temporary (Kanter, 1972, 64–74). Within the Republican Party, there is long-standing evidence that party activists who attend national conventions are more consistent in their stands on issues and more conservative than are rank-and-file Republicans (e.g., McClosky, Hoffman, O'Hara, 1960, on the 1956 presidential convention). Because such people are not easily discouraged, they continue working for the party after other, less enthusiastic, supporters leave. From this perspective, Wildavsky made a prescient assessment of the fate of those ideologues attracted to the Goldwater campaign:

Once it is understood . . . that the Goldwater movement is not a temporary aberration, but represents a profound current within the Republican Party, it becomes impossible for me to join the wishful thinkers who believe that the moderates and liberals in the party will automatically gain control after Goldwater's severe defeat in the election. A majority of party activists now support the political tendency Goldwater represented. . . . If these conservatives are to be defeated they will have to be challenged by a rival, moderate elite, willing to engage in the daily tasks of political organization over the next four years. No one has been able to tell where these people will come from, especially after the Republican Party has been swept out of office at all levels in a Johnson landslide. (Wildavsky, 1965, 411)

The consequences of involvement by purists were reflected in the 1980 state convention, where delegates voiced their approval for the stands taken by Donald Totten, state chairman of the Reagan campaign and challenger to Harold Byron Smith, Jr., as national committeeman. As one delegate said to a small group driving to the convention hall, "It's time the party responded to the conservative views of its rank-and-file members. We're in favor of Governor Reagan. We don't like what Governor Thompson is doing." An ideologically moderate office-seeker observed: "Conservatives today are very outspoken. At the local level they tend to dominate. There are lots of others who don't have strong feelings—they tend to be quiet and don't participate unless they are drawn to a particular candidate."

The patterns of interaction among party actors and their electoral success serve to legitimate purist arguments for conservatism in ways analogous to Aldrich's (1979, 120) thesis about how success legitimates ideology in other organizations. To the extent that persistent and successful party actors define legitimacy within the party, it is *their* ideology that dominates. During our interviews we were struck by the openness of conservatives, eager to discuss their beliefs even with those they perceived to be "liberal professors," whereas self-described moderates, clearly in the minority, were more diffident and concerned about the protection of their anonymity.

Yet legitimacy is also defined outside the party network—by voters—a phenomenon present wherever outsiders affect the legitimacy and continuity of organizations of which they are not a part (Meyer and Scott, 1983, 200–202). It is this dependence on the electoral environment that provides the other horn of the dilemma created by the tension between purity and size. To party actors, the question is, Who can get elected to statewide office? To some, the choice must be a moderate, as one congressional aide observed: "Some of the votes that Percy casts are anathema to the delegation. They are more conservative than he is. But some at least understand that congressmen can afford to be more conservative. My congressman says, 'I couldn't be elected statewide.'" This assessment could not be totally shared by purists, because in effect it would shake their claim to purity. What we can anticipate, then, given trends in the party at both the national and the state levels, is that dependency will continue to be met with an emphasis on the purity of conservatism, to be extended, whenever possible, to the selection of the U.S. senator and the governor.

Issues and Leaders

To purists, conservatism is of whole cloth. They disagree with the governor's aide who told us: "The governor is pro-ERA and pro-choice on abortion. But on the basis of issues, conservatives find it hard to be anti-Thompson. He's a fiscal conservative and hard on law and order." This kind of distinction was exactly the basis of Goldwater's earlier criticism of Eisenhower and Nixon, then president and vice president. To separate economic concerns from human problems is to deny that conservatism is a philosophy that takes into account the whole person (Goldwater, 1960, 9–12). Yet a philosophy has to have some guideposts, clarifying the content of beliefs and the responses appropriate to changing conditions. The breadth of those beliefs thus becomes a dimension of conservatism separate from commitment. Commitment involves the intensity of belief; breadth, the range of issues and events and the persons who are covered by them. Scope can be measured by reactions to particular issues whose salience changes over time. Informants often referred to these issues as litmus tests — emotionally charged criteria of conservative fidelity. In the words of one legislator:

Four years ago it was the Panama Canal treaty. Two years ago, it was tax limitation. There is also ERA and pro-life. But the issues don't really work as good criteria. For example, some Republican local officials [though conservative] are opposed to a tax lid. ERA is a media issue — it concerns only a handful of activists. The right-to-life issue is more important here. . . . One important conservative litmus is regionalism — that's the bedrock. By regionalism I mean concern with local autonomy.

Leaders are the creators and interpreters of ideology, but they are no more fixed symbols than are issues. They expand or contract the scope of ideological beliefs by their capacity to transform issues and events into essentially conservative themes. Their attraction may also lie in an ability to personify what is best about conservatism. In one example, a legislator responded to a question about what the Republican Party stands for:

The Republican closest to my way of thinking is Congressman Henry Hyde. Hyde has it all together in a form consistent with Republican philosophy. Phil Crane and Henry Hyde turn young people on because of their stand on single issues, for example, Hyde's stand on abortion.

We talked to another legislator about who best represents the party and, later, about what is needed for success:

The individuals I admire the most are strong conservatives. I am running as a convention delegate pledged to Phil Crane. I think Crane not only believes the conservative principles of the Republican Party, but he votes consistently with these principles. . . . Most candidates have no philosophical grounding and are unversed in important areas. A good example is that all the Republican candidates for president except Crane came out in support of limits on windfall profits. This showed an ignorance of the realities of how big business operates.

Limiting Issues

The emergence of new issues and leaders may sometimes increase opportunities for mobilizing support; more often, their principal effect is to limit interchanges in the party network. This is because they provide volatile criteria for assessing the application of conservatism to timely problems, challenging party actors to continually demonstrate their conservative credentials. When government or taxes serve as a crucial test, they acquire symbolic significance beyond their mundane properties. Barry Goldwater, in a book regarded as the conservative gospel, drew on fundamental values in writing about taxation:

One of the foremost precepts of the natural law is man's right to the possession and the use of his property. And a man's earnings are his property as much as his land and the house in which he lives. . . . How can a man be truly free if he is denied the means to exercise freedom? How can he be free if the fruits of his labor are not his to dispose of, but are treated, instead, as part of a common pool of public wealth? Property and freedom are inseparable: to the extent government takes the one in the form of taxes, it intrudes on the other. (Goldwater, 1960, 59)

Government must be limited and kept close to the local level, because this is consistent with the intentions of the Founding Fathers, who, we are told, "looked upon the institution of government as a necessary evil. They saw it as an agency required by the nature of man to suppress disorder and maintain the peace" (Evans, 1975, 29). Goldwater captured this theme well by describing the Constitution as "a system of restraints against the natural tendency of government to expand in the direction of absolutism" (Goldwater, 1960, 18). Goldwater and Evans (former president of the American Conservative Union) not only demonstrate how issues relating to government become litmus tests, but they even place the issues in the context of Burkean conservatism, with its pessimistic assessment of human nature.[7]

The period of my study was one of prominence for "single issue" movements. In particular, opposition to ERA and to abortion rights served as conservative rallying points. Yet neither was initially nor unambiguously identified as the correct conservative position. The Catholic church was, organizationally, the leading opponent of legalized abortion. Its associated lay groups, organized as a loose national coalition in the National Right

7. Rossiter (1962, 201) felt this element of orthodox conservatism was normally absent in U.S. varieties.

to Life Committee in 1968, moved from under its direct control in order
to broaden the base of support (Leahy and Mazur, 1978, 145). Meanwhile,
a woman's right to decide on the termination of pregnancy was still considered compatible with libertarian conservatism. But because pro-abortion-
rights groups quickly established a clearly liberal identity, anti-abortion
groups then mounted their opposition by appealing to conservative
Catholics (Sarvis and Rodman, 1974). At the same time, and including
the period of this study, Catholic voters have generally been more comfortable in the Democratic Party (Dionne, 1981, 310–311). For some Catholics, involvement in the anti-abortion movement has been the medium by
which they have become attached to the Republican Party. According to
a suburban committeeman: "On a Reagan–O'Neal ticket, we will get help
from a lot of pro-lifers. These will be Catholics, even those who are traditionally Democrats. We will then ask them to help other candidates."

It was pro-life groups that persuaded Republicans that theirs was the
truly conservative stance (Evans, 1975, 350–357). The result was a new consistency between ideology and partisanship for some Catholic voters. As
Rossiter observed over two decades ago:

. . . if an American were to be asked by a British visitor, "Are the principles of
the Conservative tradition taught anywhere in the States today?", he could answer
in all honesty: "Yes, imperfectly and obliquely but none the less sympathetically
in Catholic colleges and universities all over the country." (Rossiter, 1962, 234)

The momentum and moral fervor generated by opposition to abortion,
and the political conflicts it produces, are now generally recognized (*Time,*
1979). Another suburban committeeman predicted: "Pro-life is the issue
of the future. It's like abolition, though there won't be a civil war fought
over it."

The most divisive manifestations of the abortion issue in Congress and
the General Assembly actually occurred before the time of our study. During our period, Congressman Robert E. Bauman introduced an amendment to prohibit federal Medicaid funding for abortions and to stipulate
that Medicaid not be construed to require state funding; it passed 235 to
155 in December 1979. The Illinois Republican delegation was virtually
unanimous in its support, opposed only by Paul Findley, although John
Anderson signified his opposition without a recorded vote. In the General
Assembly, Senate Bill 47, requiring a 72-hour waiting period before an abortion could be performed, passed the House and Senate in June 1979. Republicans in the House were overwhelmingly in favor of the bill—72 percent of those present—compared with 56 percent of those in the Senate.
In both chambers, staunchly antiabortion legislators in suburban Cook
County contrasted with Republicans elsewhere. Contrast was sharpest in

the House, where 83 percent of the suburban Cook County Republican representatives favored the legislation. In the collar counties and in Chicago, it was 58 percent, and downstate, 67 percent.

There have been similar changes in the way the Equal Rights Amendment has been incorporated into the conservative mainstream. When introduced in Congress in 1971, it passed easily, with little partisan or ideological division. It did not pass its first introduction in Illinois in 1972, but in retrospect, it came closest to doing so then, and was least divisive of parties. Even Phyllis Schlafly, the leading opponent of ERA, recalls that she was quite indifferent in 1971: "I figured ERA was something between innocuous and mildly helpful" (quoted in Felsenthal, 1981, 239–241). But as opposition mounted, so did an anti-ERA position become defined as the correct conservative one. Schlafly played an important role in this shift, actively lobbying the Illinois General Assembly in 1978 and 1980 (Felsenthal, 1981, 249–253), as she did other legislative bodies. Unlike the general coincidence between ideology and partisanship in both Congress and the General Assembly, votes on ERA in Illinois were internally divisive for both parties, but more so for the Republicans. In the House in both 1979 and 1980, 37 percent of the Republicans and 78 percent of the Democrats voted for ERA. Republicans were notably divided by region — favorable votes came from 63 percent of the legislators in Chicago, 50 percent in the collar counties, 28 percent downstate, and 22 percent in suburban Cook County. The governor, a proponent of ERA, was in opposition not only to a majority of his own party but also to House Minority Leader George Ryan, described as "boisterous in opposing ERA" (Talbott, 1982a). Aside from Ryan, the six members of the House leadership were equally divided on ERA. Even the governor's commitment was questioned when, in 1982, he endorsed George Ryan for lieutenant governor (Felsenthal, 1982, 141).

The impact of single issues on the political process and the continuity of political parties are subject to debate among political commentators and party actors (for a review, see Crotty, 1984, 142–180). In the opinion of many party actors, the single-issue enthusiasts were potentially dangerous. A camapaign manager described them as his "least favorite kind of people. They will only work for someone because of his stand on a single issue." A candidate complained that single-issue groups "like anti-ERA or pro-life say, 'If you're against us on this issue, then you're a liberal, you're evil.'" Greatest concern was expressed by party professionals, worried that moralistic campaigns would have divisive effects on the party network. Although conceding that conservative single-issue groups had been helpful in electing Republicans to Congress in 1980, Republican National Chairman Richards was still disturbed that they were outside of party control:

"They create all kinds of mischief. They're not responsible to anyone" (Cannon, 1981).

Still, the energy brought into the political sphere by anti-ERA and anti-abortion groups struck some party actors as valuable resources. An advisor working at the district level told us:

I have been very impressed with the STOP ERA people. They have worked well within the party. They're polite; they did their homework. They raised funds for PACs earlier than the pro-ERA groups. They have worked well with both parties. I would say that the anti-abortion people are also learning to work well within the party structure.

When Donald Totten was chairman of the 1980 Reagan campaign, he gave a positive evaluation of the Moral Majority.

They are becoming much more politically active and have helped us out quite a bit. They're great. They do a lot of the work you have trouble finding people to do, because they see it as a mission. (Fairlie, 1980, 16)

Without denying the potential divisiveness of single-issue groups, some party actors still felt they could control strategies to limit interchanges. This was even the view expressed by a Republican National Committee staffer:

We need single-issue supporters for building coalitions. I don't think there is any single issue that would be sole grounds making me vote against someone. But the single-issue activists are there — if their position matches with the candidate, then they'll go along and support him. I advise candidates, no matter what they do, not to straddle the fence on touchy issues. You can't appease both sides, so there is no point in trying. Even with special-interest groups, there is a chance that the sincerity of the candidate in defending his position will neutralize many of them, who will then be prepared to judge him on broader grounds.

This possibility was explicitly denied by issue activists themselves, whose goal was deliberately to limit the distribution of aid. Prior to the 1982 election, Grace Kaminkowitz, vice chairman of ERA Illinois, said:

We've maintained all along that there was only one issue for us — ERA. We've given our members in our target districts instructions to volunteer as pro-ERA volunteers and to say they're doing so because of that. We've also given the names of our members and member organizations to legislators and candidates we've endorsed. (Wheeler, 1982)

To ERA supporters, it did not even matter that ERA would no longer come before the General Assembly. Careful distinction among friends and foes was what mattered. A similar strategy was expressed by Harriet Mulqueeny, chairman of the Eagle Forum, the organizational source of STOP ERA — "We've supported all the people who've supported us" (Wheeler, 1982).

Limiting Leaders

The rationale for limiting interchanges provided by leaders is of a different character from that associated with ideological issues. Leaders are important for their qualities as spokesmen for or embodiments of the moral nature of conservatism. As I pointed out early in this chapter, moral leadership can be separate from political power and can even be in conflict with it. Ideological leaders are especially likely to make their appeals during times when the party is undergoing a kind of "crisis of legitimacy." Because such a crisis occurs almost routinely, whenever succession to the presidency is in question, it would seem that conditions for a genuine crisis would be missing. Yet because the path to leadership itself is not routinized, claimants frequently argue their merits in terms of their greater legitimacy as true Republicans. Clearly, presidential candidates are just as likely to argue on more pragmatic grounds — who will solve economic problems better, deal with the Soviet Union more effectively, and so on — but the notion of moral superiority is never far from the surface for those who are essentially ideologues. The likelihood that such moralistic candidates will appear is probably enhanced when the party is out of office or when it has undergone some internal upheaval, as occurred for the Republicans after Watergate.

When I defined the actors in the party network, I also gave a rationale for treating the president as an offstage actor, influential in affecting events that impinge on the network without being a full participant. It was relatively easy to make this distinction prior to 1980, because there was no Republican president. Perhaps I would have made a different judgment if I had begun the research after that time, but that is unlikely, given my earlier argument that what is relevant about the presidency — especially the race for that office — is the ways it has affected relations among party actors in Illinois. Dramatic demonstration of those effects in the 1980 presidential primary can be found in the ways candidates drew on ideological sources to limit network interchanges.

At the beginning of the 1980 primary season, presidential contenders included Philip Crane (the first to enter the race), George Bush, Howard Baker, John Connally, Ronald Reagan, John Anderson, and Robert Dole. In this group there were three prominent conservatives — Connally, Reagan, and Crane. The others need not concern us here, because they appealed to a more moderate constituency and did not present themselves as ideological leaders. In a sense, this was not true of Anderson, but despite his reasonable showing in the Illinois primary — 37 percent of the "beauty contest" vote compared with 48 percent for frontrunner Reagan — he had already lost his credibility as a proponent of Republican (and hence conservative) values. Before the primary a county chairman told us:

Some idiots like John Anderson want complete gun confiscation. Does he care about the hunters? No! I'm a member of the National Rifle Association—I don't want some nut like Anderson running the country. And he calls himself a Republican. As far as I'm concerned, he's nothing more than a Kennedy—that's the worst thing I can say about a person.

Anderson's eventual move out of the Republican Party was symbolic of the moderates' loss of legitimacy. They were left without the moral justification a leader provides.

The three conservative candidates each had his own claim to legitimacy. Philip Crane's was based on a consistent advocacy of conservative positions in Congress, presidency of the American Conservative Union (which he resigned when he announced his presidential candidacy), membership on the board of Young Americans for Freedom, and public advocacy against negotiating a new Panama Canal treaty (1978). His opposition to the treaty was itself one of the conservative litmus tests. Yet despite the unimpeachable caliber of his conservatism, he was never able to achieve the kind of national recognition needed by a serious contender for the presidency.

Some conservatives were less than enthusiastic about Crane's entry into the presidential race, seeing it as a serious threat to a strong and united campaign for Ronald Reagan. Most unsettling was a series of articles by William Loeb's *Manchester Union Leader,* well known for its conservatism, questioning Crane's moral fitness (Crawford, 1980, 135–137). Even the admiration he evoked in Illinois was curiously bloodless. In his own 12th Congressional District, convention delegates agreed to present themselves as pledged to both Crane and Reagan. They had little alternative while Donald Totten, a state legislator enclaved in Crane's district and close enough to Crane to be described as his "ideological blood brother," also was Reagan's Illinois campaign chairman.

Crane's strength as a moral leader remained, but in limited ways. He could not move beyond it to achieve recognition as a political leader. He was virtually eliminated as a serious candidate during the first primary in New Hampshire (Ciccone, 1980b), and from then on had to deal with huge campaign debts and struggles between his staff and advisors such as Arthur Finkelstein and Richard Viguerie (Watson, 1979). He remained in the race until the Illinois primary as a token of support for his delegates and to participate in the candidates' televised debate. By the time of the national convention, television viewers saw an apparently offended Crane, complaining about not being included on the platform by the victorious Reagan.

Ronald Reagan was the presidential candidate with greater credibility among conservatives. Later, Crane would complain: "I knew I was a longshot, but I was convinced Reagan's support would be softer than it was in 1976" (Ciccone, 1980b). The first sign of Reagan's weakness appeared during the Iowa caucus, where George Bush won, stimulating conservatives to concentrate on Reagan's candidacy, and ending the dreams of both Crane and Connally. Until then, support for Reagan had had a peculiarly divisive quality. In 1976, that support had been an unambiguous litmus test of conservatism; in late 1979 and early 1980, there were three tests in Reagan, Crane, and Connally.

Especially troublesome to the establishment of conservative legitimacy were the rival claims of John Connally. Before the Iowa caucus, Connally appeared to be a more serious claimant than Crane to conservative leadership. To many observers and party actors, it looked like "rank-and-file Republicans for Ronald Reagan and party establishment chieftains for John B. Connally" (Evans and Novak, 1980). Everywhere Connally went among party actors in Illinois, he was met with enthusiasm. At a private dinner at the governor's mansion, where Connally reportedly "dazzled" the guests, key politicians expressed their support. One was Representative Elmer Conti, suburban chairman of the Cook County Republican central committee: "I've always been a Reaganite, but I'm getting to like Connally more and more." Another was David Shapiro, Senate minority leader and an earlier supporter of Reagan, who said, "I'm for Connally. Reagan has been holding back too long" (Talbott, 1979).

Connally ran a poor fourth in the Iowa caucus and was soon out of the race, for reasons outside the Illinois context. But we must still examine the basis of his attraction as a conservative leader in the state. A particularly parochial interpretation, typically expressed by those close to the governor, saw the Reagan-Connally rivalry as a reflection of local divisions in the Illinois party:

It's the professional conservatives, led by Don Totten, who are the governor's opponents. Totten has a burning desire to be governor. He has chosen a very anti-Thompson stance. This has hurt Reagan, because Totten, his Illinois chairman, is a professional "anti" person. All leading Illinois Republicans are for some other presidential candidate as a result.

Yet even those working on the Reagan side emphasized local issues in accounting for local leaders' choice of Connally. As one spokesman put it:

It was personal. There were still hard feelings over the Ford battle. We have built support [for Reagan] outside the party organization. Connally was perceived as the front-runner [by the establishment], and they didn't want Reagan.

We may accept this explanation as one dimension of the limiting effects of rival leadership claims. We should also consider whether they involved differing conceptions of conservatism.

John Connally had never been identified with the kind of ideological positions long associated with the other conservative opponents. In fact, he had even denied being a conservative (Crawford, 1980, 139). Consequently, it is more difficult to trace his ideological roots or to locate his brand of conservatism. He was clearly making some claims to moral leadership, but our interpretations have to be more tentative than with Reagan or Crane, because we must work more impressionistically. Connally began his political career as a Democrat, remembered in history as the Texas governor accompanying John F. Kennedy when the president was assassinated. He switched to the Republican Party in 1973, and many remained suspicious of him for being a turncoat. He became Treasury secretary in the Nixon Cabinet and was apparently President Nixon's choice for vice president after Spiro Agnew's resignation. If Watergate had not destroyed the Nixon presidency, Connally would have been Nixon's heir and the presumed 1976 presidential candidate (Phillips, 1982, 59, 70).

Kevin Phillips, conservative strategist and commentator, gives the best overview of Connally's beliefs when constructing the likely direction of conservatism in the United States. According to him:

... a "conservative" government resting on a Sun Belt base stands a better chance of moving toward the views of John Connally than of Adam Smith—toward pork barreling, crop subsidies, agribusiness, high technology and aerospace mercantilism rather than fidelity to free-market principles. (Phillips, 1982, 97)

He also identifies a corporatist style of conservatism with Connally and foretells that, if economic problems were to emerge in a Republican administration, the conservative business community would be open to business-government cooperation (Phillips, 1982, 149–159).

We can begin to infer from this insider's characterization of conservatism some of Connally's probable sources of appeal, even detecting ties with the Burkean concept of conservatism in the necessity for strong leadership (though hardly of an aristocratic sort), and in the sense of an organic community, at least one that connects business and government (Rossiter, 1962, 65). Crawford (1980, 138), a conservative who writes critically of the New Right, notes that Connally was attractive because of "an image of the tough sheriff." This resonates with the views of the county chairman who told us: "I like Connally myself. I'd go with him even if he lost the primary. He's a real Republican. He tells it like it is—he's not wishy washy. I'm a hawk. I believe you have to be strong to survive. We should get back to the basic values, read the Bible, be strong." This also helps explain the otherwise bizarre encounter with a delegate to the 1980 state convention. He presented a pessimistic view of the state of the world and felt it could be blamed on those Republicans who had not stood behind Ronald Reagan in 1976. This led me to suggest that he must be pleased with the results of the 1980 primary, with Reagan far ahead. He indicated that his enthusiasm was tempered by the failure of Connally to do better, because Connally was the best-qualified candidate: "What I would prefer is a benevolent dictator. I'm really a fascist, aren't you?" Although I was able to satisfy myself that this informant meant what he said, this does not necessarily imply that he thought Connally would have turned into a benevolent dictator. What makes his train of comments relevant is the connection he and others sensed between the Connally candidacy and what has been located as "extremism of the center," where the benign attraction of certain leaders and programs also has the potential for appealing to "apple-pie authoritarianism" (Phillips, 1982, 239).

Challenging Relations

Congressional challenges display both the importance of purism and the relevance of single, litmus test issues. Votes by Derwinski and Erlenborn in favor of the Panama Canal treaty revision opened them to broader examination as conservative purists. Similarly, local autonomy, symbolized by the Regional Transportation Authority (RTA), was in the forefront of the challenge to McClory.

In the state Senate, there were three challenges to incumbents in 1978 and two in 1980, of which one in the later year was an instance of how litmus test issues are used divisively. John Friedland, first locally endorsed to replace the late John Graham in the state Senate and then to run for his seat in the 2nd District, was challenged by Richard Fonte, who was, in turn, endorsed by Governor Thompson. I earlier discussed this situation as an instance of how, when the source of power lies in the formal structure, challenges are efforts to broaden or narrow conceptions of legitimate authority. Here we see another aspect of the dispute, when the governor accounted for his action by Friedland's failure to support his transportation program. Friedland voted against S.B.889 (given third reading in the House on September 6, 1979), a bill allowing the RTA to levy a differential sales tax hike in Cook, Kane, DuPage, Lake, McHenry, and Will counties (Serati, 1979). Friedland's "no" was identical with the vote cast by other Republicans in collar and suburban districts, and just one of the many instances when the RTA split the party along regional lines (Everson and Redfield, 1980).

Litmus test issues were raised in the other state Senate challenges, but not in ways that affected the campaigns or the outcomes. Challengers were typically less conservative than incumbents, including Forest D. Etheredge, the only successful challenger. But his defeat of state Senator Robert W. Mitchler (39th District) was more the result of a combination of factors, including Mitchler's previous investigation by the IRS, than of ideology.

It was often difficult to decide what should be considered a challenge in the multimember House, where, in a weak or changing district, even the second candidate required by law might be perceived by the incumbent as a challenger and, in fact, might be one. To avoid making judgments about such situations, I applied a conservative definition and considered a challenge to exist only where there was primary opposition to two incumbents of the same party. Under this criterion, there were three challenges in 1978 and six in 1980, and litmus test issues were present in a total of five.

In three races, challengers favoring ERA tried unsuccessfully to unseat incumbents. In the 47th District, Donna Werner was in the difficult position of facing two entrenched representatives, both of whom were opposed to ERA (Decatur *Herald-Review,* 1980). The same was true for Jo Means in the 6th District (Wheeler, 1980). In the 52nd District, Bill Brooks made an even poorer showing, although he directed his opposition to one incumbent, Timothy Johnson, who had a history of being criticized for his failure to support ERA (*Champaign-Urbana News,* 1978).

In the 38th District, which included part of Kane County (one of the collar counties surrounding Cook County, the county containing metropolitan Chicago) and parts or all of five other (more clearly downstate) counties, both representatives voted in company with other downstate Republicans in support of the Regional Transportation Authority, H.B.889, for which they aroused opposition from Roy S. Dunlop. His ostensibly conservative position was no more successful in arousing support from voters than was that of candidates campaigning for ERA.

One challenge on single-issue grounds did succeed. It was mounted in 1980 by Judy Koehler in the 45th District against incumbent Donald B. Anderson, principally on his vote for a pay raise during the preceding lame-duck session. Among those outraged by the General Assembly's action was the Peoria *Journal Star* (1980a), the major newspaper in the area. It joined Koehler in her campaign, offering its endorsement (Peoria *Journal Star,* 1980b), and adding a powerful voice to public distaste for Anderson's actions. Even support for Anderson from Governor Thompson and Congressman Robert Michel was insufficient to withstand the momentum generated by Koehler's use of the pay-raise issue.

Of the 21 races in the General Assembly, only 1 went to a challenger who campaigned primarily on a single issue, and that was an issue not even generally thought to be a litmus test. But before concluding that issues are a poor basis for challenge, we should remember that most challengers were left with the *less* conservative position. At a time when Republicans

were concerned to demonstrate the strength of their conservatism, there
were not many good issues available to challengers.

Acknowledging Dependency

Throughout this analysis, we have seen how dependence on different kinds
of supporters under changing circumstances affects relations among party
actors, with each category of actor attempting to reduce uncertainty through
the ways he uses available resources. When resources take the form of ideological postures, the most dedicated conservatives in effect deny that there
are any uncertainties. From such a perspective, unequivocal positions on
issues, and on leaders who convey an image of strength and determina-
tion, are naturally attractive. We can assume then that the circumstances
surrounding the 1980 presidential primary were especially trying for conservatives. They were able to define many of the litmus test issues and even
had a choice of leaders, but they were impeded in ensuring representation
at the national convention through the introduction of a blind primary.
Under urging by the Republican State Central Committee, the General Assembly passed a measure allowing delegates to the national convention to
be listed on the ballot unaccompanied by the names of their preferred
presidential candidates. This was a serious matter, because the primary
electorate's preferences were not binding on convention delegates; this is
the sense in which the presidential primary is merely a "beauty contest."
The intention was to elect uncommitted delegates—those without known
preferences—whom the governor could bring to the national convention.

Several explanations were given for adopting the blind primary, of which
the presumably official one was the most conspiratorial:

Illinois GOP Chairman Don Adams presents the official version. He says the party
got wind of a plot by some people to run using U.S. Rep. Phil Crane's name even
though they didn't really plan to vote for Crane at the convention. (Kieckhefer,
1979)

The more common explanation, offered by those who favored the change,
stressed the length of time between the primary (March) and the general
election (November), a period during which many unanticipated changes
could occur. One such informant questioned the criticism received:

We changed the law so that we could have an open convention. Then we got hell
for having a blind primary. But then the Democrats tried to have an open convention, which was what, in fact, we had. I don't know why the press was so critical
of us. Eight or 10 months before a convention, we shouldn't have to decide on
our presidential choice.

The blind primary gave the governor an excuse for not making a presidential choice and left him with the appearance of maximum negotiating

flexibility at the convention (Ciccone, 1980a). Some also felt that Thompson's reluctance to commit himself was tied to his own ambitions. As one newspaper commentator noted: "How can the governor posture himself for a vice presidential nod? And a few others bluntly suggest that Thompson is merely sitting back waiting to pick a winner" (Lawrence, 1980). Yet, by his unwillingness to state a preference, the governor fed the suspicions of those who felt he was motivated by opposition to Ronald Reagan. Because those closest to him, including the legislative leaders, supported Connally, the governor was assumed to have made a similar, though tacit, commitment. The blind primary was, under this reasoning, part of a deal:

The cynic's answer . . . is that Gov. James R. Thompson and former Texas Gov. John Connally have struck a deal. The deal, the story has it, is that Thompson will use the blind primary rule to gain tight control of the Illinois delegation, then deliver the state's 102 votes for Connally. Dare one whisper that the nominee for president remembers recent favors when selecting his vice presidential candidate? (Kieckhefer, 1979)

There was no question that Reagan supporters were most disgruntled.

"We think it's to our disadvantage," said Charlie Black, political director of the Reagan campaign. "I don't think there's any question it will be harder this way to elect Reagan delegate candidates. There's been some suggestion the people who proposed the law did it for this reason." (MacKay, 1980)

As a means of dealing with the uncertainties generated by dependency on the outcome of changing issues, on presidential candidates' fortunes in other states, and on internal divisions in Illinois, the blind primary was a gamble. To the extent that it was intended to increase uncertainty and thereby provide the governor with more negotiable resources, it failed. By the time of the Illinois primary, Connally was no longer a viable candidate. The two strongest contenders were Reagan and Anderson. Aided by newspapers throughout the state, their campaigns were able to make public the identity of their delegates. As a result, the primary saw the election of 43 delegates for Reagan, 26 for Anderson, 3 for Crane, and 1 for Bush, with only 19 uncommitted.

Actors and Beliefs

Several apparent inconsistencies with regard to the treatment of actors and ideology have been introduced in this chapter. By resolving them, we can arrive at a conclusion to the place of ideology.

If ideology is a medium of interchange, in which resources like power, patronage, and money are used as a channel of influence, it should be negotiable by all categories of party actors. Yet the discussion in this chapter has been based on only about half of those in the party network. How should the omissions be interpreted?

If the concept of a party network is a useful way of defining the party in action, we would expect network members to be stable over a given period. And this has been the case until the present chapter, when presidential candidates were introduced. Are they a new category of party actor, or are they somehow exceptional?

If conservatism is the dominant value system, one would anticipate that everything that falls within its scope would be intrinsically consistent. Why, then, do issues and leaders regularly change the tests for ideological purity? Each of these questions is treated in turn, illuminating the special ways ideology acts as a medium. The results demonstrate the unusual potency of ideology, leading many actors to avoid using it.

Missing Actors

This chapter provided details on the ideological actions of 10 categories of party actors: governor, senator, congressman, state senator, state representative, state House and Senate leadership, advisor, financial contributor, and interest group. Although I have quoted informants who were county chairmen or committeemen, our attention has been directed almost exclusively to public officeholders (or candidates for those offices) and to the unofficial wing of the party. Assuming that the national level campaign committees are not relevant here, because they allot money to candidates regardless of ideology, we are left to consider the omission of party officeholders or units.

Ideology is treated here principally as a negative medium of communication, like power, but unlike power, there appear to be many constraints on its use, and those constraints most affect party officials. Because ideology defines the values of the party and, in so doing, establishes legitimacy for the party, its leaders, and its programs, any effective ideologically based attack on a party component is also an attack on legitimacy. To question legitimacy is no small matter, particularly for those party actors whose positions are based on the continuity of the party organization. As we know, this is not a constraint for actors in the unofficial wing, but it is for most others, under usual circumstances. I will give several examples of the latter before examining less usual circumstances, where conflict based on ideology is unrestrained.

Candidates for statewide office may find themselves in local districts where party officials are ideologically opposed to them. Such candidates are normally more moderate than local candidates and party officeholders. Whenever this ideological disjuncture occurs, it is still customary, in general elections, for the local party apparatus to use its resources on behalf of the party candidate. A study of divisive primaries in Ohio attributed the willingness of most county chairmen who had been on the losing side to work in the general election on "a kind of professional orientation" (Comer, 1976, 128). Earlier, for example, I quoted a county chairman who told his committeemen that they must campaign for Senator Percy as a lesser evil. In another district, where there is a strong county organization, we inquired about relations with state legislators with overlapping constituencies. The county chairman responded: "If the legislators are conservatives, then we get along very well. If they're left-wingers, then we don't." In answer to our surprise that such a staunchly Republican district should have "left-wingers," the chairman identified a relatively moderate candidate and then went on to say, "We tolerate him. We list him along with all the other Republicans running. . . . We encourage straight-ticket voting."

Even the limits in interchange associated with ideological differences in Congress are governed by norms that discourage overt conflict within the state delegation. When the National Pro-Life PAC targeted nine congressmen for defeat in the 1982 election, including Paul Findley of the 20th District, four congressmen on the PAC's advisory board resigned. Congressman Henry Hyde was one of the four, even though he and Findley were sharp opposites, especially on the abortion issue (Chicago *Sun-Times,* 1981a). The importance of such partisan and regional loyalties was implied by another moderate, Congressman Tom Railsback, calling Hyde "one of my best friends" (Coffey, 1980, 20).

Ideology, in terms of either general purity or specific issues, has often been the basis of challenge to incumbent public officeholders. When Governor Thompson supported such a challenger, incumbent state Senator Friedland questioned the governor's behavior, because, as Friedland correctly pointed out, he normally supported the governor's legislative program (Serati, 1979). He could also have asked why the governor did not campaign against other legislators who had voted against him, either on a litmus test transportation bill or even on ERA. The response of many party officials, especially local ones, was to rally around the incumbent, who affirmed: "Throughout my 11 years in the House, I've tried to reflect the views of the 2nd District and I hope to continue with that conservative record in the Senate" (Serati, 1979).

I have discussed other cases where the challenge was entirely internal to a local district and, even where unsuccessful, came close to upsetting the incumbent. When that occurs, we can be sure that there are major fissures within the existing party network, which must be reconciled if the incumbent is to mount a strong campaign in the general election. So Congressman Findley was admonished to pay more attention to local concerns and to local party officials after his challenge by the mayor of Quincy. "'This is a conservative district and we don't need a liberal Republican to represent it. Findley has to try and recoup the people and demonstrate he has heard their concerns,' said Dr. Ed Ragsdale of Alton" (Lambrecht, 1980). Dr. Ragsdale was Republican county chairman for Madison County and a well-known conservative.

When a state legislator challenges a congressman on ideological grounds, each can be expected to carry with him some portion of the local party apparatus. The winner then has to decide how to treat his former opponent's friends. For the most part, there will be pressure to reintegrate all actors into the network, although informants made clear that old battles are remembered long after the principals have departed.

The one setting where constraints seem not to operate is in presidential primaries, particularly when there is no Republican incumbent. Yet even in 1976, when Reagan ran against the incumbent president, some segments of the Illinois party went with the challenger. They included, as convention delegates or alternates: a congressman — Philip Crane; state legislators — Donald Totten, David Regner, Clarence Neff; a county chairman — E. D. Taylor; and local committeemen — Bernard Pedersen, Ray Choudhry. After Reagan's defeat, informants continued to debate the aftermath, and a Ford backer felt vindicated by events: "Many people now look back at Ford with respect. As Ford comes to look better, many people are recognizing that Reagan kept him from the White House. They remember he didn't campaign for Ford." Reagan people alleged that they had immediately gone to the support of the party ticket, even when rebuffed by the Ford organization. Yet, whichever is the more accurate picture, it is certainly pertinent that, up to the time of the 1980 national convention, informants kept referring to the divisions associated with the 1976 primary.

The 1980 primary was even more unrestrained, given the larger number of candidates, the absence of organizational loyalty to an incumbent, and the finer gradations in the conservative spectrum. Pragmatic concerns were always present: Who was better qualified? Who presented a more attractive image to the electorate? Who was more likely to defeat President Carter? It was the ideological issues, however, that aroused real passion, and only those issues aroused fears that 1976 might be repeated if the losers did not pull together in the general election. At it turned out, fears were unfounded, particularly once it was clear that Governor Thompson had made an unequivocal commitment to work for Reagan's election. Those originally pledged to John Anderson may have been bitter over their rejection by the convention, but they created little trouble for the subsequent campaign, perhaps because of Anderson's own defection. They too could have left the party, but to remain a part of it, even if unenthusiastic about Reagan, they had to play down their differences.

Actors omitted from this analysis — those holding party offices or in organizational units — are similar to those included by the importance they attach to ideology. Many, in fact, became involved in the party because of an ideological commitment to particular issues or candidates. We also know that the majority shared a conservative perspective, often more conservative than that of public officeholders. They were omitted primarily because they are inhibited from using ideology as a medium of interchange. Except when there are ideologically based challenges which enlist their support because the challenger already has ties to the existing network (for example, a state legislator challenging a congressman), or where the challenges are tied to crises of legitimacy (the search for a new leader), most party officeholders will refrain from using ideological currency in punitive ways. Their greater loyalty is to the Republican Party.

Added Actors

The variety of presidential candidates is critical to understanding how leaders structure and symbolize ideological appeals. The candidates themselves, however, do not play an independent part in what I have defined as the Illinois Republican Party network. Although it is true that presidential candidates initiate actions (for example, by appealing to party actors for support) and are the recipients of actions from others (for example, through delegate pledges), this still does not make them party actors like all the others in the network. Their importance lies in the way they become part of the ideological currency used by others. That is, what is relevant to us is not what John Connally did, but how he was the focus for organizing efforts by business and political leaders in *their* conflict with actors supporting Ronald Reagan. Presidential candidates are not true members of the Illinois party network but symbols for existing party actors, constituting a part of their ideological resources.

Conservative Beliefs

Our final apparent inconsistency arises from actors' efforts to apply conservative values. As issues and leaders emerge, they are examined in light of how well they exemplify conservatism. Paradoxically, even though conservatism as an ideology should provide an explanation for unique events and a blueprint for action, it cannot totally anticipate those events or the circumstances where its blueprint needs to be applied. Its inability to encompass future conditions hardly makes it unique; ideological exegesis is a regular part of the publishing industry. But conservatism may suffer more than other ideologies: "The genuine Conservative engages reluctantly, and never really comfortably, in political speculation" (Rossiter, 1962, 20).

The basic principles of traditional conservatism spelled out in the Burkean credo have never been completely accepted in the United States.

Conservatism in this country has been more optimistic, more materialistic, and more individualistic (Rossiter, 1962, 198–201). New issues arouse concern, and new leaders ask for legitimation; both must convince potential supporters that theirs are valid claims for inclusion in the conservative value system. This was how opposition to ERA and to abortion rights came to be part of the conservative perspective.

Because the ideological underpinnings are so ambiguous, there is no way to be sure what is meant by the conservative label. This was anticipated in the study, and whenever the concept was used, informants were asked to provide their own meaning. Responses covered a range: belief in capitalism and free enterprise; anticommunism and military strength; a balanced budget; "less government"; opposition to welfare, ERA, and abortion rights. Some informants raised more general topics: the role of government; the relations between big business and the Republican Party; the place of a broader representation of groups, as opposed to "fat cats." Out of these discussions, it was possible to discern two basic strains, in the sense of both themes and tensions, in current conservative thinking.

The first strain emphasizes fiscal restraint, an orientation to business (though not necessarily big business), and the running of government as a business, especially in its goal of a balanced budget. To the extent that government is necessary, it should be local rather than national. In general, informants who expressed this brand of conservatism were close to the American tradition of individualism, materialism, and optimism. It seems appropriate then, in the U.S. context, to call this the traditional form of conservativism.

The second strain emphasizes moral causes — issues of values, lifestyle, and morality "that place uncompromising evaluations in the forefront, and appeal primarily to the emotional well-springs of communal loyalties" (Schwartz, 1981, 66). Among the adherents of this fundamentalist brand of conservatism, there may be no conscious conflict with traditional conservatism, except perhaps to question the credentials of those longtime Republicans who are also wealthy, in the upper levels of large corporations, and mainline Protestants of northern European origin. Otherwise, both strands may unite in emphasizing the moral character of the party. This was described by an informant connected with both Young Americans for Freedom and a major corporation:

Jimmy Carter stole something from the Republican Party in 1976 by casting himself as the defender of the religious and moral fiber of America. . . . In the 1980 election, Carter will not be able to pull the same thing against Reagan. The Democratic Party has never concerned itself with broad issues of morality, while the Republican Party has always had an element of morality. If Reagan wins, the Republican Party will become as competitive with the Democratic Party as it can be. . . . Reagan will take the support of groups traditionally considered Democratic — Jews and Catholics — because he is seen as God-fearing. People will be voting for morality when they vote for Reagan.

Both strands of conservatism have an unexpectedly revolutionary quality. The affinity between tradition and major change was described by House Minority Whip Robert Michel in commenting on the 1980 Republican platform:

Some critics have dismissed the Republican platform as a document of stark conservatism. I think it isn't so much conservative as it is rebellious. Our platform advocates radical change in the role of the federal bureaucracy. . . . The changes we propose in the manner in which the federal government carries out its basic responsibilities are revolutionary. Our platform advocates the abandonment of 50 years of uninterrupted dominance of American life by the federal bureaucracy. It proposes a massive shift of functionary responsibility from the bureaucracy to either individuals, the private sector, or state and local governments. (Michel, 1980, 63–64)

Phillips agrees, seeing these goals as "a revolutionary blueprint more akin to other attempts to national restoration than to conservatism's usual efforts to maintain threatened existing institutions and relationships" (Phillips, 1982, 13). He also covers the fundamentalist themes by citing New Right leader Paul Weyrich:

We are not conservatives in the sense that conservative means accepting the status quo. Today isn't the same as the 1950s, when conservatives were trying to protect what was, constitutionally, economically and morally, in the control of more or less conservative people. (Phillips, 1982, 31)

Although they use different words, it is still clear that not many of our informants were hoping to conserve the past by reinstating lost virtues. One of the few informants who expressed nostalgia — an officeholder with experience across several levels of government — did so by recognizing the inevitability of the present:

The best time, as far as I'm concerned, in this country's history was during the pioneer days. The people who survived were the strong ones. You didn't have all this pampering of criminals — they hung them. But we can't turn back . . . we've got to make do now, be strong.

Applying different concepts and working from the perspective of voters, Schneider's (1981) distinction between two dimensions of voter alignment — the partisan, based on economic issues and historical ties of religion and region; and the ideological, based on social and cultural conflict — also capture the two strains within conservatism. But by the time of my research, and particularly because of my focus on the party network, I found a strong congruence between party and ideology, with the Republican Party virtually synonymous with conservatism. Yet even though ideological consistency has increased, it has not removed the underlying sources of conflict, because, in general, ideology is a negative medium of interchange. Moreover, conservatism itself does not remove the contradictory messages of individual rights and collective morality. This was sensed by those informants who were disturbed by the stress on single issues. Even a largely disparaging account of Senator Percy's behavior at the 1980 national convention by an advisor present as a party worker could not overlook what, at the time, appeared to be dangerously extremist positions undermining the presidential campaign:

I felt Reagan was shafted over the platform because of the extreme planks — like the composition of the Supreme Court. Senator Percy, at the last minute, tried to put together a petition so he could introduce an alternative. He failed, and that's typical of Percy. He did the same sort of thing in 1976. But no one wanted a confrontation between the "baby killers" and the "AntiChrist."

My answer to the apparent inconsistency between the integrity of the conservative value system and dispute over how broadly conservative principles can be applied has to be different from the answers offered for other inconsistencies. Where previously we could argue that inconsistencies were more apparent than real, here we must recognize the insoluble problem created by the requirement for generalization, which makes the message of conservatism an unstable one. Instability is tied, for one thing, to conservative reluctance to engage in theorizing, also found among rank-and-file voters (Neumann, 1981, 1260–1263), making it difficult to respond to new issues and events. More fundamentally, however, instability is rooted in the concept of the Republican Party as a moral community. To be moral means downplaying concern with what is merely acceptable; an ideology therefore cannot be constructed primarily out of themes that are attractive to voters or even other members of the party network. Those components of the party that are the major participants in elections, however, will respond to moral themes as a means of broadening the party's appeal, the only criterion being their apparent compatibility with existing definitions of conservatism. But as new themes are placed in conjunction with those already present, participants may be left with the uneasy feeling of being forced into association with the morally unworthy.

Inconsistency in the scope of conservatism is treated as an inherent conflict between traditional capitalism and fundamentalist moral values. As expressed by conservative columnist George Will (1982, 15–16), who presents himself as spiritual heir to the British Tories under the leadership of Disraeli, there is a yearning for an age when spiritual and economic values will be congruent. Other conservative writers, like Phillips (1982) and Crawford (1980), make less benign interpretations, because they see the emphasis on morality threatening the plural character of American democracy.

In the context of the Illinois party network, ideology remains a strongly negative force, so strong that many party actors are fearful of using it. This assertion does not rest solely on the particular qualities of a conservative ideology but on the ways that any ideology demands moral commitment if actors are to be considered part of its community. In chapter 8, I deal with the final medium of interchange — the relatively positive one of money.

8

Money Talks

Money Is a Positive Medium

The conventional definition of money as a standardized, neutral unit of exchange is appropriate to its growing importance for politics based on opinion polling, electronic media, and full-time office staff, all requiring almost continuous large-scale fundraising. Raising and spending money for these purposes are not our concern, however, because they do not involve using money for interchanges within the party network. For us, money is a positive medium. Given the guidelines developed in preceding chapters, we expect it to be used to maintain relations, best exemplified in the campaign strategies of the party apparatus. It should be used as well to establish links among actors, tested under the most internally trying circumstances for the party, that is, during primary elections. We have assumed that party actors prefer orderly relations, which they try to shape through positive means. Money should then have the capacity to impose order on the network.

To understand money as a medium, it is necessary to overcome two general assumptions about its symbolic qualities. In the first, money is regarded negatively, the corrupter of political endeavors and the debaser of human relations. In the second, the symbolic properties of money are overemphasized at the expense of any intrinsic worth, an approach that loses money's deeper symbolism.

The first response is familiar from the complaints of theologians and philosophers. It echoes Shakespeare's Timon of Athens:

> Gold? Yellow, glittering, precious gold! No, gods,
> I am no idle votarist; roots, you clear heavens!
> Thus much of this will make black white, foul fair,
> Wrong right, base noble, old young, coward valiant.
> (4.3.26–29)

Where money becomes confused with its intended use, acquiring the quality of a commodity, the stage is set for the kind of alienation Marx (1971, 59–64) attributed to capitalism. In this perspective, the symbolic and intrinsic worth of money intertwines in ways useful to my own concept of money as a medium, but a totally negative assessment hinders coping with the reality of its uses. I am much closer to Parsons (1967, 307) when he states, ". . . money is 'good,' that is works as a medium" by providing positive inducements which serve to continue or establish links among party actors. Whether money should be used in this way, or whether the resulting relations are desirable, is quite beside the point. My assessment of the positive uses of money is parallel to how I treated patronage separately from any moral judgments.

I part company with Parsons's conceptualization when he attempts to exclude all issues of intrinsic worth. He builds his argument on the premise that money has no direct utility—that is, it cannot be eaten or lived in—and hence can be comprehended only in terms of how it is used. For true financial transactions to occur, there must be the kind of shared understandings that allow the constituting of a market (Parsons, 1967, 307). But by choosing to ignore other social forms, like the miser's attachment to money, Parsons's symbolic approach actually places him closer to economic rationalists, who see money expended only in the expectation of a clear return. Money, however, has broader symbolic meanings beyond the confines of narrow market conceptions.

In the party network, mundane economic transactions occur, in which money is used to buy power, acquire patronage, and gain acceptance for beliefs—uses of money that are illegitimate in Parsons's schema, as well as often illegal. There is a similar market component to other media, in which power produces access to money, as do patronage and the activation of ideology. At the same time, each medium has its own domain of operation along with its own intrinsic value. Power is used to make binding decisions and to control important resources, but for some actors control may be an end in itself, retained and used primarily as a form of self-identification. Patronage is the means of exerting influence by appointments based on partisan affiliation, but it is also valued by its beneficiaries as a sinecure and a sign of approbation. Ideology defines the boundaries of the moral community, but it manifests its intrinsic value when adherence to principle is put above all other goals. Money is at least as complex because of the confluence of its objective qualities as tokens or symbols for exchange and the subjective value it acquires through use (Simmel, 1978, 131–203).

To clarify this conception of how money is used, consider two situations where a financial contributor and a legislator prepared to exchange money. In one, a lobbyist working for the passage of ERA, Wanda Brandstetter, offered support to a freshman state representative, Nord Swanstrom (District 35), if he would vote for ERA. He interpreted her offer as a bribe, as did the Sangamon County Circuit Court (Egler, 1980b). In another instance, in 1971, two veteran state representatives, John F. Wall (District 23) and Walter "Babe" McAvoy (District 25), felt their support for a law aiding private employment agencies should be worth $20,000 from the Illinois Employment Association and several associated agencies. The final bill was vetoed by Governor Ogilvie, and subsequently the disgruntled head of an employment agency testified in the representatives' extortion trial in 1978, leading to their conviction and loss of General Assembly seats (Mooney, 1978; Fisher, 1978).

Here were the most elemental uses of money, in which the political arena was treated like the market place, with buyers and sellers clearly identified. These uses do not, however, change the fact that it is illegitimate to consider the political system as a mere extension of the economy, or the votes of legislators as commodities. Although actors may do so, they are subject to punishment when detected. No matter how widespread corrupt practices are, we cannot derive a general medium of interchange from fundamentally illegitimate premises.

Legal constraints alone are not always sufficiently clear to distinguish between freely given contributions without noticeable strings and those that imply bribery or coercion. For example, a Democratic representative, Gary Hannig, wrote to remind road-building contractors throughout the state: "I have tried to offer my friendship and support . . . and now I hope you will do the same for me." Specifically he noted his vote in favor of a four-year road program: "I voted for this bill and now I need your help. I'm being challenged in the March 18 primary and your contribution will help to ensure my reelection (and the continuation of the road program)" (Thomason and Orso, 1980; parenthetical aside in letter). One legislator, informed of the letter, called it simply "a fact of life. You can't go to the people whose interests you voted against." Mild criticism was implied by Hannig's party whip, who said that Hannig "doesn't realize its implications. To say the least, it was in poor taste." But the Coalition for Political Honesty, a watchdog organization that led the campaign to reduce the size of the House, described it as "an example of the cozy relationship between Illinois legislators and special interest groups" (Thomason and Orso, 1980). Meanwhile, others worry that "Congress is literally being bought and sold by PAC contributions" (Oakes, 1984), a concern just as applicable to state legislatures in terms of money contributed.

Yet these activities and concerns about presumed effects do not fully encompass all the money in political circulation. That is, although using money for a direct payoff occurs, probably more frequently than is ever known, this is not money's only use. For example, after a careful examination of the relations between PAC contributions and congressmen, Sabato concluded, "It is ludicrously naive to contend that PAC money never influences congressmen's decisions, but it is irredeemably cynical to believe that PACs always, or even usually, push the voting buttons in Congress" (Sabato, 1984, 140). We need to continue asking why money is contributed; we will not understand the meaning of money until we abandon moralistic presuppositions about its effects.

Money is broadly available to all categories of party actors. Our interviews make clear that party officeholders are generally involved in fundraising and in spending money for campaigning and office maintenance. Predictions of party decline to the contrary, the organizational apparatus of state parties has actually increased, especially among Republicans. In a nationwide study, the Illinois Republican Party, compared with both Democrats and Republicans in the other 49 states, was found in the bottom half of "moderately strong" organizations, whereas collectively, local units ranked 12th in strength in 50 state-by-state comparisons (Cotter et al., 1984, 29, 53). Within Illinois there is great variation in the form this organization takes: there are counties with permanent offices and full-time staff, responding to questions from constituents and keeping in regular contact with public officeholders, producing newsletters and campaign brochures, and holding regular meetings. At the other extreme are counties that rely on a corner in the home or business of the county chairman, with sporadic volunteer assistance, meeting irregularly except at election times. But in all instances, money is a necessity. The survey of precinct committeemen indicated that a third of them (based on weighted averages) had been involved in fundraising for their own relatively minor local party office in their last election, and 85 percent had participated in fundraising as part of their general responsibilities in the county.

This involvement with money is equally true for public officeholders. In their case, we supplement the information obtained from interviews with campaign-disclosure documents submitted by state legislators. These documents provide information not only about the contributions received by state senators and representatives, but also about the campaign committees, legislative leadership, Republican National Committee, governor, congressmen, interest groups, and the general category of financial contributor.

In the aftermath of the Watergate debacle, Illinois joined other states in requiring campaign disclosures. First passed in September 1974, the Campaign Financing Act was incorporated into Article 9 of the Illinois Election Laws. It requires all candidates and some political committees that receive or spend more than $1,000 in a year to make regular reports to the State Board of Elections. Using the campaign disclosure regulations in force as of January 2, 1978, we based our analysis on reports filed by legislative candidates, covering 12-month periods ending in June 30 for fiscal years

1978 through 1981. While we do not claim that these reports are totally accurate, they are clearly more complete than those filed by nonparty committees, which are more likely to be late in filing and more circumspect in disclosing expenditures (Icen, 1977).

Preparations for a primary election, which takes place on the third Tuesday in March of even-numbered years, do not come to public attention until about December of the preceding year, when nominations for candidacy must be filed with the State Board of Elections.[1] Once the primary is over, campaigning can begin for the general election, held on the first Tuesday after the second Monday in November of even-numbered years. But for incumbents, campaigning does not get seriously underway until the General Assembly goes into summer recess at the end of June. This makes data on contribution disclosures, filed for fiscal years ending June 30 in even years, appropriate for evaluating contributions to primary election candidates during 1978 and 1980. Fiscal year reports in odd-numbered years of 1979 and 1981 are treated as linked with general elections held in 1978 and 1980. There is undoubtedly some overlap in reporting but internal evidence and confirmation from the State Board of Elections both confirm that these assumptions are reasonable ones. For example, since primaries are party elections, often without contest, one can assume that the size of contributions will be smaller than during general elections. This assumption was confirmed by finding that contributions averaged $7,526 and $9,932 per candidate in fiscal 1978 and 1980, compared with $14,307 and $18,885 in fiscal 1979 and 1981.

Our combined data sources reveal that every party actor is at least a potential contributor. For example, when we asked about the interchanges between legislators and their counties, we found in smaller counties the following comment from a legislator to be typical: "I get nothing from the counties. In fact, four counties ask me for money, so I give a little to all of them." At the same time, counties and other local party units are important sources of funding for legislative candidates. In a way that parallels the likelihood of being a contributor, almost every type of actor is a potential recipient of money, including even the Republican National Committee from the state legislators and the congressman from the State Central Committee. The only type excluded is, obviously, the financial contributor, except for particular contributors who play other party roles as well.

The pervasiveness of money makes it easy to use as a medium of inter-

---

1. See Article 8-9(1) for state senators and Article 8-13 for representatives, including the stipulation that no party limit its candidates to fewer than two (State Board of Elections, 1977).

change, linking those who give and those who receive, regardless of how money is subsequently spent. Critics of money in politics generally focus on expenditures, since they think in terms of what is being bought. But I have already indicated why this is not a useful approach to understanding the links among party actors. The law supports this approach by being clearer in its requirements for reporting contributions than for detailing expenditures. The latter are simply described as "a payment, distribution, purchase, loan, advance, deposit, or gift of money or anything of value, in connection with the nomination for election, or election, of any person to public office or in connection with any question of public policy" (State Board of Elections, 1977, 271).

Minor exclusions from reporting still leave great scope to candidates or committees in determining what is a legitimate expenditure. For example, Attorney General William J. Scott told reporters that, because his public office did not allow him to enjoy the kind of income commensurate with his position, supporters pressed contributions on him: "People not only made political contributions, but they gave me gifts. They gave me clothes and ties. And some people said, 'Here's some money. Do whatever you want to with it'" (Hillman, 1979). This behavior entailed no violation of Illinois campaign expenditure law, though the IRS took a different view (Slack, 1980). It is, in fact, scrutiny from the IRS that imposes the greatest constraint on how political money is used. The fact that contributions may be stored for future use, and even retained after a legislator leaves office — a practice also found among congressmen (Chaffee, 1984) — further justifies treating contributions as the relevant medium.

Our use of legislators' campaign disclosures clearly gives them the greatest prominence, which is in keeping with their centrality in the party network. It also turns out, however, to be highly informative about the contribution patterns of most other party actors. In the four fiscal years examined, $8,092,590 was circulated among 236 candidates, excluding loans and interest on deposits but including money that candidates contributed to themselves.

Maintaining Relations

Maintenance Strategies

Money is used by all levels of the party apparatus to maintain relations among actors. For most of the central party organs — the Republican National Committee and the State Senate and House Campaign committees — support for legislative candidates is the reason for their existence. The State Central Committee and especially local party actors — defined as county, township, or ward organizations, or local affiliates such as women's groups, all of which make up the traditional source of party maintenance—have many jobs toward this end and financial support for legislative candidates may be a minor part.

To keep the party alive by sustaining existing actors and units, replacing those who leave, and staying alert to the possibility of adding to the party network involves attention to a number of simultaneous goals. Maintenance can be achieved by staying with actors who are already known to be able to win elections and who follow predictable paths in the legislature, that is, those who are incumbents.

The next step in a relatively simple expansionary strategy is to look for candidates who are likely to win. Because they are almost certainly going to take a place in the party network, welcoming contributions are highly appropriate. Without second-guessing the decisions of party actors involved, it is reasonable to assume that these candidates—"certain winners"—will be in districts with an existing strong Republican base, as evidenced by historical trends or more recent population shifts. For the state Senate, these included districts where the seat had just been vacated by a Republican (Districts 1, 3, 7, 9, 39 and 44) or those that were perceived to be leaning strongly to the Republican side (Districts 10 and 31) and then actually won with at least 58 percent of the vote.

But caution alone cannot sustain the party network in a changing electoral environment, so greater expansion requires some judicious risk-taking in what I call "horse races." I define these as Senate elections won or lost within a 45–55 percent range, specifically Districts 34, 35, 43, and 59 in 1978, and 36, 42, 48, and 54 in 1980. Again, I did not indulge in second-guessing, but characterized districts by the election outcome, including that in District 35, even though the seat had been vacated by a Republican incumbent just after the primary. In other words, I did not presume to guess how much contributors' support may have affected the margin of victory or defeat.

The remaining districts, in Chicago and southern parts of the state, especially Madison and St. Clair counties, are ones where any Republican running for the Senate had been doomed to certain defeat. For party actors to dismiss such "certain losers" without a fight entailed an admission that the electoral environment held no opportunities, not even in the near future. Yet with limited resources, how can backing losers be justified?

Because money can be used in different ways, party actors may be expected to vary in the goals they emphasize. Hypotheses follow from the characterization of party relations in chapter 3, where dimensions of central-local perspectives and centralizing or autonomy-seeking activities were distinguished.

As the collective actor that is both most central and centralizing, the

Republican National Committee puts greatest emphasis on the rationalization of party organization. When an informant from that organization
said, "Our strategy is to go where we can have the most influence—the
most bang for the buck," we can expect this to translate into support principally for horse races and certain winners.

In addition to certain winners and horse races, the state-based centralizing units should also be concerned with incumbents, because money given
to them is another way of building solidary bonds. I make this prediction
in light of the complaint by the national party staff member who worried
that money controlled by the State Senate Campaign Committee was not
going to those in need, but to "buddies," that is, to incumbents. I quoted
him earlier, in the context of analyzing relations under conditions of disjoint constituencies, where these often led to cooperation within the same
category of actors. Money to incumbents is here interpreted as positive
inducement to cooperation. In total, we would expect the statewide campaign committees to give more money to all candidates than the Republican National Committee.

Local actors in the party apparatus are anticipated to be least discrimi-
nating in the sense of giving money to all four kinds of candidates, even
gambling on candidates in contested primary elections. We expect them
to be most affected by the fear that rejection of losing candidates will eventually lead to their own local organizations becoming moribund. However, because of more limited access to financial contributors as well as
the variety of maintenance tasks they may undertake separate from candidates' campaigns, local actors are likely to have less money available than
either statewide or national ones.

For this part of the analysis, it is generally not necessary to distinguish
among fiscal years. Until it becomes germane, reference will simply be to
election years, covering both the primary and general election under a
single year.

Senate Races

Expectations are fulfilled in Tables 8-1 and 8-2 for the Republican National
Committee's contributions to state Senate candidates. For the 1978 election period (that is, fiscal years 1978–79), 85 percent of its money went
to certain winners and horse races, and for 1980 (that is, fiscal years 1980–
81), these races received all the money, with the emphasis strongly on
horse races.

Like the RNC, the State Senate Campaign Committee gave most of its
money to horse races, particularly during the 1980 election, but in support
of my hypothesis, it also paid attention to incumbents, contributing over
20 percent of its available money to them. Although certain winners ap-

Table 8-1. Money Received by State Senate Candidates from Party Apparatus (fiscal 1978–79)

Candidate Type	RNC		SSCC		Local	
	$	%	$	%	$	%
Safe incumbent[a]	3,973	11	31,432	27	18,010	31
(N = 14)	(2)		(6)		(9)	
Certain winner	15,616	44	15,731	13	4,455	8
(N = 5)	(3)		(3)		(4)	
Horse race	14,334	41	63,551	54	22,586	40
(N = 4)	(3)		(4)		(4)	
Certain loser	1,273	4	7,432	6	12,024	21
(N = 11)	(1)		(2)		(6)	
Total	35,196	100	118,146	100	57,075	100
(N = 34)	(9)		(15)		(23)	

[a]Incumbent John Roe was not counted, since he received no party money in the primary and did not run in the general election. Instead, his replacement is counted as a horse-race candidate. Republicans contested 34 of 40 Senate races.

Figures in parentheses are number funded by each agency.

pear to have been downplayed by the SSCC in terms of the proportion of total funding given, actual dollars allotted and numbers receiving money were similar to those for the RNC in the earlier election and 2.5 times more than the RNC's dollar amount in the later election. Informants for the RNC had identified seven target districts in 1980, setting aside one of them as involving an incumbent, and contributions matched this strategy. Informants for the SSCC identified eight targets without distinguishing incumbency, and made contributions accordingly. At this time, we can say nothing about the State Central Committee, which gave relatively small amounts to only three candidates, because it is not clear whether it behaved more like the RNC or the SSCC.

Although campaign disclosure records of legislative candidates document that local party organs use money as a medium of maintenance, these records give an incomplete picture of local activities, because the moneys raised and spent can have an impact on legislative elections without ever being subject to official disclosure by a legislative candidate. The only exception involves those local units that serve simultaneously as campaign committees, of which two, both in Chicago,[2] were contained in our data. A powerful county organization, for example, like the one described in

2. Surprisingly, given the weakness of the Republican Party in Chicago, four other ward organizations made contributions to candidates outside their districts. These contributions, along with those by other local units to candidates outside their districts, are not included in this analysis.

Table 8-2. Money Received by State Senate Candidates from Party Apparatus
(fiscal 1980–81)

Candidate Type	RNC $	RNC %	SSCC $	SSCC %	SCC $	SCC %	Local $	Local %
Safe incumbent[a]	0	0	25,518	21	0	0	1,298	26
(N = 5)			(2)				(1)	
Certain winner	6,000	23	15,824	13	8,593	31	2,229	44
(N = 3)	(2)		(2)		(1)		(2)	
Horse race	20,000	77	78,825	66	18,801	69	986	20
(N = 4)	(4)		(4)		(3)		(4)	
Certain loser	0	0	0		0	0	500	10
(N = 7)							(1)	
Total	26,000	100	120,167	100	27,394	100	5,013	100
(N = 19)	(6)		(8)		(4)		(8)	

[a] Robert Mitchler, who lost in the primary, and David Regner, who dropped out after the primary, are not counted. Their replacements are found under the category of Certain winner. Republicans contested 19 of 20 Senate races.

Figures in parentheses are number funded by each agency.

chapter 5 as coordinating campaign activities for all district officeholders, may carry out both its fundraising and its expenditures independently of what is reported here. Also overlooked are those county chairmen qua legislators who are given especially active support by their county organizations without the direct contribution of funds. Though these may be serious limitations, they still do not destroy the essential outlines of how money is used by local actors. My greatest reservation concerns the actual dollars in circulation, which I assume to be more than those reported through candidate disclosures.

Assuming that a county chairman or a township or ward committeeman is just as eager as a member of the State Senate Campaign Committee that his candidate win—more so, if he associates winning with access to patronage—he still confronts a different situation, in which any reasonable candidate willing to run, regardless of his chances, should be supported. This expectation was borne out only in 1978, when 21 percent of the money went to certain losers, of whom 6 of a possible 11 were supported. In that election, the difference in the number of losers supported was greater for local units compared with the two central ones. But that election also indicated local party actors' preference for incumbents, of whom 9 out of a possible 14 were supported. Although I have included a cautionary note about interpreting amounts contributed, the decrease in dollars circulated in the 1980 election period is still striking, a change that none of our informants explained and that we did not anticipate. Senate candidates supported locally also declined, from 68 percent in 1978 to 42 percent in 1980. In 1980, of the little money available, certain winners got proportionately the largest share, unlike their experience in 1978.

In contrast to central party actors, local party actors were more likely to contribute early in the election period, including the primary, and to contribute to more candidates. During the 1978 election, local actors gave over 20 percent of the money allotted during the early period (that is, in fiscal 1978 rather than 1979) and under 10 percent in fiscal 1980; central party actors combined gave less than 1 percent of each election's allotment during the primary period. The situation faced in District 39 is illustrative of the problems posed by early contributions. The seat became vacant by the primary defeat of incumbent senator Robert Mitchler, who had been abandoned by the State Senate Campaign Committee, normally supportive in just such cases of primary challenge. Later, when we asked if this had been the kind of primary in which central party actors should intervene, we were told: "I don't know. It would be hard to know what to do. Mitchler is a turkey." His victorious rival, Forest Etheredge, apparently received $270 from the SSCC during the primary period. It is unlikely that the Republicans ever were in danger of losing this seat (I counted it among "certain winners"). Yet state and national party actors quickly intervened to ensure that their generosity smooth over primary conflicts. This amounted to an additional $7,711 from the SSCC, $8,593 from the State Central Committee and $3,000 from the Republican National Committee.

House Races

By referring to "candidate types" in the preceding discussion of Senate races, I implied an ecological unit, even though my analysis remained at the individual level. Perceiving this link between levels is important, because, although money is given to individual candidates, candidates' worth is determined by their positions in an electoral setting. As we move now to the House, with its multimember districts, the unit of analysis is more explicitly ecological. This unavoidable confusion has the redeeming merit of reinforcing our emphasis on the general (rather than the individual) character of party actors, which is largely due to their environmental embeddedness.

Because of multimember districts and cumulative voting, party agencies had more difficult choices to make in giving money to candidates for the House. In the assessment of one informant: "In the House, the meaning of the game is 25 percent plus one. We target for House seats, but it's very difficult because you have to set your sights on specific numbers." I was not much more successful in developing a systematic classification of districts, but results in Tables 8-3 to 8-4 are approximately parallel to those used for Senate candidates, once we take into account that House races have to be treated as an ecological level. But whereas Senate incumbents were all safe, the same was not true in the House. The incumbency designation is then restricted to districts with two safe incumbents.

Certain winners are defined as districts that can be expected, on the basis of recent history, to elect two Republicans, although at the time of analysis they had none or only one because of incumbents' withdrawal from the House, death, or primary defeat. Primary defeats occurred in District 7 in 1978 and Districts 31 and 45 in 1980. There were 4 certain-winner districts in 1978 and 11 in 1980.

Horse races are defined as districts that fall into a narrow range of uncertainty, where the two Republican candidates together attain between 45 and 55 percent of the vote. However, as long as the other party adheres to the agreement of not running more than two candidates, at least one Republican will always win. Both the horse-race candidate and the equivalent of certain losers in Senate races are then the second-ranking Republican candidates. Districts containing certain losers may still provide some opportunity where the current Republican member is a particularly strong vote-getter whose support could be extended. For example, minority members Ralph Dunn in District 58 and Bob Winchester in District 59 each won 34 percent of all the votes cast in 1978, enabling Republicans to win the second seat in 1980, yet these districts were considered horse races at both times. The imprecision of these categories was also a problem for actors in the party apparatus, as one told us: "We worked for Wayne Miller in the 9th District and Tony Bale in the 5th, but both never made it. I really thought we could pick up those second seats in the House." By my definitions, the two districts he mentioned were classified as horse races. Including vulnerable two-incumbent districts, there were 17 horse races in 1978 and 12 in 1980 and 22 and 23 certain losers in each respective election.

The same hypotheses that were examined with more straightforward, individual-level data for Senate candidates may be tested for House candidates in Tables 8-3 and 8-4. Expectations for the Republican National Committee were more clearly supported in the 1978 election, when 91 percent of its money went to horse races alone, but they were also confirmed in 1980, when it gave about the same percentage to certain winners and horse races combined.

In 1978, both the RNC and State House Campaign Committee gave the bulk of their money in certain-loser districts to Jerry Washington (District 26). The RNC was a reluctant contributor of $2,884 in this inner-city Chicago district, where the gentleman's agreement, allowing the minority party to gain one House seat, had broken down. The third seat was in-

Table 8-3. Money Received by State House Candidates from Party Apparatus
         (fiscal 1978–79)

District Type	RNC $	RNC %	SHCC $	SHCC %	SCC $	SCC %	Local $	Local %
Safe incumbent	0	0	500	1	50	100	44,002	59
(Dist. = 16)	(0)		(1)		(1)		(11)	
Certain winner	0	0	0	0	0	0	2,225	3
(Dist. = 4)							(3)	
Horse race	40,366	91	35,926	83	0	0	21,291	29
(Dist. = 17)	(15)		(14)				(13)	
Certain loser	3,489	8	7,036	16	0	0	6,548	9
(Dist. = 22)	(2)		(2)				(5)	
Total	43,855	99	43,462	100	50	100	74,066	100
(Dist. = 59)	(17)		(17)		(1)		(31)	

Figures in parentheses are number of districts funded.

stead won by an independent, Taylor Pouncey, regarded as simply another
Democrat. From the perspective of the RNC, Jerry Washington "had no
chance, but the House Campaign Committee felt it would be good to support him, so we said we would help." The SHCC showed its commitment
to Washington by giving him $6,235. In 1980, contributions by the SSHC
in certain-loser districts indicated a supportive role for candidates who were,
in effect, certain winners, if only by default. Of these, Louis Capuzi (District
19) mounted a challenge to the incumbent, in the sense that there would
be only one Republican elected to the House, and Jesse Jackson (District
29) — not the Democratic presidential contender — had strong competition
from two independent candidates in the general election, including one
from the previous Republican incumbent, Charles Gaines, who ran as an
independent after his primary upset.

The RNC's and SHCC's contributions to House candidates were closer
to each other in amount than were the RNC's and SSCC's contributions
to Senate candidates. Because of the special character of certain-loser and
safe-incumbent House districts, both the RNC and SHCC were led to apparently "waste" their money. We also see evidence of the weaker position
of the SHCC compared with the SSCC, previously described in chapter
2. In 1978, the SHCC had fewer resources than did the RNC; by 1980 the
SHCC was able to have greater impact on House races.

As with Senate races, the State Central Committee became more prominent during the 1980 election period, but without a distinguishable pattern of giving. We are left with the judgment of a national staff member,
who commented: "The SCC gets the jobs that the campaign committees
give it, and that they don't want."

Table 8-4. Money Received by State House Candidates from Party Apparatus
         (fiscal 1980–81)

District Type	RNC $	RNC %	SHCC $	SHCC %	SCC $	SCC %	Local $	Local %
Safe incumbent	1,834	2	7,581	6	0	0	19,883	34
(Dist. = 13)	(1)		(1)		(0)		(9)	
Certain winner	26,182	32	23,267	19	0	0	20,935	36
(Dist. = 11)	(2)		(2)				(8)	
Horse race	48,737	60	82,948	66	27,443	90	13,774	24
(Dist. = 12)	(6)		(6)		(4)		(9)	
Certain loser	4,000	5	11,656	9	3,088	10	3,455	6
(Dist. = 23)	(1)		(5)		(1)		(5)	
Total	80,753	99	125,452	100	30,531	100	58,047	100
(Dist. = 59)	(10)		(14)		(5)		(31)	

Figures in parentheses are number of districts funded.

   It is in their relations with House candidates that local party actors differ most from central party actors, and not simply by conforming to my
hypothesized pattern of contributing to all four kinds of districts and to
more of them. In 1978 local party actors emphasized safe-incumbent
districts through the amounts contributed to them. In 1980 there was a
more even distribution of dollars among all districts except for certain losers, who were shortchanged. But in both election periods the dollar amounts
were very unevenly distributed. For example, Representatives Edward Mc-
Broom and George Ryan (District 43) received $37,597, 85 percent of all
the money given to safe two-incumbent districts in the 1978 election, and
$17,937, or 90 percent, in the 1980 election. McBroom was himself a county
chairman, and Ryan was the House leader. Horse-race districts 46 and 49
accounted for 56 percent of all the 1978 money in those districts and 82
percent of the 1980 money. Each of the districts had two incumbents prior
to the 1978 general election, and in the 1980 election, one defeated incumbent sought to regain his seat. These findings exemplify the uneven character of local organizational support in addition to the special quality of
House races and the advantage they give to incumbents. But just as in Senate races, local actors contributed to more candidates — 52 through the 1978
election and 51 through 1980, compared with only 17 each by national and
state actors in 1978 and 17 by the Republican National Committee, 23 by
the State House Campaign Committee, and 16 by the State Central Committee in 1980. Similarly, local actors contributed larger shares of their
money during the primary periods — 20 percent in the 1978 election period
and 11 percent in the 1980 one — whereas central party actors gave, at most,
4 percent (by the SHCC in the period 1980).

Pressure to maintain the partisan character of the House through protection of incumbents is complicated by the phenomenon, noted in Chapter 4, of increased rivalry between representatives with congruent constituencies. In one example, a representative who had served on the SHCC made sure that he received funds from the committee matching those it gave to a candidate in his district who had the prospect of winning the second seat. In another example, national staff members were concerned that a sole incumbent would "hog all the votes" by having his supporters "bullet" (cast all three votes for him). To avoid this kind of self-centered behavior, they pacified him with money.

The tendency to support incumbents by giving money to pairs of candidates in the same district resulted in RNC support for six pairs in the 1978 election and five in the 1980, which also meant giving funds to each of five incumbents in both periods. The State House Campaign Committee's selection of four and seven pairs, respectively, led to support for five incumbents in 1978 and twice that many in 1980. Similarly, local organizations funded 18 pairs in the earlier period and 20 pairs in the later, including 26 and 22 incumbents, respectively.

Giving funds to incumbents who appear assured of reelection is not simply a needlessly expensive way to maintain the status quo. Almost every race poses uncertainties, and every defeat confirms the need for defensive strategies. For example, as a staff informant explained: "In District 51, Tate was running, and the incumbent was Webber Borchers [both Republicans]. We were trying to capture more votes for the Republicans [and win the second seat]. But the result was that Tate won and Borchers lost." Our informant could also have said that the same thing had happened in 1978, when incumbent Allan Bennett lost but Borchers won. If continuing to support incumbents is a small price to pay for maintaining the party network, it is even more crucial in those settings where other Republicans are potential rivals.

This maintenance role appeared to have increasing importance for the State House Campaign Committee, which, by 1980, compared with the Republican National Committee, not only gave to more incumbents but also gave them proportionately more money. In 1978, seven House incumbents got 26 percent of RNC funds, whereas eight incumbents got 31 percent of SHCC funds. The RNC gave 8 incumbents 24 percent of their available House money in 1980, compared with the SHCC's contributions of 62 percent to 14 incumbents. In addition, the SHCC was protective of incumbents in the primaries, giving Susan Catania (District 22) $800 to face a modest challenge in 1978, and Donald Anderson (District 45) $5,000 for an ultimately losing battle in 1980. Yet even the RNC recognized the importance of sustaining relations, as reflected in the example of Nord

Swanstrom, a freshman representative who, along with his running mate, had been helped with money in 1978. Strategy was explained by a national staffer:

Nord Swanstrom was a target in 1980. This was to protect the seat. But then the 35th District was dropped when it appeared Swanstrom was doing so well. His stock went up over the Brandstetter-ERA affair. In 1980, he waited around for the kind of help he got in 1978. We told him to get going on his own.

He did not, however, have to go on his own until after the RNC had given him $3,000.

Comparisons Within the Party Apparatus

Money used for the 1978 and 1980 elections gives the appearance that each of the central party actors has different roles. Concentration on a smaller number of races, made even easier by staggered elections and supported by the largest share of financial resources, ensured a dominant role for the State Senate Campaign Committee. The ensuing self-confidence led SSCC actors to emphasize the value of centralizing tactics; we were told:

Up until 1972, money was doled out to everyone running. Now we concentrate on target districts and on incumbents who seem to be in trouble. We're putting $220,000–$225,000 into eight districts [in 1980]. We contract with a media consultant, pay for newspaper ads, handle direct mail, and other advertising. We feel direct mail appeals are best.

We're doing more and more recruiting. . . . If there's a House candidate, that's who we go for. We do discourage some people; for example, Paul Findley's son wanted to run for the Senate—he did get nominated for a House seat. We don't endorse, but we do pass the word on to the county people about whom we favor.

This rational approach to campaign financing, however, does not remove justification for supporting incumbents, even those who do not seem to be in trouble, our informant to the contrary. In general, the SSCC's strategies confirm my expectations.

Illinois, unlike some other states, puts no limits on the amount of either contributions or expenditures, including those by central party units (Jones, 1984, 193–197). Whatever constraints there are apply to the national party and affect its contributions to Senate and House races. The entry of the Republican National Committee into state legislative races began on a large scale in 1978, when $100,000 was said to have been budgeted for Illinois. Yet even without legal impediments, this news was met by an outraged reaction from Democratic House Speaker William Redmond:

I am dismayed and angered that this brand of funding, which has overtones of Watergate laundering of contributions, will be used in campaigns involving state office. Citizens will have no way of knowing whether such funding comes from the long-entrenched corporation members of the Republican eastern establishment, from Lockheed, the ghost of Howard Hughes, or Robert Vesco, who has been under the protection of Costa Rica since Richard Nixon resigned. (cited in Estill, 1978)

Redmond's argument was used by the state campaign committees to force the RNC in 1978 to give Harold Byron Smith, as a prime mover in the Finance Committee of the State Central Committee and a member of both the State Senate and House Campaign Committees, cosigning authority, although this authority in no way affected Redmond's objection to the collective identity of contributors. Clearly, the campaign committees wanted the money outright and, barring that, gave the RNC field staff little say in the selection of targeted districts. In describing earlier the conflicts between Washington and Springfield, I recorded the admission that the RNC had "bought its way in" at the outset in many states; but in Illinois, whether in efforts to totally rationalize the campaign process or to cope with environmental uncertainties by challenging state agencies, Washington staff members were unsuccessful.

When looked at in terms of election year and division by chamber, the contributions of the RNC — supplemented by those from GOPAC, the Republican Party PAC for supporting state races — appear quite moderate. In total, they were clearly substantial enough to show support for horse races and certain winners, as I hypothesized.

An increase of about $80,000 in the campaign reserves of the State House Campaign Committee suggests that it played a more authoritative role in the second election period. The special requirements of multimember districts were an obvious concern, as our informant explained:

We're encouraging team efforts, that is, running together in a district. We have spotted 10 districts that look possible for the Republicans (in 1980), and we're raising money for them. We just give money to those who need it. . . . In the primary we didn't get too active, but we did try to get to county chairmen where there were candidates who didn't look like they could win in the general election, to support the person who looked strongest.

But efforts to rationalize candidate selection and campaign activities were limited, even more than was true for the State Senate Campaign Committee, by the more fractious nature of the House, which goes beyond the consequences of multimember districts, as was described in chapters 2 and 3. As a result, hypothesized expectations were only partly fulfilled, and not until the later election period.

With an increase in activities by statewide actors and similarity in their goals, possibilities grew for some decline in conflict between the state and national apparatus. For the RNC, maintenance of the Republican Party was tied to the ability to expand the hold on state legislatures (Buchanan, 1980). That expansion was clearly also desired by state units, but not at the expense of the Republican network's current form. Parallel activities and interests required interchange, and signs that this was going on are found in reports on the size of the RNC's Illinois budgets, said to be $100,000 for 1978 and $180,000 for 1980. My own figures, based on contributions to individual candidates, come to under $80,000 for the earlier election and over $100,000 for the later one. Some of the money unaccounted for, used to pay campaign expenses shared among a number of candidates, might not be recognized by those candidates as requiring disclosure.[3] But, in addition, we were informed that some part of the added resources of the State House Campaign Committee in 1980 came from the RNC. I had no way of knowing how much money was interchanged among central party actors, yet we can anticipate that, when money is used as a medium, the boundaries between collective actors in the central party apparatus will be eased and the expression of conflicts diminished.

Autonomous localism is more strongly associated with local members of the party apparatus through their inclination to support more candidates and more incumbents and to give comparatively more money to representatives, the more locally oriented of the two kinds of legislator. My hypotheses about local party actors' strategies did not anticipate the different treatment of House versus Senate candidates. Perhaps even more significant was the decline in money used by local actors. It is a strong sign that, as the campaign committees step up their centralizing role, local actors retreat, at least in the one area of campaign financing where they cannot hope to make a comparable mark. A slight decline in the number of local units contributing money to candidates in their districts appears over the two elections: county organizations went down from 31 to 25, townships from 15 to 8, and wards from 6 to 2.

In addition, affiliated party organizations in candidates' districts were quite unimportant in using money to maintain the party network. For example, during the four years considered, and combining money given to Senate and House races, local women's affiliates gave about 5 percent of the local money in circulation. The informant who said "The people who really work for the party are the women, and they get no recognition" was expressing his own appreciation for the help they gave him. But like others who praised the way women have helped sustain the party, he was not referring to an active role in using money. Women's groups were the major

3. There was also a discrepancy of about $100,000 in the amount purportedly budgeted by the SSCC in 1980 and directly contributed to Senate candidates.

category of party-affiliated collective actors, but generalizations about them apply as well to others in this category, for example, nationality groups or the Republican members of a local government.

A brief comment about the United Republican Fund completes this review of how all levels of the apparatus contribute to party maintenance. Described earlier as the fundraising arm of the Illinois Republican Party, it was superseded by the legislative campaign committees and the State Central Committee's Finance Committee, but it still contributes directly to legislative candidates. In chapter 3, it was placed on the local dimension of the party network, both functionally and ecologically, because this seemed to accord best with its latest self-definition. In its use of money, however, it is less significant than other local party actors. Like central and local party actors, the URF's preference was for incumbents and certain winners, but in relation to legislative candidates it was a minor player. It supported only 17 candidates for the Senate and 16 for the House, and gave relatively small amounts of money to candidates. Karl Berning, a strongly entrenched conservative state Senator in District 32, received over $1,000,[4] which deviated from its normal contributions of $200 in 1978 and $100 in 1980. These numbers are unequivocal evidence that the URF, whatever its protestations to the contrary, cannot expect to be an influential voice in legislative races.

Establishing Links

Primary Strategies

Contributions to legislative candidates provide a vantage point for looking at how money is used between links with different degrees of strength in the party network. On the receiving side, the weakest links are candidates who arrive on the scene as newcomers, without previous legislative experience. On the contributing side, the weakest links are financial contributors who are part of neither the official party organs nor the candidates' immediate constituents. For the party network, the time of greatest weakness surrounds the primary election, when party unity is overridden by struggles between ideological factions, competitors for power, and ambitious individuals.

State Senate primary candidates can be classified into eight categories, depending on their electoral status — incumbent, House incumbent moving up, newcomer — and whether or not they are challenged or unchallenged

---

4. Berning was unchallenged in the primary and beat his Democratic opponent by winning 55 percent of the vote. Nevertheless, he was perceived as vulnerable, receiving $7,834 from the State Senate Campaign Committee and an additional $249 from the Republican National Committee.

in the primary. The strongest party links can be assumed in uncontested elections, first for incumbents, then movers, and then newcomers. The same candidate order follows in contested elections, ranking progressively weaker links. The seventh and eighth categories are reserved for the two weakest links — newcomers challenging movers or newcomers challenging incumbents. There were no instances of challenged movers in 1980.

In their relations with candidates, contributors indicate the importance they attach to different attributes of the party network. The earlier discussion on the importance of maintaining relations might suggest that, even during the turmoil of primaries, and even on the part of weakly linked contributors, existing *strength* is paramount. This could be manifested through giving the most money to uncontested versus contested races, or to incumbents versus others, or, at best, to incumbents with demonstrated stability. The contribution pattern emphasizing strength would then range, in descending order, from unchallenged incumbent to unchallenged mover, challenged incumbent, and challenged mover.

A somewhat different assessment of the primary period would assume that it is more essential to *protect* those who face challenges from newcomers. This would result in a pattern ranging from most contributions to challenged incumbents, then challenged movers, unchallenged incumbents, and least for unchallenged movers.

Where the party's vitality is felt to lie in its responsiveness to new circumstances, an ability to recruit new talent and a willingness to dislodge those who have grown tired are positive signs of ferment deserving of support. It is here that the establishment of *new* links becomes manifest, with money distributed accordingly. Under strategies of newness, in descending order, most money would go to a newcomer challenging an incumbent, then to a newcomer challenging a mover, a challenged newcomer, a challenged mover, and a challenged incumbent. The plausibility of these models of giving is first tested in Tables 8-5 and 8-6, using average contributions to Senate candidates in 1978 and 1980, with averages calculated on the basis of the total number of candidates in each category. Financial contributors counted here are outside-district individuals, businesses, trade and professional associations, trade unions, ideological groups, and lobbyists. Almost all candidates were funded with the exception of seven newcomers in 1978 and five in 1980.

Strengthening already strong ties with incumbents has slight support from the data only if we do not take into account the type of election. Probably more relevant is evidence of differences among candidates and between elections. In 1980, fewer races generated more money and more contributors. This becomes even more apparent if support for Senate Minority Leader David Shapiro is examined separately. When his $12,880 from

Table 8-5. Contributions to Senate Candidates from Outside District,
Nonparty Sources (primary period — fiscal 1978)
(mean $)

	No Contest		Contest	
Type of Race	N	$	N	$
Incumbents	11	2,601	3	8,522
Newcomers v. incumbents	na		2	3,637
Races	(12)		(3)	
Movers	2	2,850	3	7,183
Newcomers v. movers	na	—	2	4,983
Races	(2)		(3)	
Newcomers[a]	5	797	4	548
Races	(10)		(4)	
Mean total		6,248		21,238
Races	(24)		(10)	

[a] Includes three write-ins who then ran in the general election.

Na = not applicable.

Means are based on all candidates in each category. The base is equal
to the number of races except for contested newcomer races, when it
is doubled.

N = number of candidates actually funded.

54 contributors is subtracted from the 1978 totals, and Senator John Roe
(District 35) is excluded from the base (he received no outside-district funding and withdrew before the general election to become chief justice of
the Illinois Court of Claims), then each of the 10 remaining incumbents
received an average of $1,834 from 7 contributors. No other unchallenged
members of the Senate leadership received significant contributions, although Senator John Grotberg (District 38), added as an assistant leader
in 1980, did obtain $4,225 from 20 contributors, ranking next in this re-
gard to Senator Shapiro.

Protection of the existing network from possible disruption by challengers was the most prominent strategy. In 1978, the 3 challenged incumbents averaged $8,522 compared with the 11 unchallenged, who averaged
$2,601. The same was true, though less sharply, for challenged represen-
tatives seeking to move to the Senate compared with unchallenged movers.
The challenged movers were not involved in the 1980 election, when the
two challenged incumbents averaged $17,208 from 26 contributors, leav-
ing their unchallenged counterparts to rely on an average of only $4,767
from 16 contributors.

The full importance of protective strategies becomes manifest when com-

Table 8-6. Contributions to Senate Candidates from Outside District,
Nonparty Sources (primary period — fiscal 1980)
(mean $)

| | No Contest | | Contest | |
Type of Race	N	$	N	$
Incumbents	5	4,767	2	17,208
Newcomers v. incumbents	na	–	2	18,282
Races	(5)		(2)	
Movers	2	5,400	na	
Races	(2)		(0)	
Newcomers[a]	6	471	2	388
Races	(7)		(2)	
Mean total		10,638		35,878
Races	(14)		(4)	

[a]Two districts held no primary races. One write-in candidate who later
ran in the general election is included.

Na = not applicable.

Means are based on all candidates in each category. The base is equal
to the number of races except for contested newcomer races, when it
is doubled.

N = number of candidates actually funded.

pared with efforts at establishing new links. In 1978, protection dominated.
Of the three incumbents who were challenged in 1978 — John Graham (District 2), John Nimrod (District 4), and James "Pate" Philip (District 40) —
only Graham had, in fact, a serious fight, defeating Richard Fonte with
just over 50 percent of the vote. Yet Nimrod's 74 percent victory was matched
by almost an equal amount of money as Graham — $10,490 compared with
$11,449 — although from fewer contributors — 29 compared with 42. Philip,
also an assistant minority leader, who won with a more modest though
still secure 59 percent, received a meager $3,627 from eight contributors,
whereas his opponent, John Benzin, received nothing from these unofficial,
outside-district sources. Richard Fonte (District 2) was the sole challenging newcomer to receive significant support — $9,450 from 20 contributors.

Much of the protective contributions to movers can be attributed to support generated by Roger Keats (District 1), who received $12,100 from 31
contributors to win against Jeanne Bradner with 58 percent of the primary
vote. Less strongly supported Leonard Becker (District 7) — $5,950 from
20 contributors — defeated his totally unsupported opponent, Carl Odeen,
with an even more overwhelming 75 percent. But Thomas Miller (District
10), who hoped to move from the House in a primary battle against

newcomer Aldo DeAngelis, got only $3,500 from 11 contributors and, with 46 percent of the vote, lost to his opponent, who received $10,900.

Establishment of new links on the one hand, and protection of the existing network on the other, were the two dominant motifs in the 1980 primary. The two challenging newcomers in that primary received an average of $18,282 from 43 contributors, outdoing even the incumbents they challenged by more than $1,200 and 17 contributors. More money was not, however, sufficient to alter the election outcomes. Although Fonte received more than Friedland and Mitchler more than Etheredge, both Fonte and Mitchler were defeated.

Contributor Strength

Given that the data show some inclination to support strength and a tension between protection and the establishment of new links, especially in 1980, we can assume that these findings are affected by variations in the way contributors relate to candidates. Contributors who themselves have the strongest ties to the party network can be expected to consider candidate strength and protection paramount in determining contribution strategies. For individuals, firms, and associations with no official party status or standing as local constituents, strong ties are defined empirically as multiple links to the party network. Since the number of links may not be perfectly correlated wtih actual dollars contributed, the two need to be considered simultaneously. Candidates defined as newcomers are more likely to rely on contributions from individuals, firms, and associations who have weak ties to the party network — that is, those with few links — and who can also be expected to make relatively smaller contributions.

All those with strong links to the party network can be identified by summing the numbers of candidates they supported and the total dollars contributed over the four reporting years. If we were to follow this definition rigorously, however, we would be confined to a small number of associational contributors — Illinois Realtors Association, Illinois Medical Association, Illinois Chamber of Commerce, and Illinois Manufacturers' Association — each of which contributed over $200,000 to at least 250 candidates. The solution, displayed in Table 8-7, is to isolate the most strongly linked contributors within categories and then supplement them with those at the next level of strength. Cut-off points were determined by the natural clustering of contributors and were surprisingly easy to make.[5]

When the five types of contributors are divided according to relatively

5. The only troublesome choice was over dropping the Aurora Valley Chamber of Commerce, which contributed enough money — over $45,000 — to qualify for inclusion among moderately linked trade associations but gave to only 25 candidates.

Table 8-7. Contributors with Strong and Moderate
Links to the Party Network (fiscal 1978–81)

	$	No.
Trade Associations		
RPAC	257,335	386
IPAC	241,135	289
MPAC	203,960	262
IL Construct.	83,325	237
CAR	69,300	176
AMBIPAC	64,745	258
IL BANKPAC	46,720	186
LUPAC	35,200	172
Professional Associations		
IMPAC	216,027	353
IPACE	72,803	136
IL PHARMPAC	44,145	125
LICID	43,515	180
Firms		
Amoco	29,550	141
CIPS	24,120	86
HFC	22,675	110
Sears	12,600	42
Deere	11,275	35
CarsonPirS	11,245	70
Interlake	10,230	45
IL Bell	9,622	65
ICG	9,050	45
Trade Unions		
UAW	37,645	69
Teamsters	19,870	73
AFSCME	8,105	57
Service Empl.	6,750	38
Individuals		
W. Clement Stone	27,500	40
Bob J. Perry	7,800	10

strong, moderate, or weak links with the network and contributions are standardized by the number of Senate candidates in each category, this degree of disaggregation makes the search for patterns less reliable (Table 8-8). For the most part, we find protective strategies to be dominant. Those results that are inconclusive are principally due to the attraction to existing strength that was found in supporting incumbent Senate leader Shapiro in 1978. Although strongly linked contributors were most consistent in

Table 8-8. Contributions to Senate Candidates by Type of Primary Race and Strength of Contributors' Ties (primary periods—fiscal 1978 and 1980) (mean $)

	Contributor Ties					
	1978			1980		
Type of Race	Strong	Moderate	Weak	Strong	Moderate	Weak
Trade Associations						
No contest						
Incumbents	354	525	262	460	1,520	225
Movers	1,500	325	0	1,000	1,850	750
Newcomers	425	0	0	143	214	43
Contest						
Incumbents	1,517	703	1,100	6,900	1,650	1,620
Newcomers v. incumbents	0	83	50	750	2,300	100
Movers	1,633	367	117	na	na	na
Newcomers v. movers	333	0	0	na	na	na
Newcomers	188	0	12	0	150	0
Professional Associations						
No contest						
Incumbents	339	121	96	410	540	150
Movers	750	0	86	125	225	150
Newcomers	0	50	0	0	0	0
Contest						
Incumbents	971	217	458	500	200	675
Newcomers v. incumbents	0	1,253	0	1,250	2,355	100
Movers	800	400	33	na	na	na
Newcomers v. movers	0	0	0	na	na	na
Newcomers	63	0	0	0	0	25
Firms						
No contest						
Incumbents	300	8	271	240	90	215
Movers	250	0	125	225	625	250
Newcomers	120	20	130	0	0	0
Contest						
Incumbents	267	0	1,300	750	312	375
Newcomers v. incumbents	0	0	517	0	100	4,750
Movers	200	233	967	na	na	na
Newcomers v. incumbents	100	0	1,283	na	na	na
Newcomers	87	0	23	0	0	0
Trade Unions						
No contest						
Incumbents	63	8	17	200	0	0
Movers	0	0	0	0	0	0
Newcomers	0	0	0	42	0	0

(Continued on following page)

Table 8-8. *(Continued)*

Type of Race	1978			1980		
	Strong	Moderate	Weak	Strong	Moderate	Weak
Trade Unions (cont.)						
Contest						
Incumbents	183	0	0	0	0	0
Newcomers v. incumbents	167	50	0	738	125	125
Movers	167	83	67	na	na	na
Newcomers v. movers	0	0	0	na	na	na
Newcomers	0	0	0	63	0	0
Individuals						
No contest						
Incumbents	0	0	220	200	0	20
Movers	0	0	250	0	0	0
Newcomers	0	0	172	0	0	0
Contest						
Incumbents	150	0	957	500	0	725
Newcomers v. incumbents	0	0	1,117	0	0	4,745
Movers	1,000	0	633	na	na	na
Newcomers v. movers	0	0	1,100	na	na	na
Newcomers	0	0	113	0	0	150

Dollars contributed have been standardized by the number of candidates in each category. Refer to Tables 8-5 and 8-6 for number of candidates in each type of race and to Table 8-7 for identity of strongly and moderately linked contributors.

following strategies of protection and avoiding newness, this was the general tendency for all types of contributors, especially in 1980. The clearest manifestation of the contrary strategy—support for newness and avoidance of protection—came from weakly linked firms in 1980. Similar inclinations can also be seen for moderately linked professional associations, weakly linked individuals, and trade unions generally, all in 1980.

Without weakly linked firms, newcomers of all kinds would be almost completely disadvantaged. In 1978, Standard Oil of Indiana (Amoco) was the only strongly linked firm to give money to a weakly linked candidate—$300 to DeAngelis (a newcomer challenging a mover). It also provided money to two newcomers in competitive races, Peternard and Maitland (challenged newcomers). In 1980, there was no money from strongly linked firms to newcomers. Nor were moderately linked firms concerned with forging new links. In 1978, three such firms—Carson Pirie Scott, Sears, and John Deere—did not even participate during the primary period. Absence from the field was true as well for John Deere in 1980, when Carson's gave a meager $175. Although Sears did participate to the amount of $1,100, only one moderately linked firm in that year, Illinois Bell, gave $200 to Forest Etheredge (a newcomer challenging an incumbent). In both years, not only were weakly linked firms vitally important for challenging newcomers, but there was virtually no overlap between those who contributed to newcomers in contested races and those who funded all other candidates.

Among individual financial contributors, only one stands out — insurance executive W. Clement Stone; either alone or with his wife, he helped 40 candidates over four years with the amount of $27,500. Running a distant second is Bob J. Perry, a Texan alert to conservative candidates. He gave 10 candidates a total of $7,800 during this time. Individual financial contributors, then, are not sufficiently varied for testing my hypotheses, yet even so, they do support my expectation that those with strong links — in this case, W. Clement Stone — will give money in support of protection. During the two primary periods, he gave $5,450 to three incumbent senators and one representative moving into the Senate, all but one of whom were facing challenges. In 1980, expectations that support for newcomers challenging incumbents would come from relatively numerous small contributions were confirmed for Richard Fonte, but not for Forest Etheredge. Fonte received $8,960 from 28 individual contributors, a pattern that had also been present in 1978, when he received $3,550 from 9 contributors.

Trade unions are normally not considered one of the interest groups that are part of the Republican Party network. Informants made this clear when they criticized trade union leadership and justified the creation of political action committees to counteract the influence of unions on the Democratic Party. Given their peripheral status, when unions do contribute to Republican candidates, we would expect them to support weakly linked newcomers. Yet even unions can be differentiated according to the strength of their ties, with the United Auto Workers and the Teamsters most strongly linked. In 1978, the UAW gave $500 to Richard Fonte (a newcomer challenging an incumbent), though the more customary pattern for strongly linked unions is to support more strongly linked candidates. In 1980, however, there was a more expected bias among all union contributors to support newcomers, with the UAW giving a total of $975 to Fonte and Etheredge, and the Teamsters giving $500 to Fonte.

Trade associations dominate the contribution field, and they all followed protective strategies, with a preference for movers of all kinds. The average of $333 given to newcomers challenging movers in 1978 was the result of a contribution of $1,000 to DeAngelis from the Illinois Chamber of Commerce, which also gave $500 to his rival Miller. In 1980, as well, strongly linked contributors were largely protective. The Illinois Chamber of Commerce gave 98 percent of its campaign money to Friedland and Mitchler, and the Illinois Manufacturers' Association gave them 93 percent. However, the Illinois Realtors Association gave not only $2,300 to these two challenged incumbents but also $1,500 to opponents Fonte and Etheredge.

Of moderately linked trade associations, the Car and Truck Dealers Association was most involved in the primaries, following strategies of strength and protection. The only departure was a contribution of $1,000 to Etheredge (a newcomer challenging an incumbent). In contrast, the moderately linked Illinois Life Underwriters Association played little role in the 1978 primary but touched bases in 1980, giving $2,000 in support of strength, $1,000 to protect challenged incumbents, and $450 to the incumbents' challengers.

The professional association with the greatest contributor role was the Illinois Medical Association, which normally followed protective strategies. The one moderately linked professional association that did not conform to that pattern was the Illinois Education Association, the Illinois affiliate of the National Education Association, which represents all public school employees, making it more of a special-interest group with some trade union characteristics than a true professional association. The Illinois Education Association was the primary contributor to newcomers challenging incumbents in both primaries, indicating its search for more sympathetic legislators. Yet even the Illinois Medical Association departed from its expected role in 1980, giving $2,500 to Fonte and Etheredge (newcomers challenging incumbents), but also $1,000 to challenged incumbent Mitchler.

House Races

In order to consider House candidates, there are more complex issues to resolve, primarily regarding the meaning of competition. Because election laws required that each party nominate two candidates per district for House seats, assuming they were available, a primary election in which there were only two candidates for the House ostensibly meant there was no contest. However, in Chicago and counties like St. Clair and Madison, where Republicans could expect to win only one seat in the general election, the appearance of a second candidate, even in the primary, could be interpreted as a challenge to the incumbent. From our informants, we know that, under such circumstances, it was common to view second candidates as rivals. As a result, it is appropriate to consider anyone other than an incumbent to be a competitor and any race involving competitors to represent a contest. Just as with House races in general elections, an ecological element is involved in the analysis of primary races.

Just like primary races for the Senate, those for the House generated contributions in support of existing strength, that is, for incumbents. In uncontested primaries, mean contributions to Senate incumbents were $2,601 in 1978 and $4,767 in 1980; to House incumbents in safe two-incumbent districts, they were $2,418 in 1978 and $4,888 in 1980. In the House, leaders were singled out for support by financial contributors, regardless of their competitive position. In 1978, contribution strategies affirming strength were limited to House Minority Leader George Ryan, who received $20,950 from 42 contributors, and factional leader Donald Totten, who received $15,275 from 46 contributors. This pattern was even clearer in 1980, when Minority Leader Ryan raised $57,000 from 134 contributors.

Tables 8-9 and 8-10 concentrate on what is defined as contested races. Both unequivocally demonstrate the importance of protective strategies by contributors to House races. This pattern was especially true in 1980, when anticipation of new district boundaries made all races important, particularly those that generated competition, and resulted in an increase in money circulating. Some newcomers still were very successful in developing ties with contributors, particularly in open races with no incumbents. For example, during the 1978 primary period, John Birkinbine received $4,500 from 11 contributors compared with Dolly Hallstrom's $1,306 from 3, and both won over three other candidates in District 1. Sam Vinson, a future leader, was rewarded with a high $7,397 from 23 contributors compared with Gordon Ropp's $835 from 12, both taking seats in District 44 from among 11 primary candidates. In this same year, newcomer Clyde Robbins (District 54) had no funds from outside sources but won in the primary—and the general election—along with Glen Bower, who raised

Table 8-9. Contributions to House Candidates in Contested
Primary Races from Nonparty, Outside
District Sources (primary period—fiscal 1978)
(mean $)

	Incumbent		Challenger	
Type of Race	N	$	N	$
Two incumbents v. 1 challenger (races = 7)	14	2,574	7	736
One incumbent v. 1 challenger (races = 13)	13	1,564	13	223
v. 2 or more (races = 20)	20	2,356	51	356
No incumbent (races = 5)	na	0	26	701

N = number of candidates in each category. These are the base for calculating mean dollars.

Table 8-10. Contributions to House Candidates in Contested
Primary Races from Nonparty, Outside
District Sources (primary period — fiscal 1980)
(mean $)

	Incumbent		Challenger	
Type of Race	N	$	N	$
Two incumbents				
v. 1 challenger	10	4,716	5	1,893
(races = 5)				
v. 2 or more	2	5,118	3	233
(races = 1)				
One incumbent				
v. 1 challenger	13	4,697	13	335
(races = 13)				
v. 2 or more	15	5,495	45	1,558
(races = 15)				
No incumbent	na	0	20	1,616
(races = 4)				

N = number of candidates in each category. These are the
base for calculating means.

$1,623 from five contributors. In District 33 in 1980, however, where there
were 10 primary candidates in a race without incumbents, the candidate
most successful in attracting outside support — Richard Burnidge with
$5,650 — was narrowly defeated by Richard Klemm, who had $4,033 in outside funding, and was also surpassed in votes by Jill Zwick, who had only
$3,550.

It is evident from Tables 8-9 and 8-10 that newcomers in races where
there was already at least one incumbent were disadvantaged with respect
to funding by outside sources, but there were a number of striking exceptions. In the 1978 primary, newcomers Louis Capuzi (District 19) with $6,000
and John Hallock (District 34) with $5,270, and in 1980, Doris Karpiel
(District 2) with $4,600, Robert Kustra (District 4) with $4,680, Diana Nelson (District 6) with $6,488, Judy Topinka (District 7) with $16,647, and
"Junie" Bartulis (District 49) with $6,250 all succeeded in both raising re-
spectable amounts of outside money and overcoming competition to gain
first primary and then general election victory. Only in District 39 did 1980
primary candidates Suzanne Deuchler and Dennis Hastert receive modest
external support compared with that of at least one rival candidate and
still achieve electoral success.

The House elections that are most comparable to Senate ones, involving the extremes requiring protection and establishment of new links, are
challenges to two incumbents. In those circumstances challengers are the

most weakly linked candidates, of whom there were seven in 1978 and eight in 1980. Only two were funded by outside sources in the earlier primary and three in the later; of these, only David Barkhausen (District 31) and Judy Koehler (District 45) were successful in displacing one incumbent in 1980. In addition, in 1978, Louis Capuzi's primary victory in District 19 enabled him to gain more votes than incumbent Boris Antonovych in the general election, and then to assume the minority Republican seat for that Chicago district. Incumbent Paul Matula was upset in District 7 in the 1980 primary, allowing Judy Topinka and John Kociolko to win both seats in the general election. A similar upset removed incumbent Charles Gaines in District 29, when more votes went to former incumbent Robert Holloway and newcomer Jesse Jackson, whose famous namesake may have confused enough voters to let him win the general election.

Because contributions to House candidates were even more clearly defined than those to Senate candidates, and especially because efforts to establish links with newcomers were relatively insignificant, concern with the character of contributors to House races seems less important than it was with Senate contributors. I limit my examination, then, to two races in 1978 and four in 1980 when clashes between incumbents and newcomers generated noteworthy amounts of money for most contenders. Proceeding in this fashion, we shall encounter the unique qualities of each House race.

My choice of the term "newcomer" to describe nonincumbents is a relative one, obscuring the earlier incumbency of Robert Holloway (District 29) and Louis Capuzi (District 19). Yet neither recent nor current incumbency made much difference in forming ties with strongly linked contributors. In the only exceptions to the general pattern, Holloway received $1,000 from the Illinois Realtors Association, but the association partly compensated for this by giving $250 to incumbent Charles Gaines; the association also gave Capuzi $500 and incumbent Antonovych $200. Although Capuzi was three times as successful as Antonovych in raising external funds, he got them primarily from weakly linked sources. We can imagine that Capuzi was especially careful in this regard since his 1974 bribery conviction (later reversed), when he was charged with accepting a $200 contribution from the concrete industry (Lawrence, 1976).

In the 1978 primary race in District 6, where there were two incumbents, challenger Jo Means lost by 407 votes to incumbent Emil Boucek and by 87 votes to incumbent William Walsh. Strongly linked trade associations were the mainstay only of Walsh, who received $2,750 from them. This contrasted with contributions from the Illinois Chamber of Commerce of $300 to Boucek and $350 to Means, whose candidacy was primarily an ideological one (discussed below).

State Representative Ronald Griesheimer (District 31), in a two-incumbent district, suffered from publicity over two encounters with the courts, one for speeding (Kirby, 1979) and another for aggravated battery, reduced to simple battery (*Lake County Tribune,* 1980). As a result of the latter charge, he was not endorsed by the Lake County Republican Central Committee for the 1980 election. Yet he still managed to raise $5,150 from external sources, compared with the second incumbent's $5,085 and challenger Barkhausen's $700. Examination of contributors makes clear that, despite his personal problems, during the primary Griesheimer retained strong ties with strongly linked trade, professional, and ideological contributors.

The battle waged by newcomer Judy Koehler in District 45, a two-incumbent district, was also one in which outside funding was relatively unimportant to her but most critical to the incumbent she defeated, Donald Anderson. The $750 from the Illinois Realtors Association was the sole sign that Koehler had established ties with the most strongly linked trade associations.

The one exception of these patterns occurred in District 7, a one-incumbent district where both the *Chicago Tribune* (1980) and the Chicago *Sun-Times* (1980) unequivocally recommended that their readers "bullet" for challenger Judy Topinka. Incumbent Paul Matula, who raised $3,500, got only $900 from strongly linked sources. In contrast, Topinka raised 44 percent from strongly linked contributors, including $5,592 from the Illinois Medical Association. She stands as the sole challenger with this kind of appeal, however, even compared with the other successful challenger in her district, John Kociolko.

Ideological Contributors

Ideological contributors give us two simultaneous insights into the allocation of money in primaries because they can be classified both by strength of ties and by evident ideological position. Both characteristics confirm the importance of conservatism as the dominant force in the party network. The strongest organized manifestation of this was STOP ERA, which contributed $91,808 to 176 candidates in the four reporting years. Only the National Conservative Political Action Committee, which gave $11,750 to 48 candidates, even came close. When all the conservative groups are combined, they dominate the ideological spectrum by the number of contributions they made to candidates running for House and Senate (285) and by the amount of their contributions ($125,393). Groups considered moderate—those that supported ERA and women's interests generally—gave $48,209 in 139 contributions.

During the primary periods, the two sides contributed almost equal amounts, at the same time revealing a sharp contrast between them: 28

percent of conservative money was aimed at primaries versus 66 percent of moderate. In other words, weakly linked moderate contributors, whose best hope lies in changing the character of Republican representatives, put their money where it could be most effective. This was comparable to strategies used by ideological contributors in congressional elections (Latus, 1984, 149). My own initial findings suggest that protective strategies will be even more likely among interest groups that represent the dominant values of Republican conservatism. Conversely, those with variant values could be expected to look for prospective legislative support among newcomers, anticipating that supportive incumbents were in the minority.

As we see in Table 8-11, examining contributions to Senate candidates, in both primary years the battle was principally between strongly linked conservative groups protecting challenged incumbents or movers and weakly linked moderate groups establishing ties with challenging newcomers running against incumbents or movers. In 1978, conservative groups gave a total of $3,350 to 10 candidates, of whom 6, all challenged incumbents or movers, received $2,300; in 1980, $5,000 of the $5,600 in circulation went to the two challenged incumbents. Moderate groups gave challenging newcomers $7,500 in 1978 (the total of their contributions that year) and $1,390 in 1980 (all but $100 of their total contributions). Moderate groups concentrated their resources, giving Jeanne Bradner (District 1) $6,500 in 1978, whereas her opponent, mover Roger Keats, received only $650 from con-

Table 8-11. Contributions to Senate Candidates from Ideological Groups during Primary Periods

(mean $)

Type of Race	No Contest		Contest	
	Conservative	Moderate	Conservative	Moderate
Fiscal 1978				
Incumbents	29	0	400	0
Newcomers v. incumbents	na	na	0	333
Movers	100	0	367	0
Newcomers v. movers	na	na	0	2,167
Newcomers	0	0	125	0
Fiscal 1980				
Incumbents	0	20	2,500	0
Newcomers v. incumbents	na	na	0	645
Movers	50	0	na	na
Newcomers	71	0	0	0

See Tables 8-5 and 8-6 for basis of calculating means.

servative groups. Moderates behaved similarly in 1980, but used much less money. The $1,040 they gave to Richard Fonte (District 2) was then outdone by conservatives spending $3,250 on incumbent John Friedland.

The House presents a less clearcut picture, because incumbents were more likely to support moderate causes and were therefore also more likely to receive moderate groups' money, although contributions were generally modest. Conversely, challengers were more likely to receive conservative groups' money. But as Table 8-12 shows, in the critical case of newcomers challenging incumbents in two-incumbent districts, sole ideological support came from moderate groups. These moderate groups performed their contributor roles in highly focussed ways. Jo Means, hoping to displace one of two incumbent conservatives in District 6, received $3,150, 70 percent of all money from moderate groups to House primary races in 1978. Three candidates were given special attention to fiscal 1980 — Suzanne Deuchler (District 39) with $1,974, Diana Nelson (District 6) with $4,288, and Donna Werner (District 47) with $5,094. These three got 63 percent of that year's contributions from moderates to House candidates. Only investments in Deuchler and Nelson were successful, and their races occurred in districts where there was only one incumbent.

Table 8-12. Contributions to House Candidates in Contested Races from Ideological Groups during Primary Periods

(mean $)

Type of Race	Incumbent		Challenger	
	Conservative	Moderate	Conservative	Moderate
Fiscal 1978				
Two Incumbents				
v. 1 challenger	94	2	0	450
One incumbent				
v. 1 challenger	0	77	0	5
v. 2 or more	40	23	0	<1
No incumbent	na	na	56	0
Fiscal 1980				
Two incumbents				
v. 1 challenger	305	78	0	1,019
v. 2 or more	625	1,143	0	0
One incumbent				
v. 1 challenger	112	0	0	0
v. 2 or more	306	52	116	181
No incumbent	na	na	168	45

See Tables 8-9 and 8-10 for bases of calculating means.

My hypothesis on the way money is used to establish links with new party actors was strongly supported by ideological groups who were themselves weakly linked. Otherwise, considering all other out-of-district, non-party contributors, support for the hypothesis was more selective. Money was more often used protectively, most frequently in House races. During primary races, when party loyalty is not in question, money is still used principally as a medium for reinforcing existing ties that appear threatened, and only secondarily for beginning new relations. Even though the circumstances of primary elections would appear to give scope for the inclusion of newcomers, magnified in multimember House races, the positive quality of money is selectively used.

These findings begin to suggest the limitations of money as a medium of interchange. To the extent that money implies the existence of some kind of market, virtually unanswerable questions are raised about how prices are set and about what is being bought. Markets also imply contractual relations, in which enforceable agreements for future performance are specified within some limited context. By transferring money to candidates already known for their legislative performance, contributors both reduce their own uncertainty and avoid the appearance of demanding some future return. Giving to newcomers, however, makes overt the contractual features of the exchange. The implications of this argument, and its contrast with the uses of money discussed under maintaining relations, can be considered more conclusively when money is used for dealing with dependency.

Coping with Uncertainty

Organizational Maintenance

Support — whether legislative, electoral, or ideological — is a necessary part of continued inclusion in the party network, and actors naturally seek to acquire resources that make support more predictable. It is easy to give this the crudest possible translation when money is the medium of interchange. I cautioned against the narrowness of such a perspective, as well as the built-in illegitimacy it entails, at the outset of this chapter. Instead, we need to appreciate how money presents possibilities for interchange more varied than the mere buying of votes, or even the purchase of needed services. These possibilities occur through money's symbolic uses as a means of building ties and alliances and demonstrating intrinsic worth. Analogies can be made with Mauss's (1967) analysis of gift-giving in preliterate societies, where goods exchanged are part of a system of mutual obligations which serve to maintain and strengthen social bonds. Once there is an initial recognition that having money opens new means for recipients to conduct their political lives, then receiving money itself becomes a sign of enhanced status. Simmel (1978, 372) drew attention to this general phenomenon when he evaluated the position of women who are married after the payment of brideprice: ". . . they are valuable because one has to pay for them."

For contributors, participation in the world of political action committees and interest groups purportedly able to influence political events becomes a demonstration of political sophistication. Meyer and Rowan (1977) theorize that organizations are frequently moved to adopt the practices prevailing in related organizations, regardless of immediate usefulness, because this seems to add to their legitimacy and enhance their chances of surviving. I make a similar argument. That is, contributors signal their integration into the party network by the extent of their financial activity, an assumption I made when ranking the strength of party links for outside district contributors who are independent of the party apparatus.

But even if money is not associated with negative uses, we can detect an uneasiness that comes with its use, also recognized in the underlying theory. Although it takes no more than common sense to acknowledge the importance of power, patronage, and ideology for the operation of any political unit, the place of money is less evident. It is not the need for money that is at issue, or even its troubling consequences, which are much like those of patronage and its possibly corrupting effects. But patronage, as a medium of interchange appropriate to a political party, works well by creating obligations based on loyalty. That the resulting solidary bonds do not lead to a unified organization is less relevant than the shape they give to lively subnetwork spheres of influence. Patronage, in other words, is compatible with party coherence. Money may not be. I come to this position by contrasting the two preceding sections of this chapter in relation to the benefits of organization over markets, outlined under quite different circumstances by Williamson (1975) and Pfeffer and Salancik (1978).

The party apparatus uses money straightforwardly to maintain organizational identity. The uncertainty that the use of money is intended to control stems primarily from the behavior of the electorate, and only minimally from the future performance of candidates. Thus the central party apparatus makes contributions that avoid the primary period and seeks to augment the party network by favoring candidates who are either certain winners or in horse races. The local party apparatus, however, must sustain a base of support regardless of election outcomes, so it has to pay more attention to primary elections and to both incumbents and candidates who are certain losers.

An opposing picture appears when financial contributors without formal organizational or constituency ties with candidates participate during the most uncertain part of the election cycle. Instead of an organizational context, contributors and candidates are linked in something akin to a market situation. When partisan solidarity is put aside and untested newcomers vie for a place in the party network, uncertainty is maximized and legitimacy is put in doubt in the sense that actors appear to be contracting for future performance. Financial contributors attempt to sidestep such concerns by staying with incumbents and protecting them from challengers. Only on occasion will a strongly linked contributor, like the Illinois Medical Association, play an entrepreneurial role in supporting a challenging newcomer. It is left principally to those weakly linked ideological groups, firms, and individuals to use their money for reshaping the party network. The validity of this interpretation of how contributions are structured is given two further tests, one from the perspective of party leaders and the other from that of candidates in general.

Leaders

Using candidates for the General Assembly as the recipients, we can approach leaders and their contribution behavior in two ways. One set of leaders is made up of those formally recognized within the organizational context of the General Assembly and includes the elected House and Senate leaders and their appointed deputies. The second set consists of factional leaders, others seeking leadership positions in the General Assembly, and party leaders outside the General Assembly who would like to affect its members' behavior. In theory, these outside leaders can consist of actor types of governor, constitutional officer, U.S. senator, and congressman, although only the governor turns out to be relevant to our analysis.[6] We expect the contribution behavior of formal leaders in the General Assembly to be organizationally constrained; all others would operate in marketlike situations. On the basis of what has been learned about the activities of the party apparatus, we can generalize that money used in an organizational context is most prominent in general elections, in support of incumbents and certain winners or horse races. Marketlike behavior is harder to define, because we have assumed that contributors try to avoid it. But, at least in primaries, it has been inferred to entail support for the most vulnerable candidates, and this principle will now be extended to general elections.

The contribution patterns of Senate and House leaders, presented in

6. During the period of this study, there were no recorded instances when Senator Percy gave money to any state legislative candidate. The same was true of Attorney General Scott. Congressmen play a circumscribed role as contributors, limiting themselves to legislative candidates in their own respective districts.

Table 8-13, demonstrate that the uses of money to relate to legislative candidates were almost exclusively associated with George Ryan, first as House minority leader and then as speaker. Although Senate Minority Leader David Shapiro was the most active contributor among Senate members, neither the amount of money in use nor the number of candidates supported came near to Ryan's. Ryan also followed a procedure more common among the secondary Senate leaders in contributing to other candidates in his own district. Among those outside his district, secondary House leaders were also likely recipients of his money. Except for Celeste Stiehl, who was somehow omitted from the leaders he supported, the remaining eight received $8,450, or 21 percent of his total House money, over the four fiscal years. Arthur Telcser, himself a noncontributor who would become

Table 8-13. Contributions by Senate and House Leaders to Legislative Candidates (fiscal 1978–81)

	To House		To Senate		
	Inside	Outside	Inside	Outside	Total
Senate Leaders					
Formal					
Shapiro	0	$60	na	$3,400	$3,460
Philip	$450	450	na	0	900
Walsh	357	0	na	500	857
Weaver	133	0	na	50	183
Grotberg	20	100	na	50	170
Other					
Moore	350	150	na	7,240	7,740
House Leaders					
Formal					
Ryan	$2,850	$37,205	$3,000	0	$43,055
Stiehl	0	570	0	100	670
Conti	0	100	0	0	100
Polk	0	25	0	0	25
Telcser	0	0	0	0	0
Collins	0	0	0	0	0
Mahar	0	50	0	0	50
Daniels	432	665	300	100	1,497
Peters	0	50	0	0	50
Friedrich	100	0	0	0	100
Other					
Davis	0	1,500	0	100	1,600
Epton	0	4,300	0	1,150	5,450
Vinson	0	1,375	0	500	1,875
Totten	536	635	0	0	1,171
Reagan-Totten	0	13,637	0	100	13,737

majority leader when the Republicans won the House in the 1980 election, received $3,000, the largest single amount.

Five potential leaders, one in the Senate and four in the House, have been included in Table 8-13 because of the extent of their activity. In the House, Donald Totten has been recognized in previous chapters as a factional leader, yet initially it appeared that he was not using money in a leaderlike way because almost half of his money simply went to his district running mate. It was only after examining the contribution behavior of the Reagan presidential campaign committee, headed by Totten until he was displaced by Governor Thompson prior to the 1980 national convention, that we appear to have found Totten's surrogate for reshaping the legislature. I emphasize the connection by calling the campaign committee Reagan-Totten, which gave $13,737 to 22 candidates, all but one in the House.

Bernard Epton, who had been an assistant leader in the preceding General Assembly, behaved in ways that indicated he was hoping to acquire a firmer place in the leadership. We were told that he had begun raising money in 1980, in anticipation of a race for the speaker's position. In fact, virtually all of his campaign chest was self-contributed, containing his own $131,628, by far the largest amount any candidate gave to himself. With the intention of becoming speaker, he informed Representative Clarence Neff, then chairman of the State House Campaign Committee, that he preferred to make contributions directly to candidates rather than to the committee. At the same time, he kept his ties to the existing leadership by giving $1,150 to William Mahar, a Senate candidate whom Epton had earlier supported when Mahar was part of the House leadership, and $500 each to Telcser and to Ryan himself.

Jack Davis (District 42) attempted to find a place in the leadership during that same session, when the majority status of the Republicans opened new opportunities. This was recognized by the Reagan-Totten committee, which gave Davis $4,584 in fiscal 1979, the same amount given to his House running mate, Harry Leinenweber. Together, in that year alone, they received 68 percent of the Reagan-Totten money, but even though Davis and Leinenweber did campaign together, we have no way of knowing whether the money Leinenweber received played a part in Davis's (unsuccessful) leadership drive. Both Davis and Sam Vinson (District 44), a newcomer to the House in 1978 who would successfully enter the leadership in 1982, made their bids by avoiding any exchange of money with existing leaders.

Donald Moore, who retired from the Senate at the end of his term in 1980, sought a place in the Senate leadership in the 1979 session. His contributions were more than double those of Minority Leader Shapiro, to whom Moore gave $100, along with $500 to secondary leader Richard Walsh.

In the Senate, the contribution strategies of leaders can be compared for three types of actor – Minority Leader Shapiro, aspiring leader Moore, and Governor Thompson. The governor was the largest contributor, giving $15,841 to 12 Senate candidates, all but 1 in 1979. Moore was the most active, giving to 22 candidates a total of $7,240. Shapiro was least active, confining his $3,400 to 11 candidates. Shapiro gave 6 percent of his money during primaries; Moore, 3 percent; and the governor, 1 percent. The governor gave proportionately the least money (24 percent) to incumbents in general elections, 11 of whom were most favored by Moore with 43 percent of his money, compared with 35 percent of Shapiro's contributions. The governor, apparently hoping to alter the composition of the Senate, gave 45 percent of his Senate funds to three candidates in districts classified as certain losers and another 20 percent to four horse races. Only one of these seven candidates won, unlike the two supported certain winners. Moore gave 14 percent to five certain winners and 34 percent to three losing horse races. Shapiro divided his funds in a relatively more equal way, giving 26 percent to two certain winners, another 26 percent to three horse-race candidates, and 13 percent to two certain losers.

Moore, who was attempting to enter formal leadership, behaved in the most organizationally constrained fashion. Aside from his avoidance of primaries, his behavior most closely approximated the local party apparatus (Table 8-1). From another perspective, he can be said to have carefully avoided treating his Senate colleagues as though they were in a market situation. More expected was Shapiro's organizational behavior, resembling the State Senate Campaign Committee but also the local apparatus (Table 8-1) in support of incumbents. The governor, in contrast, acted like a participant in a more-or-less free market, placing greatest value on a future set of conditions where even long-shot candidates would have been able to fulfill his need for a Republican-dominated Senate.

Leaders' contributions to House candidates are treated in similar ways, by comparing contributions to primaries and to incumbents in general elections. I have compared formal leader Ryan with aspiring leaders Epton, Davis, and Vinson, and with the governor, who gave $19,911 to House races, all in fiscal 1979. Because the Reagan committee contributions look as though they could be Totten's, I have added them to my comparisons. Vinson supported only 7 candidates, compared with the governor's support for 14, Reagan-Totten's (including Totten's own committee) for 24, Epton's for 19, Davis's for 25, and Ryan's for 85.

Contributions during the primary periods took 44 percent of Ryan's money, 42 percent of Epton's, 40 percent of Vinson's, 17 percent of Davis's, but only 6 percent of Reagan-Totten's. Reagan-Totten's contribution behavior indicates that money was not being used to support convention delegates, elected during the primary period. The governor made no primary contributions. Ryan is not quite as comparable to Vinson and Epton as percentages might suggest because it was Ryan's running mate and his assistant leaders who received $7,550 during the primary periods. When that amount is subtracted, Ryan gave just 25 percent of his money to (other) primary candidates. Altogether, incumbents attracted 92 percent of the Reagan campaign money. Incumbents also received 94 percent of Epton's money, 84 percent of Vinson's, 78 percent of Ryan's, 54 percent of what the governor gave to House candidates, and 43 percent of Davis's.

Shifting from individuals to district types, we find that the governor concentrated on horse-race districts, giving 12 candidates 62 percent of his House money. Except for one newcomer and one incumbent, all candidates he supported won. In contrast, horse races attracted 19 percent of the Reagan-Totten money, 29 percent of Ryan's and Vinson's, 27 percent of Davis's, and 17 percent of Epton's. Except for Epton, all leaders funded from one to eight losing candidates, but because these candidates included incumbents who lost in the primaries, funding strategies can be interpreted as more often protective than innovative.

The House presents a less clear-cut picture than the Senate. Only the governor can be said to have followed marketlike strategies of a somewhat risky nature. The other leaders were all more similar to the organizational pattern set by the party apparatus, with perhaps Davis more like central party actors than local ones. But cutting across these general tendencies were Ryan's very special organizational responsibilities, carried out through strong financial support for those he had selected to be his deputies. Because he needed to deal with a House almost evenly divided between Republicans and Democrats, it was important for him to include Chicago legislators among his leaders. This ensured that he would be giving money to what have otherwise been defined as certain-loser districts. Altogether, Ryan supported 15 candidates in certain-loser districts. Not all of these were leaders, but all were given the message that he considered them valuable colleagues — most were already incumbents. For Ryan, money was a means of asserting dominance, as recognized by one lukewarm supporter who said, "George Ryan sent me $100 after the 1978 election. I sent it back. Then he got huffy, but I told him I didn't need it."

It is relevant that legislative leaders, whether actual or potential, all tended to follow a contribution pattern suggestive of the constraining demands of organizational hierarchy and continuity. Even the apparently intrusive efforts of presidential campaign committees were conducted within the confines of the existing legislative structure, aimed at reshaping the direction of leadership. Money, in itself, does not buy position; Table 8-13 was deliberately constructed to show those leaders who did not use money in their relations with other legislators. Only the governor was not bound by these organizational constraints. We should wonder whether the absence of party leaders like Percy and Scott from the money interchange was only an accident of their personal styles or an indication of the more general problems associated with the uses of money.

Candidates

It is safe to assume that candidates experience greater certainty of support through local recognition, most obviously from the electorate, but also from financial contributors. Yet certainty is also a form of dependence on the local constituency, including the local party organs. From the perspective of candidates, then, a way of decreasing dependency of this kind is to acquire financial support outside their districts. Money from outside sources can be regarded as a form of "organizational slack" (Scott, 1987, 217–218) in that it provides extra resources to compensate for the uncertainty that may be anticipated when local financial sources are not mobilized. These extra resources are also a potential springboard to other party positions.

The uses of money by ordinary candidates raised different problems from those faced by leaders, for whom whatever benefits might be expected from marketlike relations were less attractive than the greater certainty of operating within an organizational framework. Hierarchically linked relations also had the advantage of affirming leaders' dominance. What was noted as the greater risk-taking behavior of the governor, who could function outside these organizational constraints, suggests another dimension of the tension between the governor and other party actors described in earlier chapters, in which marketlike strategies can be used in the effort to reshape the party. For candidates, concern about inside and outside sources of money cuts across the distinction between markets and organizations by adding on contingencies associated with the strength of local ties.

Contributions to all candidates who received money between fiscal 1978 and fiscal 1981 were divided according to their locale, in order to find the balance between the inside and outside sources. Excluded were contributions by candidates, either to themselves or to other candidates. Not all remaining sources could be determined, however, because state law requires reporting of names and addresses only where an individual contribution is larger than $150. Treasurers of campaign funds, however, are required to keep their own tallies of all contributions of more than $20. My own analysis benefitted from the practice of many treasurers to simply pass on to the State Board of Elections all the information they had. Otherwise, small contributions are lumped together as unitemized. In total, they represent an unexpectedly large proportion of all contributions, around half in primary years and a third in general election years. Although small amounts are likely to be raised in local fundraisers like dinners, coffee hours, pig roasts, and golf outings, tickets to such events may be just as often sold to lobbyists and others outside the district as to those inside. Unitemized contributions are therefore uninterpretable and seriously affect the validity of the inside-outside distinction. For this reason, comparisons that follow are given only modest analysis.

Over the four fiscal years of this study, 234 candidates filed disclosure statements; 8 of them had all their money in the unitemized category, and another 49 had raised proportionately more money from inside than from outside sources. This contrasts with the norm of outside sources exceeding inside ones by about three to one. With 10 exceptions, those who reported more inside contributions were unsuccessful primary election contenders or, less often, unsuccessful Senate candidates. Given the data already reported, these findings are hardly surprising and need no additional comment. The atypical contribution pattern of the remaining candidates may be accounted for by the fact that most of them were newcomers to the General Assembly, generally with local party or government experience. The presence in this category of long-term incumbents Edward McBroom (District 43) and Fred Tuerk (District 46) is testimony of strong county organizations in their districts, able to mobilize large-scale local support. More surprising were contributions for state Senator Kenneth McMillan (District 47), who received $33,277, 56 percent from inside and 44 percent from outside sources. He was alone among state senators in this category. Equally surprising was the distribution of Jack Davis's $47,321 into 2 percent unitemized, 53 percent inside, and 44 percent outside. This relatively greater dependence on local sources of funding may have foretold the difficulties that both would subsequently have in expanding their political roles. Although McMillan was able to defeat incumbent Congressman Tom Railsback in the 1982 primary, he could not win in the general election, and, as already noted, Davis could not attain the speakership.

On the basis of campaign contribution information, we might infer that candidates would welcome opportunities to enlarge their network relations with central party organs, interest groups, and financial contributors beyond the borders of their districts. To the extent that most legislative candidates are successful in this effort, they alter their positions on the local dimension of the party network. But relating to the central party and to special interests through the money received from these expanded sources does not give legislators a more central, statewide perspective; instead, it increases their autonomy through dispersing their dependency. This is demonstrated through the phenomenon of what are called fetcher bills, bills routinely introduced, sometimes year after year, in order to fetch lobbyists and other interest group representatives from their indifference into a more financially communicative style. Legislative candidates may encourage the sense that a market exists in order to enhance their personal autonomy. They are constrained in this not only by legal restrictions but also by the preference of the most strongly linked contributors for the certainty of an organizational framework.

I conclude these four chapters on media of interchange with another sign of the ambiguity which accompanies the relations among party actors. The positive attributes of money in linking actors manifest themselves within the party to create two contradictory worlds. For those party actors who give money, in the sense that they are analogous to buyers in a market, it is preferable to operate in predictable, orderly contexts. These are termed organizations or hierarchies. Those party actors who receive money, to the extent that they resemble sellers in a market, have an advantage where it appears that their legislative seats have a value greater than that of run-of-the-mill candidates. This could be because of their positions as leaders or because of the certainty of their winning. In fact, they have less need for money than those candidates struggling to make their way into the legislature or the leadership. The greater risks entailed by the changes the latter seek keep many contributors from participating unless they too have weak links with the party network. Even the governor has difficulty overcoming the strength of existing links and the barriers of an unfriendly electoral environment.

9

Party Effectiveness

Is There an Ideal Party?

The sheer existence of U.S. political parties is hardly problematic; they have an assured presence in state and national politics which is recognized in state laws. But presence alone does not account for variations in how parties function. To do so requires first deciding on those elements that should be included within a party's boundaries. Only then is it possible to face the more important issue of how party elements relate to each other and, by their activities, create the living party. For this reason I began by defining the composition of the Illinois Republican Party, and only then did I go on to examine the ties among party actors. The resulting analysis is a portrait of robust organization.

In all the preceding discussion I have avoided normative commentary on the desirability or the effectiveness of what was found. I was not guided by concern for the health of U.S. political parties or by a search for ways of strengthening them. For example, a recent assessment deplored the weakening of state and local parties through the prevalence of primary elections for nominating candidates (ACIR, 1986, 98–101), but as far as this study is concerned, primaries are just another level of activity in which party actors can interact. Where Mayhew (1986, 19) sees the nomination of candidates as one of the key criteria of a traditional party organization and the loss of control over nominations as a sign of weakening parties, I have treated the impact of party actors on nominations as a variable experience, differentiating their milieus. In all this I have parallelled the assumption of contingency theorists—those who emphasize the interaction between organizations and their environments—that there is no best way of organizing (Galbraith, 1973, 2).

Even though the network of relations in the Illinois Republican Party has not been presented as if it were representative, the results of my research are largely compatible with current descriptions of U.S. political parties in general or, more specifically, with those of the Republican Party (Mayhew, 1986, 331–332; Epstein, 1986, 343; ACIR, 1986, 161, 120). We

255

may see a resemblance between where this nonjudgmental path has brought us and where Schlesinger's theory brings him:

Nothing in the model ascertains how well the parties represent the variety of interests in the society, how good they are at articulating or moderating conflict, how well they are perceived by the electorate, how successful they are in inducing popular participation, how good they are at providing effective government, nor in how "responsible" they are in providing realistic alternatives. (Schlesinger, 1984, 421)

But can we stop here? Although there may be no single form of organization that is ideal, it does not follow that all forms are equally effective (Galbraith, 1973, 2).

Writing from the perspective of one who believes that parties should be evaluated with regard to how well they play their civic roles, Crotty disputes the value-neutrality of Schlesinger's position by arguing that "every approach has its value assumptions and its weaknesses" (Crotty, 1987, 11). Crotty's criticisms can also be related to a central assumption of contingency theory: organizational forms have consequences with normative implications. That is, "the effectiveness of an organization is a sociopolitical question. . . . it reflects both an assessment of the usefulness of what is being done and of the resources that are being consumed by the organization" (Pfeffer and Salancik, 1978, 11).

It is an appropriate conclusion to this volume to put my results to an evaluative test of effectiveness. There is, however, no single concept of the ideal U.S. party to use as a standard. Instead, we must make our judgments within the context of two opposing models, described below as strong-party and weak-party models. Models of strong and weak parties are conceptions of the desirable, not descriptions of real parties. Both models are useful because they offer normative standards for evaluating the strengths and weaknesses of the Illinois Republican Party. But as useful as they are, the models still leave us without a complete conception of party functioning. For that we need to reassess this research on the Republican Party as the basis for a more general theory of U.S. party organization, something I attempt at the end of this chapter.

In the history of American politics, political parties have never had the kind of adulation reserved for symbols like the Constitution or the president (Ranney, 1975, 22–57). From the outset, the founding fathers were uneasy about the place of parties, even as they were building what are now the oldest political parties in the modern world (Chambers, 1963; Hofstadter, 1969). Regularly held up to the ridicule of critics and reformers, parties after the 1948 election faced especially trenchant criticism from a group of political scientists advocating a party system akin to the British model, one that was "democratic, responsible and effective":

An effective party system requires, first, that the parties are able to bring forth programs to which they commit themselves and, second, that the parties possess sufficient internal cohesion to carry out these programs. Such a degree of unity within the parties cannot be brought about without party procedures that give a large body of people an opportunity to share in the development of the party program.

Under this system, one party would form the government, the other, the opposition:

The fundamental requirement of accountability is a two-party system in which the opposition party acts as the critic of the party in power, developing, defining and presenting the policy alternatives which are necessary for a true choice in reaching public decisions. The opposition most conducive to responsible government is an organized party opposition. (American Political Science Association, 1950, 1–2)

This view is representative of "strong party" advocacy, in which ideal parties are programmatic, disciplined, and tied to majority rule. Such a formulation emphasizes the electoral and governmental aspects of party rather than the more comprehensive relational ones, as is the case when a political party is treated as a network of individual and collective actors whose separate activities and commitments have a partisan purpose. In the network approach used in this volume, a strong party would require centralized organization, hierarchy of authority, and ideological consistency among actors, manifested in binding party platforms and caucus solidarity. It is assumed to operate in a competitive electoral environment where it has the opportunity to win majority status at both the legislative and executive levels.

Among those rejecting the strong model of U.S. parties is Epstein (1980), who considers political parties as deriving from their social and political milieu. Simply because British political parties appear especially impressive in their governing role, he argues, "that cannot be assumed to make the American political system less effective. It is only the parties as such that may be less effective. Why should they be thought so important that their effectiveness determines the effectiveness of the system?" (Epstein, 1980, 8). To say that U.S. parties may appear less effective by some absolute standard of comparison, but quite adequate in their own context, seems, on the surface, to be tautological. Yet Epstein (1980, 351–358) holds a more purposeful view of weak parties, tying them to a pluralist conception of democracy, which requires, where there are multiple and complex societal cleavages, that political parties play broadly conciliatory roles. Similarly, Polsby and Wildavsky argue for the importance of "consensus-building parties":

Political purism might be desirable for a people homogeneous in all ways except the economic; but can a multiracial, multiethnic, multireligious, multiregional, multiclass nation like the United States sustain itself when its main agents of political action—the parties—strive to exclude rather than to include, to sharpen rather than dull the edge of controversy? (Polsby and Wildavsky, 1984, 279–280)

Although they attribute more importance to parties than Epstein does, we may still include Polsby and Wildavsky in the "weak party" camp. Again translating into our network framework, the ideal weak party is loosely linked or decentralized, with diffused authority and unprogrammatic. It would be expected to respond to a diverse electoral constituency with efforts to be broadly representative.

The ideal party is also a theme of considerable relevance to party actors. While I was cumulating individual experiences and particular events in order to understand what a party is and does, informants were eager to communicate their feelings about what the party should be. This was particularly evident when they talked about the measure of a party's success, the strengths and weaknesses of the Illinois Republicans, the party's future, and the individuals who best represented the party. Their testimony on the ideal Republican Party was a critical part of my earlier analysis and a way of viewing insiders' assessments of how well the party achieved its goals.

It is generally agreed that goals can be the main criteria for assessing organizational effectiveness (Scott, 1977). However, Scott (1987, 268–270) has also observed how difficult it is to deal with organizational goals, because they are often conceptualized differently by the organizations and by those who analyze them. This is suggested as well in regard to the weak- and strong-party models, whose underlying premises are statements about party objectives. Yet both party actors and political analysts appear to have an easy task judging a party's effectiveness, because it has a single overriding goal—electing its candidates to government office (Epstein, 1980, 361; Sartori, 1976, 64; Schlesinger, 1985, 1153). Because I consider only the kind of party whose office-seeking includes a commitment to future participation, party continuity is no more than a necessary aspect of that goal. Even the need to legislate a party program under the strongest conditions of party government, or the need for shared beliefs under the strongest condition of ideological parties, does not alter the primacy of electoral success. Party actors may simultaneously use goals rationally, as guidelines or justifications for actions; emotionally, as sources of identification; and evaluatively, as criteria of effectiveness.[1] They do so, not out of any

1. Students of organizations are inclined to treat each of the ways in which goals may be used as though they were mutually exclusive (Scott, 1987, 268). This is not being done here.

confusion about the nature of goals, but to make evident that to be a Republican is to declare a goal commitment.

The specificity of goals is a characteristic that has otherwise been viewed as a necessary prerequisite for the formalization of an organization (March and Simon, 1958; Scott, 1987, 45–48). But if we were always to associate clear and limited goals with a rational organizational structure, we would be left with an inexplicable situation in what has, from the outset of this study, been assumed to be the loosely coupled structure of the party network. Reconciliation between goals and loose coupling is accomplished by a recursive process which allows the party to continue even after electoral defeat. It is important for the party to win elections, but one cannot specify how often or how many offices. Political actors consequently operate in a setting where failure is treated as temporary and success as unstable. Even recurring failures are ambiguous, because there are no clear signals foretelling the demise of the party. The Republican Party was able to win the presidency even after two decades of Democratic dominance, once existing and emerging party coalitions had been stimulated to find new issues and new leaders (Mayer, 1967, 475–527). After generations of inactivity, the Republican Party was again able to become a potent force in the South; and in 1984, even a Republican state senator could be elected from a Chicago district. No party actor can admit that losing is inconsequential, and it may be true that an individual's fate is tied to a single outcome, but the fate of the party is not. Ambiguity about how often elections need to be won is the source of flexibility that permits continued goal specificity. Living in a city with the Cubs and White Sox teams, which regularly lose but whose fans never give up hope, highlights the parallels between sports teams and political parties. For both, winning is everything and even countless losses are merely stumbles on the road to victory.

In this chapter I use the strong- and weak-party models as preexisting standards supplying measures of effectiveness that have grown out of debates about the nature of U.S. parties. Both models lend themselves to division into three foci of analysis, related to the centralization of party activities, provision of leadership, and the extent of party responsibility or ideological coherence. As Huckshorn observes, the three characteristics are closely connected and should be understood in this interacting way: "The decentralization of the system, lack of party responsibility, and separation of powers have often combined to thwart any effort by party faithfuls to point a finger and say, 'That is our leader'" (Huckshorn, 1984, 13).

Because actors are dependent on their environment, I have added an assessment of environmental effects, even though they are not usually seen as directly characteristic of a party or fully considered in either party model. By inclusion of the environment, especially electoral conditions, I compensate for my attention to a single party. That is, at any given time and place, the Democratic Party faces environmental conditions that are the mirror image of those faced by the Republican Party. This is not to say that Democratic Party actors will respond in ways identical with those of Republican actors given identical conditions, but we would expect great similarity when, in addition to identical conditions, the two have similar preexisting relations and the same volume of resources.

The intent of this chapter is simultaneously to summarize findings of this volume, to evaluate models of party effectiveness with respect to Illinois Republicans, and to reinforce the place of political parties within organizational theory. I supplement the last by concluding with a model of an adaptive party.

Loose Coupling and Centralization

A tightly integrated organization can be approached in the same way as I have approached the Republican Party, that is, by first designating its elements. One may begin by constructing an organizational chart delineating chains of command or work flows. To end at this point, however, would result in losing the ability to incorporate all actors with a shared party name and a broadly defined community of interest into a network that defines a party in all its manifestations. This concern for inclusiveness led me to consider all levels of the federal system in locating actors, even though Illinois was the setting. Because inclusion in the network was based on activities done on behalf of the party, no matter how the party or any segment of it was specified, actors could encompass formal party positions; public positions to which a party label is added; and informal or unofficial roles with clear party ties. When actors were designated as individuals, it was in reference to a single functional position, not to a particular individual; collective actors can be individuals in the same position, group, or organization. I then presumed that, structurally, loose coupling is the result of separate actors carrying out different activities in different locations. As a presumption, it still left room to be tested within the context of the party network.

Pendleton Herring showed an early appreciation of network, first referring to it in 1940, although he gave the term a more restricted meaning, confining party at the national level to "a network of personal relations." This was his way of dismissing formal organizational charts which appeared to show a line of command from the top down, when instead, as far as the national chairman is concerned, his "strength lies in the friendships that he has established with key people over the country" (Herring, 1965, 204). It is an error, however, to completely disparage organizational charts, because they are one of the principal ways of locating party actors and defining their expected activities. Although the definitions in these charts are often, as Herring implied, inadequate predictors of action, they remain important just because they set forth expectations of what should happen and, in consequence, provide a basis of legitimacy. Their disjuncture with what actors can in fact do, given resources and environments, is the source of much of the tension among party actors. The fact that an organizational chart is not an accurate description of reality does not give us grounds for attributing network relations to personal ties. Though informants, too, were inclined to explain relations in terms of personal characteristics, actors within the network may be treated in more prototypic terms, by which means I have demonstrated an independent logic to relationships stemming from recurring activities. For example, although informants usually blamed the ineffectiveness of a central committeeman on his personal failings, I treated their comments as evidence of the difficulties that any central committeeman must have in assuming this role.

A simple and summary way of examining relationships among party actors, carried out in chapter 3, was through contacts, which indicated greatest centrality for the categories of financial contributor, advisor, and interest group, designated together as the unofficial wing. This finding appears to confirm fears of the declining significance of U.S. political parties in controlling election campaigns:

Parties are no longer the principal funders of campaigns. PACs are. Television has replaced the party as the dominant communicator of political information and, as a consequence, the preeminent influence on voter attitudes. Parties are no longer the major organizers of campaigns. Media consultants, public relations and professional experts can create "instant" parties for candidates with the funds to pay for them. As the campaign function of parties has decreased, the role of money — and hence of those who can supply it — has increased dramatically. (Crotty, 1984, 277)

Yet, granting the qualitatively different nature of election campaigns since television has become the critical campaign medium and election law reforms of the 1970s have brought more money into the political arena (Malbin, 1984), my study does not provide evidence of party decline. I was, of course, restricted by a limited time frame, but the definition of party network used here does not lead to an interpretation that party has been superseded just because candidates make direct contacts with the unofficial wing. Nor can I agree with the distorted historical reconstruction of an informant who stated: "Before the media became so important, people voted for the party. You didn't see candidates, you just voted for the party that had the principles you felt were right."

Although I cannot evaluate the possibly changing prominence of financial contributor, advisor, and interest group, I am confident that they have always been part of the network of every U.S. political party. Money has invariably been an ingredient in running campaigns and winning elections, noticeable from the time George Washington first ran for office in 1757, when a contribution was used to purchase enough spirits "for an outlay of more than a quart and a half per person" (Thayer, 1973, 25). That was considered a larger-than-average campaign contribution, and even though the future president had the means to make it himself, assistance from financial contributors was soon necessary for the conduct of other campaigns (Alexander, 1980, 4–7).

The presence of advisors has also been constant, differing in earlier times in that it did not require specialized or technical knowledge or the stake out of any kind of professional status (Sabato, 1981, 10–13). Advisors have regularly offered information and advice on campaign and political strategies premised, even when they are paid, on personal and ideological ties with candidates or officeholders. For example, Mayer writes that, when Herbert Hoover formed his Cabinet, "as usual, the posts were divided between eminent party leaders, campaign workers who deserved recognition, and personal friends of the President" (Mayer, 1967, 413). We can be sure that most of these were also advisors, in the sense used here, as were many of the "key people" mentioned by Herring. Less lofty offices than the presidency differ only in their more restricted means for rewarding advisors.

Perhaps the most doubtful category is that of interest group, because it is quite separate from a political party, especially, as Epstein (1980, 278) argues, in a two-party system. But there can be overlap along with separation when an interest group directs the majority of its demands and activities to a single party. Key (1961, 523) cautioned us that there is more likely to be "a standing alliance between party leaders and pressure-group leaders" than between a party and the majority of the interest group's members, but that is a trivial distinction here, because we are not concerned with possible voting blocs. To justify the inclusion of interest groups as a category of party actor, it is enough to establish that there are those whose political identity is essentially linked with the Republican Party.

The same contact measures also revealed the centrality of state legislators, under which I included state senator and representative. My initial surprise at their relative centrality came in part from their poor reputation, at least as expressed in the press and among reformers. Such views could lead to underestimating the focal nature of their activities and relations with other actors. They may, in fact, be the most visible component of the party in the state because of their participation in frequent elections and their service orientation to constituents. Their ties with others in the party are compounded by their ability to play multiple roles, either serially or simultaneously. A typical legislator may have experience as both a local committeeman and a county officeholder, and then later go on to serve in Congress or act as an interest-group representative. His district ties and local orientations may coexist with substantial statewide ties.

Links among party actors were also a means for discerning subsets, the most important of which were designated the party core. The core included state legislators in the House and Senate, the three components of the unofficial wing, and, more expectedly, the governor and U.S. senator. Defining the party core as actors elected locally and statewide combined with those who do not have electoral constituencies, spanning districts and the state, located in Springfield and Washington as well as points in between, is an unconventional perspective on party makeup. But it is also another demonstration of how the concept of party network operates. The network acquires its shape through linkages—not only through those created among this set of seven actors but also from those that extend to others in the party. State legislators are linked with all other local actors; the unofficial wing with all other central actors. That is, through its contacts the core set encompasses the whole network. Supporting information led to the conclusion that what actors in the core do and how they represent themselves as Republicans result in defining the party.

Most remaining actors were found in smaller subsets, linked with the core in ways that emphasize the locale in which they operated and the perspective they had on their places in the network. We generalized these as belonging to two dimensions: an ecological one that ranged from local to central arenas, and a functional-orientational one that ranged from centralization to local autonomy. In this way, for example, we could see the qualified centrality of the county chairman, stemming from his local sphere of contacts and from activities protective of his local domain.

The unique organizational character of the party, made up of actors representing different nodes of centrality, linked into subsets divisible into a two-dimensional matrix, has surprising similarities with otherwise different organizations with formally organized matrix structures (Hill and White, 1979). In a matrix structure,

the vertical lines are typically those of functional departments that operate as "home bases" for all participants; the lateral lines represent project groups or geographical arenas where managers combine and coordinate the services of the functional specialists around particular projects or areas. (Scott, 1987, 221)

An example is a department store with multiple locations whose resemblance to a political party comes from its organization on the basis of merchandise, equivalent to our functional dimension, and its dispersion of stores, equivalent to our ecological dimension. Without pushing this analogy too far, it is still instructive that the matrix form of organization institutionalizes conflict between the two principles captured by the dimensions at the same time as it gives them both legitimacy (Scott, 1987, 223). For the Republican Party, having to deal simultaneously with conflict among its actors and their claimed legitimacy is made easier to the extent that its relations can be loosely coupled. Such a result conforms to the weak-party model.

But further analysis, taking into account the effects of resource dependence, makes it necessary to qualify the relation between loose coupling and the weak-party model. Resource dependence theorists, like Thompson (1967) and Pfeffer and Salancik (1978), have been concerned with how an organization protects itself from the environment, particularly that part of the organization defined as the technical core—"one or more central sets of tasks around which the organization is built" (Scott, 1987, 182). Thompson (1967, 19) proposed that an organization attempts to buffer its technical core against environmental pressures. I suggested in chapter 4 the usefulness of thinking of a political party as having a technical core in its provision of candidates for public office. Pressures arise from the party's reliance on relatively external resources obtained from its constituency environments. The party's central task is performed even in the absence of coordinated means for selecting, slating, or endorsing candidates. At the same time, we recognize that, in company with those organizations that do not have primarily technical objectives or do not operate in market contexts, a party's tools (human and other) used for carrying out tasks tend to become ambiguous, as do the tasks themselves, given the uncertainty of elections. Such "institutionalized organizations" (Meyer and Rowan, 1977) are likely to have different relations with their environments, maintaining "high levels of interpenetration with their environments, not as a reflection of organizational weakness (as would be the case for a technical organization), but as a source of strength" (Meyer, Scott, Deal, 1983, 55). Nevertheless, the technical core remains vulnerable to detrimental penetration when an organized movement mounts a takeover like the one which occurred in the 1986 Democratic primary, when followers of Lyndon Larouche captured the offices of lieutenant governor and secretary of state.

In chapter 4, actors' links through their dependency on constituents became one way of accounting for subsequent relations. Disjoint constituencies communicated a sense of shared fate without direct competition and helped explain relative cooperation among congressmen and among state senators. The same or congruent constituencies, in contrast, promoted efforts toward insulated independence among those holding statewide offices or, under a system of multimember districts, between state representatives in the same district. Overlapping constituencies provided even less constraint on overt conflict than did congruent ones and contributed to competing power claims, like those between county chairmen and central committeemen, or the State Central Committee and the Republican National Committee.

Relations among actors were also affected by the commitment of their constituents and the size of their constituencies. For example, areas of traditionally loyal Republican support provided the kind of environmental certainty in which factionalism could thrive. Smaller constituencies could be relatively problem-free environments, but larger ones, more desirable because they were linked to greater power for actors, stimulated the use of organizational-control mechanisms.

The party and its surrounding political and social environments make available additional resources of power, patronage, ideology, and money as media of interchange among party actors. Most generally, power is used to control; patronage, to build ties of loyalty; ideology, to define the boundaries of a moral community; and money, to sustain an organizational, rather than a marketlike, framework for internal relations. Although the four media were available to all actors in the network, not all were able or inclined to use them. The most resource-rich actor was the governor, who most frequently had power relations with others in the network, especially those actors who were part of the formal authority structure. The governor also had a strong claim on patronage, but because of the phenomena of indirect and private-sector patrons, he could not dominate its use. Cadres of actors with associated workers and supporters, linked through personal obligations, could continue an independent existence throughout the party.

A sharp demarcation existed, however, among the users of ideology. Many public officeholders and those without official party status employed ideology as a test of others' worthiness and a badge of their own merit. Party officeholders may have sympathized, but they still cringed at the zealous application of ideological criteria for acceptance into the party and restrained themselves from using these criteria. Money's use was also differentiating, separating those who preferred the greater certainty of an organizational hierarchy to the risks of marketlike relations. The apparent preference for market relations included weakly linked actors and newcomers to office, both with little alternative. But at times it also described the behavior of the governor, who attempted to use money as a lever for changing relations.

Within the party network, actors became linked into particular subsets because of activities related to their positions (chapter 3), through the impact of their constituent environments (chapter 4), or by their control over and use of resources (chapters 5 through 8). Loose coupling might follow from the separateness of actor types (e.g., the county chairman compared with the central committeeman) or from rivalry within types (e.g., among state representatives). It might also follow from separate loci of operation, like those of congressman and local officeholder, or from rivalry within the same locus with overlapping constituencies, such as the Republican National Committee and the State Central Committee. At one level, this leads to the conclusion that the Republican Party is an organization of loosely coupled actors and activities. But alongside tension-filled relations and loose coupling, there is also harmony and integration, for example, in some legislative bodies and local districts. Because shared fate and common goals contribue to integration, they help to qualify any judgment of the Republican Party as conforming to a weak-party model.

We cannot assume a direct relation between loose coupling and decentralization, because centralization had multiple meanings for actors and contrasted with local autonomy, not decentralization. Centralizers have been identified as the unofficial wing, governor, Republican National Committee, State Central Committee, and, less critically, the state Senate and House leadership and the four campaign committees. For the RNC and the campaign committees, and, at times, the SCC and the unofficial wing, centralization was a means for routinizing activities seen as critical to ensuring a strong Republican presence. This interpretation has been supported by other evidence of strong centralizing trends in the national Republican Party (Jacobson, 1984, 45–51; Kayden, 1980, 263–268). But centralization had a different meaning for the governor and legislative leadership, who viewed it as a means of imposing a hierarchy of authority on the party. This view was shared at times by the SCC and segments of the unofficial wing. The equation of centralization with hierarchy was most congenial to those who expected to be at the top.

Most generally, autonomy was an orientation protective of an actor's own sphere and could be used to describe the strategies of virtually every actor except perhaps the Republican National Committee. But we also see more differentiating meanings, ranging from orientations that focus on independence, exemplified by the constitutional officer, to more actively defensive ones, like those of the central committeeman. Autonomy in the form of independence has the effect of both encouraging the loose coupling of the actor involved and keeping his fate separate from others in the party. In short, his success does not necessarily help the party achieve success for other actors. Some autonomy-seeking actors, however, also may be concerned with establishing a hierarchy of authority. This was true, for example, of those county chairmen who wanted authority over all forms of campaigning, regardless of the offices involved. Finally, what I call defensive autonomy involves strategies for retaining control over a narrow sphere of activities by treating most overtures to change as signs of hostile take-overs.

Herring's characterization of U.S. parties at the state (1965, 121) or national (1965, 210) levels as "temporary alliances of local leaders" is clearly not satisfactory for describing the Republican Party, where there are strong elements of centralization. But that still does not justify concluding that we now have an example of the strong-party model, because the move toward centralization is part of a constant struggle in which the more lasting qualities of localism, supported by other research (e.g., Crotty, 1987), are not likely to be totally defeated. Neither loose coupling nor centralization capture in full the complexity of party relationships which are, in practice, a federation of elements or actors (Epstein, 1982). That is, the party is organized hierarchically, not in terms of dominance, but in the clustering of interdependent parts (Thompson, 1967, 59).

Leadership and Power

Discussion of centralization spills over naturally to questions of leadership in ways not previously considered. Because my principal concern has been with how actors relate to each other, specified in terms of converting available resources into media of interchange, attention has been directed to uses of power, not to positions of leadership. I conclude from those uses that either a hierarchy of authority, or centralized leadership, in the strong-party model, or diffused leadership, in the weak-party model, is too simple a characterization. Although power is diffused throughout the network, it does not necessarily convert into leadership. Blocks in leadership are possible because there are three ways that media are generally used: to deal with dependency, to gain or restrict access to resources and rewards, and to maintain or challenge existing relations. Without negating the importance of leadership, in the sense that it gives direction to the party and guidance to party actors, we should see it as only one component of authority or power. Failures of leadership arise, on the one hand, because of limited authority and, on the other, through access to power by a great many actors, not primarily from the way authority is structured.

Power stems in part from the authority of position, that is, from the recognized right of those occupying a position to make decisions binding on others. We found in chapter 5 that about half the actor types in the network had such positions, and of these, only five displayed significant authority in dealing with dependency. In addition to the governor, who used power with most actors in efforts to establish his dominance, they were the state senator and representative, the county chairman, and the congressman. In contrast, party officeholders, in their authoritative capacity, used power primarily to restrict access to resources by, for example, controlling the ability to tap party workers. With the governor the center of authority, he was also most often subject to challenges, in which the legitimacy of his activities was questioned on the grounds that he was either too strong or too weak.

One reason for the difficulty of establishing authoritative leadership lies with the broad availability of power for dealing with uncertainty. Because uncertainty is the hallmark of any political party operating in a competitive environment, party actors who can claim resources that will purportedly reduce uncertainty are guaranteed at least a modicum of power, as they are in most other kinds of organization (Hickson et al., 1971; Thompson, 1967, 127–136). Information is one important resource, used, for example, in efforts to rationalize campaigning. Offering to provide information, however, is experienced by possible recipients as a manifestation of the drive toward centralization and thus as a challenge to existing autonomy, even when, as in the case of relations between the State Central Committee and the Republican National Committee, the former had its own centralizing aspirations. When resources took the form of campaign workers or of credit for services to constituents, both party and public officeholders acted protectively to block access. Money, treated as a medium in its own right, becomes an aspect of power in dealing with dependency. It was basic to the struggle of competing actors to control its fundraising and dispersement, and helped account for the continuing power of the United Republican Fund in the face of rival, and more official, claimants.

A second source of limitation on leadership stems from the sanctions available to actors. Although power is primarily a negative avenue of interaction with others, its efficacy is ambiguous unless it is backed by the threat of truly consequential sanctions, such as the state's threat of force or threat of exclusion from a valued group. It was clear from information supplied by informants, as well as from other sources, that authoritative actors had little in the way of severe sanctions. The absence of official sanctions, whose threatened use could be taken seriously enhanced the potency of measures used to cope with uncertainty, regardless of the status of actors who used them; and it also demonstrated the limits of authority. In addition, it anticipated what was confirmed in chapter 7, how, independently of authority, ideology could be the basis of control, much as recent organization theorists speak of the cultural control of organizations (Scott, 1987, 291).

The difficulty in exercising authority is exemplified by meanings of asymmetrical relations. Although it was expected that contacts made but not reciprocated would most likely be expressions of request for help and directed to those with greater resources, there were also important instances when those presumably of higher status made contacts that remained un-reciprocated. These contacts were interpreted as efforts by the initiating actors to dominate and control. Lack of reciprocity was a protective strat-egy adopted even against authoritative actors who could be rebuffed with-out serious cost. This form of asymmetry was another manifestation of the contest between centralization and autonomy.

Lawrence and Lorsch (1967), in their study of loose coupling in plastic-manufacturing companies, found that the main integrating mechanism is specially created roles for bridging and resolving conflicts. Scott admon-ishes us to see, however, that the argument for integration comes from a rational-system perspective most appropriate for market-oriented produc-tion organizations, where "conflict interferes with goal attainment; and its resolution is associated with greater effectiveness of performance" (Scott, 1987, 253). That is, integration is not necessarily desirable where loosely coupled elements can operate autonomously. In the party this occurred, for example, whenever some offices were won despite the inability to ob-tain support for others. But the successful results of autonomous actions do not eliminate concern about conflict itself causing harm to the Repub-lican cause. This was a particularly sensitive issue to many party actors, described by one prominent county chairman in terms that we might in-terpret as a diagnosis of the Republican disease:

Republicans have the tendency to cut each other up—stab each other in the back. . . . I think we're a party made up of individualists. We value our personal rights. A unified spirit probably contradicts the tendency to be an individualist. . . . we've got to work on this. . . . unity doesn't mean giving up on being an individual.

The reduction of conflict should be one rationale for the emergence of bridging roles in the party. In general, brokers are expected to "arise in communities of actors with a common fate because of exposure to similar environmental contingencies" (Aldrich, 1982, 290). In network terms, brokers are actors who simultaneously have relations with others who are themselves related only through the intermediation of the broker. I described such actors as members of articulated sets, and rather than bridge rela-tions, they appeared to block them. The principal examples were the cen-tral committeeman and the State Central Committee.

Although party brokers did not occur under the rubric of specific posi-tions or actor types, they were present *within* actor types, for example, in Congress or the state House, when individuals act to reconcile differences and serve as subgroup leaders. This supports Aldrich's generalization about the importance of common fate, because each person acted as a broker with others in his own kind of disjoint electoral environment. It contrasted with those in articulating positions who were in sets where members had quite different constituent environments. Brokers were also found among individuals with limited office ambition, who could present themselves as impartial exponents of the party interest. The most prominent example during the time of the study was Harold Byron Smith, Jr., who served as a broker not only because he had renounced public office but also because he simultaneously held a number of pivotal party offices.

Limits on authority, a reflection on the difficulty of achieving leadership under either party model, led to complaints that emphasize personal qualities. As voiced by one party officeholder: "The Republican Party has no muscle, no leadership. The party wins now because of the appeal of particular Republican candidates. For it to succeed there has to be less emphasis on the personality cult and more on working within the party." But what we have learned from other studies of large organizations is that *decentralized* authority is likely to increase with greater formalization (Scott, 1987, 243–245; 275–276). Although the uncertainties that are the essence of a party's environment may restrict the growth of formal organization, they do not inhibit the dispersion of power. In the face of this, the continuing search by party actors for ways of achieving dominance goes on and spills over to media other than power, giving a special attractiveness to patronage and money because they can be positive inducements. That is, they can be used to maintain existing relations, not challenge them; to establish links, not restrict access; and to cope with dependency by contributing to orderly relations of dominance.

Patronage, as a traditional component of partisanship, is important to authoritative actors, especially the governor. But in identifying both patrons and patronage, all actors are affected by the ambiguity associated with contemporary limits on patronage that take the form of low-level government jobs. As we found in chapter 6, one consequence of ambiguity is the creation of new forms of patronage, including some in the private sector, that are removed from control by party officials. Another is that, after governmental patronage is distributed, it is generally reallocated by "indirect" patrons who reap the benefits of loyal clients without necessarily passing these benefits on to the "direct" patrons. Because indirect patrons have created their own subgroups, they are insatiable and therefore often dissatisfied with the results of their efforts to obtain additional patronage for maintaining their fiefdoms. Patronage remains an essential ingredient for sustaining bonds of personal loyalty, but because it is not possible to monopolize its sources or control its distribution, the dominance it provides remains subdivided among various actors. To the extent that it is associated with leadership, patronage demonstrates the diffuseness of the weak-party model. Unlike business corporations, where demands for loyalty are a symptom of more general efforts to avoid uncertainty (Kanter, 1977, 49), in the party, some form of patronage is an important counterweight to the predictability that is built into efforts at formalization.

Money as a positive inducement has even more troublesome qualities than patronage, just because it is so impersonal. On the one hand, it means that all contributions, regardless of source, are valuable. This is another confirmation of the weak-party model's assertion of diffuse leadership. On the other hand, it appeared in chapter 8 that candidates who looked like winners received contributions almost as though they were of interchangeable value. The opportunities that money appears to provide for reconstituting the nature of the party—for example, to elect those more supportive of the governor, or to select a more ideologically moderate slate—were used relatively infrequently and were not often successful. Instead, the potential of money to add to the centralizing thrust of the party was focussed on continuing or adding to a winning streak, with minimal disruption of existing relations. The uses of money indicated the adaptive capacity of party elements to harness resources for their own maintenance.

The achievement of power is another way of describing the office-seeking goals of a party; the prevalence of power relations is another demonstration of how all resources are convertible into power. For these reasons, both party models seem inadequate when they concentrate solely on leadership. Even the conceptions of leadership implied in both models do not address the existence of "stratarchy," hierarchies of authority within locally defined party components (Eldersveld, 1964, 9, 98–117). A more accurate interpretation needs to take into account how leadership, and power in general, represent one manifestation of the continuing tension between centralization and local autonomy.

Ideology and Responsibility

Controversy among academic observers over the need for party responsibility and among activists who argue for ideological consistency boil down to a similar concern. As Sorauf has observed:

The scholars who favor party government (or responsibility) and the ideologues of the left and right in American politics both want the major American parties to present more specific and differentiated programs. Both groups also want the parties to govern by carrying their programs into public policy. To the extent that such goals require some degrees of consensus on basic values and long-term philosophies, they both also want greater ideological clarification and commitment within the parties. (Sorauf and Beck, 1988, 448, 450)

Both groups can be cheered by evidence from the Illinois Republican Party, where conservatism is the dominant ideology. During the study period, conservatism was manifested in the self-identifications of party actors and in roll-call votes, both in the General Assembly and in Congress. On issues preselected by special-interest groups, legislators in Springfield and Washington were consistently separated from their Democratic counterparts along a single dimension of conservatism, with only a few exceptions even in the diverse, multimember state House. In chapter 8, conservative interest groups were collectively among the major financial contributors to legislative candidates. They acted on the conviction that their place in the party was secure by concentrating their contributions during general elections. Their ideological rivals, in contrast, behaved as though they could not make an impact on the network unless they altered its composition; this was manifested in their giving the majority of contributions in the primary period.

I find it difficult to imagine, in the U.S. political system, what kinds of behavior would demonstrate a responsible party system as advocated in the strong-party model, and I made no effort in that direction. Elling, who admits to a similar problem, nevertheless examined legislative performance in Illinois and Wisconsin between 1947 and 1971. During that time, by making four party-state comparisons, he found that the Illinois Republicans were least likely to fulfill campaign pledges (Elling, 1979, 388–389). Recognizing that the partisan role of the governor had a strong bearing on these results (Elling, 1979, 393), he leaves us with the problem of how to interpret their bearing on party responsibility.

Meanwhile, proponents of the weak-party model view the ideological ascendancy in both parties with dismay. To the extent that the United States may be approaching a situation where the major national parties become "parties of advocacy," Polsby and Wildavsky see a danger to democracy:

What is lost, in our view, is a capacity to deliberate, to weigh competing demands and to compromise so that a variety of differing interests each gain a little. This loss would not be so great if the promise of policy government — to select efficacious programs and implement them successfully — were likely to be fulfilled in performance. But, on the record so far, this is doubly doubtful. (Polsby and Wildavsky, 1984, 275)

Informants, who were not burdened by such theoretical concerns, had a great deal to say about the programmatic aspects of the party. They connected the achievement of the party's office-seeking goals with the instituting of Republican programs by saying, for example, that "success is getting a candidate who is not only personable but who can come up with constructive solutions." It was in this capacity that informants were most optimistic, seeing their party as one that can "solve problems" and that, "on basics, on issues of inflation and economy, . . . can do a better job." Comparing the two parties, they expected the Republicans to succeed because of the Democratic Party's inability to deal with "rampant inflation and its disastrous foreign policy. The Republicans offer the hope of acting as a unified entity for the good of all the people."

In the ongoing struggle to confirm commitment, ideological purists challenged even incumbent congressmen whose conservative credential had seemed intact. And although challengers lost, they served notice to the party that commitment cannot be taken for granted. Purists exhibited even more strength when they denied access to resources to those judged ideologically deficient. The dependency created by unequal power was met with principled choices, without fear that these might impede success. Such purist strategies might be expected to limit the growth of the party, an evaluation made even by informants, like a Chicago-area legislator, who put it bluntly:

The first name in this game is winning. If you don't want to win, you shouldn't be in politics. The party is going in the right direction, but unfortunately it's made up of some groups who are too rigid — people who would rather lose an election than support someone they don't like, people who would rather hang on to rigid and outdated values but who will eventually lose.

But this assessment turns out to be incorrect for reasons that are irrefutable to party actors. Claims to moral superiority are supported by the ability of purist candidates to win at district levels and by the devotion of purist party workers to their causes, regardless of temporary defeats. Simply put, conservatives are successful and thereby establish the legitimacy of their perspective. In their objective to make the party machinery subservient to ideology, they were helped by party officeholders, reluctant to enter such a potentially explosive debate.

The scope of ideology raises questions about the meaning of conservatism under changing conditions. The answers do not lie in the refinement of a conservative dogma but in the search for new issues and causes to use as litmus tests for disqualifying those less than orthodox. Such issues were most often involved in challenges to state legislators. Expanding the scope of conservatism also encourages the emergence of new leaders who attempt to ratify their legitimacy by symbolizing the purest form of conservatism. This translates into a limiting role by excluding the legitimacy of other claimants. Whatever dependency is implied by the application of ideology was met head on, with the denial of uncertainty.

There are dangers in using ideology, but only party officeholders appeared explicitly constrained. Otherwise, there was little concern about how attacks on legitimacy could generate uncontrollably destructive forces in the party network. The ascendancy of ideologists within either party could, according to Sorauf, have worrisome consequences for the electorate:

The educated, sophisticated, and involved political minority may impose a new kind of political tyranny on the less involved, lower SES segments of the electorate. It increasingly tries to impose an ideological politics that lacks salience and may indeed be incomprehensible to the less sophisticated. At the same time, it contributes to the decline of the most useful cue-giver, the major political party. (Sorauf and Beck, 1988, 494)

To see how conservative dominance was achieved in the network is to understand some of the costs associated with the strong-party model of programmatic, disciplined parties. On the positive side, the capacity of ideological values to encourage party actors' commitment and identification as Republicans is a means of ensuring the continuing relevance of values for selecting and defining goals. But in the form of ideology, value integrity may become an end in itself, threatening to reorder the primacy of the party's office-seeking goal. As a medium of interchange, ideology has negative qualities, like power. But unlike other media that are convertible into power, ideology stands alone in its capacity to define legitimacy, not in relation to power and authority, but through judgment of moral correctness. It is not enough to identify as a conservative or to act according to some conservative precepts. Ideology demands continuing displays of commitment and continuing willingness both to enlarge and to refine the scope of conservatism. As I wrote in chapter 7, "Ideology gives primacy to the party, not as a vehicle for winning votes or gaining office, but as a moral community."

Electoral Environment

The dynamic element affecting the persistence of the party network is its changing environments, experienced by party actors as more or less pervasive uncertainty, to be faced by a search for sustained support. The generality of this common fate is essentially modified by variations in the kinds of support on which actors depend and by the likelihood of their sharing that support. A true sense of common fate, then, is limited to those who depend on the same kind of environment, but do not compete for the same supporters. All others can be expected to interact with some degree of tension or conflict, which are themselves aspects of dynamism. Actors whose fate is tied to electoral constituencies probably confront the greatest uncertainty, but those constituencies also confer the benefit of allowing dependent actors to hold claim to the greatest legitimacy. Actors who operate in a nonelectoral environment perceive different priorities, perhaps because they experience less urgent pressures. The electoral calendar affects them differently, allowing more concern with party maintenance. They are also more likely to try to adopt strategies of an organizationally rational kind, including centralization.

One argument for studying the Republican Party in Illinois is its presence in a lively two-party system. Evidence presented in chapter 2 defended that view by emphasizing the size and stability of the Republican component in the General Assembly and in Congress and Republican access to the governorship. Yet the aggregate strength of the two parties cannot obscure Illinois's identity as a Republican state from the realignment of 1896 to the present (Jensen, 1971; MacRae and Meldrum, 1960; Beggs and Schwartz, 1984). What this means is that most of the 102 counties, disregarding their unequal size, continue to vote for Republican candidates. Changes that occurred as a result of the New Deal did not alter the basic disparities:

After 1932 Democratic strength in Illinois tended to be concentrated in the most metropolitan centers with the highest proportion of foreign-born (mostly eastern European and Catholic) and Negroes, and in the traditionally Democratic Little Egypt section of southern Illinois, where most of the residents were white Anglo-Saxon Protestants. (Fenton, 1966, 196)

Even though the population composition has altered, the voting patterns have remained.

Related to these geographic disparities are ones tied to offices. For example, partisan voting for congressional offices shifted more slowly than for the presidency or U.S. Senate (MacRae and Meldrum, 1960; Beggs and Schwartz, 1984). During the time of this study, covering the 1978 and 1980 elections, Republicans were more successful in Congress; since then, the tides have turned. Even more striking is the failure of the Republican Party to penetrate the state's major urban center. Republican mayors disappeared from Chicago with the New Deal realignment, and with them, the possibility of major Republican representation on the city council. According to one old-timer, acceptance of this outcome, which he extended to all Cook County, allows the party's office-seeking goal to slip away:

The Republican Party is just less ambitious than it once was. I remember when there used to be spirited fights around the election of the county board president, sheriff, and state's attorney. The Republican Party now accepts the Democratic Party's dominance of Cook County with more docility. They have a defeatist attitude.

Dependence on the environment is the principal underlying theme rationalizing the weak-party model's emphasis on decentralization as a means

of coping with diversity. In the hands of those who emphasize the heterogeneity of the U.S. electorate, the most effective weak party is one that
is broadly representative, aggregating the widest possible range of social
interests. Informants found fragmentation worrisome, as a participant in
the unofficial wing expressed it:

The Republican Party is fragmented in Illinois. It has no strong organization. The
party represents two different sets of interests — urban/rural, metropolitan/down-
state. This split makes it difficult to build a state party, because one set of interests
is being played off against the other.

But from the perspective of the weak-party model, this would be reassur-
ing evidence that the Republican Party is taking its representative role
seriously.

For strong-party modelists, electoral representativeness is, at best, secondary to a majoritarian goal. Because coherence is as essential for the
party's programmatic role as it is for ideology, too broad a representation
of interests may be presumed incompatible and even harmful. In the
responsible-party argument, the opposition party is expected to take up
the slack by absorbing support from excluded interests.[2] In this view it
seems quite reasonable for a public officeholder to say that it is "not good
to get elected by appealing to all people. There are more receivers than
producers, and I don't give a damn about receivers . . . [though] I don't
want them to starve."

As long as so many Republican candidates are able to win office, what
difference does it make that they are not evenly distributed by region or
across offices? When I raised a comparable question in the context of Canadian society, I was dealing with parties that participated in a system of
responsible government requiring disciplined parties. That is, Canadian
parties are much like the strong-party model. My answer then was that
a regionally biased party's effectiveness will be limited in carrying out
policies and programs that have nation-building objectives (Schwartz, 1974,
308). In other words, simple majorities are not enough. Similar weaknesses,
some reported in our interviews, can be detected in Illinois. If downstate
Republicans consider Chicago "Gomorrah on the Lake," they are un-
prepared to recognize any contribution that Chicago makes to the well-
being of the state. Secession is raised as a viable alternative. Interests and
population groups not bound to the main body of Republican support

2. An alternate route for coping with electoral dependency is proposed by strong-party
advocates in the form of broader participation *within* party offices and deliberative bodies.
Arguments for such participation were contained in the American Political Science Association (1950) proposal, and they have shaped reforms in the Democratic Party (Price, 1984,
106–107; Polsby and Wildavsky, 1984, 217–222) but remain largely irrelevant to Republicans.

can be ignored or rejected.[3] And never far behind is the specter of racism, with Lincoln's party preferring to represent only white interests (Berler, 1983; Kleppner, 1985). In general, the Republican Party responds to its environment in ways that make it appear effective in the strong-party model but ineffective in the weak-party one. It does so by selecting strategies in keeping with ideologically compatible goals of success, strengthening ties to existing constituencies, and discouraging efforts to mobilize new ones.

The Adaptive Party

In the 200-year history of the United States, the essential structure of a two-party system has remained unchanged despite the disappearance of the Federalists, the nineteenth-century birth of the Republican Party, the ebb and flow of different forms of Progressivism, and even lengthy periods of regional adherence to a single party. The democratic process of government as we know it has existed only with free parties and probably could not survive without them. It is these features of continuity and apparent indispensibility that justify speaking of robust organization as characteristic not only of the Illinois Republican Party but also of U.S. parties generally. These features also make irrelevant further search for theories of party existence. This sounds much like Epstein (1986, 344) in his "belief that American parties will persist, with merely incremental changes, in a now-settled mold." But in affirming party continuity I do not suggest that a political party is an unchanging structure. It is a continually emerging set of relations in which actors may increase or decrease their centrality, their access to resources, or their overall power. What is lacking, then, is a theory of party adaptability.

In asking what makes for adaptive parties, the party models introduced in this chapter are no longer particularly helpful. They tell us what parties *should be,* especially the strong-party model, and they describe what parties *do,* most completely in the weak-party model. But neither directly addresses what parties *can be.* To do so requires a theoretical basis for selecting the qualities that make for adaptive parties, beginning with the premise that adaptability is the ability to change in response to changing environmental conditions. It is in this regard that the strong-party model, with its emphasis on responsible parties, has been strongly criticized[4] for

3. A similar argument is made to explain Republican policies on cities generally (Mollenkopf, 1983).

4. Although it is true that the responsible-party model has been most severely criticized on grounds that, as the reforms it stimulated have been introduced, it has not produced more effective parties (e.g. Ranney, 1975, 195–210; Polsby and Wildavsky, 1984, 210–222), that is not our concern here.

ignoring the environmental context of the party system (e.g., Keefe, 1972, 1; Banfield, 1964, 26; Blank, 1980, 235). Harmel and Janda (1982, 58–73), using cross-national data, should put to rest any doubts about the environment-party relation, particularly with regard to the environmental constraints under which U.S. parties operate. Although the weak-party model has been better in its attention to environmental factors, it still does not move beyond a basically unidirectional perspective, in which constraint comes from the environment but parties themselves have little they can do to affect their relations with it.

Four principles of party adaptability are identified below. Though I have hedged them with numerous qualifications, I do not depart from the principles themselves.

Without in any way diminishing the importance I have attributed to local and state conditions or to the temporal limits of this analysis, one can still see how, in general, the success of the Republican Party has been tied to the richness of its existing resources of ideology and money and to its identification with the business community, making the move to rationalize the party apparatus and its activities so attractive. Like department store chains that respond to changed environments by creating internal specialty shops or boutiques and sloughing off lower-producing product lines aimed at lower-status and -income levels (Barmash, 1986), the Republican Party has ensured its niche in a changing political environment. But in observing the Republican Party's past successes, we should not simply conclude that it has become the model of an adaptive party. The Illinois Republican Party is, however, the empirical basis for my concluding generalizations.

1. An adaptive party is a loosely coupled system, not simply as a descriptive characteristic, but also out of necessity. Only through the loose coupling of actors and activities can functional and ecological divisions remain present with coequal legitimacy. Because loose coupling goes along with relatively permeable boundaries, new actors, either as individuals or categories, can be incorporated into the network of relations as circumstances change. We found this exemplified in the ways that candidates can directly relate to the unofficial wing without the intermediary of formal party organs or, conversely, how local party actors can rebuff efforts at control from central party actors.

Loose coupling, however, is not synonymous with lack of party integration. If it were, there would be no limits on who could intrude into the network, altering the nature of the party and making adaptability impossible. This highlights a defect in the weak-party model's otherwise close attention to the social and political environment as its affects parties, because the model has no way of dealing with continuing changes in the environment. In consequence, there has not been sufficient recognition of how an increasingly competitive, and hence uncertain, electoral environment can stimulate greater ideological consistency within each party. This happens as party actors respond to uncertainty by closing ranks and tightening their coupling:

Not only has the spread of competition to all regions meant greater voting cohesion within the Congress; it has also reduced the range of ideological differences within the parties. Liberal Republican congressmen like Donald Riegle of Michigan and John Lindsay of New York came to find the Democratic party a more congenial home. Conservative Democratic congressmen such as Phil Gramm of Texas and Andrew Ireland of Florida follow Strom Thurmond's path to the Republican party. Finally, as Senator Richard Lugar (1984) pointed out in a recent appeal for funds for Republican lawmakers: "there is no such thing as a 'safe' seat anywhere." Candidates need all the help they can get; they are finding that the best place to get it is from their fellow partisans. (Schlesinger, 1985, 1168)

Limits on loose coupling for adaptive parties also come about because of the demands of actors' positions. For example, after Governor Thompson's adversary, Donald Totten, lost his 1982 primary bid for lieutenant governor, he stayed on the sidelines, his sole Illinois office, Schaumberg Township committeeman. Elected Cook County chairman in 1984, he assumed the conciliatory role of building the county party into a unified and potent state presence (Neal, 1986). Then required to interact with a broadened range of party actors, most recently increased by the conversion of disaffected Chicago Democrats after the 1987 mayoral election, many of his difficulties could have been anticipated. If he had been guided primarily by ideological purism, the extension of relations with other actors would have suffered. If, conversely, he had allowed too easy penetration of the Cook County party by people like former Cook County Democratic chairman Edward Vrdolyak, he would have risked compromising the integrity of the Republican Party. Apparently these difficulties were insurmountable and led to his eventual defeat in the 1988 chairman race (Hardy and Dold, 1988b). Even a ward committeeman in ideological sympathy with Totten admitted: "Totten is a good Republican, but he's too much of an ideologue to face practical political problems. And he doesn't know how to deal with weak Republican areas" (Gorman, 1988). Totten's problems were compounded by opposition from Cook County sheriff James O'Grady, himself a former Democrat but now the only Republican officeholder in the county and the employer of Totten's challenger, former Democrat James Dvorak. O'Grady had been busy establishing ties with others by hiring relatives of local committeemen and selecting one influential suburban committeeman, Dave Brown, to serve as his lobbyist with the state legislature.

These kinds of integrative activities gave O'Grady enough influence over Governor Thompson to lead to the latter's endorsement of Dvorak. Totten had not been successful in bending from his ideological position—for example, by his support for Jack Kemp's presidential aspirations—leading a former governor's aide to conclude, "The Thompson-Totten marriage was never really consummated" (Hardy and Dold, 1988a).

It would be a mistake to confuse loose coupling with party decline. For example, when Governor Thompson won an unprecedented fourth term in 1986, he revealed greater partisan strength than any idealized party spokesman. His only serious challenger, James Nowlan, chose not to enter the primary. A former Cabinet member, Nowlan decided that political parties were no longer of any significance—a view he shared with John Anderson, for whom he worked during the 1980 presidential primary—and hence he avoided the primary and ran as an independent candidate for governor (Lawrence, 1985). It was a short-lived campaign, because, as we know, non-party candidates have little support.

2. An adaptive party is a rational, goal-directed system. This would seem to go without saying, both because the Republican Party is an organized entity and because of the prominence given to winning elections. But the obvious needs repeating when some party actors are prepared to sacrifice electoral success to other goals, despite how this reduces the party's adaptability. The value of rationality for adaptability comes from the advantages that technically efficient modes of organizing and campaigning give to their users, despite nostalgia for earlier ways of behaving. Mayhew's (1986) documentation of the declining influence of party machines is proof of the adaptive superiority of more rationalized organizational forms. Adaptability is also reflected in the behavior of financial contributors who give money to legislative incumbents as though they are interchangeable in quality.

Reliance on technically rational devices like public-opinion polling to identify voters' judgments of electable candidates exemplifies the limits of rationality by allowing the environment, in the form of the voting public, to determine the party's character. In my earlier report of how a member of the Republican national staff complained when local political actors refused to pay attention to such poll results in selecting a candidate for a legislative seat, I accepted the staffer's assessment of the subsequent election's unsuccessful outcome as evidence of the superiority of centralized technical control. But now it is best to acknowledge the errors of both national and local actors. National actors, by emphasizing the rational choice of candidates, wanted to permit the environment to do the choosing without trying to shape it. Local actors, by assuming that the environment was essentially passive, omitted attention to the possibility of rational choices.

Emphasis on candidates' electability can be pushed too far when more primitive qualities of personal appeal are disregarded. I do not refer here to popularly understood definitions of charisma but to the relations between political entrepreneurs and their personally loyal following. This general category of political entrepreneur may enter the party network as a candidate for legislative or executive office, but he may also be a candidate for party office, a financial contributor, or an interest-group leader. Entrepreneurs' contributions to party adaptability are recognized within the network on the basis of past performance, that is, because they have won an election, given money, provided advice, or demonstrated a following. But it is less usual to acknowledge the value of entrepreneurs who originate outside the usual pool of party adherents. For example, it is common to hear complaints about candidates because they have not paid their dues as party workers before competing for office. Similarly, there is little inclination to recognize the highly personal ways entrepreneurs use their resources. Our best example concerned the activities of private-sector patrons, whose forms of patronage were used to ensure close bonds of loyalty. Despite the traditional ways they may behave, more appropriate for an old-fashioned party machine, these entrepreneurs contribute a dynamic element to the party network that can supplement the drabness of technical efficiency.

3. An adaptive party is a cultural system, emphasizing its distinctiveness from other parties and providing more potent symbols for adherence than are conveyed by the mere acceptance of the party label. Since I first had the idea of studying the Republican Party organization, Ronald Reagan won the presidency twice, also winning over most foes in his own party. Today, the Bush supporter who had warned in 1980, "Now we can't elect a Reagan. We'd go back to highbutton shoes and rank and file order," would likely disavow his words. I would argue that this is not so much a sign that the president had become a member of the Illinois party network as that he continued to play a symbolic role in the interchange among party actors. He had simply lost the capacity to test the scope of conservatism, just as we can be sure that presidential hopefuls in 1988 once again served this purpose. To the extent that presidential candidates did not play a similarly symbolic role for the Democratic Party, testing the scope of central beliefs, it was a sign of that party's lesser adaptability.

A political party without adequate ideological direction is like a company without pride in its product. In the competition for markets, such a company is left trailing those that can rely on a solidary and committed workforce, which ensures the excellence of the services and products offered (Ouchi, 1981). The achievement of such commitment is more likely to come about in what Lindblom calls a "preceptoral control system," where rationality rests on an ideology which once taught to the individual gives him both a "correct" understanding of the social world and guidelines for his own decisions. Although a preceptoral system depends on simple moral and emotional appeals to supplement the rational, the core element in the creation of the new man is his ideological education, a genuine attempt to raise the level of his conscious, thoughtful, deliberated understanding. (Lindblom, 1977, 59)

But given that Lindblom's primary example of a preceptoral system is the Chinese regime under Mao, we must be struck by the authoritarian implications of ideological commitment. Similarly, we sense the constraints when firms evaluated as excellent "are marked by very strong cultures, so strong that you either buy into their norms or get out" (Peters and Waterman, 1982, 77).

Up to this point, the strong-party model has been valuable because of the importance it attaches to ideology, probably the most important aspect of party culture. Reformers who advocate even greater ideological choice between the two major parties will not likely be convinced by Harmel and Janda (1982, 37–39), who find U.S. parties already as programmatically distinct as British parties. Although the cohesion of the legislative parties in the United States may be low compared with other countries, it still has the potential for becoming higher, despite environmental conditions (Brady, Cooper, Hurley, 1979). The strong-party model, in other words, neglects the existing and potential consistency of current parties. Yet in this regard the model is still superior to the weak-party model's underestimation of ideological and programmatic differences between the parties, rooted in the history of their separate existences.

The culture of the party is its core, the soul that keeps its boundaries from being eroded. But as I suspected at the beginning of this research, the culture of conservatism can be a serious limit on organizational rationality. This was demonstrated in 1984 with Congressman Tom Corcoran's unsuccessful primary challenge to Senator Percy. The fissures from that primary battle contributed both to Percy's defeat by Democrat Paul Simon and to Percy's subsequent employment in a nonpartisan position in Washington. In 1986, the race was against popular Democratic Senator Alan Dixon. When presumably strong candidates like Secretary of State James Edgar proved reluctant to take on Dixon, Representative Judy Koehler announced her willingness to enter the race. This was met first with disparagement by those who hoped to find a better-known candidate, followed by gratitude for her courage. Then, after months of indecision and demands for unqualified support, former Congressman Tom Corcoran entered the race, only to drop out again, still struggling to pay debts incurred in his 1984 primary race against Senator Charles Percy and worried about another primary contest (Dold, 1986). The battle was left to Koehler and businessman George A. Ranney, Jr., to argue over who was the better conservative (Talbott and Schott, 1986). Koehler's primary victory, whatever it did to establish the primacy of her conservatism, did not alter the destructiveness of the battle or her ultimate defeat in the general election.

4. An adaptive party is a system of power, directed to achieving control over uncertainty. We found it revealing in earlier chapters to consider a whole range of power sources and uses rather than to look at just those based on legitimate authority. Legitimacy itself is not fixed. This does not make a political party a defective organization, nor is the lack of clear leadership a sign of party disintegration. The pressures of uncertainty should keep most elements of an adaptive party alert to ways in which power is acquired and used.

The richness of power sources can, of course, make a party prone to conflict, especially in the face of recurring tension between the pressures toward centralization and the preservation of local autonomy. As the discussion on loose coupling already made clear, this is a tension that has no resolution, because it is built into the nature of the U.S. political system and hence of its parties. Actors in an adaptive party will temper their uses of power to enhance information flows and curtail internecine struggles.

In describing each attribute, I have also quite candidly outlined its limitations. Further problems arise when the four attributes are combined, because they create two fundamental dilemmas. The first dilemma arises from the simultaneous need for loose coupling along with the rational pursuit of goals. Living in a loosely coupled party milieu, actors find it easy to lose sight of how the goals for which they strive have broader application to the party network. And because goals of electoral success are so crucial, actors will search for the most efficient means of achieving them, leading some to embrace the value of tightly coupled, centralized organizational forms.

The second dilemma arises from the presence of an ideology alongside the striving for power. The energy generated by participation in a common culture creates a dynamic party and, given free rein, places ideology above any other rationale for party existence. Power, however, provides a contrary rationale, whereby all resources channelled into media of interchange should ultimately be convertible to power. For an adaptive party to thrive in the face of these dilemmas is no easy matter. An adaptive party is a changing party, constrained by its past and its immediate conditions while attempting to take advantage of the opportunities it finds. But because a party is a network of relations, how it experiences constraints and how it confronts opportunities are dependent on the interchanges among its actors.

The lesson to be learned from examining the life of the Illinois Republican Party is one of robust organization, not adaptability. In its robustness, the party displays an overall vigor, separate from the situation of particular actors or segments, that enables it to continue despite recurring defeats. It is robust in the roughness of its structure, shrinking and expanding under changing environmental conditions without being bound to a set pattern. Like statisticians who speak of robustness in relation to measures that are unaffected by extreme cases (Andrews, 1978), we may see the Republican Party as sturdy enough to survive the extremes of internal dissent or electoral rejection. Robustness is necessary for an adaptive party, but it does not cause one to emerge. If an adaptive party is truly a model of what a party can be, then robustness needs to be harnessed to bring it about.

*Directory of
Party Actors
and Performers*

References

Index

Directory of Party Actors
and Performers

Actors

U.S. senator

Governor

Performers

Carver, Richard, 21, 42, 72
Corcoran, Tom, 185, 282
Daly, Lars, 21
Dirksen, Everett C., 19, 20, 21, 44, 62, 63, 74,
    121, 139–140, 153
[Dixon, Alan J.], 21, 23, 97, 282
Goldwater, Barry, xiii, 173, 177, 187, 187n,
    188–189, 190, 191
Hull, William E., 140
Koehler, Judy, 282, 283
O'Neal, Dave, 21, 40, 136, 192
Percy, Charles, 19–22, 44, 49, 62, 74, 88, 98,
    105, 113, 121, 135, 137, 140, 143, 176, 181,
    182, 185, 189, 204, 209, 247n, 252, 282
[Pucinski, Roman], 49
Ranney, George, 283
Schlafly, Phyllis, 21, 185
Scott, William J., 21, 97
[Seith, Alex], 21, 135
Senate Steering Committee, 183
[Simon, Paul], 282
Smith, Ralph, 19, 20, 21, 69, 125
[Stevenson, Adlai, III], 19, 21, 42
Witwer, Samuel E., 129

Altorfer, John, 22
Carpentier, Charles, 140
[Kerner, Otto], 22, 68
Nowlan, James, 280
Ogilvie, Richard B., 19, 20, 22, 24, 33–34, 49,
    59, 68n, 69, 70, 73, 98, 104–105, 113, 125,
    129, 131, 135, 146, 154, 157, 159, 162–163,
    213
Percy, Charles, 140

287

Performers include officeholders, staff, and contenders, including unsuccessful ones. Democratic performers are enclosed in square brackets.

References

Advisory Commission on Intergovernmental Relations (ACIR). 1986. *The Transformation in American Politics: Implications for Federalism.* Washington, D.C.

Aldrich, Howard E. 1979. *Organizations and Environments.* Englewood Cliffs, N.J.: Prentice-Hall.

Aldrich, Howard E. 1982. "The Origins and Persistence of Social Networks." Pp. 281–293 in Peter V. Marsden and Nan Lin, eds., *Social Structure and Network Analysis.* Beverly Hills: Sage.

Aldrich, Howard E., and David A. Whetten. 1981. "Organization-Sets, Action-Sets, and Networks: Making the Most of Simplicity." Pp. 385–408 in Paul C. Nystrom and William H. Starbuck, eds., *Handbook of Organizational Design,* Vol. 1, *Designing Organizations and Their Environments.* New York: Oxford University Press.

Alexander, Herbert E. 1980. *Financing Politics. Money, Elections and Political Reform.* 2nd ed. Washington, D.C.: Congressional Quarterly.

Althoff, Phillip, and Samuel C. Patterson. 1966. "Political Activism in a Rural County." *Midwest Journal of Political Science* 10 (Feb.): 39–51.

American Political Science Association. 1950. *Toward a More Responsible Two-Party System. Report of the Committee on Political Parties.* New York: Rinehart.

Andrews, David F. 1978. "Data Analysis, Exploratory." Pp. 97–107 in William H. Kruskal and Judith M. Tanur, eds., *International Encyclopedia of Statistics,* Vol. 1. New York: Free Press.

Bales, Robert F., Fred L. Strodtbeck, Theodore M. Mills, and Mary E. Roseborough. 1950. "Channels of Communication in Small Groups." *American Sociological Review* 16 (Aug.): 461–468.

Banfield, Edward. 1964. "In Defense of the American Party System." Pp. 21–39 in Robert A. Goldwin, ed., *Political Parties, U.S.A.* Chicago: Rand McNally.

Barmash, Isadore. 1986. "Piece by Piece, the Big Stores Rebuild." *New York Times* (Sept. 21): F1, F8.

Beggs, Jack, and Mildred A. Schwartz. 1984. "Defining Party Strength." Unpublished manuscript, Chicago.

Benedict, Michael Les. 1985. "Factionalism and Representation: Some Insight from the Nineteenth Century United States." *Social Science History* 9 (Fall): 361–398.

Benson, J. Kenneth. 1977. "Organizations: A Dialectical View." *Administrative Science Quarterly* 22 (Mar.): 1–21.

Berler, Ron. 1983. "Bridgeport's Great White Hope." *Chicago* (July): 120–130.

297

Berry, Jeffrey M. 1984. *The Interest Group Society.* Boston: Little, Brown.

Beyer, Janice M. 1981. "Ideologies, Values, and Decision-Making in Organizations." Pp. 166–202 in Paul C. Nystrom and William H. Starbuck, eds., *Handbook of Organizational Design,* Vol. 2. New York: Oxford University Press.

Bibby, John F. 1979. "Political Parties and Federalism: The Republican National Committee Involvement in Gubernatorial and Legislative Elections." *Publius* 9: 220–236.

Blank, Robert H. 1980. *Political Parties: An Introduction.* Englewood Cliffs, N.J.: Prentice-Hall.

Blau, Peter M. 1963. *The Dynamics of Bureaucracy.* Rev. ed. Chicago: University of Chicago Press.

Blau, Peter M. 1977. *Inequality and Heterogeneity.* New York: Free Press.

Boczkiewicz, Robert E. 1977. "Mrs. Schlafly Decides Not to Oppose Percy." *St. Louis Globe-Democrat* (Jan. 7).

Boissevain, J. 1974. *Friends of Friends: Networks, Manipulators and Coalitions.* Oxford: Blackwell.

Brady, David W., Joseph Cooper, and Patricia Hurley. 1979. "The Decline of Party in the U.S. House of Representatives, 1887–1968." *Legislative Studies Quarterly* 4 (Aug.): 381–407.

Buchanan, Christopher. 1980. "National GOP Pushing Hard to Capture State Legislatures." *Congressional Quarterly* (Oct. 25): 3188–3192.

Burke, Edmund. 1971. "Thoughts on the Causes of the Present Discontents." *Collected Works,* Vol. 1. Boston: Little, Brown. (Original 1770.)

Burt, Ronald S. 1976. "Positions in Networks." *Social Forces* 55: 93–122.

Burt, Ronald S. 1980. "Models of Network Structure." *Annual Review of Sociology* 6: 79–141.

Burt, Ronald S. 1983a. "Range." Pp. 176–194 in R. S. Burt and M. S. Minor, eds., *Applied Network Analysis.* Beverly Hills: Sage.

Burt, Ronald S. 1983b. "Cohesion Versus Structural Equivalence as a Basis for Network Subgroups." Pp. 262–282 in R. S. Burt and M. S. Minor, eds., *Applied Network Analysis.* Beverly Hills: Sage.

Campaign Briefs. 1978. "Endorsements Told Primary Vote Near." Elgin *Daily Courier-News.*

Cannon, Lou. 1981. "GOP Chief Decries Independent Efforts to Target Democrats on 'Single Issues'." *Washington Post* (Apr. 28): A3.

Carroll, Glenn R., ed. 1988. *Ecological Models of Organizations.* Cambridge, Mass.: Ballinger.

Cartwright, Bliss C., and R. Stephen Warner. 1976. "The Medium Is Not the Message." Pp. 639–660 in Jan J. Loubser et al., eds., *Explorations in General Theory in Social Science,* Vol. 2. New York: Free Press.

Chaffee, Kevin. 1984. "Money under the Mattress: What Congressmen Don't Spend." *Washington Monthly* (Sept.): 32–38.

Chambers, William N. 1963. *Political Parties in a New Nation.* New York: Oxford University Press.

Champaign-Urbana News. 1978. "Johnson's 'No' on ERA, His Most Famous Vote." (March 17).

Chicago *Sun-Times.* 1980. "More for Illinois House." (Feb. 26).

Chicago *Sun-Times.* 1981a. "4 Congressmen Quit Group over 'Hit List'." (June 4).

Chicago *Sun-Times.* 1981b. "All Reported Clear in Lobbyist Paula Case." (Aug. 29).

Chicago Tribune. 1978. Editorial, "Keeping the U.R.F. Alive." (July 22).

Chicago Tribune. 1980. "Illinois House Endorsements." (Mar. 13).

Ciccone, F. Richard. 1980a. "Gov. Thompson Holds His Tongue." *Chicago Tribune* (Feb. 17).

Ciccone, F. Richard. 1980b. "First to Enter Race Says 'Never Again'." *Chicago Tribune* (July 16).

Ciccone, F. Richard, Daniel Egler, Mitchell Locin. 1981. "The Good, the Bad, and the Unbelievable. (A General Assembly Review)." *Chicago Tribune Magazine* (Sept. 13): 30–36.

Clarity, James F., and Warren Weaver, Jr. 1984. "Washington Talk: Endorsement Squabble." *New York Times* (Mar. 16): 12.

Clark, Peter M., and James Q. Wilson. 1961. "Incentive Systems: A Theory of Organizations." *Administrative Science Quarterly* 6 (Sept.): 129–166.

Coffey, Raymond. 1980. "Ever the Thunder from the Right." *Chicago Tribune Magazine* (Mar. 23).

Cohen, Michael D., and James G. March. 1976. "Decisions, Presidents, and Status." Pp. 174–205 in James G. March and Johan P. Olsen, *Ambiguity and Choice in Organizations.* Bergen, Norway: Universitetsforlaget.

Colby, Peter W., and Paul Michael Green. 1979. "The Consolidation of Clout: The Voting Power of Chicago Democrats from Cermak to Bilandic." *Illinois Issues* 5 (Feb.): 15–24.

Comer, John. 1976. "Another Look at the Effects of the Divisive Primary." *American Politics Quarterly* 4 (Jan.): 121–128.

Cook, Robert E. 1982. "Lobbyists and Interest Groups." Pp. 113–122 in James D. Nowlan, ed., *Inside State Government. A Primer for Illinois Managers.* Urbana: Institute of Government and Public Affairs.

Cotter, Cornelius P., and John F. Bibby. 1980. "Institutional Development of Parties and the Thesis of Party Decline." *Political Science Quarterly* 95: 1–27.

Cotter, Cornelius P., and Bernard C. Hennessy. 1964. *Politics Without Power: The National Party Committees.* New York: Atherton.

Cotter, Cornelius P., James L. Gibson, John E. Bibby, Robert J. Huckshorn. 1984. *Party Organizations in American Politics.* New York: Praeger.

Crane, Edgar G., Jr. 1980. "The Office of Governor." Pp. 60–86 in Edgar G. Crane Jr., ed., *Illinois: Political Processes and Governmental Performance.* Dubuque: Kendall/Hunt.

Crane, Philip M. 1978. *Surrender in Panama.* Ottawa, Ill.: Green Hill.

Crawford, Alan. 1980. *Thunder on the Right.* New York: Pantheon.

Crotty, William J. 1984. *American Parties in Decline.* 2nd ed. Boston: Little, Brown.

Crotty, William J., ed. 1987. *Political Parties in Local Areas.* Knoxville, Tenn.: University of Tennessee Press.

Crozier, Michel. 1964. *The Bureaucratic Phenomenon.* Chicago: University of Chicago Press.

Cyert, Richard M., and James G. March. 1963. *A Behavioral Theory of the Firm.* Englewood Cliffs, N.J.: Prentice-Hall.

Davis, James A., and Samuel Leinhardt. 1972. "The Structure of Positive Interpersonal Relations." Pp. 218–251 in Joseph Berger, Morris Zelditch, Jr., and Bo Anderson, eds., *Sociological Theories in Progress,* Vol. 2. Boston: Houghton Mifflin.

Decatur *Herald-Review.* 1980. "ERA Backers Zero In on Key Legislative Races." (Mar. 4).

Derthick, Martha. 1975. *Uncontrollable Spending for Social Service Grants.* Washington, D.C.: Brookings.

Dill, William R. 1958. "Environment as an Influence on Managerial Autonomy." *Administrative Science Quarterly* 2 (Mar.): 409–443.

Dionne, E. J., Jr. 1981. "Catholics and the Democrats: Estrangement but Not Desertion." Pp. 307–325 in S. M. Lipset, ed., *Party Coalitions in the 1980s.* San Francisco: Institute for Contemporary Studies.

Dold, R. Bruce. 1986. "Corcoran Backs Out of Campaign." *Chicago Tribune* (Jan. 7).

Dunn, Charles W. 1972. "Cumulative Voting Problems in Illinois Legislative Elections." *Harvard Journal on Legislation* 9: 627–665.

Duverger, Maurice. 1963. *Political Parties.* Trans. Barbara and Robert North. 2nd rev. New York: Wiley. (Original 1951).

Egler, Daniel. 1980a. "Thompson Seeks Loyal . . ." *Chicago Tribune* (Mar. 9).

Egler, Daniel. 1980b. "ERA Lobbyist Guilty of Vote Bribery." *Chicago Tribune* (Aug. 23).

Ehrenhalt, Alan. 1982. *Politics in America. Members of Congress in Washington and at Home.* Washington, D.C.: Congressional Quarterly.

Elazar, Daniel. 1970. *Cities of the Prairie.* New York: Basic.

Eldersveld, Samuel J. 1964. *Political Parties: A Behavioral Analysis.* Chicago: Rand McNally.

Eldersveld, Samuel J. 1982. *Political Parties in American Society.* New York: Basic.

Elling, Richard C. 1979. "State Party Platforms and State Legislative Performance: A Comparative Analysis." *American Journal of Political Science* 23 (May): 383–405.

Elrod v. Burns, 427 U.S. 347 (1976).

Emerson, Richard M. 1962. "Power-Dependence Relations." *American Sociological Review* 27 (Feb.): 31–40.

Emerson, Richard M. 1972. "Exchange Theory, Part II: Exchange Relations and Network Structures." Pp. 58–87 in Joseph Berger, Morris Zelditch, Jr., and Bo Anderson, eds., *Sociological Theories in Progress,* Vol. 2. Boston: Houghton Mifflin.

Epstein, Leon D. 1980. *Political Parties in Western Democracies.* New Brunswick, N.J.: Transaction.

Epstein, Leon D. 1982. "Party Confederations and Political Nationalization." *Publius* 12 (Fall): 67–102.

Epstein, Leon D. 1986. *Political Parties in the American Mold.* Madison: University of Wisconsin Press.

Erickson, Bonnie H. 1982. "Networks, Ideologies, and Belief Systems." Pp. 159–172 in Peter V. Marsden and Nan Lin, eds., *Social Structure and Network Analysis*. Beverly Hills: Sage.

Estill, Bob. 1978. "Redmond's Feud with the RNC." Springfield *State Journal-Register* (Feb. 28).

Evans, Rowland, and Robert Novak. 1980. "Bush Fire in the Prairie State." Chicago *Sun-Times* (Feb. 6).

Evans, M. Stanton. 1975. *Clear and Present Dangers*. New York: Harcourt Brace Jovanovich.

Everson, David H., and Kent Redfield. 1980. "Regional Interests Further Party Decline." *Illinois Issues* (Mar.): 12–13.

Fairlie, Henry. 1980. "Born Again Bland." *The New Republic* (Aug. 2–9): 16–20.

Felsenthal, Carol. 1981. *The Sweetheart of the Silent Majority*. Garden City, N.Y.: Doubleday.

Felsenthal, Carol. 1982. "How Feminists Failed." *Chicago* (June): 139–142, 152–157.

Fenton, John H. 1966. *Midwest Politics*. New York: Holt, Rinehart and Winston.

Fetridge, William Harrison. 1976. *With Warm Regards*. Chicago: Dartnell.

Fish, C. R. 1904. *The Civil Service and Patronage*. Cambridge: Harvard University Press.

Fisher, Dennis D. 1978. "2 Convicted Legislators to Lose Assembly Posts." Chicago *Sun-Times* (Feb. 25).

Flament, Claude. 1963. *Applications of Graph Theory to Group Structure*. Englewood Cliffs, N.J.: Prentice-Hall.

Galbraith, Jay. 1973. *Designing Complex Organizations*. Reading, Mass.: Addison-Wesley.

Goldwater, Barry. 1960. *The Conscience of a Conservative*. Shepherdsville, Ky.: Victor.

Gonet, Phillip, and James D. Nowlan. 1982. "The Legislators." Pp. 69–91 in James D. Nowlan, ed., *Inside State Government. A Primer for Illinois Managers*. Urbana: Institute of Government and Public Affairs.

Gorman, Tom. 1988. "GOP Officials Discuss Problems." *Hyde Park Herald* (May 4).

Gosnell, Harold F. 1937. *Machine Politics: Chicago Model*. Chicago: University of Chicago Press.

Gouldner, Alvin W. 1967. "Reciprocity and Autonomy in Functional Theory." Pp. 141–169 in Nicholas J. Demerath III and Richard A. Peterson, eds., *System, Change, and Conflict*. New York: Free Press.

Gove, Samuel K., Richard W. Carlson, Richard J. Carlson. 1976. *The Illinois Legislature. Structure and Process*. Urbana: University of Illinois Press.

Granovetter, Mark S. 1973. "The Strength of Weak Ties." *American Journal of Sociology* 79 (May): 1360–1380.

Griffin, William. 1978. "Comptroller Race a Test of Power." *Chicago Tribune* (Mar. 19).

Hardy, Thomas, and R. Bruce Dold. 1988a. "GOP Chief Loses Thompson Backing." *Chicago Tribune* (Mar. 24).

Hardy, Thomas, and R. Bruce Dold. 1988b. "O'Grady's Candidate Elected to County GOP Post." *Chicago Tribune* (Mar. 29).

Harmel, R., and Kenneth Janda. 1982. *Parties and Their Environments.* New York: Longmans.

Hartley, Robert E. 1979. *Big Jim Thompson of Illinois.* Chicago: Rand McNally.

Hennessy, Bernard. 1968. "On the Study of Party Organization." Pp. 1–44 in William Crotty, ed., *Approaches to the Study of Party Organization.* Boston: Allyn and Bacon.

Herring, Pendleton. 1965. *The Politics of Democracy.* New York: Norton.

Hershey, Robert D., Jr. 1982. "$22,000 Divided by Four Dozen Races Equals a Busy Day for One Committee." *New York Times* (Oct. 13).

Hickson, D. J., C. R. Hinings, C. A. Lee, R. E. Schneck, J. M. Pennings. 1971. "A Strategic Contingencies' Theory of Intraorganizational Power." *Administrative Science Quarterly* 16 (June): 216–229.

Hill, Raynard E., and Bernard J. White. 1979. *Matrix Organization and Project Management.* Ann Arbor: University of Michigan Press.

Hillman, G. Robert. 1979. "Gifts from Many Helped Him Live Better: Scott." Chicago *Sun-Times* (Apr. 11).

Himmelstein, Jerome L. 1983. "The New Right." Pp. 13–30 in Robert C. Liebman and Robert Wuthnow, eds., *The New Christian Right.* New York: Aldine.

Hofstadter, Richard. 1969. *The Idea of a Party System.* Berkeley: University of California Press.

Holderman, James B. 1963. "Rebuilding the Republican Party in Illinois." *Illinois Government* 16 (Jan.): 1–4.

Howard, Robert P. 1978. "Senator Charles H. Percy." *Illinois Issues* (June): 8–10.

Hucker, Charles W. 1978a. "Illinois Primary: Anderson Survives Challenge." *Congressional Quarterly* (Mar. 25): 749.

Hucker, Charles W. 1978b. "Explosive Growth: Corporate Political Action Committees Are Less Oriented to Republicans than Expected." *Congressional Quarterly Weekly Report* (Apr. 8): 849–854.

Huckshorn, Robert J. 1976. *Party Leadership in the States.* Amherst: University of Massachusetts Press.

Huckshorn, Robert J. 1984. *Political Parties in America.* 2nd ed. Monterey, Calif.: Brooks/Cole.

Icen, Richard H. 1977. "New Effort Set to Close Loopholes." Decatur *Herald-Review* (Mar. 12).

Jacobson, Gary C. 1984. "Money in the 1980 and 1982 Congressional Elections." Pp. 38–69 in Michael J. Malbin, ed., *Money and Politics in the United States. Financing Elections in the 1980s.* Chatham, N.J.: Chatham House.

Jensen, Richard J. 1971. *The Winning of the Midwest.* Chicago: University of Chicago Press.

Jewell, Malcolm E., and David M. Olson. 1988. *Political Parties and Elections in American States.* 3rd ed. Chicago: Dorsey.

Johnston, Michael. 1979. "Patrons and Clients, Jobs and Machines." *American Political Science Review* 3 (July): 385–397.

Jones, Ruth S. 1984. "Financing State Elections." Pp. 172–213 in Michael J. Malbin, ed., *Money and Politics in the United States. Financing Elections in the 1980s.* Washington, D.C.: American Enterprise Institute.

Kanter, Rosabeth M. 1972. *Commitment and Community.* Cambridge: Harvard University Press.

Kanter, Rosabeth M. 1977. *Men and Women of the Corporation.* New York: Basic.

Katz, Richard S. 1980. *A Theory of Parties and Electoral Systems.* Baltimore: Johns Hopkins University Press.

Kayden, Xandra. 1980. "The Nationalizing of the Party System." Pp. 257–282 in Michael J. Malbin, ed., *Parties, Interest Groups, and Campaign Finance Laws.* Washington, D.C.: American Enterprise Institute.

Keefe, William. 1972. *Parties, Politics, and Public Policy in America.* New York: Holt.

Keller, Bill. 1981. "Congressional Rating Game Is Hard to Win." *Congressional Quarterly* (Mar. 21): 507–517.

Keller, Bill. 1982. "Washington Diarist – Beer." *The New Republic* 187 (Dec. 13): 43.

Kemeny, John, Laurie Snell, Gerald L. Thompson. 1966. *Introduction to Finite Mathematics.* Englewood Cliffs, N.J.: Prentice-Hall.

Key, V. O., Jr. 1949. *Southern Politics.* New York: Knopf.

Key, V. O., Jr., 1961. *Public Opinion and American Democracy.* New York: Knopf.

Key, V. O., Jr., 1964. *Politics, Parties, and Pressure Groups.* 5th ed. New York: Crowell-Collier.

Kieckhefer, Robert. 1979. "Blind Primaries: A Brick on a Top-Heavy Load?" *Illinois Issues* (Sept.): 34.

Kirby, Joe. 1979. "'Speedy' Legislators in for Surprise?" Waukegan *News-Sun* (Mar. 1).

Kleppner, Paul. 1985. *Chicago Divided. The Making of a Black Mayor.* De Kalb, Ill.: Northern Illinois University Press.

Kluckhohn, Clyde. 1951. "Values and Value Orientations in the Theory of Action: An Exploration in Definition and Classification." Pp. 388–433 in T. Parsons and E. A. Shils, eds., *Toward a General Theory.* Cambridge: Harvard University Press.

Lake County Tribune. 1980. "Ruling Lets Rep. Griesheimer Keep Legislative Seat, License." (Feb. 1).

Lambrecht, Bill. 1980. "Findley Abandoning Bedfellows." *St. Louis Post-Dispatch* (Mar. 26).

Latus, Margaret Ann. 1984. "Assessing Ideological PACs: From Outrage to Understanding." Pp. 142–171 in Michael J. Malbin, ed., *Money and Politics in the United States. Financing Elections in the 1980s.* Washington, D.C.: American Enterprise Institute.

Laumann, Edward O., and Peter V. Marsden. 1979. "The Analysis of Oppositional Structure in Political Elites: Identifying Collective Actors." *American Sociological Review* 4 (Oct.): 713–732.

Laumann, Edward O., and Franz U. Pappi. 1976. *Networks of Collective Action.* New York: Academic.

Lawrence, Mike. 1976. "Cement Bribery Trial." *Illinois Issues* (Dec.): 6–12.

Lawrence, Mike. 1980. "Thompson Shops for Right Candidate." Decatur *Herald-Review* (Mar. 7).

Lawrence, Mike. 1985. "Jim Nowlan: The Travail of an Independent Candidate for Governor." *Illinois Issues* 11 (Dec.): 6–9.

Lawrence, Paul R., and Jay W. Lorsch. 1967. *Organization and Environment.* Cambridge, Mass.: Harvard University Press.

Leahy, Peter, and Allan Mazur. 1978. "A Comparison of Movements Opposed to Nuclear Power, Fluoridation, and Abortion." *Research in Social Movements, Conflict and Change* 1: 143–154.

Leiserson, Avery. 1958. *Political Parties and the Study of Politics.* New York: Knopf.

Lemieux, Vincent. 1977. *Le Patronage politique.* Québec: Les Presses de l'université Laval.

Lempinen, Edward W. 1980. "Double-Dip Bonanza for State Legislators." Chicago *Sun-Times* (Feb. 17): 50.

Lindblom, Charles E. 1977. *Politics and Markets.* New York: Basic.

Locin, Mitchell. 1984. "Dan Crane's Wrong Didn't Hurt Him with the Right." *Chicago Tribune* (Sept. 20).

Lowi, Theodore J. 1968. "Forward to the Second Edition." Pp. v–xviii in Harold F. Gosnell, *Machine Politics.* Chicago: University of Chicago Press.

Luce, R. D. 1950. "Connectivity and Generalized Cliques in Sociometric Group Structure." *Psychometrica* 15 (June): 169–190.

Luce, R. D., and A. D. Perry. 1949. "A Method of Matrix Analysis of Group Structure." *Psychometrica* 14 (May): 95–116.

McAdam, E. L., Jr., and George Milne. 1963. *Johnson's Dictionary.* New York: Random House.

McCarthy, John L., and John W. Tukey. 1978. "Exploratory Analysis of Aggregate Voting Behavior." *Social Science History* 2 (Spring): 292–331.

McClosky, Herbert, Paul Hoffman, and Rosemary O'Hara. 1960. "Issue Conflict and Consensus among Party Leaders and Followers." *American Political Science Review* 54 (June): 406–427.

MacKay, Robert. 1980. "Some Foresight on Blind Primaries." *Illinois Issues* (Mar.): 31.

MacKay, Robert. 1981. "How Block Grants Stack Up." *Illinois Issues* (Nov.): 37.

MacNeil, Neil. 1970. *Dirksen: Portrait of a Public Man.* New York and Cleveland: World.

McNitt, Andrew D. 1982. "Campaign Organizations in Michigan and Illinois." Paper presented to the annual meeting of the Midwest Political Science Association, Milwaukee.

MacRae, Duncan, Jr., and James A. Meldrum. 1960. "Critical Elections in Illinois: 1888–1958." *American Political Science Review* 54 (Sept.): 669–683.

Malbin, Michael J., ed. 1984. *Money and Politics in the United States. Financing Elections in the 1980s.* Chatham, N.J.: Chatham House.

Manning, Al. 1979. "Maneuver by Thompson Thwarted." Springfield *State Journal-Register* (Dec. 27).

Manning, Al. 1980. "Rep. Findley's Seat No Longer Safe." Springfield *State Journal-Register* (Mar. 25).

March, James G., and Johan P. Olsen. 1976. *Ambiguity and Choice in Organizations*. Bergen, Norway: Universitetsforlaget.

March, James G., and Herbert A. Simon. 1958. *Organizations*. New York: Wiley.

Martin, Maureen, 1980. "Rather Than Seek Office, He Helps Those Who Do." *Suburban Trib* (Feb. 27).

Marx, Karl. 1971. *The Grundrisse*. Ed. and trans. David McLellan. New York: Harper and Row.

Mauss, Marcel. 1967. *The Gift. Forms and Functions of Exchange in Archaic Societies*. Trans. Ian Cunnison. New York: Norton.

Mayer, George H. 1967. *The Republican Party*. 2nd ed. New York: Oxford University Press.

Mayhew, David R. 1986. *Placing Parties in American Politics*. Princeton: Princeton University Press.

Mechanic, David. 1962. "Sources of Power of Lower Participants in Complex Organizations." *Administrative Science Quarterly* 7 (Dec.): 349–362.

Merton, Robert K. 1957. *Social Theory and Social Structure*. Rev. and enlarged. Glencoe, Ill.: Free Press.

Meyer, John W., and Brian Rowan. 1977. "Institutionalized Organizations: Formal Structure as Myth and Ceremony." *American Journal of Sociology* 83 (Sept.): 340–360.

Meyer, W. John, and W. Richard Scott. 1983. "Centralization and the Legitimacy Problems of Local Government." Pp. 199–215 in W. J. Meyer and W. R. Scott, eds., *Organizational Environments. Ritual and Rationality*. Beverly Hills: Sage.

Meyer, John W., W. Richard Scott, Terrence Deal. 1983. "Institutional and Technical Sources of Organizational Structure: Explaining the Structure of Educational Organizations." Pp. 45–67 in John W. Meyer and W. Richard Scott, eds., *Organizational Environments. Ritual and Rationality*. Beverly Hills: Sage.

Michel, Robert H. 1980. "A Primer for Platform Reading." *Commonsense* 3 (Summer): 59–66.

Michels, Robert. 1949. *Political Parties*. Trans. Eden and Cedar Paul. Glencoe, Ill.: Free Press.

Mollenkopf, John H. 1983. *The Contested City*. Princeton: Princeton University Press.

Monroe, Alan D. 1980. "Elections: Political Culture, Public Opinion, Sectionalism and Voting." Pp. 156–166 in Edgar G. Crane, Jr., *Illinois: Political Processes and Governmental Performance*. Dubuque: Kendall/Hunt.

Mooney, William F. 1978. "2 Convicted Legislators to Lose Assembly Posts." Chicago *Sun-Times* (Feb. 18).

Moore, Gwen. 1979. "The Structure of a National Elite Network." *American Sociological Review* 44 (Oct.): 673–692.

Mouton, Jane S., Robert R. Blake, Benjamin Fruchter. 1960a. "The Reliability of Sociometric Measures." Pp. 320–361 in J. L. Moreno, ed., *The Sociometry Reader*. Glencoe, Ill.: Free Press.

Mouton, Jane S., Robert R. Blake, Benjamin Fruchter. 1960b. "The Validity of Sociometric Responses." Pp. 362–387 in J. L. Moreno, ed., *The Sociometry Reader.* Glencoe, Ill.: Free Press.

Munger, Frank, and Karen Hoffman. 1980. "Ideology, Issue Preference, and Candidate Choice: The 1976 Contest between Ford and Reagan." Paper prepared for the Midwest Political Science Association meetings. Chicago, Apr. 25.

Neal, Steve. 1986. "Totten Wants a Major League GOP." *Chicago Tribune* (Feb. 6).

Neumann, W. Russell. 1981. "Differentiation and Integration: Two Dimensions of Political Thinking." *American Journal of Sociology* 86 (6): 1236–1268.

Nie, Norman H., Sidney Verba, John R. Petrocik. 1976. *The Changing American Voter.* Cambridge, Mass.: Harvard University Press.

Nowlan, James D. 1965. "Leaderless Politics: The Story of Structured Disjunction in the Illinois Republican Party, 1960–1965." MA thesis, Department of Political Science, University of Illinois at Urbana.

Nowlan, James D. 1982. "Patronage and Personnel." Pp. 53–68 in J. D. Nowlan, ed., *Inside State Government. A Primer for Illinois Managers.* Urbana: Institute of Government and Public Affairs.

Oakes, John B. 1984. "The PAC-Man's Game: Eating Legislators." *New York Times* (Sept. 6).

Olson, David M. 1978. "U.S. Congressmen and Their Diverse Congressional District Parties." *Legislative Studies Quarterly* 3 (May): 239–264.

Ouchi, William G. 1981. *Theory Z.* Reading, Mass.: Addison-Wesley.

Parsons, Talcott. 1967. *Sociological Theory and Modern Society.* New York: Free Press.

Parsons, Talcott. 1969. *Politics and Social Structure.* New York: Free Press.

Peoria *Journal Star.* 1978a. "Castle Says Thompson May Have Problems." (Jan. 27).

Peoria *Journal Star.* 1978b. "Mail Order Nightmare." (Mar. 12).

Peoria *Journal Star.* 1980a. Editorial. (Mar. 2).

Peoria *Journal Star.* 1980b. Editorial. (Mar. 14).

Peters, Thomas J., and Robert H. Waterman, Jr. 1982. *In Search of Excellence.* New York: Harper and Row.

Pfeffer, Jeffrey. 1977. "Power and Resource Allocation in Organizations." Pp. 235–265 in Barry Staw and Gerald Salancik, eds., *New Directions in Organizational Behavior.* Chicago: St. Clair.

Pfeffer, Jeffrey. 1981. "Who Governs?" Pp. 228–247 in Oscar Grusky and George A. Miller, eds., *The Sociology of Organizations.* 2nd ed. New York: Free Press.

Pfeffer, Jeffrey and Gerald R. Salancik. 1974. "Organizational Decision Making as a Political Process: The Case of a University Budget." *Administrative Science Quarterly* 19 (June): 135–151.

Pfeffer, Jeffrey, and Gerald S. Salancik. 1978. *The External Control of Organizations.* New York: Harper and Row.

Phillips, Kevin P. 1982. *Post Conservative America: People, Politics, and Ideology in a Time of Crisis.* New York: Random House.

Pierson, James E., and T. Smith. 1975. "Primary Divisiveness and Election Success: A Re-examination." *Journal of Politics* 37 (May): 555–562.

Polsby, Nelson W., and Aaron Wildavsky. 1984. *Presidential Elections. Strategies of American Electoral Politics.* 6th ed. New York: Scribners.

Poole, Keith T. 1981. "Dimensions of Interest Group Evaluation of the U.S. Senate, 1969–1978." *American Journal of Political Science* 25 (Feb.): 49–67.

Poole, Keith T., and Howard Rosenthal. 1984. "The Polarization of American Politics." *Journal of Politics* 46 (Nov.): 1061–1079.

Price, David E. 1984. *Bringing Back the Parties.* Washington, D.C.: Congressional Quarterly.

Raines, Howell. 1982. "Meteors in the Campaign Managing Firmament." *New York Times* (Nov. 25).

Rakove, Milton. 1975. *Don't Make No Waves: Don't Back No Losers.* Bloomington: Indiana University Press.

Ranney, Austin. 1960. *Illinois Politics.* New York: New York University Press.

Ranney, Austin. 1975. *Curing the Mischiefs of Faction: Party Reform in America.* Berkeley: University of California Press.

Riordan, William L. 1948. *Plunkitt of Tammany Hall.* New York: Knopf.

Roberts, James C. 1980. *The Conservative Decade.* Westport, Conn.: Arlington House.

Robinson, Mike. 1978. "Philip Crane No Longer Shy about Presidential Question." Elgin *Daily Courier-News* (Jan. 27).

Rose, Richard. 1974. *The Problem of Party Government.* New York: Free Press.

Ross, Diane. 1984. "Pate Philip: The Unambiguous Leader of the Senate GOP." *Illinois Issues* 10 (Mar.): 30–32.

Rossiter, Clinton. 1960. *Parties and Politics in America.* Ithaca: Cornell University Press.

Rossiter, Clinton. 1962. *Conservatism in America.* 2nd ed., rev. New York: Vintage.

Royko, Mike. 1981. "Bump the Bumpkins. Keep the Taxes Here." Chicago *Sun-Times* (May 29): 2.

Sabato, Larry. 1981. The Rise of Political Consultants. New York: Basic.

Sabato, Larry. 1982. "A Survey of Costs and Services of Political Consultants." *Campaigns and Elections* 2 (Winter): 42–47.

Sabato, Larry. 1984. *PAC Power: Inside the World of Political Action Committees.* New York: Norton.

St. Louis *Globe-Democrat.* 1978. "Republicans Blair, Castle Bid for Post." (Mar. 16).

Sartori, Giovanni. 1976. *Party and Party Systems,* Vol. 1. Cambridge: Cambridge University Press.

Sarvis, Betty, and Hyman Rodman. 1974. *The Abortion Controversy.* 2nd ed. New York: Columbia University Press.

Sawyer, Jack, and Duncan MacRae, Jr. 1962. "Game Theory and Cumulative Voting in Illinois: 1920–1954." *American Political Science Review* 56: 936–946.

Schattschneider, E. E. 1942. *Party Government.* New York: Rinehart.

Schilling, Tom. 1980. "As Always, Skinner's Bid Is Unorthodox." *Lake County Trib* (Mar. 12).

Schlafly, Phyllis. 1964. *A Choice Not an Echo.* 3rd ed. Alton, Ill.: Pere Marquette.

Schlesinger, Joseph A. 1965. "Political Party Organization." Pp. 764–801 in James G. March, ed., *Handbook of Organizations.* Chicago: Rand McNally.

Schlesinger, Joseph A. 1966. *Ambition and Politics.* Chicago: Rand McNally.

Schlesinger, Joseph A. 1984. "On the Theory of Party Organization." *Journal of Politics* 46 (May): 369–401.

Schlesinger, Joseph A. 1985. "The New American Political Party." *American Political Science Review* 79 (Dec.): 1152–1169.

Schneider, William. 1981. "Democrats and Republicans, Liberals and Conservatives." Pp. 179–231 in S. M. Lipset, ed., *Party Coalitions in the 1980s.* San Francisco: Institute for Contemporary Studies.

Schwartz, Mildred A. 1974. *Politics and Territory: The Sociology of Regional Persistence in Canada.* Montreal: McGill-Queens University Press.

Schwartz, Mildred A. 1981. *The Environment for Policy-Making in Canada and the United States.* Montreal and Washington, D.C.: C. D. Howe Institute and National Planning Associates.

Scott, W. Richard. 1977. "Effectiveness of Organizational Effectiveness Studies." Pp. 63–95 in Paul S. Goodman and Johannes M. Pennings, eds., *New Perspectives on Organizational Effectiveness.* San Francisco: Jossey-Bass.

Scott, W. Richard. 1981. *Organizations. Rational, Natural, and Open Systems.* Englewood Cliffs, N.J.: Prentice-Hall.

Scott, W. Richard. 1987. *Organizations. Rational, Natural, and Open Systems.* 2nd ed. Englewood Cliffs, N.J.: Prentice-Hall.

Seligman, Lester G. 1961. "Political Recruitment and Party Structure: A Case Study." *American Political Science Review* 55 (Mar.): 77–86.

Serati, Ray. 1979. "Sen. Friedland Unable to Convince Governor to Support Candidacy." Elgin *Daily Courier-News* (Dec. 21).

Shakman, Michael L., and Paul M. Lurie, et al. v. The Democratic Organization of Cook County et al. 1979. No. 69C2145. U.S. District Court for the Northern District of Illinois. *Partial Summary Judgment,* September 24; *Consent Judgment,* 1981.

Simmel, Georg. 1978. *The Philosophy of Money.* Trans. T. Bottomore and D. Frisby. London: Routledge and Kegan Paul.

Simon, Roger. 1981. "Crime Does Pay — for Bill Scott." Chicago *Sun-Times* (Oct. 9).

Simon, Roger. 1982. "Blowhard Faces 80-Candle Cake." Chicago *Sun-Times* (May 4).

Slack, Steve. 1980. "Scott's Justice." *Illinois Issues* 6 (Dec.): 4–8.

Snowiss, Leo M. 1966. "Congressional Recruitment and Representation." *American Political Science Review* 60 (Sept.): 627–639.

Sorauf, Frank J. 1959. "Patronage and Party." *Midwest Journal of Political Science* 3 (May): 115–126.

Sorauf, Frank J. 1963. *Party and Representation.* New York: Atherton.

Sorauf, Frank J. 1964. *Political Parties in the American System.* Boston: Little, Brown.

Sorauf, Frank J. 1984. *Party Politics in America.* 5th ed. Boston: Little, Brown.

Sorauf, Frank J., and Paul Allen Beck. 1988. *Party Politics in America.* 6th ed. Glenview, Ill.: Scott Foresman.

Star Publications. 1980. "Derwinski Not a True Conservative, Savard Says." (Jan. 17).

State Board of Elections. 1977. *Election Laws: State of Illinois.* Springfield.

Stevenson, Carol. 1978. "Republican Hopefuls Gather to Outline Their Positions, Knock Their Opponents." Elgin *Daily Courier-News* (Feb. 18).

Street, David. 1981. "Welfare Administration and Organizational Theory." Pp. 285–300 in George T. Martin, Jr., and Mayer N. Zald, eds., *Social Welfare in Society.* New York: Columbia University Press.

Sweet, Lynn. 1982. "Rep. Epton Calls GOP Businessmen 'A Joke'." Chicago *Sun-Times* (Aug. 7).

Talbott, Basil, Jr. 1979. "Connally Dazzles Illinois GOP at Thompson Party." Chicago *Sun-Times* (June 20).

Talbott, Basil, Jr. 1980. "Jim Finally Gets Digits Dirty." Chicago *Sun-Times* (Jan. 24).

Talbott, Basil, Jr. 1982a. "Thompson's ERA Blunder" Chicago *Sun-Times* (June 24).

Talbott, Basil, Jr. 1982b. "A GOP Veteran Looks Back." Chicago *Sun-Times* (July 17).

Talbott, Basil, Jr.1982c. "GOP: Gutting Own Party." Chicago *Sun-Times* (Oct. 14).

Talbott, Basil, Jr. 1982d. "2 GOP Groups Prepare a Joint County Effort." Chicago *Sun-Times* (Nov. 23).

Talbott, Basil, Jr. 1983a. "Corcoran in Race against Sen. Percy." Chicago *Sun-Times* (June 14).

Talbott, Basil, Jr. 1983b. "GOP Fund-Raising Tiff Keys on Abe." Chicago *Sun-Times* (July 20).

Talbott, Basil, Jr. 1984a. "State Republicans Split — Note the Two Jims Contest." Chicago *Sun-Times* (Feb. 2).

Talbott, Basil, Jr. 1984b. "GOP Wants Minorities, Not VIPs." Chicago *Sun-Times* (May 21): 3.

Talbott, Basil, Jr., and Dean Schott. 1986. "2 in GOP Senate Race Fight to Be Right." Chicago *Sun-Times* (Jan. 7).

Tarrant, David. 1980. "'Liberal' Senators Facing Tough Re-election Fights Moderated Their 1979 Votes." *Congressional Quarterly* (Apr. 26): 1111–1127.

Thayer, George. 1973. *Who Shakes the Money Tree?* New York: Simon and Schuster.

Thomason, Arthur J., and Jim Orso. 1980. "Lawmaker's Letter Puts Price on Friendship." St. Louis *Globe-Democrat* (Mar. 7).

Thompson, James. 1967. *Organizations in Action.* New York: McGraw-Hill.

Tichy, Noel M. 1981. "Networks in Organizations." Pp. 225–249 in Paul C. Nystrom and William H. Starbuck, eds., *Handbook of Organizational Design,* Vol. 2. London: Oxford University Press.

Time. 1979. "The Fanatical Abortion Fight." (July 9): 26–27.

Tocqueville, Alexis de. 1945. *Democracy in America,* Vol. 1. New York: Norton.

Truman, David B. 1971. *The Governmental Process.* 2nd ed. New York: Knopf.

Uslaner, Eric M., and Ronald E. Weber. 1977. "Partisan Cues and Decision Loci in U.S. State Legislature." *Legislative Studies Quarterly* 11 (Nov.): 423–444.

Van Der Slik, Jack R., and Jesse C. Brown. 1980. "Legislators and Roll Call Voting in the 80th General Assembly." Pp. 109–118 in Edgar G. Crane, ed., *Illinois: Political Processes and Government Performance.* Dubuque: Kendall/ Hunt.

Viguerie, Richard. 1981. *The New Right: We're Ready to Lead.* Falls Church, Va.: Caroline House.

Warren, Ellen. 1983. "Dan Crane Admits Sex with Page." Chicago *Sun-Times* (July 15).

Wasburn, Philo. 1982. *Political Sociology.* Englewood Cliffs, N.J.: Prentice-Hall.

Watson, Jerome. 1978. "Crane Downgrades Percy as More Liberal Than Adlai." Chicago *Sun-Times* (Sept. 13).

Watson, Jerome. 1979. "Crane Shapes Up Campaign Staff" Chicago *Sun-Times* (May 4).

Weber, Max. 1978. *Economy and Society.* Ed. Guenther Roth and Claus Wittich. Berkeley: University of California Press.

Wheeler, Charles N., III. 1980. "GOP Legislative Contests Hot in 3 Regional Districts." Chicago *Sun-Times* (Feb. 8).

Wheeler, Charles N., III. 1982. "ERA Lives On—In Assembly Races." Chicago *Sun-Times* (Oct. 19).

Wildavsky, Aaron. 1965. "The Goldwater Phenomenon: Purists, Politicians, and the Two-Party System." *Review of Politics* 27 (July): 386–413.

Will, George. 1982. *The Pursuit of Virtue and Other Tory Notions.* New York: Simon and Schuster.

Williamson, Oliver E. 1975. *Markets and Hierarchies: Analysis and Antitrust Implications.* New York: Free Press.

Wilson, James Q. 1961. "The Economy of Patronage." *Journal of Political Economy* 69 (Aug.): 369–380.

Wilson, James Q. 1966. *The Amateur Democrat.* Chicago: University of Chicago Press.

Wilson, James Q. 1973. *Political Organizations.* New York: Basic.

Wolfinger, Raymond. 1974. *The Politics of Progress.* Englewood Cliffs, N.J.: Prentice-Hall.

Zucker, Lynne G., ed. 1988. *Institutional Patterns and Organizations. Culture and Environment.* Cambridge, Mass.: Ballinger.

Index

311